TRAVEL◆S[
WESTERN C

TOTEM POLES IN VANCOUVER B.C.

John Elk III

TRAVEL ★ SMART®

WESTERN CANADA

Second Edition

Lyn Hancock

AVALON
TRAVEL

TRAVEL✦SMART: WESTERN CANADA

2nd EDITION

Lyn Hancock

Published by
Avalon Travel Publishing
1400 65th Street, Sute 250
Emeryville, CA 94608, USA
Printing History
2nd edition—January 2001
5 4 3 2

Please send all comments, corrections,
additions, amendments, and critiques to:

TRAVEL✦SMART
WESTERN CANADA

AVALON TRAVEL PUBLISHING
1400 65th STREET, SUITE 250
EMERYVILLE, CA 94608, USA
e-mail: atpfeedback@avalonpub.com
www.travelmatters.com

ISBN: 1-56691-225-3
ISSN: 1096-4061

Editors: Angelique Clarke, Suzanne Samuel
Graphics Coordinator: Erika Howsare
Production: Amber Pirker
Design: Marie J.T. Vigil
Index: Naomi Dancis
Cover Design: Janine Lehmann
Map Editors: Mike Ferguson, Michael Balsbaugh
Cartography: Mike Morgenfeld, Doug Beckner, Kathy Sparkes

Front cover photo: large—Peyto Lake (Michael J. Howell/Index Stock), small—Vancouver (John Elk III)
Back cover photo: Banff, Canada (Mach 2 Stock Image)

Distributed by Publishers Group West
Printed by R.R. Donnelley

Acknowledgements

Thank you, Frank, for keeping me sane during the hurricane that raged around us while this book was researched and written. No matter what you volunteered to do, you supported me with rare dedication. Thank you, Jim Cant, Barry Campbell, Ted Owens, and fellow PWAC-er, Laura Winopol, for your help, and particular thanks to Marla Daniels and Christie Makowichuk of Edmonton Tourism for your enthusiastic assistance.

TRAVEL SMART: Western Canada
A GUIDE THAT GUIDES

Most guidebooks are primarily directories, providing information but very little help in making choices—you have to guess how to make the most of your time and money. *Travel Smart: Western Canada* is different: By highlighting the very best of the region and offering various planning features, it acts like a personal tour guide rather than a directory.

TAKE THE STRESS OUT OF TRAVEL

Sometimes traveling causes more stress than it relieves. Sorting through information, figuring out the best routes, determining what to see and where to eat and stay, scheduling each day—all of this can make a vacation feel daunting rather than fun. Relax. We've done a lot of the legwork for you. This book will help you plan a trip that suits you—whatever your time frame, budget, and interests.

SEE THE BEST OF THE REGION

Author Lyn Hancock has lived in Western Canada for 38 years. She has hand-picked every listing in this book, and she gives you an insider's perspective on what makes each one worthwhile. So while you will find many of the big tourist attractions listed here, you'll also find lots of smaller, lesser-known treasures, such as the Silly Boat Race in Nanaimo or Carey's Beachcombing Pacific Treasures in Sandspit. And each sight is described so you'll know what's most—and sometimes least—interesting about it.

In selecting the restaurants and accommodations for this book, the author sought out unusual spots with local flavor. While in some areas of the region chains are unavoidable, wherever possible the author directs you to one-of-a-kind places. We also know that you want a range of options: one day you may want to have afternoon tea in Victoria's opulent Empress Hotel, while the next day you would be just as happy (as would your wallet) with fish and chips. Most of the restaurants and accommodations listed here are moderately priced, but the author also includes budget and splurge options, depending on the destination.

CREATE THE TRIP YOU WANT

We all have different travel styles. Some people like spontaneous weekend jaunts, while others plan longer, more leisurely trips. You may want to cover as much ground as possible, no matter how much time you have. Or maybe you prefer to focus your trip on one part of the region or on some special interest, such as history, nature, or the outdoors. We've taken these differences into account. Though the individual chapters stand on their own, they are organized in a geographically logical sequence, so that you could conceivably fly into Vancouver, drive chapter by chapter to each destination in the book, and end up close to where you started. Of course, you don't have to follow that sequence, but it's there if you want a complete picture of the region.

Each destination chapter offers ways of prioritizing when time is limited: In the Perfect Day section, the author suggests what to do if you have only one day to spend in the area. Also, every Sightseeing Highlight is rated, from one to four stars:

★★★★   must see
 ★★★   highly recommended
  ★★   worthwhile
   ★   see if you have time

At the end of each sight listing is a time recommendation in parentheses. User-friendly maps help you locate the sights, restaurants, and lodging of your choice.

And if you're in it for the ride, so to speak, you'll want to check out the Scenic Routes described at the end of several chapters. They take you through some of the most scenic parts of region.

In addition to these special features, the Appendix has other useful travel tools:
- The Planning Map and Mileage Chart help you determine your own route and calculate travel time.
- The Special Interest Tours show you how to design your trip around any of six favorite interests, ranging from wineries to First Nations tribal culture.
- The Calendar of Events provides an at-a-glance view of when and where major events occur throughout the region.
- The Resource Guide tells you where to go for more information about national and state parks, individual cities and counties, local bed-and-breakfasts, and more.

HAPPY TRAVELS

With this book in hand, you have many reliable recommendations and travel tools at your fingertips. Use it to make the most of your trip. And have a great time!

WHY VISIT
WESTERN CANADA?

Several decades ago I left my home in Australia and set off to see the world, traveling through Asia, Africa, and Europe before ending up in Canada. I lived in Eastern Canada for one year, but it wasn't until I went west that I was inspired to stay. I call it God's Country; others call it Lotus Land or Shangri-La.

What's so alluring about Western Canada? What does it have that attracts immigrants and tourists and makes it the fastest-growing region in Canada? Diversity of climate, landscapes, and wildlife; of people, cities, and cultures. Immensity of mountains, forests, and prairies; of sky and light that lift spirits and trigger dreams. Beautiful British Columbia. Wild Rose Country Alberta.

It takes less than one hour to fly across Western Canada—from the reef-ridden beaches and rainforest jungles of the Pacific Coast and the island-studded fjords of the Inland Passage; over the ice-capped mountains of the Coast Range, the sagebrush hills, and rolling grasslands, the lakes and rivers of the Interior Plateau; over the Canadian Rockies; and then to flat, patterned prairie. West of the Rocky Mountains is the magnificent chaos of British Columbia; east of the Rockies is the contrasting orderliness of Alberta.

Yet, it takes more than one lifetime to see it all. Despite Western Canada's expansive network of roads and ferry routes, it is still largely unexplored. You will have to make choices.

Take a boat trip through the Gulf Islands or the Inland Passage. Hike and camp in a Rocky Mountain national park. Ride a horse in the Cariboo Mountains or raft the Chilcotin River. Ski at Whistler, Kelowna, or Jasper. Visit a vineyard along Okanagan Lake. Drive the Alaska Highway or the Icefields Parkway. Fish for salmon on the Queen Charlotte Islands or for trout in one of the pristine northern lakes. Connect with human history by viewing totem poles in Ninstints or a buffalo jump at Head-Smashed-In, by hiking the Chilkoot Pass Trail, or by visiting a fur-trading post or heritage park.

The best reason to visit Western Canada is for the great outdoors, but even its cities are attractive. See cosmopolitan Vancouver, dynamic Calgary, megamalled Edmonton, or fabled Victoria, and seek out other towns such as charming Kimberley, spectacular Atlin, or picturesque Telegraph Cove.

"Go West" is advice as good today as it was yesterday.

THE LAY OF THE LAND

British Columbia, the westernmost province of Western Canada, is known around the world for beautiful landscapes. The words on B.C. license plates are true: Beautiful British Columbia. Visitors who are inhibited by high snowcapped mountains may prefer Alberta, which shares the Rocky Mountains on its southwestern edge, but stretches east to the Great Plains and north to the rocky Canadian Shield. Whichever route you take, you will be awestruck by the variety of landscapes.

In the far west, the land rises from the Pacific Ocean in a necklace of islands, the largest of which are the Queen Charlotte Islands, Vancouver Island, and the Gulf Islands. These help to protect British Columbia's fjord-indented coastline and are part of the Inland Passage to Alaska. Towering over the islands are the Coast Mountains, the some of the highest in North America—Mount Waddington is 13,175 feet and 4,016 meters.

The only flat areas of British Columbia are the rich Fraser River delta and the Peace River Lowland in the northeast that merges with the Peace River Lowland in northwestern Alberta.

British Columbia's drier interior, between the coast and the Rocky Mountains, is a region of high plateaus (the Cariboo-Chilcotin), deep lakes and valleys (the Okanagan), and even more mountain ranges (Cassiar, Omineca, Monashee, Selkirk, and Purcell).

Between the interior plateau and the Rockies lies the Rocky Mountain Trench, a huge gash in the landscape through which major rivers such as the Columbia flow. The Rockies mark the Continental Divide, a height from which some rivers flow west to the Pacific Ocean, others flow north to the Arctic Ocean, and still others flow east across Canada to empty eventually into the Atlantic Ocean. Mount Robson, at 13,048 feet—3,977 meters—is the range's highest point.

Remnants of the last Ice Age can be seen in the popular Columbia Ice Fields and the Athabasca Glacier.

Sloping eastward from the Rockies are the forested foothills of Alberta. About three-quarters of Alberta is flat prairie grassland, now tamed into neat farmland. The plain is gashed by deep valleys, such as the North and South Saskatchewan Rivers, and by dry gulches such as the Badlands near Drumheller. In the north, the prairie gives way to boreal forest and the ancient rocks and lakes of the Canadian Shield.

FLORA

Timber covers almost two-thirds of British Columbia. Huge trees, many of which are more than 300 feet tall and 1,000 years old— Douglas fir, western red cedar, western hemlock, Sitka spruce—dominate Western Canada's wild and wet west coast. Take a walk through Cathedral Grove or follow a trail in Clayuquot Sound to appreciate the best of these world-famous rainforests. Gnarled Garry oak and shiny arbutus grow in pockets of rocky outcroppings on Vancouver and the Gulf Islands. On the rain-shadow side of the mountains, at higher elevations or more northerly latitudes, the coast and boreal forests give way to parklands and grasslands dotted with groves of alder, birch, and aspen. Most of the southern prairie, however, has no trees at all.

There is a greater variety of flowering plants in British Columbia than anywhere else in Canada. Southwestern British Columbia's mild climate brings flowers out earlier than in other parts of Western Canada; Victorians like to boast of roses blooming during the December holidays, and the city has the highest flower count in the country each February. Spectacular wildflowers appear in spring the high alpine meadows of Manning Park and Mount Revelstoke. The provincial flower of British Columbia is the Pacific dogwood; Alberta's is the wild rose.

FAUNA

No place in Canada is home to as many wild animal species as British Columbia. Including fish, there are 1,083 different species. Off the west coast, many tour operators will take you to see seals, sea lions, orca and gray whales, and even sea otters, which are making a comeback after near extermination. The forests in both British Columbia and Alberta are home to cougars, deer, elk, moose, wolves, and black bear; the mountains shelter mountain sheep and goats. Many of these can be seen from more than 60 wildlife viewing areas that are being set up throughout British Columbia by the government. Contact the Wildlife Branch,

B.C. Environment, 780 Blanshard Street, Victoria, British Columbia V8V 1X5; 250/387-9767.

Tour operators will take people to see the rare white kermode bear on Princess Royal Island and the endangered grizzlies of the Khutzeymateen Valley. But you don't necessarily have to trek to the wilderness to see Western Canada's famous wildlife—cougars have been spotted on several occasions on the grounds of the Empress Hotel in downtown Victoria!

Ornithologists flock to see Western Canada's birds. More than one million birds migrate along the Pacific Flyway, and thousands stop to nest. Victoria and Vancouver are favorite wintering areas for ducks, geese, and eagles, and Victoria's holiday season bird count is often the highest in Canada.

Popular viewing areas are the Reifel Refuge at the mouth of the Fraser River, Brackendale near Vancouver, and Witty's Lagoon near Victoria. Visitors are often amazed to see colorful tropic-like birds such as tufted puffins and rhinoceros auklets swimming close to shore or nesting in offshore colonies. The many sloughs and potholes in British Columbia's Cariboo region and on the Alberta prairie provide nesting grounds for ducks, geese, swans, and white pelicans. Some towns celebrate the annual return of wildlife, such as Parksville's Brant Festival, Nanaimo's Sea Lion Festival, and Ucluelet's and Tofino's Whale Festivals.

Alberta is well known for its bird conservation efforts, especially regarding birds of prey. Several centers encourage visitors to have a close-up look at the raptors in their care. Try Alberta Birds of Prey Centre near Lethbridge, 800/661-1222, and the Canadian Wildlife Service Peregrine Falcon Hatchery near Wainwright, 403/842-5513. McLennan, north of Edmonton, calls itself the Bird Capital of Canada: it's at the center of three major flyways and annually hosts 17,000 shore birds and 250,000 land birds. For guided tours, check out Kimiwan Birdwalk, 403/324-3065. In the far north, Wood Buffalo National Park is the last remaining natural nesting ground of the whooping crane.

HISTORY AND CULTURES

In earlier times the two provinces of Western Canada—British Columbia and Alberta—were kept largely separate by the two north-south series of mountain ranges: the Coast Range and Rocky Mountains. The indigenous people occupied land on all sides of these barriers for at least 10,000 years. To the west lived the Coast Salish, Nootka, Kwakiutl, Bella Coola, Haida, Tsimshian, and Tlingit; to the east lived the Interior Salish, Beaver, Chipewyan, Blackfoot, Blood, Cree, Peigan, and Sarcee. Formerly dubbed Indians or Aboriginals, the distinctly varied tribes are now collectively referred to as First Nations people.

Coastal tribes fished for salmon, hunted whales, gathered berries, and harvested furs and cedar trees for clothing and canoes. Easy living produced a rich culture. Inland tribes living in a harsher climate had to work harder. They relocated their homes and traded obsidian, buffalo skins, and mountain-goat wool for the much-valued eulachon oil of their coastal cousins.

Europeans looking for the Northwest Passage and rich trade items of their own began exploring Western Canada in the late 1700s. From the west by sea came Russians, Spaniards, Americans, and British, who established a fiercely competitive trade with China in the sea otter furs that they obtained from First Nations tribes along the Pacific Coast.

From the east by land came British and Americans who set up fur-trading posts for the Northwest Company and Hudson's Bay Company. The Northwest Company's Alexander Mackenzie used native trading routes to find his way across Western Canada to the Pacific Ocean, and, in 1793, he became the first person to cross the continent. As the sea otter and beaver were vital trade items in what was to become British Columbia, so was the buffalo—or plains bison— in what was to become Alberta.

Few visitors settled in Western Canada until the gold rush, which began in 1858, first along the Fraser River, then the Cariboo, and by 1898, the Yukon. In 1866, the two colonies of Vancouver Island and mainland British Columbia became one. Five years later, British Columbia joined other provinces to become partners in the Dominion of Canada—after very nearly joining the United States!

The next great influx of settlers came to Western Canada after 1886, when the Canadian Pacific Railway reached the Pacific Coast. One year later, the logging settlements in Burrard Inlet became part of the new port city of Vancouver, which quickly outstripped Victoria as the capital of British Columbia. Other railway lines followed, and lumbering became the province's most important industry.

Meanwhile, in Alberta, the Northwest Mounted Police, who came west to maintain law and order, built Fort Macleod and Fort Calgary; the once-vast throngs of plains bison were decimated through overhunting; treaties were signed with the First Nations people; and in the 1880s, surveyors marked the prairie into 160-acre (65-hectare) squares. The foothills and short-grass prairie combined with the railway and warm Chinook winds from the west were ideal for agriculture and ranching.

In the early 1900s, settlers from the Ukraine, Great Britain, Germany, Scandinavia, and the United States streamed into Western Canada in response to the Canadian government's offer of free land. In 1905, Alberta became a province and, along with Saskatchewan, joined the Confederation. As a result of its strategic location for people heading north to the Klondike Gold Rush and, later, the Alaska Highway and Canol pipeline construction, Edmonton flourished and became the provincial capital.

It was the discovery of oil in 1914 at Turner Valley, southwest of Calgary, and, more importantly, in 1947 at Leduc, near Edmonton, that really put Alberta on the map. Alberta's economy shifted from agriculture to oil and gas. Western Canada's natural resources—fish, lumber, grain, oil, gas, and coal—combined with an abundance of energetic immigrants have brought wealth to the area.

Today the tourist industry buffers the otherwise boom-and-bust economy. And adventure travel and ecotourism are the fastest-growing segments of the industry. Tourists flock to Western Canada for its geography: to climb mountains, camp, raft rivers, watch whales, and catch fish.

Tourists also come to sample Western Canada's many different cultures, which follows a recent pique in interest and pride in First Nations cultures. On the Queen Charlotte Islands, visitors watch Haida artists at work; at the Gitxsan villages of the Skeena River, they tour longhouses and watch masked dancers. At Writing-on-Stone Provincial Park along the Milk River, tourists view North America's largest concentration of pictographs and petroglyphs; and at Head-Smashed-In Buffalo, they learn how Plains Indians killed and used bison.

The arts and cultures brought to Western Canada by various immigrant groups make it a fascinating place to live and visit. See Victoria for its British heritage; Calgary for its Calgary Stampede and a peek at Western American culture; Cardston to learn about the Mormon way of life; Edmonton to savor a Ukrainian lifestyle; and Castlegar for its Doukhobor culture.

The newest wave of immigrants comes from Asia. British Columbia, a Pacific Rim province, and its port city of Vancouver are benefiting most from Asian influences. The Asian market purchases 40 percent of British Columbia's exports, and many Chinese from Hong Kong, in particular, have bought land and invested in businesses in Greater Vancouver. Vancouver's Chinatown is the second largest on North America's West Coast.

ARTS

The arts are alive and very well in Western Canada. Along with a recent resurgence in, and greater appreciation of First Nation art such as Haida carvings, there has been a tremendous growth in all arts. Ballroom dancing is making a big comeback in British Columbia, and of course, square dancing has always been a hit in Alberta.

The arts flourish on the west coast, particularly on the Gulf Islands. Because of the diverse scenery, more and more Hollywood films are being produced in Western Canada, especially in Vancouver, Victoria, and Nelson. Each town's daily newspapers and weekly tabloids list current arts and entertainment events. In addition, Vancouver has an Arts Hotline at 604/684-ARTS.

It's worth taking in a show or symphony at Vancouver's refurbished Orpheum Theatre just to see this concert hall's original splendor. Visit the Vancouver Art Gallery and Victoria's Emily Carr Gallery to view the works of Emily Carr, an eccentric painter who captured the essence of the wild west coast. Shows of international significance take place at Vancouver's Queen Elizabeth Theatre, Victoria's MacPherson Playhouse, Calgary's Centre for the Performing Arts, the Calgary Jubilee Auditorium, and the Edmonton Jubilee Auditorium. Sometimes the showcase is as intriguing as the event, as in the Vancouver Symphony's annual concert at the top of Whistler Mountain, and Victoria Symphony's performance on a barge in Victoria's Inner Harbor.

Festivals of all kinds are held everywhere, especially in summer. Check out the Edmonton Folk Music Festival, the Edmonton Jazz City International Festival, the Edmonton Street Performers Festival, and Edmonton Dreamspeakers. Try the Whistler Country and Blues Festival, Whistler's Showcase of Street Entertainment Festival, the Victorian International Festival, Banff Festival of the Arts, Harrison Hot Springs Festival of the Arts, and Chemainus Festival of Murals. Don't miss the Fringe Festival of streetside theatrical events held in Victoria and Vancouver. One of Victoria's newer events is First People's Festival in early August. There are also many arts and crafts fairs and venues where you can see local artists in action.

Museums that shouldn't be missed are Victoria's Royal British Columbia Museum, Calgary's Glenbow Museum, B.C. Forest Museum in Duncan, Head-Smashed-In Buffalo Jump Interpretive Centre near Fort Macleod, Vancouver's Museum of Anthropology, the Royal Tyrrell Museum in Drumheller, and Passing of the Legends Museum in Kananaskis Country.

CUISINE

The diversity of Western Canada naturally leads to an equally diverse cuisine. British Columbia salmon and seafood dominate west coast restaurants. Alberta's steaks, which are as big as dinner plates are favorites on the prairie.

An increasing number of restaurants in and around Vancouver serve northwest coast First Nations cuisine such as bannock bread, alder-grilled salmon, and soapberry ice cream. Fresh lamb is a specialty of Saltspring Island. Fresh Okanagan fruit is bought in boxes from roadside stands, and Okanagan grapes are the basis for a thriving wine industry. Armstrong cheeses are especially tasty. And buffalo and lake trout are popular in the north.

The effects of immigration on cuisine are seen everywhere. The British custom of afternoon tea is a popular ritual at the Empress Hotel, and dozens of other restaurants, in Victoria. Ukrainian perogies and cabbage rolls are easy to find in Edmonton, as is Russian borscht in Grand Forks.

OUTDOOR ACTIVITIES

You name it, you can do it—depending on the season—and retail stores offer guidebooks to help you decide where and how to do it: walking, hiking, mountaineering, climbing, cycling, swimming, canoeing, kayaking, white-water rafting, Sea-Dooing (marine motorbiking), powerboating, sailboating, houseboating, scuba diving, windsurfing, gliding, parachuting, parasailing, hot-air ballooning, horseback-riding, hunting, fishing, bird-watching, wildlife-watching, whale-watching, golfing, caving, gold-panning, snowmobiling, snowshoeing, skiing—or suntanning and hot springs soaking.

And what spectacular settings for outdoor activities! British Columbia has five national parks, more than 450 provincial parks and recreational areas, 131 ecological reserves, an increasing number of specially protected areas, additional Forest Service recreation areas, and municipal recreation areas. Alberta has four national parks, 143 provincial parks, 159 Forest Service recreation areas, and additional municipal recreation areas. Be sure to plan early—some of the more popular national park trails restrict numbers.

PLANNING YOUR TRIP

WHEN TO GO

Western Canada's weather is as varied as its geography, but generally it rains a lot more on the west side of the mountains, is drier in the central interior and the prairie, and is cooler the farther north or the higher you go. British Columbia is the rainiest—and the balmiest—province, and Alberta is the sunniest.

June to August are the most popular months to travel in Western Canada, and, of course, it's when the weather is warmest, which is a lot warmer than visitors expect from a country that is known for its cold. In fact, in July the prairie sizzles, and in the Osoyoos desert you can fry an egg on the pavement. But summer months can be crowded, so consider the advantages of shoulder seasons. Spring and fall are beautiful in the Okanagan Similkameen, which is also

Remember to dress in layers and be ready for everything—a lightweight, hooded jacket and windbreaker for the unpredictable mountains, especially at night; gumboots and umbrellas for rain on the west coast any time of year; and swimsuits and shorts for the dry, lake-splashed interior in summer.

the best wine-tasting time. Spring, when the flowers burst open, is the best time of year in Victoria and Vancouver. If you visit the northern half of Western Canada in fall, when the leaves turn gold and orange, you will avoid mosquitoes and can catch more fish. Winter in the Rocky Mountains and the Okanagan is ideal for skiing. Take at look at the climate chart and the calendar of events for each destination while you are making your plans.

HOW MUCH WILL IT COST?

Traveling in Western Canada is less expensive than in Europe, but more expensive than in the United States. Goods and services are generally more expensive in Canada and, except in the Yukon, Northwest Territories, Nunavut, and Alberta, additional taxes must be paid: the Provincial Sales Tax (PST) is 7 percent in British Columbia; the much-hated Goods and Services Tax (GST) is also 7 percent; and an additional nonrefundable tax on hotel and motel accommodations is 8 percent in British Columbia and 5 percent in Alberta.

Nonresidents can have the GST refunded on some accommodations and nonconsumable products if the goods are bought for use *outside* Canada and taken out of the country within 60 days of purchase, and if the rebate is claimed within a year of purchase. You must buy a minimum of $100 worth of goods and have paid at least $7 GST, and you must submit original receipts. Rebate application forms are available from most Canadian duty-free shops, tourist information centers, and Canadian embassies and consulates; or you can mail your application to Revenue Canada, Customs and Excise, Visitor Rebate Programme, Ottawa, Ontario K1A 1J5. For further information, call 800/66-VISIT in Canada, or 613/991-3346 outside Canada.

Elderhostel Canada is an excellent way to enjoy a rewarding holiday. For as little as $400 a week all-inclusive, you live on college campuses or in conference centers, marine biology field stations or environmental study centers, and enjoy the accompanying cultural and recreational resources. Elderhostel is a blend of education and travel for participants who are at least in their mid-50s. There are usually lectures for about 90 minutes a day, but with no homework or exams, which makes it easy to enjoy many extracurricular activities suited to the elderhostel's location.

American visitors have the advantage of a U.S. dollar that is usually worth 30 percent more than the Canadian dollar. At the time of this writing, American visitors received approximately $1.40 Canadian for every U.S. dollar; shop around for the best exchange rates. All prices quoted in this book are given in Canadian dollars. (To convert to approximate U.S. dollars, divide by 1.4.) In addition to the usual $5, $10, $20, $50, $100, and larger bills, Canada has a couple of intriguing coins: the "loonie," worth $1 and engraved with a loon; and the "toonie," worth $2 and en-graved at the center with a "gold" polar bear. They are so striking that you may want to keep one or two as souvenirs.

Prices for hotel and motel accommodations in this resort-rich region vary greatly according to where and when you go—from less than $30 a night in the off-season in the backwoods or on the edge of town, to more than $2,000 a night in high season for a suite in a top-flight Banff resort. The average price for a motel or hotel room is $80 to $125, but competition for the tourist dollar brings on a variety of specials based on location and time of year, with such add-ons as free breakfasts and dinners. You can get good rooms for $40 to $50, and less if you choose university and hostel facilities—and that doesn't mean a bunk bed. Bed-and-breakfast accommodations usually cost less than hotels, though not always as these meet-the-people establishments are mushrooming and some are becoming mini-resorts. Camping costs range from $10 to $20 per party, one vehicle per site, and include the GST. Hostel prices are similar.

Meals vary greatly in price as well. You can get a hearty breakfast at a neigh-borhood café for as little as $2.99, and a gourmet dinner at a fancy hotel for about $40, but an average dinner at a good restaurant costs about $20—excluding drinks, appetizers, and desserts. Buffets and chain restaurants are eco-nomical. Often, the higher the price for a meal, the less food on your plate.

Overall, a family of four traveling in Western Canada should expect to pay about $350 a week if camping, $900 a week if staying at motels and using kitch-enette facilities, and $2,500 a week if choosing moderate- to high-end hotels and dining out.

Budget-minded travelers can take buses and trains, use campgrounds in provincial and national parks, and travel midweek. If you happen to be a British Columbian senior over the age of 65, you can travel free during midweek on government-operated ferries.

There are programs to suit every interest in Western Canada: Pacific Coast marine life at the Bamfield Marine Station or aboard a 65-foot motor vessel; Vancouver gardens at a college campus; the Kootenays with a camera or paint-brush from a platformed, double-walled teepee; the Ukrainian culture from a hotel in Smoky Lake; or Calgary by bicycle. For a catalog of Elderhostel adven-tures, contact Elderhostel Canada, 4 Cataraqui St., Kingston, Ontario K7K 1Z7; or email ecmail@elderhostel.org.

ORIENTATION AND TRANSPORTATION

Three major roads cross Western Canada from the coast to the interior to the Rockies: Highway 3 through Osoyoos and Cranbrook, the most southerly route and the one closest to the U.S. border; Highways 1 and 5 via Kamloops to Banff and Calgary; and Highway 16 through Prince Rupert, Prince George, Jasper and Edmonton. Two major roads run north to south: Highway 97 through Cache Creek, Prince George, and the Alaska Highway; and Highways 2 and 35 through Fort Macleod, Calgary, Edmonton, and High Level.

A circular tour via public transportation that is popular with international travelers is to take the train east from Vancouver to Kamloops, Jasper—and possibly Edmonton—a second train west from Jasper to Prince George and Prince Rupert, then ferry south to Port Hardy on Vancouver Island, take a bus down to Victoria, and, finally, ferry over to Vancouver.

The major airports of Vancouver, Calgary, and Edmonton are served by just about every major airline, notably Air Canada and Canadian Airlines International. Cut costs by purchasing tickets in advance, by being alert to special deals, and by flying with no-frills discount charter airlines such as Canada 3000. If you depart from Vancouver's International Airport, you must pay an Airport Improvement Tax of $10 (provincial) and $15 (international).

Once in Western Canada, the best way to travel is either by car or in some kind of recreational vehicle. The scenery is ever-changing, there's much to see and do in concentrated areas, and the highways provide circular routes. In British Columbia, myriad logging roads provide after-hours and weekend access to a variety of remote countryside and free camping areas. Maps are free and available from the B.C. Forest Service, Recreation Section, 4595 Canada Way, Burnaby, British Columbia V5G 4L9; 604/660-7500. A four-wheel-drive vehicle is usually necessary only in the most remote mountainous areas or in accessing snow activity areas in winter.

To get from Vancouver Island to the United States without battling the bottleneck of busy Vancouver, take the Duke Point ferry from just south of Nanaimo to Tswwassen terminal just south of Vancouver.

Ferries form an integral part of the highway system; B.C. Ferries runs many routes that interconnect and provide a delightful way of hopping between the islands and the mainland. The Inside Passage Ferry between Port Hardy and Prince Rupert, and the newer Discovery Coast Ferry between Port Hardy and Bella Coola are really mini-tours. Between June and September, artists are often on board to entertain or to display and sell their work. Inland ferries are free for all, and on other ferries, seniors with B.C. Pharmacare cards can travel free Monday through Thursday—excluding holidays. Count on long lines in summer on the more popular routes. It is possible to reserve space under certain conditions. For more information, contact B.C. Ferries, 1112 Fort Street, Victoria, British

Columbia V8V 4V2; 604/669-1211 in Vancouver, 250/386-3431 in Victoria, and 800/663-7600 anywhere else. Other ferries ply the waters between Victoria, Seattle, and Port Angeles; and between Sidney and Anacortes.

U.S. drivers must carry proof of financial responsibility. The Yellow Card is accepted as a nonresident interprovincial motorvehicle liability insurance, obtainable from your own insurance company. Radar detection of speeders is controversial, but it's widely used in British Columbia. Seat belts and child restraints for children under six are mandatory in Western Canada, as are helmets for cyclists and motorcyclists. The Alaska Highway and Mackenzie Highway are paved—or as good as paved—but watch your windshield and avoid logging trucks on the Liard Highway, which is still gravel.

Gas is cheaper in the United States than in Canada, so if you are near the U.S. border, fill up on the American side. Gas is also cheaper east of the Rockies. Officially, Canada is on the metric system, but there has been some resistance to changing from Imperial measurement, and recently Canadians have begun using both, especially in grocery stores.

All major cities are linked by Greyhound Bus, while smaller bus companies provide economical connections between many other communities. Train travel is more costly and limited in scope, but it's more relaxing and often follows more scenic routes. The Rocky Mountain Railtour between Vancouver and Jasper, Banff, and Calgary is highly regarded as the most spectacular train trip in the world. For further information, contact VIA Rail at 800/561-8630 in Canada, B.C. Rail at 604/631-3500, and Rocky Mountaineer Railtours at 800/665-7245 in Canada and the United States.

RECOMMENDED READING

People who live in, or even visit, this area are smitten with a love of the landscapes and their inhabitants, and feel compelled to write about them. The following is a list of some of the more recent publications:

Kim Goldberg's recent *Where to See Wildlife on Vancouver Island* (Harbour Publishing, 1997) is a welcome addition to the British Columbia government's own guide to the province's wildlife viewing areas. *Wild Mammals of Western Canada,* by Arthur and Candace Savage (Western Producer Prairie Books, 1981), gives a scientific but popular overview of western wildlife. For a definitive guide to the natural history of the province, look at *British Columbia: A Natural History* by Richard Cannings and Sidney G. Cannings (Greystone Books, 1996).

Many books are available for different ages on specific Western Canadian animals. *There's a Seal in My Sleeping Bag,* by Lyn Hancock (Harper Collins, 1972), is a Canadian classic. It describes the author's life flying, boating, and meeting

Western Canada's people and wildlife. *There's a Raccoon in My Parka, Love Affair with a Cougar,* and *An Ape Came out of My Hatbox,* on similar themes, are all out of print but available in libraries. Also, check out *Tell Me, Grandmother, The True Story of Jane and Sam Livingston,* about the first settlers in what was to become Calgary.

The Fraser River, by Alan Haig-Brown (Harbour Publishing, 1996), describes a river that flows through much of British Columbia's landscape. In its historical, geographical, cultural, and economical importance, the Fraser is British Columbia.

For a racy raconteur's rendition of life on the West Coast, there is *Raincoast Chronicles* (there are more than 17), by Howard White of Harbour Publishing; and a similar look inland, *Down the Road: Journeys through Small-Town British Columbia* and *Backroading Vancouver Island,* both by Rosemary Neering (Whitecap Books, 1991).

A Traveller's Guide to Aboriginal B.C., by Cheryl Coull (Whitecap Books, 1996), is the latest of many books on Western Canada's original inhabitants. Any books by author and illustrator Hilary Stewart on Western Canada's First Nations people and their culture are well worth reading. Try *Cedar* and *Looking at Totem Poles* (Douglas and McIntyre, 1993).

Kids will enjoy *Fun BC Facts for Kids,* by Mark Zuelke (Whitecap Books, 1995), and the novel *Buffalo Sunrise,* by Diane Swanson (Whitecap Books, 1995). Zuelke also wrote *The BC Fact Book, Everything You Ever Wanted to Know,* and *The Alberta Fact Book* (Whitecap Books, 1995). For kids too, in the *Hello Canada* series, read *British Columbia* by Vivien Bowers (Lerner Publications, 1995), *Alberta* by Sarah Yates (Lerner Publications, 1995), and *Destination Vancouver* by Lyn Hancock (Lerner Publications, 1998).

For history, a classic is *British Columbia, A History of the Province,* by well-respected George Woodcock (Whitecap Books, 1993). For a lighter look, try *Bowering's BC, A Swashbuckling History,* by poet George Bowering; and *British Columbia, An Illustrated History,* by Geoffrey Molyneux. Heather Harbord concentrates on *Nootka Sound* (Heritage House, 1996), where the non-native discovery of British Columbia began. This book is both a history and a paddling guide for kayakers. Another classic is *I Heard the Owl Call My Name,* by Margaret Craven (Clarke-Irwin, 1967), the story of a dying Anglican minister who spent two years with Coast Indians.

For an airborne look at a grandiose province, you can't do better than *Over Beautiful British Columbia* and its accompanying video, recently released by *Beautiful British Columbia Magazine* (Pacific Publishers, 1996). It's heavy on photographs and too light on text, but great for the coffee table. *Beautiful British Columbia Magazine* also publishes the regularly updated *BC Explorers Travel Guide* for a mile-by-mile description of British Columbia and Rocky Mountain roads.

Read *Great Bear Rainforest: Canada's Forgotten Coast,* by Ian and Karen McAllister and Cameron Young (Harbour Publishing, 1997), for a glimpse into the life and habitat of the white (Kermode) bear, an elusive denizen of the province's forested inlets.

Western Canada inspires a flood of pictorials and guides. Try Bruce Obee's *The Canadian Rockies* (Whitecap Books). Altitude Press publishes most of the Rocky Mountains guidebooks such as *Classic Hikes in the Canadian Rockies,* by Paul Graeme. Lone Pine Publishing publishes many of the guides to Alberta's natural history, including the useful *Alberta Wildlife Viewing Guide.* There are dozens of guidebooks written about the different methods—hiking, biking, boating, driving—of experiencing Vancouver Island, such as the *Hiking Trails and Island Adventures* series by Richard K. Blier.

WESTERN CANADA CLIMATE

Average daily high and low temperatures in degrees Celsius, plus monthly precipitation in millimeters (inches in parentheses). To convert degrees Celsius to Fahrenheit, multiply by 1.8 and add 32.

	Victoria	Vancouver	Banff	Calgary
Jan.	6.5/0.3	6.3/0.2	-5.3/-14.9	-3.6/15.4
	141 (5.6)	149.8 (6.0)	31 (1.2)	12.2 (0.5)
Mar.	10.2/1.9	10.1/1.8	3.8/-7.9	3.3/-8.4
	72 (2.9)	108.8 (4.4)	21.5 (0.9)	14.7 (0.6)
May	16.3/6.5	16.8/6.4	14.2/1.5	16.4/3.0
	33.5 (1.3)	61.7 (2.5)	57.5 (2.3)	52.9 (2.1)
July	21.8/10.4	22.0/11.1	22.1/7.4	23.2/9.5
	17.6 (0.7)	36.1 (1.4)	51.2 (2.1)	69.9 (2.8)
Sept.	19.1/8.4	19.0/8.3	16.1/2.4	17.4/3.8
	36.6 (1.5)	64.4 (2.6)	43.8 (1.8)	48.1 (1.9)
Nov.	9.4/2.5	9.2/2.3	0.5/-8.2	2.9/-9.0
	139.2 (5.6)	169.9 (6.8)	30.4 (1.2)	11.6 (0.5)

1
VANCOUVER

Ahh, Vancouver. Lotusland! Shangri-La! City of Dreams! Clichés? Yes, but for this gateway to Western Canada, the superlatives are really true. Consider the statistics: Vancouver is British Columbia's largest city; Canada's third-largest city; and the fastest-growing city in North America, with a 1.8 million population and a 3 percent annual growth rate. According to the Corporate Resources Group of Geneva, an agent of the World Tourist Council, Vancouver is the world's best city in which to live. It has a healthy, clean environment where you can sail or golf in the morning, ski in the afternoon, and pick roses in winter. It's the number-one destination in North America for tour buses. A favorable dollar exchange basically gives Americans every third day of their stay for free. Can seven million visitors each year be wrong?

Get a Vancouver City Passport of complimentary coupons from The Inn at False Creek, 800/663-8474.

Vancouver sprawls across islands and peninsulas separated by rivers, inlets, fjords, and bays, between a backdrop of rugged mountains and a lush apron of fertile farmland. And the variety of its terrain makes it third only to Los Angeles and New York as a North American film and television production center. Vancouver caters not only to sports lovers and outdoor enthusiasts, but also to connoisseurs of good books, coffee, wine, restaurants, and the arts. Vancouver boasts the highest ratio of foreign-born residents of any city in the world. This mix of cultures only adds to its appeal.

A PERFECT DAY IN VANCOUVER

Start the day at either the Georgia Street, Alberni, or the Beach Avenue entrance and walk or bicycle the seawall around Stanley Park, a Vancouver tradition. Stroll the beaches of English Bay to the Aquatic Centre, then take a False Creek ferry to Granville Island for lunch—either a stand-up snack at the Public Market or a sit-down meal at a dockside restaurant. False Creek, once a derelict industrial area, now hosts trendy cafés, condos, pubs, and marinas. If it is raining, pop into the Vancouver Museum, the Vancouver Maritime Museum, Science World, or a pub at Stamps Landing. Take the SkyTrain through downtown from Main Street station to Waterfront Station at Canada Place, then the SeaBus ferry to the North Shore of Burrard Inlet. Finish your day with a Skyride up Grouse Mountain for dinner.

ORIENTATION

To get yourself around Greater Vancouver, remember that the mountains are to the north (the North Shore), the sea to the west (Georgia Strait and English Bay), and that the city and its surrounding communities (West Vancouver, North Vancouver, Coquitlam, Burnaby, Richmond, Delta, and Surrey) are divided by waterways spanned by many bridges.

The Vancouver International Airport is located on Sea Island in the mouth of the Fraser River, one of the islands in this delta. The artwork and architecture of the international wing is a destination in itself. Don't miss the dramatic Haida Jade Canoe opposite the food outlets.

Note that Vancouver is on the lower mainland, and Victoria, BC's capital, is on Vancouver Island, a short ferry ride across Georgia Strait to the southwest.

It is useful to know that, except for the downtown core, which is a peninsula, Vancouver streets run north-south and avenues run east-west. The dividing line between west and east is roughly Main Street. West of Main, avenues are preceded by a "W" for west; east of Main, they are preceded by an "E" for east.

Vancouver can be reached by plane, train, bus, or cruise ship, or by car via Highway 1 (the Trans Canada), the main route from the east, or Highway 99, a northern extension of the U.S. Interstate 5 from the south. Via Rail's western transcontinental train "The Canadian" is a relaxing three-day ride from Toronto.

Once in Vancouver, use the city's public transit system, which is the most extensive in Canada. Get a copy of *Discover Vancouver on Transit* from a tourist

GREATER VANCOUVER

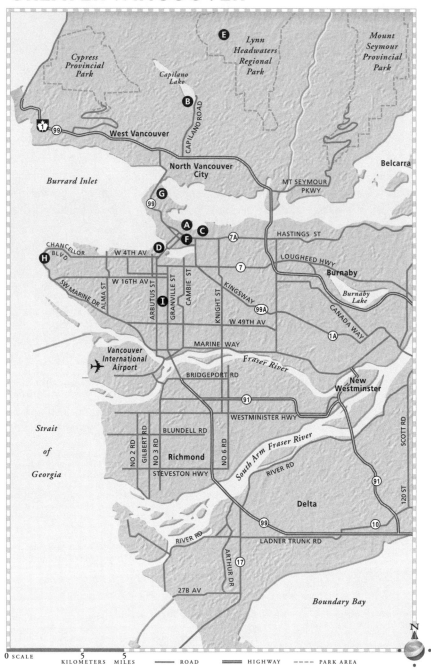

bureau or TransLink, 604/540-3000. It lists most of the attractions and shows you how to get to them. Take the SkyTrain from Vancouver to Burnaby, New Westminster, and Surrey. Use the SeaBus between Vancouver and the North Shore. Both connect directly with buses and trolleys. And don't forget to walk the waterfront. There's lots of it.

SIGHTSEEING HIGHLIGHTS

★★★★ CANADA PLACE

Georgia and Granville Streets used to mark the social center of downtown Vancouver. Now crowds stroll the promenades of stunningly beautiful Canada Place, a pier that juts into Burrard Inlet from the corner of Burrard and Howe Streets. The white, Teflon-coated sails that form the roof of the Vancouver Trade and Convention Centre are an irresistible subject for camera-toting tourists and residents alike. The largest cruise ships in the world tie up on either side of the convention center, and the cruise ship terminal is underneath. Saturday is the time to watch the ships arrive and depart, then have lunch in the luxurious Pan Pacific Hotel (see Lodgings)—the jewel of Canada Place—with the offices of the World Trade Centre below.

Inside the convention center is the CN IMAX Theatre with its five-story screen and sensational films that pull you in with wraparound images and sound.

Details: (IMAX) 604/682-4629 for further info, 604/280-4444 for tickets, or if out of town 800/582-4629, khurvey@imax.com, www.imax.com/vancouver; open Apr.–Oct. daily noon–10 P.M.; Nov.–Mar. noon–4 P.M., 6–10 P.M. $9.50 adults, $8.50 seniors, $7.50 students. (2 hours)

SIGHTS

Ⓐ Canada Place
Ⓑ Capilano Canyon Suspension Bridge and Park
Ⓒ Dr. Sun Yat-Sen Classical Chinese
    Garden and Chinatown
Ⓒ Gastown
Ⓓ Granville Island
Ⓔ Grouse Mountain
Ⓕ Library Square
Ⓖ Stanley Park
Ⓗ UBC Museum of Anthropology
Ⓖ Vancouver Public Aquarium
Ⓘ Van Dusen Gardens

Note: Items with the same letter are located in the same area.

★★★★ GRANVILLE ISLAND
Information Centre, 1592 Johnston St., near Public Market, 604/666-5784

A center for sawmills and other industries in the 1920s and 1930s, this mudflat island in False Creek was largely deserted after World War II. In 1973, it received a facelift and became a popular people place, with a houseboat community, a waterpark, tennis courts, three theaters, a brewery, a Kids Only market, and the unbeatable Public Market where you can watch artisans make pottery, tapestries, silk paintings, and other arts and crafts.

Details: Open 9 A.M.–6 P.M. year-round (except Monday in winter). Getting to Granville Island is an adventure in itself. Moorage in front of the market is free for two hours if you arrive in your own boat, and little ferries leave from the south foot of Hornby Street every few minutes. Price is $1.75 with discounts for seniors and children. Buses #50 and #51 are a great way to go. Ferries also run to Vanier Park, Stamps Landing and Science World. (3 hours)

★★★★ GROUSE MOUNTAIN
6400 Nancy Greene Way, North Vancouver, 604/986-6262, info@grousemtn.com, www.grousemountain.com

Only 15 minutes from downtown, Grouse Mountain offers ski runs in winter, hikes the rest of the year, a fun family outing, an escape to paradise, and wonderful views across the Lower Mainland to Vancouver Island and down to the United States. Of course, such a "foreverland" should be experienced on a clear day.

A 100-passenger car glides smoothly up the mountainside to 1,100 meters (3,600 ft) above sea level in only eight minutes at a cost of $16.95, discounted for seniors, children, and families. The cost includes the Peak Chairlift, a multimedia presentation on British Columbia, an unforgettable view of the toy-like city of Vancouver laid out below, an art-in-the-forest tour that features 26 giant Douglas fir chainsaw sculptures, and, in summer, a logger sports show. In winter, this price includes a snocat-drawn sleigh ride. In summer, use the picnic spots or hike the one-hour trail around Blue Grouse Lake. There's also an adventure playground for kids, a beer garden alongside the Peak Chair lift, and the new Hiwus Feasthouse where guests enjoy First Nation hospitality, dances, stories and a five-course meal; 604/984-0661.

Helicopter tours, 604/270-1484, of the surrounding mountains range from $45 to $95 per person, depending on tour length. For skiers, there are two aerial trams, four double chairs, one T-bar, and two rope tows, and 13 runs.

Details: 20 minutes by car over the Lions Gate Bridge, or take the #246 bus and transfer to #232 Grouse. (3 hours)

★★★★ STANLEY PARK

The pride and centerpiece of Vancouver, Stanley Park is one of the finest and largest (405 hectares/1,000 acres) natural city parks in North America. Bordered on three sides by water, it guards the entrance to Vancouver's spectacular natural harbor and sets the scene for the rest of the city's attractions. The park is ringed by a paved road and a 10.5-kilometer (6.5-mile) seawall walk/bike path. Vehicle traffic runs one way, counterclockwise.

You can golf, bowl, or play tennis; watch grass hockey, cricket, rugby, or soccer; swim in a saltwater pool; or relax on manicured lawns and smell the roses. You can identify birds in Beaver Lake and Lost Lagoon, photograph totem poles, ogle the boats at the Royal Vancouver Yacht Club, watch cruise ships sail under Lions Gate Bridge from Prospect Point, ride a miniature steam railway, take a horse-and-carriage tour, pet farmyard animals, see

The BC Ferry system is the largest domestic ferry service in the world.

Theatre Under the Stars at the Malkin Bowl, watch the sun set from the Teahouse Restaurant at Ferguson Point, and listen to the firing of the Nine O'Clock Gun—a nightly tradition. And you can also escape into the park's heavily forested interior by a crisscross of trails and forget that a frenetic downtown is only minutes away. Be as social or as solitary as you like. Stanley Park appeals to people of all ages and interests, in all seasons.

Details: At the foot of Georgia St., Stanley Park is a peninsula in the Vancouver Harbour. Open daily, 24 hours. Free, but there's a small parking fee, $5/day or $1 for two hours. A free shuttle bus operates mid-May to mid-September, passing stops every 10 minutes. (4 hours)

★★★★ UBC MUSEUM OF ANTHROPOLOGY
6393 N.W. Marine, 604/822-3825

Drive the beaches to this award-winning building on the campus of the University of British Columbia, brilliantly designed by famous Vancouver architect Arthur Erickson. Situated on the Point Grey Bluffs overlooking English Bay, the museum focuses on the art of the Northwest Coast First Nations people. You will be awed by its carved front doors, monumental totem poles, and massive sculptures of the Great Hall.

Details: *Open Tues. 11 A.M.–9 P.M., Wed.–Mon. 11 A.M.–5 P.M., closed Mon. in winter; $6 adults, with discounts for children, seniors, and families; free on Tue. (2 hours)*

★★★★ VANCOUVER PUBLIC AQUARIUM
604/659-3474, www.vanaqua.org

This major must-see attraction in Stanley Park features orcas (killer whales), beluga whales, seals, sea lions, and sea otters. Daily showings emphasize education. The aquarium's board room must be Vancouver's most innovative meeting room-adults conduct business watching orcas cavort through the windows.

Details: *Open daily Jun. 26–Sept. 6, 9:30 A.M.–7 P.M., the rest of the year 10 A.M.–5:30 P.M.. $12 adults, $9.50 senior citizens and ages 13–18, $7.50 ages 4–12, $33 family rate (two adults and three children). (2 hours)*

★★★ CAPILANO CANYON SUSPENSION BRIDGE AND PARK
3735 Capilano Rd., North Vancouver, 604/985-7474, capilano@istar.ca, www.capbridge.com

Capilano Canyon carves its tempestuous way through Capilano River Regional Park within minutes of downtown. Plunging cliffs, white water rapids, and towering timbers and totem poles in a misty rainforest make it an awesome setting. Add a salmon hatchery with fish ladders and other outdoor displays, a 61-meter (200-foot) Giant Fir, and the famous

If you want an aerial experience that won't cost anything, cross the 73-meter (240-foot) suspension bridge in Lynn Canyon Park. Walk the trails and visit the ecology center. Access is by car or by SeaBus and Phibbs Exchange/Westlynn bus #229 (2 hours).

Suspension Bridge that is the longest and highest suspended footbridge in the world—450 feet/137 meters long, 230 feet/70 meters high.

Details: *Access is by car off Capilano Rd., or by SeaBus to Lonsdale Quay, then bus #246 and #232 (in summer, #236 goes right by the park); Open daily Apr.–Oct. 8:30 A.M.–dusk, 9 A.M.–5 P.M. Nov.–Mar. $8.25 adults, discounted for seniors and students. (2 to 6 hours)*

★★★ DR. SUN YAT-SEN CLASSICAL CHINESE GARDEN AND CHINATOWN
578 Carrall St., 604/268-6363, sunyatsen@bc.sympatico.ca, www.discovervancouver.com/sun

Step through time and space into this bustling "other world" centered on East Pender Street between Carrall Street and Gore Street. Vancouver's Chinatown is second only to San Francisco's in size, and some of its architecture—recessed balconies, ornamental rooflines, and curved roof tiles—is unique to this city. Nearby, beside a free public park, is the Dr. Sun Yat-Sen Classical Chinese Garden, a beautiful walled sanctuary where every Friday night from June to September you can experience an Enchanted Evening in the garden while you sip tea, watch a one-hour Chinese music program, and stroll under the soft light of handmade lanterns.

For a reasonably priced and innovative experience, take a MAXimum Skyhigh to China Tour, which includes a panoramic view of Vancouver from the Lookout! on top of the Harbor Centre Tower, a tour of the Dr. Sun Yat-Sen garden, a nine-course dinner at Park Lock Chinese Seafood Restaurant and admission to a film at the CN IMAX Theatre. All for $42. Book through the Dr. Sund Yat-Sen Garden.

Details: *Jun. 15–Sept. 15 daily 9:30 A.M.–7 P.M.; May 1–Jun. 14 daily 10 A.M.–6 P.M.; Sept. 16–Apr. 30, 10 A.M.–4:30 P.M.; $6 adults, discounted for children, seniors, and families. (1 hour)*

★★ GASTOWN

"Gassy Jack" Deighton, a saloon owner and, in 1867, the first non-native inhabitant of the area, is Gastown's *raison d'être*. After a huge fire destroyed Vancouver in 1886, this area surrounding Water Street between Richards and Columbia Streets was rebuilt, largely with hotels and warehouses that became an early Skid Row from the Great Depression through the early 1960s. A masterly plan turned this shopping area into a historic site; cobblestone streets and gas lamps lent authenticity, overhead wires were buried, and trees added beauty.

Crowds gather to see the world's first steam clock, still operating, listen to its quarter-hour whistle, and see its on-the-hour spumes of steam, all within earshot of Gassy Jack's statue at the intersection of Water and Cambie Streets.

Details: *Free 90-minute tours led by costumed historians depart daily from Gassy Jack's statue at 2 P.M. in summer. (2 hours)*

★★ LIBRARY SQUARE
350 West Georgia at Homer St., 604/331-4045

Depending on point of view, a strangely modern nine-story coliseum-type structure nestling beside a 22-story office tower and filling a complete city block, Vancouver's Public Library is either a building of grace and beauty or a hideously pretentious and controversial eyesore. The library has a six-story, light-filled atrium, a vertical and horizontal electronic conveyor system to move books and other materials, automated checkouts, a language library allowing self-tutoring in 90 languages, and a computerized lab, and is surrounded by promenades, shops, restaurants, espresso bars, and a bookstore.

Details: *Tours are available of the library's interior. May–Sept. Mon.–Wed. 10 A.M.–9 P.M., Thur.–Sat. 10 A.M.–6 P.M., Sept.–Apr. Sun. 1–5 P.M. (1 hour)*

★★ VAN DUSEN BOTANICAL GARDENS
5251 Oak St. at 37th Ave., 604/878-9274

Once a golf course, this tranquil retreat is now ranked as one of the world's top ten botanical gardens. It has one of North America's three Elizabethan hedge mazes. Weather permitting, guided tours are offered in the afternoons from April to October, or pick up a self-guided tour sheet at the entrance.

Details: *Jun.–Sept. 10 A.M.–9 P.M.; the rest of Sept. 10 A.M.–6 P.M.; the rest of the year 10 A.M.–4 P.M.; the Festival of Lights is open nightly Dec. 11–Jan. 3, 5–9:30 P.M.; $5 adults, discounted for seniors, children, and families. (2 hours)*

FITNESS AND RECREATION

Vancouverites spend more money on sports equipment than any other Canadians. The possibilities are endless and easily accessible. You can walk and cycle the waterfront along Burrard Inlet, False Creek, and the Fraser River, or through an impressive network of city parks; hike, ski, and climb in the North Shore mountains (Grouse Mountain, Cypress Bowl, and Mount Seymour, or the 41.5-kilometer [26-mile] Baden-Powell Trail across the city's backdrop); sail, powerboat, paraglide, kayak, windsurf, fish, dive, and swim in the city's many waterways; ride horses in Southlands, Vancouver's rural equestrian neighborhood; play tennis on dozens of free city park courts; and golf on a variety of scenic courses along Howe Sound and the Fraser River (for transportation and bookings to the top local courses try the **West Coast Golf Shuttle,** 604/878-6800). If you are a birder, don't miss the more than 250 species to be seen in peak season (April through October) at the **George C. Reifel Bird Sanctuary** on Westham Island, 604/946-6980. If you can do only one activity, walk the seawall in Stanley Park. No outfitters needed.

FOOD

Vancouver is a culinary paradise, with an overwhelming choice of restaurants, many of them Asian. Consult the weekly Vancouver newspaper, *Georgia Strait,* for updated listings at the time of your visit.

Choose a restaurant with a view. Join Vancouverites for an inexpensive summer lunch or Sunday brunch at **Bridge's,** 1696 Duranleau, Granville Island, 604/687-4400. It has a dining room, bistro, pub, and large patio overlooking the boats and ferries of False Creek.

You get a more industrial view of the Burrard Inlet waterfront at the refitted **Cannery,** 2205 Commissioner, near the north end of Victoria, 604/254-9606. It's more expensive, but decorated in the rustic style of the West Coast fishing industry, and it's one of the city's oldest and most dependable seafood restaurants. You are closer to the view if you sit by the window of the **Five Sails Restaurant** in the Pan Pacific Hotel, 999 Canada Place, 604/662-8111. It's expensive, but this is the heart of Vancouver and worth it.

Perhaps the most panoramic view of both downtown Vancouver and the North Shore mountains is **Seasons in the Park,** in Queen Elizabeth Park, W. 33rd Ave. and Cambie St., 604/874-8008. Choose a seat in the dining room under a broad-leafed fig tree. The food is moderately priced and as good as the ambiance, especially the seafood. My favorites on the menu are B.C. grilled salmon and seared prawns and scallops.

Looking south, the view is still good at the long-established and fairly expensive **Salmon House on the Hill** at 2229 Folkestone Way, West Vancouver, 604/926-3212. West Coast First Nations artifacts adorn the walls, and the chef is known for such creations as alder-grilled salmon marinated in single-malt Scotch whiskey, lemon grass, and golden sugar with lemon and ginger butter. A newer, trendier place continuing the West Coast theme and serving oven-baked

DOWNTOWN VANCOUVER

SCALE

0.5 MILES

0.5 KILOMETERS

0 SCALE

ROAD ─── HIGHWAY ──── PARK BOUNDARY

Coal Harbour

English Bay

Sunset Beach Park

Mole Hill

Gastown

Chinatown

Sun Yat Sen Garden

Vanier Park

Hadden Park

To Stanley Park

To G

WATER ST
E CORDOVA ST
E HASTINGS ST
E PENDER ST

TERMINAL AV
QUEBEC ST
99A 1A
GEORGIA VIADUCT
PACIFIC BLVD
CAMBIE ST
Cambie Bridge
To O P
R
a
U
HOMER ST
SEYMOUR ST
HOWE ST
BURRARD ST
THURLOW ST
G
To B H Y C

W CORDOVA ST
W HASTINGS ST
DUNSMUIR ST
SMITHE ST
Sky Train
7A
W
E D
T
Z
Q
J
L
F

MELVILLE ST
GEORGIA ST
COAL HARBOUR RD
W PENDER ST
99N 1A
GEORGIA ST
JERVIS ST
ROBSON ST
NELSON ST
DAVIE ST
NICOLA ST
BEACH AV
PACIFIC BLVD
BEACH AV

DENMAN ST
CHILCO ST
PARK LN
LAGOON DR
To Stanley Park
N V b
S
X
I
M

Granville Bridge
Burrard Bridge
CHESTNUT ST
OGDEN AV
To A
K

wild salmon is moderately priced **Raintree at the Landing,** 375 Water St. near Cordova St., 604/688-5570. The view is inside at Vancouver's only First Nations restaurant, the **Liliget Feast House,** 1724 Davie near Denman, 604/681-7044. Low tables are surrounded by log columns and concrete platforms and walls hung with Northwest Coast art, which give you the feeling of going through a walk in the forest and entering a First Nation longhouse. Try the reasonably priced Potlatch Platter for two. It features alder-grilled salmon, mussels, prawns, oysters, venison and wild rice. Side dishes include sea asparagus, fiddlehead ferns and yams.

Famous chef Umberto Menghi owns several popular but more expensive restaurants that reflect his passion for traditional Italian food. His signature restaurant, **Il Giardino di Umberto,** 1382 Hornby St. at Pacific Ave., 604/669-2422, is known for its hearty pastas, game dishes, and garden decor. If you want family fare and family prices, go instead to the **Old Spaghetti Factory** in Gastown, 53 Water St., near Abbott St., 604/684-1288, where you can sit in an old streetcar while you eat, and have the kids mess with paper and crayons. This restaurant's been around for 30 years and is proud of its good service and reasonable prices.

They are expensive, but if you want the best of food and wine, along with elegant and exclusive surroundings, choose a dining room In one of the city's downtown hotels. All get rave reviews and win awards: **Chartwell** in the Four Seasons Hotel, 791 W. Georgia St., 604/689-9333; **Diva at the Met,** in the

---

FOOD

- Ⓐ Bread Garden
- Ⓑ Bridge's
- Ⓒ Cannery
- Ⓓ Chartwell
- Ⓔ Diva at the Met
- Ⓕ Five Sails Restaurant
- Ⓖ Il Giardino di Umberto
- Ⓗ Isadora's Cooperative Restaurant
- Ⓘ Liliget Feasthouse
- Ⓙ Old Spaghetti Factory
- Ⓚ Planet Veg
- Ⓛ Raintree At The Landing
- Ⓜ Romano's Macaroni Grill at the Mansion

FOOD *(continued)*

- Ⓝ Salmon House on the Hill
- Ⓞ Seasons In the Park
- Ⓟ Tojo's
- Ⓠ Tsunami Sushi
- Ⓡ William Tell

LODGING *(continued)*

- Ⓢ English Bay Inn
- Ⓓ Four Seasons Hotel
- Ⓣ Hotel Vancouver
- Ⓤ Kingston Hotel B&B
- Ⓥ Lighthouse Retreat Bed and Breakfast
- Ⓦ New Backpackers Hostel

LODGING *(continued)*

- Ⓕ Pan Pacific Hotel Vancouver
- Ⓧ Sylvia Hotel
- Ⓨ Waterlily
- Ⓩ Wedgewood Hotel
- ⓐ YWCA Hotel Residence

CAMPING

- ⓑ Capilano Mobile RV Park
- ⓒ Park Canada Recreational Vehicle Inn

Note: Items with the same letter are located in the same area.

Metropolitan Hotel, 645 Howe St. near Georgia St., 604/602-7788; and **William Tell,** in the Georgian Court Hotel, 765 Beatty St., 604/688-3504. The landmark William Tell has been famous for its consistently good Swiss-French cooking since owner and chef Erwin and Josette Doebeli opened it in 1964.

Tojo's, 777 W. Broadway Ave. at Willow St., 604/872-8050, is regarded as the best and one of the most expensive of Vancouver's Japanese restaurants. Some people prefer the more affordable floating sushi bar at **Tsunami Sushi,** 604/238-1025, Robson St., 604/687-8744. Sit on stools and select your dishes of sushi as they float along a river of flowing water set in the counter in front of you.

You can get cheap eats in the city. The **Bread Garden** is a chain of budget eat-in or take-out restaurants for those who want inexpensive and healthy soups, sandwiches, and salads available any hour of the day or night. The waitfolk are friendly and energetic. Try the carrot and basil soup, Thai chicken wraps, and cheese-filled tortellini with pesto salad. The chocolate mousse cheesecake is legendary. There are 10 locations in Vancouver; try the one at 1880 W. First at Cypress, 604/738-6684.

Romano's Macaroni Grill at the Mansion, 1523 Davie St., 604/689-4334, an affordable but distinctive restaurant, is in a wonderfully restored heritage house said to be haunted—a great place to eat on Halloween. Dishes and decor are based on Philip Romano's memories of his Mama Rosa's home in Italy, featuring an open kitchen, white gladiolas, and paper-covered tables. Weekend brunch is a good deal: all the Italian you can eat for a very affordable price, with Caesar salad and foccacia included.

As an alternative to the ubiquitous Macdonald's, take the kids to **Isadora's Cooperative Restaurant,** 1540 Old Bridge, Granville Island, 604/681-8816, for a weekend brunch; the earlier the better because it's popular. A local favorite of vegetarians is the family-owned and operated **Planet Veg,** 1942 Cornwall St., 604/734-1001. It's nothing much to look at, but the food is cheap and healthy. Try the samosas.

LODGING

Out of Vancouver's more than 16,000 rooms, rates will vary from as little as $15 to more than $1,000 per night. The best deals are offered in the city's off-season, October 17 through May 31. During that time Alberta, Washington, and California residents can take advantage of "Discover the Spectacular" program rates of as much as 50 percent off, offered through Tourism Vancouver hotel partners.

Some of the most expensive hotels are landmarks and worth the splurge.

One of the most spectacular of the newer hotels is the **Pan Pacific Hotel Vancouver** (Canada Place pier and convention center), 999 Canada Pl. at the foot of Howe St.; 800/663-1515 in Canada, 800/937-1515 in the U.S. Rooms are probably among the most expensive in Vancouver, but you get an outstanding downtown location, an eight-story atrium lobby lined with totem poles, a lounge and café with 40-foot glass walls, a panoramic view of Vancouver Harbor, and probably the best hotel health club in Canada. Even if you don't stay there, do visit.

Those who want nostalgia and tradition in the grand style will be more attracted to the much older but newly renovated **Hotel Vancouver,** 900 W. Georgia St., 604/684-3131 or 800/441-1414. It's one of the famous and historic Canadian Pacific Railway hotels where you expect crystal and chandeliers—expensive, but conveniently located and worth the money.

The **Four Seasons Hotel,** 791 W. Georgia St., 604/689-9333 or 800/268-6282, in Canada, 800/332-3442 is also expensive, but it's in the center of Vancouver's main shopping district, it pampers children and pets, as well as adults. Kids get complimentary milk and cookies on arrival. Pets get bottled water served in a bowl on a sterling silver platter.

Highly recommended, and expensive, is Eleni Skalbania's intimate boutique-style **Wedgewood Hotel,** 845 Hornby St., 604/689-7777. It is noted for its elegant antique furniture and the superb food served in its Bacchus Ristorante and Lounge, which resembles an authentic Tuscan inn.

Another Vancouver landmark is the much-loved grande dame **Sylvia Hotel,** 1154 Gilford St., 604/681-9321. With views of English Bay beaches and sunsets, and extremely reasonable rates given its fame and location, this ivy-cloaked stone, heritage hotel is understandably popular; reserve very early. Smaller and pricier, but in the same style is the **English Bay Inn** in a quiet spot at 1968 Comox St., a block from the beach and Stanley Park, 604/683-8002. This 1930s house is renovated in British private-club style with sleigh and four-poster beds, and offers sherry and port in the parlor each afternoon. The European-style **Kingston Hotel B&B,** 757 Richards St., 888/713-3304, has a great downtown location, is close to theaters, has an English-style pub in the same building, yet has moderate rates.

Bed-and-breakfasts are multiplying rapidly in Vancouver. For a private romantic suite near Lighthouse Park only 20 minutes from downtown via scenic Marine Drive, try the **Lighthouse Retreat Bed and Breakfast,** 4875 Water Ln., 604/926-5959, lighthouse@vancouver-bc.com, www.vancouver-bc.com/LighthouseRetreat. The double rooms are huge and moderately priced. If you like sleeping near water and waking up with nature by your window, try a floating bed-and-breakfast called **Waterlily,** one of three River Run Cottages at

4551 River Rd., West Ladner, 604/946-7778. It has a queen-size loft bed, a claw-foot tub, potbellied stove, private deck, and a kayak, rowboat, and bicycle for exploring the surrounding farmland and fishing village. It's one of the more expensive bed-and-breakfasts and is 30 minutes to downtown by freeway; but to some, an intriguing romantic lodging is worth it.

University residences, YMCA/YWCAs, and youth hostels are abundant in this two-university city and provide good budget accommodations. The **YWCA Hotel Residence** at 733 Beatty St., 604/895-5830, hotel@ywcavan.org, www.ywcahotel.com, has 11 floors of downtown hotel rooms with an incredible choice—singles, doubles, twins, triples, and quaint rooms with hall, shared or private bathrooms—a far cry from traditional YMCA and YWCA accommodations. The free services of a Health and Wellness Center, a 15-minute walk away, is a bonus. Of the several hostel-type hotels in Vancouver, try **The New Backpackers Hostel,** 347 W. Pender St., near Gastown, 604/688-0112. It's more upscale with larger rooms and the same prices.

CAMPING

You can pitch your tent or park your RV just minutes from downtown Vancouver. **Capilano Mobile RV Park,** 295 Tomahawk Ave., West Vancouver, 604/987-4722, has an incredibly choice location by the Capilano River, under the Lions Gate Bridge, opposite Stanley Park, and beside a beach and the popular Park Royal shopping center. Another choice site at the southern end of the city is **Park Canada Recreational Vehicle Inn,** 4799 Highway 17 (exit north on 52nd St.) in Delta, 604/943-5811. It's handy to the Tsawwassen ferry terminal for Victoria and Nanaimo. Nearby provincial parks such as Garibaldi Provincial Park and Golden Ears Provincial Park also offer a wide selection of natural camping sites. Reservations can be made through Discover Camping at 604/689-9025.

NIGHTLIFE

All the big-name artists come to Vancouver. It's more than probable that they want an excuse to see the city—and be paid for it—as much as they enjoy Vancouverites' enthusiastic reception.

Half a million people watch a glorious display of fireworks set to music at the annual summertime Symphony of Fire International Fireworks over English Bay in the West End, 604/738-4304; or world-class live performances at one of the many and varied theaters. The traditional place for shows is the **Queen Elizabeth Theatre** (big productions) and **Playhouse** (intimate plays) on the

THE SUNSHINE COAST
AND THE GULF ISLANDS

Travel just 30 minutes to two hours out of Vancouver by ferry, rail, air, bus, car, or bike and you have a lifetime of choices.

Take a trip to Squamish by BC Rail's Royal Hudson steam train followed by a 20-minute stopover flight along the glaciers of the Coast Mountains, and return to Vancouver by way of Howe Sound on the MV Britannia. Phone Harbour Cruises at 800/663-1500 or 604/688-7246 for reservations. The season runs June to September, Wednesday through Sunday, and holiday Mondays. If you want just the glacier experience, phone Glacier Air in Squamish at 800/265-0088.

For an unusual, fun, and educational excursion into what makes much of the economy of Vancouver and British Columbia tick, take a paddle-wheel cruise on the Fraser River from New Westminster, once the capital of British Columbia, to Fort Langley, a Hudson's Bay Company fur-trading post and the birthplace of British Columbia. You will see the log booms, sawmills, and fishing ports of a working river while you enjoy lunch and some historical drama at the same time. For more information call Paddlewheeler River Adventures, 604/525-4165.

corner of Hamilton and Georgia Sts., 604/665-3050. The **Orpheum Theatre** at Smithe and Seymour, 604/665-3050, built in 1927 and restored lavishly in 1977, is worth seeing for its ornate decor, its painted dome ceiling, and its gilt ornamentation. It's home to the Vancouver Symphony. The **Vancouver East Cultural Centre,** 1895 Venables, 604/254-9578 or 604/251-1363, was once a turn-of-the-century East End church. If it's not raining and you are feeling nostalgic, sit outdoors by the bandshell in Stanley Park at the **Theatre Under the Stars,** 604/687-0174, and watch a lively musical.

Vancouver has nightclubs to suit every taste. Wine and dine as you revolve through the view in the **Cloud 9 Lounge,** Landmark Hotel, 1400 Robson St., 604/662-8328 or at The Top of Vancouver, one level up from The Lookout! in the **Harbour Centre Tower,** 555 W. Hastings St., 604/669-2220. The 1950s atmosphere of the **Waldorf Hotel,** 1489 E. Hastings St., 604/253-7141, is presently in vogue, as are the singing and dancing at the **Blarney Stone,** 216 Carrall St., Gastown, 604/687-4322.

One of the hottest nightspots in town is the **Purple Onion Cabaret,** 15 Water St., in the heart of Gastown, 604/602-9442. It has two rooms: the jazz cabaret is small, intimate, and furnished in 1950s style; and down the hall is a large nightclub for those who want to dance the night away. Cabaret acts change frequently.

Scenic Route: The Georgia Strait

From Horseshoe Bay in West Vancouver, take Highway 101 up the Sunshine Coast to Powell River via the Langdale and Saltery Bay ferries, cross Georgia Strait to Comox and Courtenay, and drive down the east side of Vancouver Island to Crofton. Then take the Saltspring Island ferry to Vesuvius Bay, meander through Saltspring Island to the charming village of Ganges, and take another ferry from Fulford Harbour across the strait to Tsawwassen and Vancouver. Ask B.C. Ferries for schedules and special CirclePac rates.

This enchanting, 300-kilometer (180 mile) coastal tour takes you through cottage country and appeals to artists and boaters. Take your time and spend several days poking into its many nooks and crannies. Explore the detours. It's worth the water-taxi ride from Lund to cruise to the distinctive white sandy beaches of tropical-looking Savary Island. Don't miss the marine parks in Desolation Sound and Princess Louisa Inlet, either in your boat or on a trip with Bluewater Adventures, 604/980-3800. Gibson's Landing, on the Sechelt Peninsula between Langdale and Earls Cove is world-famous as the location for the internationally popular CBC Television series The Beachcombers. Reminisce with the locals over a cup of coffee at Molly's Reach Café, the same watering hole featured in the show.

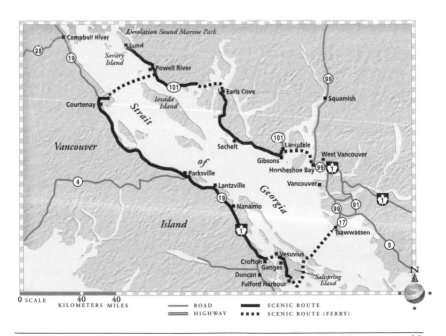

2
WHISTLER AND THE
SEA TO SKY HIGHWAY

The Squamish Highway or, as it is more romantically called, the Sea to Sky Highway, climbs out of the picturesque seaside village and ferry terminal of Horseshoe Bay in West Vancouver, sidles along Howe Sound under a rim of overhanging mountains to Squamish, and slices up through forests to reach Whistler at 675 meters (2,214 feet).

Whichever season you choose, try to spend a few days at Whistler Resort. Named after the whistling marmots of Whistler Mountain, this is a world-class, European-style, four-season resort. Three major North American ski publications have rated it the number-one ski resort in North America, not only for the greatest vertical drop in the continent (1,609 meters/5,280 feet), the largest ski area (more than 2,800 hectares/7,071 acres), and the most extensive high-speed lift system in the world (32 lifts serving more than 200 marked runs and 12 alpine bowls, including three glaciers), but also for its scenery, dining, and après-ski activities. Since Whistler Village opened in 1980 at the base of Whistler and Blackcomb Mountains, it has become a self-contained community with a year-round population of more than 8,600—a number that jumps to almost 30,000 during the winter.

A PERFECT DAY IN WHISTLER
In summer, wake up from your slopeside suite that is as far up Blackcomb Mountain as possible, take a gondola or open-air chairlift to the top of either

Whistler or Blackcomb Mountains, and hike one of the alpine trails, which vary in length from 30 minutes to more than three hours. If weather permits and the pocketbook allows, join a helicopter tour to get even higher into the mountains for heli-hiking or a picnic lunch at one of the glaciers; **Whistler Heli-hiking,** 604/932-4105. Then, hike or mountain bike down the mountain and browse through the shops and art galleries at Whistler Village, sip a drink at a café, listen to some streetside entertainment, and finally find a delicious place for dinner. It doesn't get better than that.

HIGHWAY SAFETY

The Sea to Sky Highway is a spectacular mountain drive, but between Vancouver and Squamish it is squeezed between the sea and the mountains in a high rainfall area subject to mudslides. It is narrow, winding, and can be dangerous. For up-to-date road reports, call Talking Yellow Pages, 604/299-9000; listen to Mountain FM Radio West Vancouver-Squamish at 107.1; or watch hourly reports between November and April on the Weather Channel. For road safety assistance, phone the B.C. Automobile Association, 800/663-2222.

ORIENTATION

Get to Vancouver and then drive the Sea to Sky Highway (Highway 99) north to Squamish and the Whistler Resort (2 hours) or take the train or bus. The Whistler Express bus departs daily from the Vancouver International Airport (for schedules, call 604/266-5386). B.C. Rail's Cariboo Prospector, 800/663-8238 or 604/984-5246, departs the North Vancouver terminal daily at 7 A.M. for the Whistler train station with free connecting bus service to the village. It's better to drive your own vehicle so you can complete a circle tour back to Vancouver via Lillooet and Cache Creek, or perhaps a wider circle through the Okanagan. Walking is the best way to get around Whistler Village, although other methods are available as well —horses, bikes, in-line skates, helicopters, fixed and float planes, four-wheel-drive vehicles, and public buses.

SIGHTSEEING HIGHLIGHTS

★★★★ BRACKENDALE EAGLE RESERVE
Located in Brackendale 10 kilometers (6 miles) north of downtown Squamish on Hwy. 99
The Brackendale Art Gallery at 41950 Government Road sponsors

WHISTLER AND THE SEA TO SKY HIGHWAY

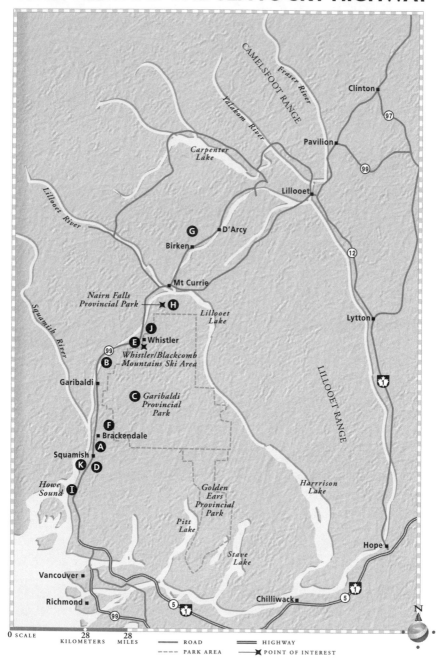

CAMELSFOOT RANGE

Fraser River

Yalakom River

Clinton

97

Pavilion

Carpenter Lake

99

Lillooet

Lillooet River

G ● D'Arcy

Birken

Mt Currie

12

Nairn Falls Provincial Park — ✕ H

Lillooet Lake

Lytton

J
E ✕ Whistler
Whistler/Blackcomb Mountains Ski Area

99

B

Garibaldi

C Garibaldi Provincial Park

LILLOOET RANGE

F
● Brackendale

A

Squamish ■
K ● D

Howe Sound ● I

Golden Ears Provincial Park

Harrrison Lake

Pitt Lake

Hope

Stave Lake

Vancouver ■

1

Richmond ■

99

5

1

Chilliwack ■

5

1

N

0 SCALE   28 KILOMETERS   28 MILES

ROAD — — — HIGHWAY

- - - - PARK AREA   ✕ POINT OF INTEREST

an annual January eagle count. Brackendale is home to the largest gathering of bald eagles in North America. In 1994, a record 3,700 bald eagles were counted in one day. Eagles gather along the Squamish and Cheakamus Rivers to feed on spawning salmon. During January weekends, members of the Brackendale Eagle Reserve Society guide visitors to the best viewing sites along the dikes. You can also view the eagles from a raft or on horseback.

Details: *Brackendale Art Gallery, Box 100, Brackendale, BC, V0N 1H0; 604/898-3333, gallery@mountain-inter.net.*

★★★★ GARIBALDI PROVINCIAL PARK
Highway 99 between Squamish and Whistler, 604/898-3678
You can ski or walk from Whistler Mountain to neighboring Garibaldi Provincial Park via Singing Pass and Russet Lake, but it isn't easy. Better to access this stunningly beautiful park, with its striking volcanic peaks, lush alpine meadows, and remote lakes, via various signposted trails that take off from the Sea to Sky Highway (Hwy. 99). Or you can take the train to Garibaldi Station and hike from there.

Some people prefer to access the park by helicopter to the top

---

SIGHTS
- Ⓐ Brackendale Eagle Reserve
- Ⓑ Brandywine Falls Provincial Park
- Ⓒ Garibaldi Provincial Park
- Ⓓ Stawamus Chief Provincial Park
- Ⓔ Whistler Resort

FOOD
- Ⓔ Bear Foot Bistro
- Ⓔ Christine's
- Ⓔ Crab Shack
- Ⓔ Il Caminetto di Umberto
- Ⓔ Old Spaghetti Factory
- Ⓔ Rendezvous
- Ⓔ Rimrock Café and Oyster Bar

FOOD *(continued)*
- Ⓔ Roundhouse Lodge
- Ⓔ Thai One On
- Ⓔ Trattoria di Umberto
- Ⓔ Val d'Isere
- Ⓔ Zeuski's Taverna

LODGING
- Ⓔ Blackcomb Lodge
- Ⓔ Canadian Pacific Château Whistler Resort
- Ⓔ Chalet Luise
- Ⓔ Edelweiss Pension
- Ⓔ Hostelling International-Whistler
- Ⓔ Pan Pacific Lodge Whistler
- Ⓔ Residence Inn by Marriott
- Ⓔ Shoestring Lodge
- Ⓔ UBC Lodge

CAMPING
- Ⓕ Alice Lake Provincial Park
- Ⓖ Birkenhead Lake Provincial Park
- Ⓗ Brandywine Falls Provincial Park
- Ⓒ Garibaldi Provincial Park
- Ⓗ Nairn Falls Provincial Park
- Ⓘ Porteau Cove Provincial Park
- Ⓙ Riverside Campground
- Ⓚ Shannon Falls Provincial Park

Note: Items with the same letter are located in the same area.

instead of trekking uphill through the trees. A favorite Garibaldi hike is into Garibaldi Lake from the Rubble Lake parking lot 39 kilometers (23 miles) north of Squamish. Camp overnight in alpine meadows, then climb Black Tusk 2,315 meters (7,595 feet)—or as much of its rocky peak as you dare. Cheakamus Lake and Diamond Head are the park's other two main natural attractions. Late July to early September is the most popular visiting time, but snow may linger on the ground until well into July.

Details: *For further info, contact District Manager, Alice Lake Provincial Park, Box 220, Brackendale, B. C. VON 1H0; 604/898-3678. (1 day)*

★★★★ **WHISTLER RESORT**
120 km (75 mi) north of downtown Vancouver on Hwy. 99. Whistler Resort Association, 4010 Whistler Way, 800/944-7853 or 604/6654-5625, www.whistler-resort.com

Whistler has rapidly become world famous as a year-round playground for local families, not just celebrities or wealthy globetrotting skiers. Backdropped by two dramatic side-by-side mountains—Blackcomb and Whistler—Whistler Resort comprises several European-style villages and residential neighborhoods, and more are being built all the time. Whistler is third only to Vancouver and Victoria in attracting tourists. It is consistently rated as the Number One Ski Resort in North America and is the only one to offer summer skiing—on Horstman Glacier.

Whistler's abundant snowfall (an average of 9.14 meters/30 feet) allows exceptional downhill, cross-country, and heli-skiing; snowboarding; snowshoeing; snowmobiling; ice skating; ice hockey; and sleigh-riding. Its mile-high vertical runs mean you can easily mountain-ski until early June and glacier-ski and snowboard mid-June to mid-August. By helicoptering to the glaciers, you can ski almost year-round (lift operates June 12 through August 3). Buy dual mountain lift tickets so you can ski both mountains economically.

For 80 years before Whistler became a ski resort, the area was a popular summer resort for the local residents. It now boasts some of the world's best golf courses and mountain-bike trails. Whistler's mild coastal climate means golfing can begin in May. Riding chairlifts and gondolas to the top of the mountains make it easy to go alpine hiking, horseback-riding, and paragliding. The temperate months of July through October is the best time for hiking in alpine areas, but there are many miles of marked hiking trails along Whistler's lakes and valleys. Daring mountain bikers switchback down the mountain by a thrilling trail known simply as The Descent. You can be guided down or do it yourself.

Five nearby lakes and numerous local streams encourage swimming, sunbathing, boardsailing, canoeing, kayaking, sailing, rafting, jet-boating, and fishing. Climbing is popular, whether it's on a granite rock high in the mountains or the Climbing Wall in Whistler Village itself. In-line skating is currently very trendy, and Whistler offers a paved 20-kilometers (12-miles) Valley Trail shared by cyclists and walkers.

Anything is possible at Whistler Resort. Practically every month has its own festival or special event. From June through October, the cobblestone plazas come alive with constant entertainment. Children, especially, have lots to keep them occupied—from ski camps, day camps, and language camps, to climbing walls, windsurfing, and even a trapeze. Some of the many tours such as guided nature walks on the top of Blackcomb Mountain, are free.

Details: To book tours and buy lift tickets, contact the Whistler Activity and Information Centre at the front doors of the Whistler Conference Centre in the main village, 601/932-2394. For direct contact, call Whistler/Blackcomb Relations, 604/932-3434. Customized packages (lift tickets, lodging, and ground transportation to and from Vancouver International Airport), are available from Whistler Resort, 800/944-7853 or 604/664-5625. Package prices vary depending on the season. (1 day)

★★ BRANDYWINE FALLS PROVINCIAL PARK
37 km (23 mi) north of Squamish off Hwy. 99, 604/898-3678
Take a break and walk the short 10-minute forest trail to a viewpoint over 60-meter high (195-feet) Brandywine Falls. Views of the falls and surrounding mountains of Garibaldi Provincial Park are impressive. You can fish, picnic and camp.

Details: (30 minutes)

★★ STAWAMUS CHIEF PROVINCIAL PARK
About 1 km (0.6 mi) south of Squamish off the east side of the highway, 604/898-3678.
Its main feature is the 652-meter (2,139-foot) Stawamus Chief, one of the world's largest freestanding monoliths and a rock sacred to the Squamish First Nation. The rock annually attracts more than 160,000 hikers and rock climbers.

Details: Open year-round. (1 to 2 hours)

FITNESS AND RECREATION

Unless you just sit in your car and gaze at the scenery or sit in a café, you can't help being physically fit, whatever the season. There is so much to do. In addition to its innumerable year-round outdoor activities that include four of the world's top golf courses, Whistler has several indoor fitness centers. **Meadow Park Sports Centre,** 604/938-PARK, boasts the most facilities including an indoor rock climbing wall.

FOOD

Many of the more cosmopolitan restaurants in Whistler Resort are expensive—as much as $100 for a full-course meal for two. The following are some of the more reasonably priced restaurants where you get the best value. But if you like seafood, splurge at the elegantly rustic **Rimrock Café and Oyster Bar,** 2117 Whistler Rd. (Creekside), 604/932-5565 or 604/938-1411. It's in the high-end price range, but is revered for its ambiance, food, and service. Part of the rock on which it is built is inside the restaurant, along with pine floorboards and a huge fireplace. **Val D'Isere,** in the bottom level of the Sheraton Suites in the Town Plaza area, 604/932-4666, serves expensive, classic French cuisine, but the food and ambiance are also worth the price. Famous Chef Umberto Menghi has two popular Italian restaurants at Whistler with moderate to high prices, but the quality is always first-class with fresh hand-picked ingredients: fine dining at **Trattoria di Umberto,** in the Mountainside Lodge, 604/932-5858, and the less expensive, more family oriented **Il Caminetto di Umberto,** in Whistler Village, 604/932-4442.

The **Bear Foot Bistro,** adjoining the Listel Hotel in Whistler Village, 604/932-1133, serves expensive, but incredibly good steaks. The Bistro has a separate room for drinking fine Scotch whiskey and smoking cigars, and artists-in-residence often create while you dine. **Thai One On,** in the Upper Village at the base of Blackcomb Mountain, 604/932-4822, serves Thai food at reasonable prices; **Zeuski's Taverna,** in Whistler's new Town Plaza, 604/932-6009, serves reasonably priced Greek food. The **Crab Shack,** across from the Coast Whistler Hotel in Whistler Village, 604/932-4451, is a local favorite for steak and seafood and has a separate pub with an oyster bar and pool table. Families on a budget like the ever-popular **Old Spaghetti Factory,** in the Crystal Lodge at 4154 Village Green West, 604/932-1081. Lots of food and affordable.

You can literally eat your way up the mountains, from the cheap cafeteria-style fare in the **Rendezvous** at the top of the Solar Coaster lift on Blackcomb Mountain, 604/932-3141 to upscale cafeteria food in the new

Roundhouse Lodge at the top of the lift on Whistler Mountain, 604/905-2367; to the dearer continental cuisine and linen-and-silverware ambiance at **Christine's** atop Blackcomb Mountain, 604/932-7437.

LODGING

With more than 115 lodgings available, Whistler offers something for everyone, from high-priced luxury hotels to friendly bed-and-breakfast inns and budget hostels. Off-season rates usually apply in November, December (excluding Christmas season), January, and in some places, April. Some hotels offer family packages. The quickest way to book accommodations is to call **Whistler Central Reservations,** 800/WHISTLER, www.whistler-resort.com. Whistler is one place where you will want to splurge. Consider it similar to a trip to Europe.

The new **Pan Pacific Lodge Whistler** at the top of Whistler Village beside the Excalibur Gondola leading to Blackcomb Mountain, and also close to the base of Whistler Mountain, is a full-service lodge; every "room" is a luxury suite with hotel service advantages. Lots of wood in the decor and a fireplace in every suite give it a warm, cozy feel, and high quality spa amenities provide extra luxury. Contact Pan Pacific at 604/905-2999 or 888/905-9995, whistler@pan pacific-hotel.com, and www.panpac.com\hotel

Hotels such as **Canadian Pacific Château Whistler Resort,** 4,599 Château Blvd., 800/606-8244 or 604/938-8000, are worth visiting just to appreciate the architecture (do stroll through the marvelous glass and stone-walled lobby), or to browse the shops. If you can afford the splurge, stay here and revel in the grandeur. **Residence Inn by Marriott,** a ski-in/ski-out resort on the slopes of Blackcomb Mountain, 4899 Painted Cliff Rd., 800/777-0185 or 604/905-3400, offers more affordable studios and one- and two-bedroom suites that look out onto the chairlift. The Marriott offers a complimentary serve-yourself breakfast and a shuttle to the town center. The hotel also provide generous servings of happy hour complimentary food. **Blackcomb Lodge,** 4220 Gateway Dr. in the town center, 800/667-2855 or 604/932-4155, is cheaper, centrally located, and has kitchens.

The closest pension-type bed-and-breakfast within walking distance of Whistler Village is **Chalet Luise,** 7461 Ambassador Crescent, 800/665-1998 or 604/932-4187. Its charm lies in its alpine-style architecture and Swiss hospitality. Rates are reasonable and include a full breakfast and complimentary afternoon tea. The **Edelweiss Pension,** 7162 Nancy Green Dr., 800/665-2003 or 604/932-3641, is just as pretty and has similar rates that include a full breakfast and complimentary afternoon tea/cake.

Whistler's most affordable quality accommodation, with a restaurant and pub on site, is the **Shoestring Lodge,** 7124 Nancy Green Dr., about 2 kilometers (1.3 miles) north of Whistler Village, 604/932-3338, shoe@direct.ca and www.whistler.net/boot/string.html. It has both private and dormitory accommodation. **Hostelling International-Whistler,** 5678 Alta Lake Rd., 604/ 932-5492, 604/932-4687, whistler@hihostels.bc.ca; and **UBC Lodge,** 2124 Nordic Estates, 604/932-6604 or 604/822-5851, also offer both shared and private accommodations for budget travelers.

Many accommodation rental companies such as **Powder Resort Properties,** Box 1044, Whistler, BC V0N 1B0, 800/777-0185 (Can. and U.S.) or 604/932-2882, rent out one- to four-bedroom condos and hotel rooms throughout Whistler at a moderate cost.

CAMPING

Several provincial parks along the Sea to Sky Highway offer picnicking or overnight camping: **Porteau Cove, Shannon Falls, Alice Lake, Garibaldi, Brandywine Falls, Nairn Falls,** and **Birkenhead Lake.** All can be accessed at 604/898-3678. At Diamond Head camping is restricted to cleared tent spaces; a day shelter is at Red Heather Campground; and there is an overnight shelter with 34 bunks at Elfin Lakes Campground. At Garibaldi Lake and Black Tusk, camping is allowed only at Taylor Meadows and the west end of Garibaldi Lake, where there are cleared tent spaces and day shelters. Otherwise, camping is restricted to the west end of Cheakamus Lake and the northwest end of Wedgemount and Russet Lakes.

Closer to Whistler Resort are several immaculate places for day picnicking and water sports: Lost Lake, Alpha Lake, and the largest, Alta Lake, which features Rainbow Park, Lakeside Park, and Wayside Park. (My personal favorite is Rainbow Park.) A new addition is **Riverside Campground,** about 2.5 kilometers north of Whistler Village, 604/932-5469. It has 100 RV sites, 80 tenting sites, three group sites, 14 small cabins and all upscale amenities including a small grocery store and eventually a mini-golf course and a nature walk.

NIGHTLIFE

Mountain Sports and Living (formerly *Snow Country* magazine) ranked the big **Longhorn Saloon and Grill,** in the Carleton Lodge at the base of Whistler Mountain, 604/932-5999, as the best après-ski bar in Canada. It has a ski-in location, substantial portions of food at fair prices, ice-cold draught beer, plus DJs spinning classic and modern rock during the week and live music on weekends. It offers 29 different burgers and perhaps the "best damn nachos in town." Its

Live at the Longhorn Concert Series attracts world-class performers. Other people prefer **Buffalo Bill's Bar and Grill,** next to the Conference Centre in the heart of Whistler Village, 604/932-6613, with lots of space for dancing, playing pool, eating lunch or dinner, watching sports events on a big-screen TV, trying out the ski simulator, or listening to the occasional live entertainment.

Another popular gathering place favored by locals is the **Cinnamon Bear Bar**, in the Delta Whistler Resort, 604/932-1982, open from 11 A.M. to 1 A.M. daily. The **Savage Beagle,** in Whistler Village, 604/932-3337, offers a variety of music, from hip-hop to jazz; a wine and cigar bar lounge upstairs and a dance club downstairs. **Garfinkel's,** 604/932-2323, is a Whistler Village club in which you can dance until 2 A.M. **Dub Linn Gate Old Irish Pub,** in the lobby of the new Pan Pacific Lodge, 604/905-4047, is the place where people of all ages are flocking, especially for an après-ski beer (it offers 32 different draft beers from around the world), live entertainment nightly in the busy season, or just relaxation in front of a fire. The pub was built in Ireland by Guinness Breweries and rebuilt at Whistler, and John Reynolds, one of the famous Irish Rovers, plays there regularly. There isn't anything more authentic than that.

3
VICTORIA

In contrast to Vancouver, its boisterous big sister on the Lower Mainland, Victoria on Vancouver Island is a sleepy English seaside village—although that image is changing. Victoria's hills are gentle, smooth, rocky outcrops softened by glaciers and clothed with meadows of shiny arbutus, twisted oaks, and glorious wildflowers. Victoria, like the queen after whom the city is named, is, genteel. Twenty percent of Victoria's residents are over 65, and in the past it's been said that the city rolls up its sidewalks at night, but that image is changing, too.

The site of a former Hudson's Bay Company trading post (1843), Victoria is the oldest city in Western Canada and the capital of British Columbia. It's known world-wide for its charm and friendliness (according to *Condé Nast Traveler* magazine, it has been rated as the top city in the world for friendliness and ambiance), meticulously groomed year-round gardens and hanging baskets, Victorian-era architecture, and the best weather in Canada. The city attracts artists, naturalists, and retirees. Travel writers call it the Garden of Eden, as did city's founder, James Douglas, in 1843.

A PERFECT DAY IN VICTORIA

Hit all the high spots in a London-style double-decker bus, horse-drawn carriage, or *kabuki* (pedicab). Stroll the Inner Harbour to look at yachts and mingle with the crowds in the city's central core; eavesdrop on a wedding in Beacon

EMPRESS HOTEL, VICTORIA

_ee Foster

Hill Park; follow the yellow footprints that mark the scenic Marine Drive; have a drink at the Snug in the Oak Bay Beach Hotel; dash back to the Empress Hotel for afternoon tea; and meander along every road to the water on the Saanich Peninsula. Then, cap the day with dinner and fireworks at Butchart Gardens. So much for traditional Victoria, but if you want a walk on the wild side, book an ecotour with the Royal British Columbia Museum, or any adventure travel operator, and spend a day offshore, perhaps watching whales.

ORIENTATION

Victoria at the southern tip of Vancouver Island is the western terminus of the Trans-Canada Highway (Hwy. 1), but you will probably arrive in Swartz Bay by ferry from Vancouver and Tsawwassen and drive to Victoria by Highway 17—the Pat Bay Highway—through the Saanich Peninsula, by ferry from Anacortes or Port Angeles in Washington State, or fly into Victoria's International Airport. The prettiest way is the ferry ride through the Gulf Islands from Vancouver and Tsawwassen to Swartz Bay. If you come via Seattle, take the _Victoria Clipper_ ferry or the luxury _Princess Marguerite_ vehicle and passenger ferry.

It's easy to get around Victoria by bus (pick up Victoria by Bus from BC Transit 250/382-6161), but it's better to explore the downtown area by horse-drawn wagon or kabuki. Whether walking or driving, keep to the waterfront as

GREATER VICTORIA

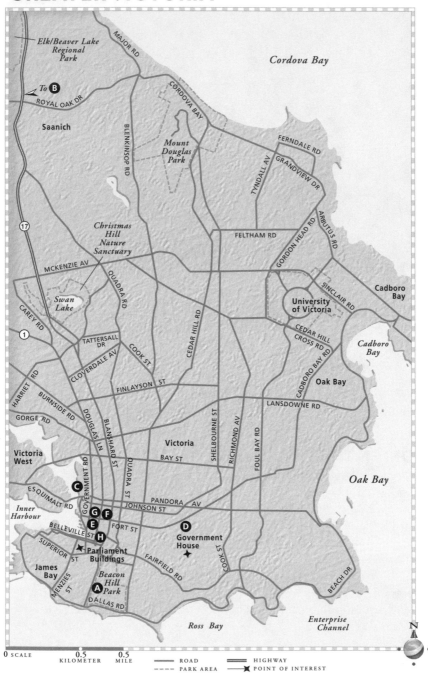

Elk/Beaver Lake Regional Park

MAJOR RD

Cordova Bay

To **B**

ROYAL OAK DR

CORDOVA BAY

Saanich

BLENKINSOP RD

Mount Douglas Park

FERNDALE RD

TYNDALL AV

GRANDVIEW DR

ARBUTUS RD

17

Christmas Hill Nature Sanctuary

FELTHAM RD

GORDON HEAD RD

SINCLAIR RD

Cadboro Bay

MCKENZIE AV

QUADRA RD

University of Victoria

CAREY RD

Swan Lake

CEDAR HILL CROSS RD

Cadboro Bay

1

TATTERSALL DR

COOK ST

CEDAR HILL RD

CADBORO BAY RD

HARRIET RD

CLOVERDALE AV

FINLAYSON ST

Oak Bay

BURNSIDE RD

DOUGLAS LN

LANSDOWNE RD

GORGE RD

BLANSHARD ST

Victoria West

Victoria

SHELBOURNE ST

RICHMOND AV

FOUL BAY RD

BAY ST

Oak Bay

ESQUIMALT RD

GOVERNMENT RD

QUADRA ST

C

Inner Harbour

PANDORA AV

G **F**

JOHNSON ST

E

BELLEVILLE ST

FORT ST

H

D

COOK ST

Government House

SUPERIOR ST

★ Parliament Buildings

FAIRFIELD RD

James Bay

MENZIES ST

Beacon Hill Park

A

BEACH DR

DALLAS RD

Ross Bay

Enterprise Channel

N

0 SCALE
0.5 KILOMETER
0.5 MILE
——— ROAD
═══ HIGHWAY
--- PARK AREA
★ POINT OF INTEREST

much as possible and be sure you take in the magnificent houses and gardens of the Uplands and Marine Drive areas of Oak Bay.

SIGHTSEEING HIGHLIGHTS

★★★★ BUTCHART GARDENS
800 Benvenuto Ave., Brentwood Bay, 250/652-4422, groupres@butchartgardens.bc.ca
Jenny Butchart started it in 1904 with a yen to beautify an old quarry. Now this 20-hectare (50-acre) showplace near Brentwood Bay, 21 kilometers (13 miles) north of Victoria, is a world-famous destination featuring distinctive formal gardens, outdoor musical and theatrical performances, the Ross Fountain, restaurants, nightly illuminations June 15 through September 30, and a truly fantastic music-and-thrills fireworks display every Saturday night in July and August. Your best bet is to spend Saturday at the gardens. Enjoy a romantic gourmet picnic basket for two, or splurge on dinner in the Dining Room Restaurant, watch the fireworks, and stroll the gardens in the moonlight. Christmas illuminations are also spectacular.
   Details: Open daily at 9 A.M. (including holidays), closing hour depends on season; adults $15.75 (high season) discounted for children and groups; reduced admission Nov.–Mar. (3 hours)

★★★★ EMPRESS HOTEL
721 Government St., reservations 800/441-1414, direct 250/384-8111, www.cphotels.ca
Built in 1908 by the Canadian Pacific Railroad (CPR) in elegant château-style, the newly renovated Empress is justly famous for the magnificence of its traditional decor, as in the Palm Court and Crystal Ballroom. New traditions are seen in Tony Hunt's Kwakiutl totem pole in the confer-

---

SIGHTS

- Ⓐ Beacon Hill Park
- Ⓑ Butchart Gardens
- Ⓒ Chinatown
- Ⓓ Craigdarroch Castle
- Ⓔ Empress Hotel
- Ⓕ Inner Harbour
- Ⓕ Munro's Bookstore
- Ⓖ Old Town
- Ⓗ Royal British Columbia Museum
- Ⓔ Victoria Bug Zoo

Note: Items with the same letter are located in the same area.

---

ence center lobby beside the rebuilt Conservatory. Afternoon tea in the Tea Lobby is expensive, but it's a traditional Victorian ritual that you shouldn't miss, with silver trays of cucumber, watercress, and egg salad sandwiches; scones with Devonshire cream; seasonal berries with crème Chantilly; and a tea blend unique to the hotel. A piano or string quartet plays soothing background music. Splurge, and leave your jeans at home. The Empress's afternoon tea is popular, so book three days in advance, 250/389-2727. New is the Bengal Patio beside the Rose Garden, a quieter lunch venue than Victoria's other patio restaurants that are on busy streets. Try the Bengal's famous curry buffet lunch.

Details: (2 hours)

★★★★ THE INNER HARBOUR

It's worth being touristy in Victoria, so make the stone-walled Inner Harbour, edged by Johnson, Wharf, Government and Belleville Streets in the heart of Victoria's downtown area, your first stop. Several famous attractions are near here—the Empress Hotel, the Parliament Buildings, the Royal British Columbia Museum—but also the **Royal London Wax Museum,** 250/388-4461, **Miniature World,** 250/385-9731, **Crystal Garden, 250/381-1213, and** Pacific Undersea Gardens, 250/382-5717. Your kids will love them all, especially the Chamber of Horrors in the wax museum.

Wander the wheelchair-accessible waterfront and take a ferry across the harbor to Ocean Pointe Resort, the Coast Harbourside Hotel or the boats, float planes and float houses at Fisherman's Wharf. Pick up brochures and free coupons at the **Victoria Travel Info-Centre,** 812 Wharf St., 250/953-2033, then read them on a bench overlooking the harbor while listening to street-busker music or the bell tunes of the museum's carillon. Don't forget to take your own photo of Victoria's favorite postcard—the "Welcome to Victoria" floral sign on the lawn in front of the Parliament Buildings. Gaze up at the bronze statue of Captain Vancouver looking down from the roof of the legislature and holding the flag that he used in 1792 to claim this northwest corner of the continent in the name of the British Crown. Come back at night to see the legislature outlined in lights.

Details: (2 hours)

★★★★ OLD TOWN

In the downtown area between Wharf and Government Streets, this is where Victoria began. A flourishing seaport at the turn of the century, Victoria has preserved and remodeled more than 200 old warehouses, factories, offices, stores, and seedy hotels to produce a vibrant strolling area of colorful courtyards and alleyways that cater to historians, architects, artists, shoppers, diners, and browsers. **Bastion Square,** where Sir James Douglas established Fort Victoria in 1843, houses the **Maritime Museum of British Columbia,** 250/385-4222, its vast collection of model ships, and the tiny but real vessels Tilikum and Trekka whose stories raise eyebrows—and hair! Multilevel Market Square has intriguing shops, bars, and restaurants surrounding a courtyard that often hosts free musical and other special events.

Details: The Maritime Museum is open daily 9:30 A.M.–4:30 P.M.; adults $5, discounted for seniors, students and families. (2 hours)

★★★★ ROYAL BRITISH COLUMBIA MUSEUM
675 Belleville St., 250/387-3701 or 888/447-7977, www.rbcn1.rbcn.gov.bc.ca

As one of the world's best museums, it's active enough to intrigue the whole family. The life-size hand-carved Haida canoe, with its naked Haida whalers, and the stunning rain forest curtain that used to dominate the lobby have been relegated to storage; some say to avoid offending prudish sensibilities, others say to save space. However, the museum has plenty of other wonderfully realistic dioramas and three-dimensional sensory displays of the province's tidal marshes, seabird colonies, old-growth forests, First Nations longhouses, sawmills, gold-diggings, and frontier towns. Real-life totem poles stand tall on either side of the escalator.

Check what's showing on the six stories-tall screen at the **National Geographic IMAX Theatre** within the museum. For 24-hour show information phone, 250/953-IMAX (4629).

Outside the museum in Thunderbird Park are full-size totem poles, a half-size Kwakiutl ceremonial house, and a carvers' workshop and demonstration area. Listen to the Netherlands' Centennial Carillon, the gift of Dutch residents of British Columbia to commemorate Canada's centennial in 1967. It's the largest carillon in Canada.

Details: Museum open daily 9 A.M.–5 P.M.; adults $7 discounted for seniors, youths, students and families; audio tours in several languages available for a small fee (museum); adults $9 discounted for seniors, students, and youth (theater); combination passes for museum and theater available. (2 hours). Thunderbird Park open daily dawn–dusk. Free. (1 hour)

★★★ BEACON HILL PARK

Once a swampy forest, this 74-hectare (183-acre) inner-city park (entrance is at the foot of Douglas Street) is now a mostly manicured retreat, walking destination, and birding spot for residents and tourists alike. It has formal flower beds, bird-filled ponds, graceful trees, stone-walled bridges, picnic sites, playing areas, and a children's farm. No food concessions, but there are free musical concerts in summer. Joggers, walkers, and dogs stretch their legs daily along the scenic Dallas Road waterfront, a very Victorian tradition.

Details: *Open daily dawn–dusk. Free. (1 hour)*

★★★ CHINATOWN

Gate is located at the intersection of Government and Fisgard Sts.

Chinatown covers little more than Fisgard Street, but is packed with shops, restaurants and on-street vegetable stalls. Fan Tan Alley, Canada's narrowest thoroughfare, barely permits two people to stand side by side. The **Gate of Harmonious Interest** is an impressive entranceway to Chinatown.

Details: *(1 hour)*

★★★ CRAIGDARROCH CASTLE

1050 Joan Crescent, 250/592-5323, ccastle@islandnet.com

This sandstone extravagance, which looks as if it came from Disneyland, was built by coal baron Robert Dunsmuir for his wife in the late 1880s. He promised her a castle if she would go with him to Vancouver Island, but Dunsmuir died before he could live in it. The castle, overlooking the city, features turrets, leaded-glass windows, tiled floors, and intricately carved woodwork. It also houses Victorian furnishings and changing exhibits of the period. Squeeze through the front door built just wide enough to defend with a sword and gaze up four stories and a spiral staircase to the ceiling.

Details: *Open daily Jun. 15–Sept. 9 A.M.–7:30 P.M., the rest of the year 10 A.M.–5 P.M., adults $7.50, discounted for groups, students, children, Canadian Military, all proceeds go to the ongoing restoration of castle. (1 hour)*

★★★ MUNRO'S BOOKSTORE

1108 Government St., 250/384-2464

Probably the best-stocked bookstore in Victoria, it's also worth visiting for the elegance of its Neoclassical architecture. This restored 1909 heritage building once housed a bank. It has been touted as "the most magnificent bookstore in Canada, possibly North America."

Details: *(15 minutes plus browsing time)*

★★★ VICTORIA BUG ZOO
1107 Wharf St., 250/384-BUGS, cmaier@bugzoo.bc.ca, www.bugzoo.bc.ca

Victoria's popular new hands-on attraction is not only for kids. People of all ages—even bug haters—will remember the prickly feeling of a giant African millipede or a praying mantis crawling up their arms, or hissing cockroaches, or scorpions that glow in the dark. If you're in a group, try a sleepover one Saturday night (bring your own sleeping bag) and enjoy chocolate-covered bugs for snacks.

Details: *Open daily Mon.–Sat. 9:30 A.M.–6 P.M., Sun 11 A.M.–6 P.M.; $6 adults, $5 students and seniors, $4 children 3–16. (.5 hour)*

FITNESS AND RECREATION
There's lots to do year-round in balmy, coastal Victoria. Walking or jogging the Dallas Road waterfront in all weather is a popular pastime. Golfers can't beat the scenery at **Victoria Golf Club,** situated on a peninsula jutting into the Juan de Fuca Strait, but to play at this exclusive course you will need an introduction from another golf club, 250/598-4224. Also extremely scenic is the new **Olympic View Golf Club** at 643 Latoria Rd., 250/474-3671. Imagine a setting that overlooks the Olympic Mountains in neighboring Washington and a signature 17th hole that is a 60-foot waterfall cascading over a natural rock monolith. Birders head for **Clover Point, Whiffin Spit, Witty's Lagoon,** and the boardwalk of the **Swan Lake-Christmas Hill Nature Sanctuary,** or they ogle bald eagles scavenging spawned-out salmon at the Eagle Festival in fall at **Goldstream Provincial Park.**

Cyclists, hikers and horseback-riders appreciate the recently developed 42-kilometer (26-mile) **Galloping Goose Trail** through Victoria's west coast communities. Swimmers use the magnificent new indoor **Saanich Commonwealth Place** aquatic center, built for the 1994 Commonwealth Games at 4636 Elk Lake Dr., 250/727-7108; or nearby lakes such as Thetis, Elk, and Beaver (warmish); or such rare sandy beaches as Willows and Island View (a tad chilly). The new **Gowlland Tod Provincial Park** is a scenic hiking trail and day-use area on the edge of Finlayson Arm and Tod Inlet. Offshore offers many opportunities for boating, fishing, diving and the new passion for whale-

and wildlife-watching—and, of course, in a city that caters to all ages, lawn bowling and croquet.

You can book a variety of activities—convenient one-stop shopping—at the centrally located **Victoria Marine Adventure Centre** at 950 Wharf St., 800/575-6700 or 250/995-2211.

FOOD

When you're wondering where to go for a meal or nightspot in Victoria, pick up a copy of the weekly *Monday Magazine* (it comes out on Wednesday) or *Victoria Dining Guide* (a good spot is Sam's Deli on Government Street beside the Inner Harbour).

Barb's Fish and Ships (yes, really!) is a floating fish-and-chips take-out shop moored alongside the fishing boats and floathouses of Fisherman's Wharf at 310 St. Lawrence St., 250/384-6515. It's very popular because of its location and if you ask first, you can get your fish and chips wrapped traditionally in newspaper.

For healthier alternatives, try sit down fish and chips at a restaurant such as the **Garlic Rose,** 1205 Wharf St. in Bastion Square, 250/995-2796. Here, enthusiastic, dedicated owner and chef Moses Hanna serves healthy, herb-filled, reasonably priced meals, breakfast, lunch and dinner, seven days a week, year-round. "If you're not satisfied with your meal, I guarantee it will be free," is his promise. "And healthy!" Patrons say that the food is so good at the **Re-bar,** 50 Bastion Square, 250/361-9223, that most people don't notice that it's vegetarian. This juice bar serves freshly squeezed fruit, vegetable and wheatgrass drinks. People flock to **Sam's Deli,** 805 Government St., 250/382-8424, for huge "build-it-yourself" sandwiches they can eat on the street at Victoria's busiest intersection. Close by, right on the dock beside the even busier Inner Harbour and therefore good for people and boat watching, is **Milestone's,** 812 Wharf St., 250/381-2244, which serves familiar food at affordable prices. You view the food, not the scenery, at **Pounders,** 535 Yates St., 250/388-3181, a Mongolian Style Stir Fry franchise where you pick out your meat, vegetables and spices, hand them to the chef to cook, and pay by the pound.

Whenever sweet-toothed guests come to town, I rush them to the **Dutch Bakery and Coffee Shop,** 718 Fort St., 250/385-1012, to drool over this Victorian institution's impeccable pastries and little cakes.

You must try some of the other venerable Victorian institutions: the opulent **Empress Room** at the Empress Hotel, famous for its tapestry-covered walls, its elegant candle and fire-light atmosphere and fine dining; the **Blethering Place Tea Room and Restaurant,** 2250 Oak Bay Ave., 250/ 598-1413, a favorite with the older crowd where you can sit all day people-watching over a pot of tea; and the cozy Tudor-style **Oak Bay Beach Hotel,** 1175 Beach Dr., 250/ 598-4556. You can rely on their distinctive British ambiance and the consistently good quality of their food and service. The **Princess Mary Restaurant,** 358 Harbour Rd., just west of the Johnson Street Bridge, 250/386-3456, is the top deck of an actual sailing ship, the *Princess Mary,* that sailed the local waters for 40 years. Residents don't rave about the food—unremarkable burgers, sandwiches, soup, and seafood—but for decades they have brought their out-of-town visitors to this Victorian institution and habits die hard. If you like fine dining amid luxury boats and looking at seals, try the much classier and very popular **Marina Restaurant in Oak Bay,** 1327 Beach Dr., 250/598-8555.

Camille's Fine Westcoast Dining is an intimate French restaurant at 45 Bastion Square, 250/381-3433, and is well known for its impeccable food and service and its extensive wine list, but I prefer the heated outdoor courtyard ambiance of the Italian-style **Il Terrazzo** restaurant nearby at 555 Johnson Street off Waddington Alley, 250/361-0028, a hole-in-the-wall recently renovated by an award-winning architect and now getting rave reviews as the best place in Victoria to kiss and propose marriage. It has a retractable roof, wood fireplaces in the walls and tables strewn with real rose petals.

Three popular hot spots that are always crowded are **Pagliacci's,** 1011 Broad St., 250/386-1662; **Café Brio,** 944 Fort St., 250/383-0009; and the recently opened **Med Grill,** 1010 Yates St., 250/360-1660. You may have to line up to get in, but the food (West Coast cuisine with a Latin heart) is worth waiting for, the prices reasonable and the atmosphere lively.

Your best bet for Chinese food is the old standby, **Don Mee's Seafood Restaurant** at 538 Fisgard St., 250/383-1032, and the newer, more expensive, but highly respected **Hunan Village** at 546 Fisgard St., 250/382-0661. For traditional and homemade East Indian food, the family-run **Spice Jammer** at 852 Fort St., 250/480-1055, is popular. For good Greek cuisine accompanied by customary belly dancing, don't miss the landmark windmill that soars over **Millos** at 716 Burdett St., 250/382-4422, one block from the Empress Hotel. **Periklis** at 531 Yates St., 250/386-3313, is another long-established Greek restaurant and the favorite of top Victorian restaurateurs.

For more formal and expensive dining, Victoria has several world-acclaimed restaurants in its hinterland. Three have spectacular locations. Lunch on the terrace of the **Deep Cove Chalet,** 11190 Chalet Rd., North Saanich, 250/656-3541 and treat yourself to sweeping lawns, beautiful gardens, and exquisite food, especially the Sunday seafood buffet. Go for dinner (French cuisine) and the sunset over Saanich Inlet is free. **Sooke Harbour House,** a country inn at 1528 Whiffen Spit Road, Sooke, on the southwest coast of the island,

DOWNTOWN VICTORIA

N

To B K

CADBORO BAY RD

BAGGIE ST

ROCKLAND AV

RICHARDSON ST

To Beach Dr.

ST. CHARLES ST

FAIRFIELD RD

DALLAS RD

JOAN CRESCENT

FERNWOOD RD

BAY ST

PRINCESS AV

PANDORA AV

JOHNSON ST

YATES ST

FORT ST

RICHARDSON ST

MOSS ST

COOK ST

VANCOUVER ST

L

QUADRA ST

C

COOK ST

DALLAS RD

BLANSHARD ST

U

HUMBOLDT ST

To E F

PRINCESS AV

DISCOVERY ST

HERALD ST

FISGARD ST

S

W

H

O V

N

Beacon Hill Park

DOUGLAS ST

T

Bastion Square

DOUGLAS ST

GOVERNMENT ST

GOVERNMENT ST

To R Z a b d

G

P

D

M I

STORE ST

J

WHARF ST

GOVERNMENT ST

Upper Harbor

Q

MENZIES ST

BELLEVILLE ST

X

SONGHEES RD

SUPERIOR ST

NIAGARA ST

ESQUIMALT RD

KIMTA RD

OSWEGO ST

CRAIGFLOWER RD

CATHERINE ST

Victoria Harbor

A

ERIE ST

SIMCOE ST

DALLAS RD

Victoria

FERRY TO SEATTLE WA

FERRY TO PORT ANGELES WA

OLD ESQUIMALT RD

LAMPSON ST

ESQUIMALT RD

Y

BEWDLEY AV

PARK TERRACE

FRASER ST

PLACE OF INTEREST

FERRY

PARK BOUNDARY

ROAD

MILE

KILOMETER

0 SCALE

250/642-3421, hosts a restaurant known continent-wide for its local seafood served with fresh herbs and fresh flowers grown in adjacent gardens.

Butchart's Gardens, 800 Benvenuto Ave., Brentwood Bay, is famous for its flowers, but with the **Dining Room Restaurant's** recent focus on fine dining 250/652-8222, you'll now find flowers on your plate—pansies on your butter, violets in your vinaigrette, roses in your chicken marinade. Choose a table that overlooks the Italian Garden and soak up more flowers with the view. You'll not find better service or ambiance anywhere.

In June, plan to eat out nightly at the annual **Victoria Folk Fest,** in Centennial Square behind City Hall. You'll get almost nonstop free entertainment as well as a variety of ethnic foods.

LODGING

The first hotel on everyone's list is the historic, ivy-clad **Empress Hotel,** overlooking the Inner Harbour at 721 Government St., 800/441-1414, 250/384-8111, 250/381-5959, right in the swing of things downtown. Grand rooms, even grander lobbies, the renowned Bengal Room for curries and drinks, the daily afternoon tea ritual, arcades of expensive shops—the Empress

FOOD

- Ⓐ Barb's Fish and Ships
- Ⓑ Blethering Place Tea Room and Restaurant
- Ⓒ Café Brio
- Ⓓ Camille's Fine Westcoast Dining
- Ⓔ Deep Cove Chalet
- Ⓕ Dining Room Restaurant
- Ⓖ Don Mee's Seafood Restaurant
- Ⓗ Dutch Bakery and Coffee Shop
- Ⓘ Empress Room
- Ⓙ Garlic Rose
- Ⓚ Hunan Village
- Ⓙ Il Terrazzo
- Ⓚ Marina Restaurant in Oak Bay
- Ⓛ Med Grill

FOOD (continued)

- Ⓜ Milestone's
- Ⓝ Millos
- Ⓚ Oak Bay Beach Hotel
- Ⓞ Pagliacci's
- Ⓟ Periklis
- Ⓟ Pounders
- Ⓠ Princess Mary Floating Restaurant
- Ⓓ Re-bar
- Ⓘ Sam's Deli
- Ⓡ Sooke Harbour House
- Ⓢ Spice Jammer
- Ⓣ Victoria Folk Fest

LODGING

- Ⓤ Abigail's Hotel
- Ⓘ Empress Hotel
- Ⓥ Green Gables Inn
- Ⓚ Oak Bay Beach Hotel

LODGING (continued)

- Ⓦ Ocean Island Backpackers' Inn
- Ⓧ Ocean Pointe Resort
- Ⓥ Olde England Inn
- Ⓘ Union Club of British Columbia

CAMPING

- Ⓩ All Fun RV Park and Campground
- ⓐ Fort Victoria RV Park
- ⓑ Goldstream Provincial Park
- ⓒ Island View Beach RV/Tent Camp
- ⓓ Thetis Lake Campground

Note: Items with the same letter are located in the same area.

is a tourist destination in itself. Celebrities hit the hotel regularly. This is a hotel that is well worth a splurge despite its high-end rates. Ask for its low season and package rates.

For less history and more modern razzmatazz, look across the Inner Harbour to the similarly priced **Ocean Pointe Resort,** 45 Songhees Rd., 800/667-4677, 250/360-2999, www.oprhotel.com, which arguably has better views of what's going on in Victoria than the venerable Empress. Rather than walking across the Johnson Street Bridge to the Ocean Pointe Resort, a fun way to get there is by water, on a perky tug-like ferry. In addition to superlative views from its dining rooms (the Victorian and the Boardwalk), health-conscious menus, its own wine shop, and artwork from around the world, the Ocean Pointe is the only hotel in Western Canada with a complete European-style spa. If you have money to burn, try the New Year's Delight, an Ancient Roman Bathing Ritual, or five computerized facial treatments. But that's after whale-watching, squash, tennis, and golf.

Tourism Victoria's handy toll-free line for accommodation information and advance reservations, 800/663-3883, offers lots of choices.

If you think Victoria is losing some of its highly touted English charm, stay at the less expensive **Olde England Inn,** 429 Lampson St., 250/388-4353. All rooms have seventeenth- and eighteenth-century antiques, some have open fireplaces and canopied beds used by European monarchy, and family suites are available. This distinctive half-century-old inn is part of a reconstructed English village that includes replicas of William Shakespeare's birthplace and Anne Hathaway's thatched cottage. You'll enjoy traditional English fare such as roast beef, steak-and-kidney pie, sherry trifle, scones, and crumpets served by costumed wenches in the Shakespeare Dining Room. The **Oak Bay Beach Hotel,** 1175 Beach Dr., 800/668-7758 or 250/598-4556, is also a Tudor-style establishment, but with a waterfront advantage and reasonable rates. Similarly priced is the current home of the **Union Club of British Columbia** (est. 1879), 805 Gordon St., 800/808-2218, 250/384-1151, www.unionclub.com. This historic private club was built in 1911 and has a truly Victorian atmosphere. Rates include a continental breakfast, a free health spa, daily paper, use of seven dining rooms and lounges, a billiard room, library, and a reading room.

As a tourist mecca, Victoria has an abundance of bed-and-breakfast places. Five of the nine lodgings that achieved a five-star rating "luxurious: among the best in Canada" are in the Greater Victoria area. One of these is **Abigail's Hotel,** a romantic heritage building located at 906 McClure St., 800/561-6565, www.abigailshotel.com.

For more ordinary and less expensive lodgings which are clean, modern, and conveniently located downtown, try **Green Gables Inn,** 850 Blanshard, 250/385-6787. The cheapest accommodation in Victoria and one that is getting rave reviews for its decor and services is **Ocean Island Backpackers' Inn,** a newly renovated 1893 heritage building at 791 Pandora Ave., 888/888-4180, 250/385-1788, get-it@oceanisland.com, www.oceanisland.com. Rooms are shared or private. This special type of hostel offers Internet, computer and fax access, a music room with instruments, nightly movies, free morning coffee, bike storage, vehicle parking for $3 a day, discounts at local businesses, guided day trips, and a fun brochure to appeal to the young at heart.

CAMPING

Kids will like **Fort Victoria RV Park,** 340 Island Highway 1A, 250/479-8112. From its log palisade, it really does look like a fort, but with the new Inland Highway running along one side, it can be noisy. **All Fun RV Park and Campground,** 2207 Millstream Rd., 250/474-4546, entices families with its adventure golf and driving range, waterslides, Go-karts, batting cages, bumper boats, and auto racetrack. **Thetis Lake Campground,** adjacent to Thetis Lake Regional Park at #1-1938 Trans-Canada Highway, Thetis Lake, 250/478-3845, is close to excellent boating, swimming, and hiking. **Island View Beach RV/Tent Camp,** 3 kilometers (2 miles) east of Highway 17 at the end of Island View Rd., 250/652-0548, open April to October, runs along a beautiful beach of sand and fine pebbles, the best in Victoria.

For more natural camping, use the regional and provincial parks. **Goldstream Provincial Park,** 2930 Trans-Canada Highway, 250/391-2300, emphasizes old-growth forests, fall salmon-spawning, and the Freeman King Nature Centre.

NIGHTLIFE

No longer are the sidewalks rolled up at night in staid Victoria. "Happenings," Victoria's weekly entertainment calendar in the *Times-Colonist* newspaper, and the weekly *Monday Magazine* each feature current events. The **McPherson Playhouse,** 250/386-6121, located in a restored heritage theater in the center of town is the major venue for live performances year-round. The **Royal Theatre,** 805 Broughton St., 250/386-6121, is the home of the Victoria Symphony Orchestra, which performs a Symphony Splash on a barge in the Inner Harbor each summer to an open-air audience of more than 40,000, if it doesn't rain. It is billed as North America's largest outdoor classic event. The **Belfry Theatre,** 1291 Gladstone, 250/385-6815, features comedy revues and music hall shows.

The **Fringe Theatre Festival** is a popular city-wide alternative theater event in August. You buy a ticket to a smorgasbord of different shows—comedy, dance, plays, skits and other dramas—that are held in different locations around the city.

Pubs and brewpubs are popular in British-like Victoria. The oldest and most acclaimed—**Spinnakers Brew Pub,** at 308 Catherine St., 250/384-6613, and the prettiest—the flower-filled **Swans Brew Pub** with its Millennium Jazz Club, 506 Pandora Ave., 250/361-3310, are two of the most popular and well-located. A rooftop patio with live entertainment, four multilevel cricket-themed rooms, and the world's only rooftop sand volleyball court, make the unique **Sticky Wicket Pub and Restaurant** in the Strathcona Hotel, 919 Douglas St., 250/383-7137, a fun place to go. You can even watch the sun go down as it slices between the buildings. Two popular new brewpubs in Victoria are **Hugo's** adjoining the new Magnolia Hotel, 625 Courtney St., 250/920-4844, which caters to the thirty-somethings before 9 P.M. and the younger crowd later; and the **Harbour Canoe Club,** the only marine brewpub in B.C., at 450 Swift St., 250/361-1940.

Ballroom dancing is very trendy right now. Dance to the view at **McMorran's Beach House** overlooking sandy log-strewn Cordova Bay, 5109 Cordova Bay Rd., 250/658-5527.

4
HIGHWAY LOOPS
AND ISLANDS

The "Island," as British Columbians affectionately call Vancouver Island, is larger than most people think (450 kilometers/280 miles long). And a lot of it is inaccessible except for a maze of restricted logging roads.

Diversity is part of the Island's appeal. On the west coast, mountains and rainforest that are sliced by fjords plunge into the reef-ridden, storm-tossed Pacific Ocean. On the east side, homes, farms, and gardens that overlook placid, protected passages tame a drier, gentler land south of Campbell River. In high places, forests and logging swamps open out onto colorful alpine meadows and perpetually snowcapped peaks. Underground is a labyrinth of caves; around its edge, a necklace of islands and islets.

The island can be traversed in a few hours via the new Inland Island Highway, but take time to travel the backroad loops of the old Island Highway as well. And whenever possible, take ferries to offshore islands. A foot ferry has opened between Telegraph Cove, Alert Bay, Sointula, and Port McNeill. An entire season can be spent looping and island-hopping up and down the east coast of Vancouver Island.

A PERFECT DAY ON THE ISLAND HIGHWAY

Go whaling from Telegraph Cove. This charming boardwalk community of a dozen permanent residents (at the most), located 438 kilometers (270 miles) up-island from Victoria, was owned from 1912 until 1985 by the late Fred Wastell, whose father originally chose it to serve as a telegraph station. Over the years, the station has gone through many metamorphoses, from fish-box factory to post office, but today it is the Fred Wastell Manor, a quaint hotel run by Telegraph Cove Resorts, which currently owns the cove. Head to Stubbs Island Whale Watching where you can cruise on Wastell's boat "Gikumi" in the Johnstone Strait, the most accessible and predictable location in the world for seeing orcas (killer whales). And only 20 kilometers (12 miles) from the strait is the Robson Bight Ecological Reserve, where whales can be seen rubbing themselves on the gravel beach. And if there aren't any whales in sight, just enjoy the charm of B.C.'s most photogenic community.

ORIENTATION

Getting up and down the east coast of Vancouver Island is simple. Begin in Victoria and drive up-island to Port Hardy on the new Inland Island Highway (Highways 1 and 19), which is scheduled for completion in 2002. Leave it often in order to drive a loop of the old meandering coastal highway (now Highway 19A) and take a ferry to one or more of the islands of your choice. If you absolutely have to save time—or if you are on the way back to Victoria—take the new Nanaimo Parkway, a 21-kilometer expressway that bypasses the busy city, and the 125-kilometer Inland Island Highway that bypasses coastal communities between Parksville and Campbell River (it's incomplete north of Courtenay).

Access Saltspring Island from Crofton; Thetis Island from Chemainus; Gabriola and Newcastle Islands from Nanaimo; Lasqueti Island from French Creek; Hornby and Denman Islands from Fanny Bay; Quadra and Cortes Islands from Campbell River; Cormorant and Malcolm Islands from Port McNeill; and then from Port Hardy, as many islands as you like. You can also ferry to Alaska.

For further information, call 250/953-4949, and make sure you buy detailed maps of each region, or *The BC Explorers Travel Guide* published by *Beautiful British Columbia Magazine*. For ferry information, pick up current schedules from each town's Info Centre or write Ferries Corporation, 1112 Fort St., Victoria, B.C. V8V 4V2, 888/223-3779, 250/386-3431, or check www.bcferries.bc.ca.

SIGHTSEEING HIGHLIGHTS

★★★★ CHEMAINUS
**Art and Business Council of Chemainus, Box 1311, B.C.
V0R 1K0, 250/246-4701, 250/246-3251,
abc@tourism.chemainus.bc.ca, www.ibnd.commurals.html**

This is the Little Town That Did—or, rather, did *not* die when its local sawmill closed. Instead, it transformed itself into the world's largest outdoor art gallery. Each summer, artists gather to paint giant murals on building walls that depict local history. It is now a popular and colorful destination for the whole family, with sidewalk cafés, ice cream parlors, tea rooms, antique stores, a dinner theater, and a horse-drawn carriage to more easily see it all.

Details: *(3 hours)*

★★★★ **COWICHAN NATIVE VILLAGE**
200 Cowichan Way, Duncan, 250/746-8119, info@ cowichannativevillage.com, www.cowichannativevillage.com
Stop in Duncan, the City of Totems, and follow the yellow footprints that start at the Cowichan Valley Museum in the 1912 train station and lead to 41 totem poles around town, then visit the Cowichan Native Village. This living history museum and art gallery dedicated to the culture of the Northwest Coast Indians offers demonstrations of carving, weaving, silversmithing, beadwork, and dancing, along with theatrical presentations, and a midday salmon barbecue.

Details: *Open mid-May–mid-Oct. daily 9 A.M.–5 P.M.; $8 adults, $7 seniors and students, $3.50 children; guided tours on the hour, multimedia presentations on the half-hour. (1 to 2 hours)*

★★★★ **DENMAN AND HORNBY ISLANDS**
Denman/Hornby Tourist Services, 250/335-2293 or 250/335-2731
Here you can visit two neighboring rural islands practically for the price of one—they are so closely connected by ferry. From Buckley Bay, 20 kilometers (13 miles) south of Courtenay, it's a 15-minute ferry trip to Denman, where there is a 15-minute drive to catch a connecting ferry to Hornby. Don't miss Fillongley Provincial Park and the many artisan studios that can be found on Denman. Take advantge of the scenery and clean air by going on a 5-kilometer (3-mile) hike around Helliwell Provincial Park and swim at Tribune Bay Provincial Park, which has some of the warmest waters and finest white sandy beaches in the province. Hornby Island, dubbed "the undiscovered Hawaii of British Columbia," is fun for the whole family, whether you drive, cycle, or hike.

Details: *(1 day)*

HIGHWAY LOOPS AND ISLANDS

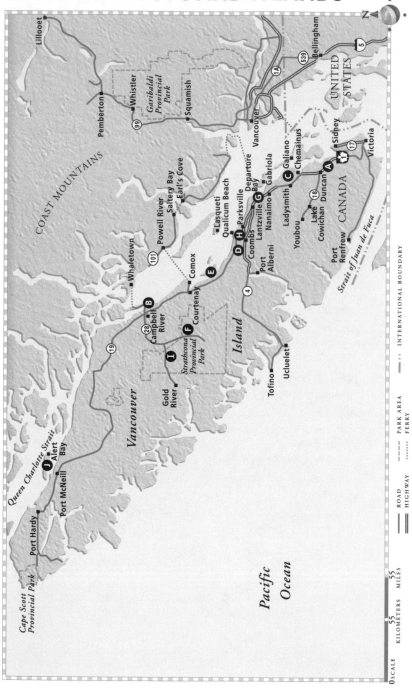

★★★★ **MOUNT WASHINGTON ALPINE RESORT**
Mount Washington, Box 3069, Courtenay, B.C. V9N 5N3, 250/338-1386
Now accessible from Courtenay by the 40-kilometer (25-mile) paved Strathcona Parkway is this reasonably priced alpine ski area, which has special programs and facilities for kids and disabled skiers. The area's alpine trails and wildflowers, the view from the chairlift, and the possibility of seeing the rare Vancouver Island marmot, are also a delight in summer. Mount Washington's Village Centre is expanding rapidly with shops, hotels, and restaurants.

Details: *Drive, bus, or take Via Rail's E and N Dayliner train from Victoria to Courtenay, 800/561-8630. (1 to 2 days)*

★★★★ **NANAIMO**
Tourism Nanaimo Info Centre, Beban House, 2290 Bowen Rd., B.C. V9T 3K7, 800/663-7337 or 250/756-0106, info@tourism.nanaimo.bc.ca, www.tourism.nanaimo.bc.ca
Nanaimo is also called The Hub or Harbor City. Take a walk along the waterfront, past two parks and Swy-A-I ana Tidal Lagoon, buy fresh seafood from Fisherman's Wharf, and listen to the noon cannon fired by costumed guards at the Hudson's Bay Company's Bastion, the oldest remaining structure of its type in North America. In July, contestants in the **Great International Nanaimo Bathtub Race** shoot 55 kilometers (34 miles) across the Strait of Georgia to Vancouver in bathtubs fitted on flat planing boards and powered by 7.5-horsepower outboard motors. In the **Annual Silly Boat Race,** competitors are given a short time to concoct zany boats from a variety of fun materials, then race them in the harbor. Nanaimo is gaining a reputation for the best scuba diving in North America. One artificial reef, the

---

SIGHTS

- **A** British Columbia Forest Museum
- **B** Campbell River
- **C** Chemainus
- **D** Coombs Emporium and Frontier Town
- **A** Cowichan Native Village
- **E** Denman and Hornby Islands
- **F** Mount Washington Alpine Resort
- **G** Nanaimo
- **H** Parksville and Qualicum Beaches
- **I** Strathcona Provincial Park
- **J** U'mista Cultural Centre

Note: Items with the same letter are located in the same area.

HMCS *Saskatchewan,* has generated more than 15,000 dives since it was sunk in 1997.

Take the five-minute people-only ferry across the harbor to Newcastle Island Provincial Marine Park. It's a marvelous destination for a day with the family. Don't miss swimming in Kanaka Bay (a shallow, warm-water lagoon), hiking the trail that circles the island, then ferrying across to neighboring Protection Island for a drink or a meal at the Dinghy Dock Marine Pub and Bistro (see Food section).

At the **Bungy Zone,** 35 Nanaimo River Rd., 250/716-7874 or 250/753-5867, jumpers can plunge 43 meters (140 feet) into the Nanaimo River Gorge and spring back from oblivion just before hitting the water. Kids (adults, too) will like **Cyber City Adventures,** 1815 Bowen Rd., 250/755-1828, an adventure park where they can have fun with lasers, mountain bikes, Go-karts, power balls, golf balls, and a virtual reality arcade. Winding around and up and down the town, watch for wildlife murals on the buildings, the work of local artist Jeff King. Finally, find a Nanaimo Bar. No, it's not the local watering hole; it's a sweet chocolate-and-the-works concoction laden with calories.

Details: *Newcastle Island Ferry, 661 Hunter St., B.C., V9S 1P9, 250/753-5141; Newcastle Island Pavilion, 250/753-1931; Newcastle Island Provincial Marine Park, 250/754-7893. (2 days)*

★★★★ **PARKSVILLE AND QUALICUM BEACHES**
Parksville Chamber of Commerce, Box 99, Parksville, B.C., V9P 2G3, 250/248-3613, parksvil@nanaimo.arc.com, www.nanaimo.arc.com/~parksvil/index.html
Qualicum Beach Visitor Centre, 2711 West Island Hwy., Qualicum Beach, 250/752-9532, info@qualicum.bc.ca, www.qualicum.bc.ca
These two seaside resort and retirement villages are famous for their sun and sandy beaches. At low tide, the sea recedes to leave the hard sand exposed for hundreds of yards, ideal for beachcombing and sandcastle-building; and when the tide returns, it's perfect for swimming. Each summer, Parksville hosts an annual **Sandcastle Competition.** Each April a **Sea Brant Festival** celebrates the arrival of thousands of Brant geese on their migration stop between Mexico and Alaska. There's plenty to keep you occupied in the Parksville-Qualicum area, but also use its central position to explore the rest of the island. Try to

see the Big Qualicum River Fish Hatchery, Englishman River Falls, and Horne Lake Caves.
Details: *(1 day)*

★★★ CAMPBELL RIVER
Campbell River Visitor Infocentre, 1235 Shoppers Row, 250/287-4636
Campbell River, half way up the Island, is famous for fresh and saltwater fishing, and scuba diving. It is headquarters of the Tyee Club whose members must catch a salmon of 30 pounds or more. Fish for free from Canada's first fully equipped saltwater fishing pier, the 183-meter-long (600-foot) Campbell River Fishing Pier next to the Government Wharf downtown. It has shelters for dry fishing on rainy days, lights for night fishing, as well as fish-cleaning stations, seating, built-in rod holders and bait stands. It's also a favorite spot for strolling and watching the cruise ships pass by on their way to Alaska. The whole waterfront downtown, **Discovery Harbour Centre,** has been revitalized and is a pleasant place to stroll and browse. Check with the Campbell River Museum at 250/287-3103 for boat trips to the bird colony on Mitlenatch Island.
Details: *(1 day)*

★★★ STRATHCONA PROVINCIAL PARK
Box 1479, Parksville, V9P 2H4, 250/954-4600
This rugged mountain wilderness almost in the center of the island is the province's first and largest provincial park. Many of the hikes are uphill, but the alpine scenery at the top is worth the climb. Golden Hinde, at 2200 meters (1875 feet), is the island's highest peak. Della Falls, one of the highest waterfalls in Canada, has an overall drop of 440 meters (275 feet) in three cascades. Comox Glacier is the Island's last remaining glacier. Hike to Paradise Meadows, Battleship Lake, and Forbidden Plateau (easy); and to Marble Meadows and Flower Ridge (more difficult). This park is accessed off Highway 28 from Campbell River or at Forbidden Plateau outside Courtenay.

In the park on Highway 28, 38 kilometers (22.8 miles) west of Highway 19 near Campbell River, is a private resort, **Strathcona Park Lodge and Outdoor Education Centre**, 250/286-3122, info@strathcona.com, www.strathcona.bc.ca, a superb base for such outdoor activities as hiking, climbing, cross-country skiing, and canoeing; and indoor activities such as quilting, yoga, wellness strategies, and other year-round special-interest programs. Strathcona is both a scenic place to stay and an outdoor education center.

Details: *(2 days)*

★★★ U'MISTA CULTURAL CENTRE
In Alert Bay on Cormorant Island, 250/974-5403, umista@island.net

Take the ferry from Port McNeill, 194 kilometers (116 miles) north of Campbell River, to the fishing village of Alert Bay, turn left at Front Street and continue for 2 kilometers to see this fine collection of elaborately carved masks and other artifacts that depict the Potlatch Ceremony of First Nations people. At a potlatch (ceremonial feast and dance), the host, perhaps an important chief, distributes gifts such as copper, masks, and blankets. The more gifts distributed, the higher the status of the giver. Copper, in particular, is a sign of wealth. Also in Alert Bay is a 53-meter (173-foot) totem pole featuring 22 carved figures, which was considered the world's tallest until a taller totem was erected in Victoria in 1994. Pick up a totem pole guide from the Info Centre for an explanation of the various totems in 'Namgis Burial Grounds that can easily be seen from the roadway.

Details: *Open May–Sept. daily 9 A.M.–6 P.M.; rest of year weekdays 9 A.M.–5 P.M., $5 adults, $4 over 64, $1 under 12; $2 guided tour. (1 hour)*

★★ BRITISH COLUMBIA FOREST MUSEUM
2892 Drinkwater Rd., Duncan, 1.5 km (1 mi) off Hwy. 1, 250/715-1113

Kids will love riding the steam train through the forest while parents learn the history of logging at this outdoor museum.

Details: *Open May–Sept. daily 10 A.M.–6 P.M.; $8 adults, $7 over 65 and ages 13–18, $4.50 ages 5–12. (2 to 3 hours)*

★★ COOMBS EMPORIUM, GENERAL STORE, OLD COUNTRY MARKET AND FRONTIER TOWN
2326 Alberni Hwy., 9 km (5.4 mi) west of Parksville, 250/248-6272

Kids will love the goats that live and graze on the grass-covered roof of the main market building. In addition to its novelty shops, outdoor cafés, and street entertainment, rapidly proliferating Coombs is a great place to pick up bread, pastries, fruits, veggies and flowers.

Details: *(2 hours)*

FITNESS AND RECREATION

The east coast of Vancouver Island, a mecca for retirees, has endless opportunities for recreation. Name almost any activity and you can do it here on the Island's gentle side. Golfing year round is popular with locals and visitors; many hotels offer golf and accommodation packages (**Fairwinds Schooner Cove Resort,** 3521 Dolphin Dr., Nanoose Bay, 800/663-7060), and often retirement complexes are clustered around a golf course (**Arbutus Ridge Golf and Country Club,** 3515 Telegraph Rd., Cobble Hill, 250/743-5100). **Crown Isle Golf and Country Estates** at 399 Clubhouse Drive in Courtenay 800/378-6811, 250/338-6811, is a new championship course rated No. 1 on Vancouver Island by *Golf Digest.*

Water sports are understandably popular. Fishing has always attracted visitors and in spite of the ups and downs of the sports fishing industry, it still is. Use an outfitter to get to the hot spots. Two good ones are **Megan Cruising,** 2753 Vargo Rd., Campbell River, 250/286-9610, cell 250/830-7435, and **Codfather Charters and Lodge,** 6465 Hardy Rd., Port Hardy, 250/949-6696, codfthr@island.net. With Codfather, fishing is available year-round and accommodations are in deluxe waterfront resorts.

For whale watching, contact, **Stubbs Whale Watching,** Box 2-2, Telegraph Cove, British Columbia V0N 3J0, 800/665 3066, 250/928-3185 stubbs@ island.net, www.stubbs-island.com. For full-day or longer trips, see **Mackay Whale Watching Charters of Port McNeill,** 250/956-9865.

FOOD

Make the most of the ambiance when you eat out on the Island— dine in a pub, on an island, near water, on a ship, in a heritage house, on a golf course, or in a vineyard. If you can afford only one splurge, do it at the **Aerie Resort** overlooking Finlayson Arm on top of Malahat Mountain, 25 minutes by road from Victoria along the Vancouver Island Highway. Take the Spectacle Lake Provincial Park turnoff at the north end of the Malahat Drive and follow the signs to the resort, 250/743-7115. Intimate, formal, seven-course dinners and three-course lunches are expensive, but both the restaurant and hotel have won more awards than probably any other place in Western Canada.

You will find less expensive ambiance as you travel north. At **Vigneti Zanatta,** a romantic Italian farm winery at 5039 Marshall Rd., Duncan, 250/748-2338, sit outdoors on the wraparound terra-cotta verandah of a 1903 farmhouse overlooking a vineyard. Appetizers, different daily risottos, and hardy pastas—simple rustic Italian fare—are the family's specialties. Go there for an affordable weekend brunch, particularly if you enjoy wine.

The Nanaimo area has several interesting and affordable restaurants that combine food and ambiance. An old standby, **The Grotto,** 151 Stewart Ave., 250/753-3303, is delightfully decorated in a marine style. It has expanded its West Coast seafood menu to include a sushi bar and other Asian enticements. **Dar Lebanon,** 347 Wesley St., in the Old City Quarter of Nanaimo, 250/755-9150, is another winner for traditional food at reasonable prices. It is delightfully housed in a heritage home where the owners are also the chefs and live upstairs. With its archways, murals, and brass charcoal burners, you will think you are in the Middle East as soon as you step inside. For value, try the Mixed Grill and finish with a Lebanese dessert.

For the best deal in town, paddle, cruise or ferry across Nanaimo Harbour from the Harbourfront Walkway to **Dinghy Dock Marine Pub and Bistro** on Protection Island, 250/753-2373 or 250/753-8244. Drink, dance, and dine while watching the boats and the striking sunsets over Nanaimo's mountains. The best deal on the menu is barbecue ribs, chicken, and smoked sausage with a giant stuffed spud and a Caesar salad on the side. The pub closes between November and March.

Everybody likes the award-winning **Mahle House,** 2104 Hemer Rd. in Cedar, 250/722-3621. This family-run operation prides itself on serving fresh organic produce from the adjacent garden, its heritage house atmosphere, an award-winning wine list, and local art work. Go in a group of four on Adventurous Wednesdays when for about $25 a multicourse dinner chosen by the chef is placed at your table. Or go on Grazing Platter Thursdays when two or more people graze their way through a colorful ceramic platter piled with pork loin, calamari, prawns, lamb chops, sausages, chicken wings, Thai salad, grilled vegetables—and more—for less than $20. Nearby at 2313 Yellow Point Rd., 250/722-3731 is the **Crow and Gate.** It's a "meat and potatoes" pub (no TV or loud music) set in the middle of a field, and its loyal clientele likes its low ceilings, Tudor-style architecture, English specialties (bangers and mash, steak-and-kidney pie, and Melton Mowbray pie), and reasonable prices.

Vancouver Island still reveals much of its English heritage so pubbing is popular. See Island Pubbing *by Robert Moyes.*

Moving north, you can't beat the reasonable prices, charming decor and gardens of the **Old House Restaurant,** 1760 Riverside Ln., Courtenay, 250/338-5406.

LODGING

As with restaurants, the Island has lots of charming lodges. Let's start with the opulent. The **Aerie Resort** on Malahat Mountain, 800/518-1933, 250/743-7115, aerie@relaischateaux.fr, www.aerie.bc.ca, is a great splurge for lodging as

The Gourmet Trail, a comprehensive luxury wining, dining, and lodging tour arranged by First Island Tours, 800/970-7722 or 250/658-5367, in Victoria, will take you to The Aerie and several other high-end hotel restaurants including Hastings House Country House Hotel, Sooke Harbour House, Wickaninnish Inn and Pointe Restaurant, and the Empress Hotel.

well as dining. A magnificent assembly of multitiered, red tile-roofed mansions in the mountains, the Aerie overlooks misty fjords and islands. Touted as one of North America's 12 best country inns and one of the best 500 hotels in the world, it has been featured on the American TV program *Run Away with the Rich and Famous*. Go in winter when rooms are less costly and when you have more excuse for staying indoors to enjoy the luxury.

Like the Aerie, **Hastings House Country House Hotel**, 160 Upper Ganges Rd., Saltspring Island, 800/661-9255, 250/537-2362, is part of the Relaix and Chateaux chain of luxury country inns. This elegant Tudor-style manor house built in 1939 was fashioned after the owner's eleventh-century ancestral home in Sussex, England. Unlike the Aerie, barns and farmhouses have been reconstructed as charming garden cottages. For a fun alternative to eating in the dining room, sit with the chef in the kitchen for a behind-the-scenes dining experience.

Deer Lodge Motel, behind the fence at 2529 on the Island Highway in Mill Bay, 800/668-5011, 250/743-2423, is a charming, downplayed version of Hastings House. With its flower gardens and gorgeous views over Saanich Inlet to Mount Baker, it scarcely should be called a motel. You'll get very friendly service at the **Fairburn Farm Country Manor**, 3310 Jackson Rd., Duncan, phone/fax 250/746-4637, fairburn@gec.net, www.gec.net\fairburn. Once a millionaire's country estate, it is now a working farm a few miles southwest of Duncan, in the peaceful Cowichan Valley. The Archer family offers affordable cottage or bed-and-breakfast accommodations. Guests may help with chores that may include herding water buffalo and making cheese from buffalo milk. Most of the food served is home-grown, and lamb is the farm specialty.

Yellow Point Lodge, 3700 Yellow Point Rd. (near Ladysmith), 250/245-7422, is a popular log and stone retreat in the forest beside the ocean that appeals to eccentrics, romantics and outdoor types, especially those who like beaches and water sports. Conveniently situated on Highway 19A at Long Lake

HIGHWAY LOOPS AND ISLANDS

Lillooet

Whistler

Garibaldi
Provincial
Park

Squamish

Pemberton

99

Bellingham

5

539

1A

UNITED
STATES

COAST MOUNTAINS

Saltery Bay
Earl's Cove

Powell River

Lasqueti

Qualicum Beach

Parksville

Departure
Bay

Vancouver

Sidney

Victoria

Galiano

Gabriola

S

I

T

A

17

D

Chemainus

F

G

Nanaimo

Ladysmith

Duncan

CANADA

Coombs

Lantzville

K

P

18

Lake
Cowichan

Youbou

101

Whaletown

Comox

V

Port
Alberni

4

Port
Renfrew

Strait of Juan de Fuca

R

E

Courtenay

C

Campbell
River

H

28

Island

19

U

Gold
River

Strathcona
Provincial
Park

Vancouver

J

Tofino

Ucluelet

Queen Charlotte Strait

Alert Bay

N

Port McNeill

Pacific
Ocean

Cape Scott
Provincial Park

Q

Port Hardy

O SCALE   55   KILOMETERS   55   MILES

ROAD — — —   PARK AREA - - -

HIGHWAY ═══   FERRY · · · · · ·

· · · · · · INTERNATIONAL BOUNDARY

O

L

M

B

N

5 kilometers north of Departure Bay in Nanaimo is the more modern **Long Lake Inn Resort,** 800/565-1144, reservations@longlakeinn.com, www.longlakeinn.com. Its three levels of well-illuminated rooms reflected in the waters of the adjacent lake make it a welcome jewel on a dark or rainy night. Unlike the ocean, the lake beside your door is always serene enough to use the hotel's kayaks, canoes, and paddleboats.

Also handily located on the highway and the ocean further north yet set amid trees is **Tigh-Na-Mara Resort Hotel,** the popular log masterpiece of hotel rooms, condos, and cottages, at 1095 East Island Highway, Parksville, 800/663-7373, 250/248-2072, info@tigh-na-mara.com, www.tigh-na-mara.com. Locals love it too, especially for its Sunday Brunch. Ivy-clad, Tudor-style **Qualicum College Inn,** 427 College Rd., Qualicum Beach, 800/663-7306, 250/752-9262, qcihotel@nanaimo.ark.com, www.vquest.com/qcihotel, was once a private boys' boarding school and this adds to its charm. The Inn hosts regular Murder Mystery Weekends and rates are very reasonable, but Qualicum can also be an unexpected southern location for seeing the northern lights. If entertaining kids is a priority, stay at the inexpensive **Paradise Seashell Motel** (and RV Park), located at 411 W. Island Highway., Parksville, 877/33RELAX (7-3529), 250/248-6171, seashell@bcsupernet.com, www.bctravel.com/ci/seashell (see CAMPING section).

Knight Inlet Lodge (fishing, eco-adventures, grizzly bear viewing) is a breathtaking 30-minute float plane ride from Campbell River on Vancouver Island. It is a new place, high end, but a great place to view grizzlies; www.grizzlytours.com.

FOOD

- Ⓐ Aerie Resort
- Ⓑ Crow and Gate
- Ⓑ Dar Lebanon
- Ⓑ Dinghy Dock Marine Pub and Bistro
- Ⓑ The Grotto
- Ⓑ Mahle House
- Ⓒ Old House Restaurant
- Ⓓ Vigneti Zanatta

LODGING

- Ⓐ Aerie Resort
- Ⓔ April Point Lodge
- Ⓕ Deer Lodge Motel
- Ⓖ Fairburn Farm Country Manor

LODGING *(continued)*

- Ⓗ Haig-Brown House
- Ⓘ Hastings House Country House Hotel
- Ⓙ Knight Inlet Lodge
- Ⓚ Long Lake Inn Resort
- Ⓗ Painter's Lodge Holiday and Fishing Resort
- Ⓛ Paradise Seashell Motel
- Ⓜ Qualicum College Inn
- Ⓝ Telegraph Cove Resort Hotel
- Ⓞ Tigh-na-mara Resort Hotel
- Ⓟ Yellow Point Lodge

CAMPING

- Ⓠ Cape Scott Provincial Park
- Ⓡ Miracle Beach Provincial Park
- Ⓢ Montague Harbour Provincial Park
- Ⓛ Paradise Adventures Mini Golf and RV Park
- Ⓛ Rathtrevor Beach Provincial Park
- Ⓣ Ruckle Provincial Park
- Ⓤ Strathcona Provincial Park
- Ⓥ Tribune Bay Provincial Park

Note: Items with the same letter are located in the same area.

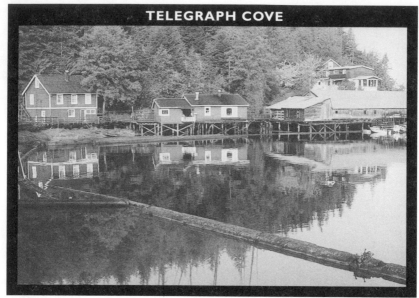

TELEGRAPH COVE

Campbell River appeals to anglers, naturalists and literary types. A special bed-and-breakfast right on its banks is **Haig-Brown House,** 2250 Campbell River Rd., (Hwy. 28) in Campbell River, 250/286-6646, www.oberon. ark.com/~kdbhbh. It is the former home of British Columbia's favorite fisherman-author-philosopher, Roderick Haig-Brown. **Painter's Lodge Holiday and Fishing Resort,** 1625 Macdonald Rd., 800/663-7090, 250/286-1102, obmg@pinc.com, www.obmg.com, open from March to October, and the more secluded **April Point Lodge,** April Point Rd. (on nearby Quadra Island), 800/663-7090 or 250/285-2222, are world-famous oceanfront salmon-fishing resorts. Stay here and watch the celebrities even if you don't fish.

Don't miss renting a room in the Wastell Manor or a self-contained historic cottage on the boardwalk of Telegraph Cove from **Telegraph Cove Resorts,** Box 1, Telegraph Cove, V0N 3J0, 800/200-HOOK or 250/928-3131. No TV or phones, but unforgettable atmosphere and a variety of prices to suit all budgets and group sizes.

CAMPING

Vancouver Island and the Gulf Islands have an abundance of camp spots, both public and private, to match the diversity of the area. Choose the provincial park campsites first. Contact B.C. Parks at 250/387-4550, www.discovercamping.ca.

The most popular and scenic ones are **Strathcona,** near Campbell River, 250/954-4600; **Rathtrevor Beach,** near Parksville, 250/248-3931; **Ruckle,** on Saltspring Island, 250/387-4363; **Montague Harbour,** on Galiano Island, 250/391-2300; **Miracle Beach,** near Courtenay, 250/248-3931; **Tribune Bay,** on Hornby island, 250/335-2359; and way up north at the end of the island, the remote and incomparable **Cape Scott,** 250/954-4600.

Of the private campgrounds, don't miss **Paradise Adventures Mini Golf and RV Park,** on the Island Highway, Parksville, 250/248-6612. Kids will be fascinated by its Disneyland look. They can play on the giant-sized Big Shoe, Castle, Water Wheel, and Old Sailing Ships on Treasure Island, while parents play minigolf or prepare dinner on the barbecue grill before trooping off to the beach.

NIGHTLIFE
Go to bed early to be ready for outdoor adventures the following day.

5
WEST COAST OF
VANCOUVER ISLAND

"God's Country" is how Vancouver Island's west coast has been described. When I arrived by boat here in 1962, it rained for six weeks, but when the sun finally shone through the fog, I knew I had truly reached paradise.

At that time, I was fortunate enough to explore this magnificent meeting of land and sea—its graveyard reefs, surf—pounded beaches, wind-lashed forests—by float plane and rubber boat. Only the hardiest of tourists tackled the trails that traversed Vancouver Island's central mountains and sliced through rainforests into the land of cougars, whales, eagles and sea otters. Only the most adventurous boaters penetrated the reef-ridden waterways that knifed through the jungle to meet the mountains. Since then, the west coast of Vancouver Island has become more easily accessible. You can now reach this rugged wilderness coast in about 90 minutes, by a paved Pacific Marine Highway (Hwy. 4), from Port Alberni to Pacific Rim National Park Reserve that is flanked by the villages of Ucluelet and Tofino. To explore further, you must travel by boat or float plane. From Port Alberni, the Gateway to the West Coast, you can also drive to the boardwalk village of Bamfield through a maze of logging roads, or you can cruise down the Alberni Canal and through Barkley Sound to Bamfield and Ucluelet.

A PERFECT DAY ON THE WEST COAST OF VANCOUVER ISLAND

Pick a sunny one, and at 8 A.M. board the MV *Lady Rose* or MV *Frances Barkley* at the Harbour Quay in Port Alberni for a trip down the Alberni Canal into Barkley Sound and through the Broken Group Islands. You will arrive in Ucluelet at 1 P.M. Arrange for a rental vehicle or a friend with a car to meet you in Ucluelet, and let your friend board the boat at 2 P.M. for the return journey to Port Alberni while you go back later by the Pacific Rim Highway.

In Tofino, stop at the end of the road, where the highway meets the ocean at Long Beach, and take a walk on the sand and a swing through the Pacific Rim Park Information Centre. Afterward, stop again for another walk on Chesterman Beach and sit down for a cup of clam chowder at the newly built Wickaninnish Inn. Be sure to choose a long summer day so you can complete at least part of the drive back east along the Pacific Rim Highway in daylight. Savor the drive along Cameron Lake, and, if you have time, pause at Cathedral Grove in MacMillan Provincial Park to gaze up at some of the last and largest remaining Douglas fir trees.

ORIENTATION

Fewer than a dozen roads cut across the central mountains of Vancouver Island to meet the long inlets and ragged edges of the west coast: Highway 14 to Port Renfrew, Highway 10 to Bamfield, Highway 4 to Tofino, Highway 28 to Gold River and Tahsis, other unnamed logging roads to Zeballos, Fair Harbour, Port Alice, Coal Harbour, Holberg, Winter Harbour, and now San Josef Bay at the very tip of the island. Here you can hike the Cape Scott Trail to Cape Scott and stroll the Cape Scott Sand Neck where both sides of Vancouver Island come together. This is as west as you can go.

The most popular route is Highway 4, the Pacific Marine Highway, which begins at Craig's Crossing near

Remember that Port Alberni is the Gateway to the West Coast: this is the signpost to look for from Highway 19, not Ucluelet, Tofino or Pacific Rim National Park Reserve.

Parksville, 26 kilometer (15.6 miles) north of Nanaimo on Highway 19—the new Vancouver Island Inland Highway—and reaches tide water at Port Alberni in just 47 kilometer (28 miles). Continue for another 93 kilometers (56 miles) to the Ucluelet-Tofino junction. Turn right (north) for Pacific Rim National Park Reserve and Tofino. Turn left (south) for Ucluelet. Alternatively, take the sea route Port Alberni-Barkley Sound-Ucluelet by the *Lady Rose* or the *Frances Barkley*.

WEST COAST OF VANCOUVER ISLAND

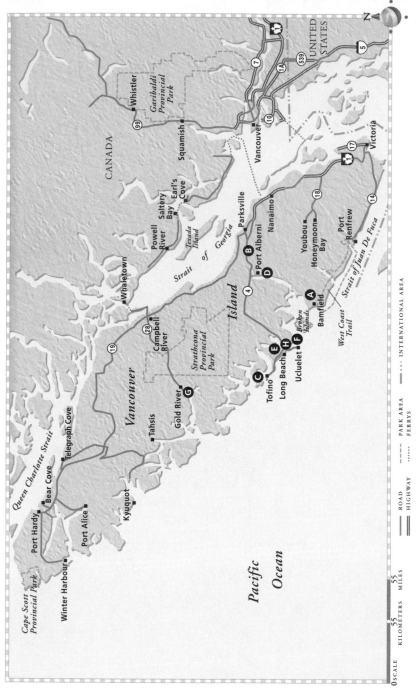

SIGHTSEEING HIGHLIGHTS

★★★★ MV *LADY ROSE*
Lady Rose Marine Services, Box 188, Port Alberni, B.C., V9Y 7M7, 800/663-7192, 250/723-8313, (April–September business hours)

A west coast legend, the Lady Rose has delivered mail, cargo, and passengers to isolated villages, fishing resorts, and logging camps for more than 50 years. This historic freighter also takes visitors on all-day cruises to Bamfield or Ucluelet, and picks up and drops off kayakers bent on paddling in Barkley Sound or hikers tackling the West Coast Trail. Year-round schedule Port Alberni-Ucluelet and Port Alberni-Bamfield with stops at Sechart in the Broken Group Islands of Barkley Sound on request, and in summer, additional sailings to Ucluelet.

Details: *Full-day round-trip to Ucluelet costs $40–$46, children 8–15 half-fare, under 8 free when accompanied by an adult; reservations recommended in summer. (1 day)*

★★★★ PACIFIC RIM NATIONAL PARK RESERVE
Box 280, Ucluelet, BC V0R 3A0, 250/726-7721

Almost 500,000 people visit this park each year. It stretches 125 kilometer (80 miles) from near Tofino in the north to Port Renfrew in

---

SIGHTS
Ⓐ Bamfield
Ⓑ Cathedral Grove (MacMillan Provincial Park)
Ⓒ Clayoquot Sound
Ⓓ MV *Lady Rose*
Ⓔ Pacific Rim National Park Reserve
Ⓒ Tofino
Ⓕ Ucluelet
Ⓖ MV *Uchuck III*

FOOD
Ⓕ Canadian Princess Restaurant
Ⓒ Crab Bar
Ⓒ The Pointe Restaurant
Ⓒ Schooner Restaurant
Ⓗ Wickaninnish Restaurant

LODGING
Ⓐ Bamfield Lodge and Cottages
Ⓕ Canadian Princess Resort
Ⓒ Clayoquot Wilderness Resort

LODGING (continued)
Ⓒ Middle Beach Lodge
Ⓒ Pacific Sands Beach Resort
Ⓒ Paddlers' Inn B&B
Ⓒ The Snug Harbour Inn
Ⓒ Vargas Inn
Ⓗ Wickaninnish Inn
Ⓒ Wilp Gybu (Wolf House) B&B

CAMPING
Ⓒ Bella Pacifica Resort and Campground
Ⓔ Green Point Campground
Ⓕ Ucluelet Campground

Note: Items with the same letter are located in the same area.

the south, although not continuously. It contains sandy beaches, dense rainforests, rugged headlands, and rocky islands. There are three separate areas in the park.

Long Beach is named for an 11-kilometer (7-mile) curve of smooth, hard, surf-swept sand exposed to the open Pacific Ocean. Overlooking Long Beach is **Wickaninnish Centre,** the park's headquarters, which houses a restaurant, a theater, exhibits, and is the starting point for both guided and self-guided tours.

The magnificent **Broken Group Islands** in the middle of Barkley Sound have recently become very popular destinations for canoeists and kayakers. A cheaper alternative to having the *Lady Rose* drop you off is to launch your boat from Toquart Bay, 16 kilometers (12.8 mile), which is reached by a rough road off Highway 4 (follow the sign).

The arduous but popular **West Coast Trail** follows the coast for 72 kilometers (45 miles) between Bamfield and Port Renfrew. Built along the route of a former telegraph line hung from tree to tree in the 1890s to help survivors of ships wrecked in this Graveyard of the Pacific, it was known as the Lifesaving Trail or the Shipwrecked Mariners' Trail. A quota system governs the number of hikers permitted to start each day at any one of the three access centers: Pachena Bay, Gordon River, and Diti-daht First Nations' Nitinat Lake Visitor Centre.

You can get conveniently from Victoria, Duncan, or Nanaimo to the Bamfield starting point (295 kilometers/177 miles) by West Coast Trail Express, 250/477-8700, at a cost of $46.73.

Details: *Contact the Superintendent, Pacific Rim National Park Reserve, Box 280, Ucluelet, B.C. V0R 3A0; 250/726-7721. The Park Information Centre, 250/726-4212, and the Wickaninnish Centre are open daily mid-March–Sept. 9:30 A.M.–5 P.M.. Admission for private vehicles is by daily permit ($5) March–October. Parking lots sell permits at vending machines that accept Visa, MasterCard, coins, or bills. There is no fee to drive through the park without stopping. Buy a copy of the Official Guide to Pacific Rim National Park Reserve, $14.95. (1 to 3 days)*

★★★★ TOFINO

Tofino Chamber of Commerce, Box 476, 380 Campbell St., BC V0R 2Z0, 250/725-3414

From mid-March to mid-April, Tofino, the western terminus of the Pacific Rim Marine Highway joins the adjacent national park to celebrate the **Pacific Rim Whale Festival.** This is when thousands of Pacific gray whales migrating north from the Baja Peninsula in Mexico to feeding grounds in Alaska are seen close to shore. Each whale travels up to 16,000 kilometers (10,000 mile) annually, the longest migration of any mammal in the world. Tofino, once a sleepy fishing village, is now a thriving tourist destination with several companies eager to take you closer to the whales. Some of the gray whales, and occasionally, humpback whales have been known to remain in the area until fall, when they rejoin the migration back to Mexico.

Tofino is an excellent base for spring and fall whale-watching, bird-watching, storm-watching, fishing, kayaking, exploring **Pacific Rim National Park Reserve** to the south, and flying or cruising to Hot Springs Cove in **Maquinna Provincial Park** to the north. Grice, Chesterman, and Mackenzie Beaches are the best of the local beaches.

Details: *For whale-watching tours in rigid hull rubber Zodiacs, Mar.–Oct., try Remote Passages Marine Excursions, 71 Wharf St., 800/666-9833, 250/725-3330, remote@island.net, www.remotepassages.com. To explore First Nations sites or experience the indigenous culture, contact Nuu-chah-nulth Booking and Information Centre, 300 Main St., Box 453, Tofino V0R 2Z0, 800/665-9425 or 250/725-2888. (2 hours)*

★★★ **BAMFIELD**

Bamfield Chamber of Commerce, Box 5, B.C. V0R 1B0 (no phone) or Bamfield Marine Station, 250/728-3301
In this charming little fishing village, 102 kilometers (61 miles) south of Port Alberni by logging road, or accessible by boat via the Alberni Canal, the main street is an inlet leading to Barkley Sound, and the pavement is a boardwalk linking the buildings. Walk to picturesque **Brady's Beach, Cape Beale Lighthouse,** or **Pachena Bay,** which is the beginning of the West Coast Trail. Tour the Marine Biological Station, which was once a cable station, or use Bamfield as a base for fabulous fishing, kayaking and scuba diving.

Details: *(1 day)*

★★★ **CLAYOQUOT SOUND**

This revered waterway consisting of inlets and islands between Kennedy Lake and Hesquiat Peninsula, including Flores, Vargas, and Meares Islands, is surrounded by the largest expanse of low-elevation old-growth temperate rainforest left in North America. In the aftermath of confrontations between loggers and preservationists, logging has been limited, First Nation cultural sites acknowledged, and new trails and new provincial parks established in the area. Walk the 16-kilometer (9.6-mile) **Ahousat Wild Side Heritage Trail** on Flores Island; the 3-kilometer (1.8-mile) **Meares Island Big Cedar Trail** leading to the **Hanging Garden Cedar** believed to be over 2000 years old; and the 29-kilometer (17.4-mile) **Clayoquot Valley Witness Trail** about 45 kilometers (27 miles) west of Port Alberni off Highway 4. Walk the sandy beaches of Vargas Island. Boat or fly by float plane to **Hot Springs Cove,** 37 kilometers (22.2 miles) northwest of Tofino in Maquinna Provincial Park and then walk the boardwalk to Vancouver Island's only known hot springs.

Details: Phone 250/670-9531 or 250/670-9602 (Flores Island); 250/725-3309 (Vargas Island Inn); 250/725-3233 (Tla-o-qui-aht the First Nation name for Clayoquot Valley Witness Trail). (1 day)

★★★ **UCLUELET**
Ucluelet Chamber of Commerce, Box 428, V0R 3A0, 250/726-4641 or 250/726-7289
The best way to appreciate Ucluelet, a logging, fishing, and now a tourist village 8 kilometers (5 miles) southeast of the Ucluelet-Tofino-Port Alberni junction on Highway 4 is to explore its coves and beaches by foot, wander along its waterfront, and browse its arts and crafts shops. **Amphitrite Point Lighthouse** is now automated, but is a good destination for a short hike around He-tin-kis Park, to look for Pacific Gray whales or to sit on the rocks and see the sunset. The newly developed **Wild Pacific Trail** starts here. You can now walk north along the coast to Tofino by linking with trails in Pacific Rim National Park Reserve. Like Tofino, Ucluelet is a good base to watch for whales during the Pacific Rim Whale Festival every March.

Details: (1 day)

★★ **CATHEDRAL GROVE (MACMILLAN PROVINCIAL PARK)**
31 km (18 mi) west of Parksville on Hwy. 4; B.C. Parks, 250/387-5002
A violent storm felled some of the trees in this park during the winter of 1996–1997, but it is still worth stopping along Highway 4 west of Parksville to stroll one of the looped trails in this awe-inspiring forest of 800-year-old Douglas firs. The largest tree measures 3 meters (10 feet) in diameter, 9 meters (30 feet) around, and 75 meters (240 feet)

high. Forest baron H. R. MacMillan donated these trees to the province in 1944. A visitors' center opened in 1997.

Details: *(minimum 1 hour)*

★★ **MV UCHUCK III (WEST COAST CRUISES)**
Nootka Sound Service, Box 57, Gold River V0P 1G0,
250/283-2325/15, mvuchuck@island.net,
www.island.net/~mvuchuck
You'll combine history, geography, economy and enjoy a cruise to the birthplace of Western Canada if you take a trip on this historic coastal freighter that provides year-round passenger and freight service from the logging town of Gold River to Nootka Sound, where in 1778 at Yuquot (Friendly Cove), the British Captain James Cook met the Mowachaht Chief Maquinna in the first contact between Europeans and B.C. First Nations. The Uchuck III continues through Tahsis and Esperanza Inlets to Kyuquot Sound where you will see re-established sea otters, a species that was exterminated in B.C. after Cook's visit spurred a world trade in sea otter pelts. Contact Nootka Sound Services for various schedules and corresponding fares. Day cruises are available or use the boat's drop-off service.

Details: *(1 to 2 days)*

FITNESS AND RECREATION

The possibilities are endless in this ocean and forest playground. You can be as organized (or not) as you like. Hike the many trails in **Pacific Rim National Park Reserve,** kayak the islands in Clayoquot Sound off Tofino, surf the waves off Long Beach, fish for salmon in Barkley Sound, dig for clams and oysters in Toquart Bay, dive for wrecked ships in the Graveyard of the Pacific, or soak in the natural hot springs of Hot Springs Cove. Do-it-yourself or let an operator do it for you. Here are some of the best.

Tofino Sea Kayaking Company, 320 Main St., Tofino, Box 620, 800/TOFINO-4, 250/725-4222, paddlers@island.net/~paddlers, www.island. net/~paddlers, provides one-stop shopping. Not only does it rent kayaks, teach kayaking, arrange kayaking tours of various lengths including overnight stays on popular Vargas Island, but it has a building on the waterfront in downtown Tofino that serves as an inn, bookstore and coffeeshop. If you are a woman, check out Wimmin Seeking Wild, a six-day kayak trip for women only.

Remote Passages Marine Excursions, 71 Wharf St., Box 624, Tofino V0R 2Z0, 800/666-9833, 250/725-3330/3163, remote@island.net, www.remotepassages.com, also offers educational kayak trips in Clayoquot Sound, as well as whale-watching trips by inflatable 19- and 24-foot rigid hull Zodiacs March to October, the most extensive whale-watching season on Vancouver Island. Combine a cruise to Hot Springs Cove with black bear-watching May/June, August/September, and salmon-watching September/October.

If you want a bigger boat and Tofino is your base, get food and accommodation, nature cruises, guided or do-it-yourself fishing trips, at **Weigh West Marine Resort,** 634 Campbell St., 800/665-8922, 250/725-3277, wwest@ weighwest.com, www.weighwest.com. In Ucluelet, book with **Canadian Princess Resort,** a steamship anchored in Ucluelet Harbour, Peninsula Rd., Box 939, Ucluelet V0R 3A0, 800/663-7090, 250/726-7771, www.obmg.com.

For one-to-one concentration on fishing, here's a couple of highly recommended fishing operators: David Murphy of **Stamp Pacific Sportfishing,** 5915 Beaver Creek Rd., Port Alberni, V9Y 8H9, 250/723-2772, mmurphy@ island.net, www.westcoastfishing.com; Doug Ferguson, **Coastline Salmon Charters,** Box 105, Bamfield, V0R 1B0, 250/728-3217.

And up there in Kyuquot Sound, try the Levine family at memorably named **Slam Bang Lodge,** a small floating fishing lodge on Union Island, 250/332-5313, www.rmid.com/slambang. You'll get good fishing year-round (prime fishing April through September), as well as intimate encounters with eagles, seals, and sea otters. The Levines and their neighbors, the Kayras, who own the store and the Miss Charlie Restaurant in Kyuquot, have lived and fished in this area for decades. Watch out for Miss Charlie, the harbor seal who lives in the wild, but who has been a family pet for almost 40 years.

FOOD

When you tire of do-it-yourself picnicking on a west coast beach, let atmosphere dictate your choice of restaurant. Try to get a window seat overlooking the surf. The best location is the stunning glass-walled **Pointe Restaurant and On-the-Rocks Bar,** in the Wickaninnish Inn at Chesterman Beach, 800/333-4604, 250/725-3100. You get a 240-degree view from a dining room that features soaring ceilings, cedar post-and-beam construction, and a circular wood-burning fireplace. The chef specializes in gourmet west coast seafood, perhaps a little pricey, but the place and the food are worth it. Two cheaper restaurants in Tofino that specialize in good food, although they lack a waterfront location are the **Schooner Restaurant,** 331 Campbell St., 250/725-3444, whose clam chowder gets rave reviews from the locals, and the **Crab Bar,** in a cozy cottage at 601 Campbell St., 250/725-3733, whose fresh crab is highly praised. Down the road in the Wickaninnish Centre at the national park headquarters, is the busy **Wickaninnish Restaurant,** 250/726-7706. It's not as intimate, but it's more affordable than the new Wickaninnish Inn and it has panoramic views of legendary Long Beach. Be prepared to wait, since this restaurant advertises "seafood, sunsets, and romance." In Ucluelet, an appropriate place for seafood dining is the **Canadian Princess Restaurant,** 250/726-7771, located in a 236-foot ship in the Boat Basin overlooking the fishing fleet.

LODGING

Unless you want to take chances and spend all night on the beach, you had better book ahead for any lodging near Pacific Rim National Park Reserve in the popular summer months. Tofino is the place to go for the most options. First the unique. Newly opened is **Clayoquot Wilderness Resort,** c/-450 Campbell Rd., Box 728, Tofino, V0R 2Z0, 888/333-5405, 250/726-8235 www.greatfishing.com. It's a high-end floating fishing lodge anchored in Quaint Bay, a 20-minute boat ride from Tofino. But you don't have to fish, you can revel in the rainforest, hike, kayak, or ride horses on adjacent trails.

This part of the Pacific Rim has several other upscale, wilderness cedar-and-glass inns set amid trees on rocky beaches overlooking the wild west coast. You'll love their wraparound boardwalks and cedar plank decks for ocean-viewing. **Middle Beach Lodge,** 3 kilometers (2 miles) south of Tofino along Pacific Rim Highway, 250/725-2900, lodge@middlebeach.com, www.middlebeach.com, is situated on a private peninsula in the middle of a forest and has a variety of rooms, suites and cabins to suit a variety of tastes and budgets. This hotel actually has two lodges on the site, one adult-oriented and the other for families.

Not quite so private is **The Wickaninnish Inn,** on Osprey Lane at Chesterman Beach, 800/333-4604, 250/725-3100, wick@wickinn.com, www.wickinn.com. A local resident, his family, and friends have recreated the rustic elegance of Long Beach's former Wickaninnish Inn, now the park interpretive center. Guest rooms feature floor-to-ceiling picture windows, private balconies with soaker tubs inches from surf-lashed rocks, and furniture fashioned from recycled old-growth timber and driftwood. Handicap-equipped rooms are available. The Inn specializes in winter storm-watching, a growth industry in this part of the world, between November 1 and February 27.

I like the oceanfront cottages and suites with kitchens or kitchenettes at the ever popular **Pacific Sands Beach Resort,** 800/565-2322, 250/725-3322, info@pacificsands.com, www.pacificsands.com. Its back door is 1421 Pacific Rim Highway, 7 kilometers (4 miles) south of Tofino, but its front door is at the south end of magnificent (and sandy) Chesterman Beach, where waves crash beneath your window, and rock pinnacles beg for a camera.

Much kinder on the budget is **Wilp Gybu (Wolf House) B&B,** 311 Leighton Way, 250/725-2330, wilpgybu@island.net, www.vancouverisland-bc.com/WilpGyuuBB. Cheaper still is **Paddlers' Inn B&B,** 320 Main St., 800/TOFINO-4, 250/725-4222, paddlers@island.net, www.island.net/~paddlers. It is basic, but comfortable, reasonable, and conveniently located. In the same building is a bookstore, coffeeshop, and kayak touring store. Island lovers will head for yet another affordable and fun place to stay, **Vargas Inn,** 250/725-3309. This is a laid-back wilderness resort on Vargas Island within sight of Tofino. Vargas Island is a gem: more sand beaches than any other on the west coast, some of the best sportfishing, and a snack bar for feeding gray whales. Prices include boat transportation and meals, but vary according to time of year, length of stay, number of people, and type of lodging.

There's less choice in Ucluelet. Nostalgic people will stay at the **Canadian Princess Resort,** an historic west coast steamship permanently anchored on Peninsula Road in Ucluelet Harbour, 800/663-7090, 250/726-7771, www.obmg.com. It's open March 10 to September 30 and specializes in whale-watching, fishing packages, and nature cruises. Romantic people will stay at **The Snug Harbour Inn,** 460 Marine Dr., 888/936-5222, 250/726-2686, asnughbr@island.net, www.ucluelet.com/asnugharbourinn. It overhangs an oceanfront cliff, looks down on a private beach and features fireplaces beside the bed and jetted tubs. It's not cheap, but it's great for Valentine's Day, storm watching, and special getaways.

In Bamfield, stay in the action center of town at **Bamfield Lodge and Cottages,** 575 Boardwalk, 250/728-3419, bamlodge@cedar.alberni.net, www.anglingbc.com/bamfield lodge. It's nothing fancy, but offers everything at reasonable prices.

CAMPING

The west coast is the place for camping and you should contact the Pacific Rim National Park Reserve, 800/689-9025, for detailed information on the many sites available. Your first choice should be **Green Point Campground,** a shell's throw from Long Beach. It has 94 year-round sites for tents, trailers, and RV units, along with heated washrooms. Additional tent camping is available at 33 walk-in beach sites and 20 walk-in forest sites nearby. This campground is highly popular between April and October, so book ahead or face a long wait. From late June through early September, illustrated lectures, films, and audiovisual presentations are given nightly; free for registered campers, $2 for non-registrants, parking included. There's also a more primitive walk-in campsite on the beach at the end of the Schooner Trail.

If you can't find space in the park, try **Bella Pacifica Resort and Campground,** on the Pacific Rim Highway 3 kilometers (2 miles) south of Tofino on sandy Mackenzie Beach, with private nature trails to Templar Beach; 250/725-3400. In Ucluelet, try the **Ucluelet Campground,** at Seaplane Base Rd., overlooking Ucluelet Harbor and adjacent to a boat launch, 250/726-4355.

If west coast romance leads to popping the question, see West Coast Wilderness Weddings, 5151 Wilkinson Rd., Port Alberni, 250/723-0650.

NIGHTLIFE

Spend your evenings watching the sun set over the Indian Ocean or the surf crash on the rocks from either a tent or your waterfront inn window. Swap tales of the fish you hooked or the whales you spotted.

6
PORT HARDY
TO THE CARIBOO

Cariboo Country is similar to old California—it's British Columbia's Wild West cow and cowboy country laced with gold diggings. It extends from the fjords and rainforests of the central coast, east to the mountains and canyons of the Chilcotin, east again to the lakes, grasslands, and rolling sagebrush hills of Cariboo proper, almost to the Alberta border. This part of Western Canada is for hunters and anglers, hikers and horseback-riders, paddlers and gold-panners.

Traditionally, coastal First Nation tribes accessed the area by way of the Nuxalk-Carrier Grease Trail, a native trading route along the Blackwater River between Bella Coola and the Fraser River near present day Quesnel. In 1793, Sir Alexander Mackenzie, the first person to cross continental North America, reached the Pacific Coast by the same trail. Following the 1859 gold discovery near Horsefly, gold seekers rushed into the area on the arduous Cariboo Waggon Road (sic). Lillooet marks Mile 0 of the original wagon road to Barkerville and the richest gold-bearing streams in the Cariboo, and communities along the way (70 Mile House, 100 Mile House, and 108 Mile Ranch) still bear the old names. Cars, not wagons and camels, now zip along this Gold Rush Trail, officially named Highway 97 and Highway 26.

COUNTRY ROAD IN NORTHERN B.C.

Spectrum Stock

A PERFECT DAY IN THE CARIBOO

Where to start? Perhaps, a day re-living Barkerville history; canoeing the Bowron Lakes; paddling Lava Canyon in Chilko Lake; hiking the Rainbow Range Trail; fly-in fishing from Nimpo Lake; rafting the Fraser River; driving the Gold Rush Trail; or watching the Williams Lake Stampede.

Some people prefer chartering a plane for a personalized aerial tour of Mount Waddington—British Columbia's highest mountain, and nearby Homathko Ice Fields, or a flight through Tweedsmuir Provincial Park from Nimpo Lake to include Hunlen Falls, but some budgets would probably settle for a day (or week) of horseback-riding.

The Cariboo is chock-full of guest ranches and working ranches where you can ride with cowboys, fish or bird-watch at one of the many lakes, go for a hay ride, and sing around the evening campfire. If visiting The Hills Health and Guest Ranch or the 108 Ranch near 100 Mile House, add a swim and Jacuzzi soak—or maybe a massage, wrap, or facial.

ORIENTATION

You can fly there, but to get the feel of the country and its people, take or rent a car or camper and budget for one splurge later on into the mountains by plane or chopper. Most people drive to the Cariboo by Highway I (the Trans-Canada), following the Fraser River Canyon north from Vancouver to Lytton, and the Thompson River north to meet Highway 97 at Cache Creek. Highway 97 between Cache Creek in the south and Prince George in the north is the main artery through the Cariboo. To the west are the twisted plateaus and high mountains of the Chilcotin where horse and float plane are the best modes of transport. To the east are the lakes and streams, and a network of backcountry gravel roads that leads you to the best inland fishing in Western Canada. To get to this Interlakes region, take Highway 24, the Fishing Highway, east from near 100 Mile House.

The coastal First Nation tribes traded eulachon (fish) for furs, obsidian, and other goods with the interior First Nations along a route that was named the Grease Trail for the eulachon oil that leaked from wooden containers in which the oil was carried.

B.C. Ferries' Discovery Coast ferry takes you from Port Hardy on Vancouver Island to Bella Coola on the northern mainland, transports your vehicle so you can then drive east on Highway 20 through the Chilcotin Country to meet Highway 97 at Williams Lake. Highway 20, nicknamed "Freedom Road" (freedom to reach the outside world) was built in 1953 by a couple of entrepreneurial residents who grew tired of waiting for a government that said it couldn't be done. Be prepared for "The Hill," a narrow, precipitous rollercoaster ride of 19 kilometers (11.4 miles) between Bella Coola and the road's summit at Heckman Pass.

You can also take the train. BC Rail's "Cariboo Prospector" parallels much of the original gold seekers' route from North Vancouver to Lillooet, Williams Lake, Quesnel, and Prince George.

SIGHTSEEING HIGHLIGHTS

★★★★ BARKERVILLE
From Hwy. 97 head east from near Quesnel on Hwy. 26 for 82 km (51 mi), 250/994-3332
The Gold Rush to the Cariboo comes to life again in this restored ghost town, 8 kilometers (5 miles) from Wells. When Billy Barker struck gold here in 1862, Barkerville quickly became the most populated city west of Chicago and north of San Francisco. The town is open year-round, but the full interpretive program of historical characters dressed in period costume, guided tours of its 125 original and restored build-

ings, live theater, displays, shows, and demonstrations operates only in summer. It's educational and entertaining for the whole family.

Details: *Barkerville Historic Town, Barkerville Post Office, Barkerville, B. C. V0K 1B0; or Barkerville/Wells Visitors Infocentre, 250/994-3302 or 250/994-3332. Townsite open mid-May–Sept. 30, daily dawn–dusk, program times may vary; entry fees good for two days, adults $5.50, over 65 and ages 13–17 $3.25, ages 6–12 $1; family rate $10.75, free the rest of the year. (1 to 2 days)*

★★★★ BOWRON LAKE PROVINCIAL PARK
Drive 23 km (19.8 mi.) north from Hwy. 26 turnoff via Bowron Lakes Rd. (between Wells and Barkerville), 800/663-6000, 250/398-4414, 250/992-3111

The 115-kilometer (72-mile) canoe circuit of lakes, streams, and portages through this park, set amid the 2,425-meter (8,000-foot) peaks of the Cariboo Mountains, is one of the most beautiful canoe trips in the world. It's unique in that canoeists can return to the starting point without backtracking. Most people take eight days to travel the full circuit, but it can be completed in six if necessary. Peak use occurs the last week of June through the first week of September, but avoid crowds by traveling at the end of May or the first week of October. Be prepared for rain and cold weather in any case. Reserve through Supernatural B.C., 800/663-6000, well in advance although a limited number of drop-in canoeists permitted if space available. Only 27 canoes allowed onto the circuit each day to maintain the wilderness experience.

Details: *Fees for full circuit are $119.26/two-person canoe/kayak; stay limited to 14 days, paddlers must register at Bowron Lake Registration Centre May 15–Sept. 30 and view video. (6 to 8 days)*

★★★ DISCOVERY COAST PASSAGE
Depart Port Hardy on Vancouver Island via BC car and passenger ferry to Bella Coola on mainland via McLoughlin Bay, Shearwater, Klemtu and Ocean Falls, 888/223-3779 or 250/386-3431.

In the early 1960s I had the good fortune to travel up and down British Columbia's forested fjord-cut coast by float plane and rubber dinghy. In those days, First Nations and sawmill communities, fishing villages, and boardwalk canneries were alive with far more people and activities than they are today.

In recent years, in an attempt to begin a new era in tourism, the

PORT HARDY TO THE CARIBOO

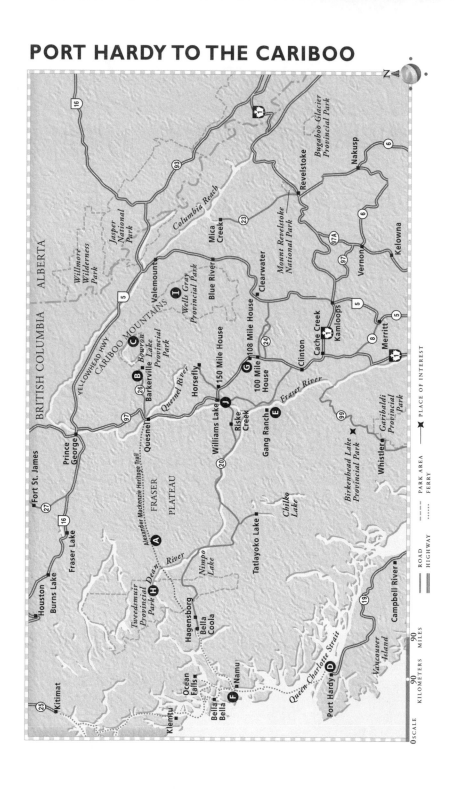

British Columbian government launched a new ferry, the *Queen of Chilliwack*, to cruise what it dubbed the Discovery Coast Passage, between Port Hardy and Bella Coola. The new ferry loads and unloads freight and passengers at or near each of its milk-run stops: Finn Bay, known coast-wide for its huge chinook salmon; Namu, with a former cannery and a 10,000-year-old archeological site; Bella Bella, home to about 1500 First Nations people; Shearwater fishing resort; Ocean Falls, a former mill town; and Klemtu, once a thriving cannery, now a First Nations community of 200. The new ferry allows kayaks to be loaded and unloaded at all stops, creating another vast waterway for exploration.

The Discovery Coast ferry is more like a miniature cruise boat, with deck golf, Bingo, showers, engine-room tours, and on-board entertainment. Although onshore facilities are still being built, passengers are offered walking tours, salmon barbecues, fishing trips, dance demonstrations, and visits to First Nations longhouses. You can sail to Bella Coola on a 15-hour day cruise, or extend the voyage all summer by getting on and off the ferry as many times as you want. If you can afford only one stopover activity, paddle in a canoe across Lama Passage with Heiltsuk native Frank Brown and pick up the ferry again at Shearwater. The trip can be booked on the ferry. Campgrounds and accommodations along the route are limited, so reservations and prior planning are advisable. You can sleep on reclining chairs in the lounge or set up tents in the solarium. I like sleeping on the benches in the cafeteria —they're narrow but quiet and uncrowded.

The only road out of Bella Coola is Highway 20, the Freedom Road with its infamous "Hill," which switchbacks up a narrow 20-kilometer (12-mile) gravel road with up to 18-percent grades to reach its highest point at 1524 meters (5,000 feet). Highway 20 then goes 436 kilometers (285 miles) through the lake country of the Chilcotin to meet the town of Williams Lake at Highway 97.

SIGHTS

- **A** Alexander Mackenzie Heritage Trail
- **B** Barkerville
- **C** Bowron Lake Provincial Park
- **D** Discovery Coast Passage
- **E** Gang Ranch
- **F** Hakai Provincial Recreation Area
- **G** 108 Resort and 108 Heritage Site
- **H** Tweedsmuir Provincial Park
- **I** Wells Gray Provincial Park
- **J** Williams Lake

Note: Items with the same letter are located in the same area.

Details: Cost of car and driver between Port Hardy and Bella Coola is $330 one-way and $110 for each additional passenger with reductions for students, seniors and the disabled. Buses and RVs cost more, bikes less. Kayaks and canoes get stowed for $40.75. Tent rental (includes bedding) is $25 for two nights. Season runs June–September. Routes, schedules, and cruise lengths vary, so contact B.C. Ferries, 1112 Fort St., Victoria, B.C. V8V 4V2. (3 to 6 days)

★★★ TWEEDSMUIR PROVINCIAL PARK
West entrance located 51 km (30.6 mi) east of Bella Coola, 54 km from east entrance, on Hwy. 20, contact B.C. Parks, Bag 5000, Smithers, B.C. V0J 2N0; 250/847-7320; or B.C. Parks, 301-640 Borland St., Williams Lake, B.C. V2G 4T1; 250/398-4414

This is the second-largest provincial park in B.C. after Tatshenshini. When the Kenney Dam was built to power the hydroelectric plant at Kemano and the aluminum smelter at Kitimat, the water levels of the park's northernmost lakes rose, resulting in an eyesore of drowned trees and floating debris hazardous to boaters. However, the central and southern areas offer a variety of wilderness attractions: the colorful Rainbow Mountains, an ancient volcanic area composed of lava and other rock that have eroded to expose vivid hues; the Dean River, one of British Columbia's best fly-fishing areas; the Atnarko River, which supports the largest population of chinook salmon on the central coast and where visitors to Stuie can view spawning fish; and an arduous nine-hour hiking trail leading to Hunlen Falls. Fly to Tweedsmuir Wilderness Camp with Tweedsmuir Air Services from Nimpo Lake, 800/668-4335, and spend a few days canoeing the Hunlen Valley chain of lakes. Nearby is the village of Hagensborg, established in the late 1890s by Norwegians, who chose the area because it reminded them of their homeland. Tweedsmuir is a wilderness park with few amenities so be prepared.

Details: Minimum 1-hour drive through park on Hwy. 20, or 2-hour trail hike north from Burnt Bridge at the west entrance to Tweedsmuir Park to view Stupendous Mountain, or an extended camping trip of your choice. (1 day to several weeks)

★★★ WELLS GRAY PROVINCIAL PARK
Leave Hwy. 5 at Clearwater and head north 35 km to park entrance, or drive gravel road west from Blue River, 250/587-6150

Nicknamed "the Waterfalls Park" for the beauty and abundance of its waterfalls and waterways, Wells Gray's best-known cascade is Helmcken Falls. Like Tweedsmuir, it offers an infinite variety of superb scenery: in the north, a multitude of unnamed peaks and glaciers; in the south, extinct volcanoes, lava beds, and mineral springs. Unlike Tweedsmuir, Wells Gray has an extensive trail system leading to its main attractions and many campsites.

Details: Contact B.C. Parks, 1210 McGill Rd., Kamloops, B.C. V2C 6N6; 250/828-4494. Hiking trails range from 30-minute nature walks to week-long backpacking trips. (1 day to several weeks)

★★★ WILLIAMS LAKE
On Hwy. 97 15 km (9 mi.) north of 150 Mile House.
Williams Lake Infocentre, 250/392-5025
It's best known for hosting the **Williams Lake Stampede,** B.C.'s largest stampede, a four-day celebration held at the Stampede Grounds, 250/392-6585, on the July 1 weekend. It includes both traditional and modern professional rodeo events—wild cow milking, team cattle penning and pony chariot races—chuckwagon races and bull fighting. Add a parade, barn dances and a downtown street party for a popular time to visit Williams Lake. See the **Museum of the Cariboo-Chilcotin,** 113N Fourth Ave., 250/392-7404, B.C.'s only museum devoted solely to rodeo, for a history of the Williams Lake Stampede.

Xats'ull Heritage Village is a First Nations (Shuswap) heritage site on the edge of the Fraser River at Soda Creek, approximately 32 kilometers (19.2 miles) north of Williams Lake, 250/297-6323 or 250/297-6467. It features ancient petroglyphs, pit houses, a sweat lodge, cultural programs and salmon cooked over open fires if arranged in advance.

Details: (1 to 2 days)

★★ ALEXANDER MACKENZIE HERITAGE TRAIL
Alternatively named the **Nuxalk-Carrier Grease Trail,** this is a 420-kilometer (250-mile) recreation trail between the confluence of the Blackwater and Fraser Rivers near Quesnel, and Sir Alexander Mackenzie Provincial Park in Dean Channel near Bella Bella, where a monument marks the end of the fur trader's historic 1793 journey across Canada. Mackenzie was the first person to record such a journey (more than 10 years before the similar Lewis and Clark expedi-

tion across the United States). The Alexander Mackenzie Heritage Trail takes you from British Columbia's interior plateau country through mountainous Tweedsmuir Provincial Park, along the Bella Coola Valley, to coastal fjords and the Pacific Ocean, almost the width of B.C. The 80-kilometer (50-mile) trail section inside the park takes about five to seven days to travel and is perhaps the most scenic part of the route.

Hikers can walk the entire trail in 18 to 24 days, although three weeks is more relaxing. Day-trippers can do shorter walks from several road-accessible trailheads. Local outfitters offer guided pack trips.

Details: *For a variety of trail guides, contact the Alexander Mackenzie Trail Association, Box 425, Stn. A, Kelowna, B.C. V1Y 7P1. For other trail info, phone the Ministry of Forests, 250/982-2000. (3 weeks)*

★★ HAKAI PROVINCIAL RECREATION AREA
Launch a kayak from the B.C. Discovery Coast ferry at Shearwater near Bella Bella and paddle 43 km (27 mi.) south to the Hakai. Or charter a boat or float plane.
This extensive and scenic archipelago centering on Hunter and Calvert Islands is the largest marine park on British Columbia's west coast. Accessible only by boat or plane and blessed with spectacular white sand beaches and sheltered inlets, it's an ideal playground for boaters, fishers, kayakers, and divers. Hakai Pass is world-famous for salmon-fishing and is home to a number of floating fish camps and resorts, including the 136-foot *Marabell* (Oak Bay Marine Group, 800/663-7090). Nearby is **Fiordland Provincial Recreation Area,** a visually stunning area that embraces Mussel and Kynock inlets, a four-hour boat ride south of Bella Bella.

Details: *(4- or 5-day organized trips)*

★★ 108 RESORT AND 108 HERITAGE SITE
Travel 13 km (7.8 mi) north of 100 Mile House on Hwy. 97 to the 108 Mile Ranch, 108 Resort, 250/791-5211 or 800/667-5233, 108 Heritage Site, 250/791-5228 or 250/791-1971, Hills Health and Guest Ranch 250/791-5225
This former cattle ranch is now a 263-hectare (650-acre) recreational community and a roadside reconstruction of the original log buildings from the 108 and 105 Ranches. Accommodations and dining, plus year-round activities that include cross-country skiing, golf, horseback-riding, hiking, canoeing, and swimming are offered.

Details: *Unless you are passing through and just glimpsing the historic buildings from the road, stay overnight. (1 day)*

★ **GANG RANCH**
Gang Ranch Post Office, Gang Ranch, B.C. V0K 1N0
250/459-7923 (Can be difficult to find)
Once billed as the largest ranch in North America, this historic, million-acre working ranch that stretches south of Williams Lake from the Fraser River to the Coast Mountains, offers a tour of the original cook house, store and post office, a small guest house and unguided activities such as horseback-riding (bring your own horse), hiking, photography, and viewing of the world's second-largest herd of California bighorn sheep.
Details: *Approximately 2.5 km south of Hwy. 97, take Hwy. 20 to Dog Creek Rd. Follow Dog Creek Rd. for 1.5 to 2 hours to the Gang Ranch. (1 day or drive through)*

FITNESS AND RECREATION

The Cariboo is a recreational paradise—from cruising, kayaking and saltwater fishing on the coast; to hiking, freshwater fishing, canoeing, rafting, hang-gliding, horseback-riding, and skiing in the interior; to my favorite-heli-hiking in the mountains.

Take a guest ranch vacation with **Chilcotin Holidays,** 250/238-2274, chilcotin_holidays@bc.sympatico.ca, www.chilcotinholidays.com. One of the owners is a member of the famous Bracewell family who, four generations ago, pioneered ranching and guide-outfitting in the Chilcotin-Cariboo region. Take a guided packhorse trip with **Bracewell's Alpine Wilderness Adventures,** 250/476-1169, 250/476-1165, or Chilanko JJ Channel H492-430. As well as offering hunting, fishing, wildlife viewing, glacier touring, prospecting, bird-watching, and survival skills, the Bracewells include guests in seasonal ranch activities and take them aerial sightseeing by bush plane or helicopter. Back at the ranch, you stay in a 10,000-square-foot log house.

Choose your own adventure, whether it is riding a horse, hiking, biking, skiing, snowmobiling, or fly-in fishing at one of **Stewart's Lodge and Camps,** 250/742-3388, 800/668-4335. Bob and Ginny Stewart pioneered fly-in fishing from a tent back in 1953 and now their children fly guests to a variety of outpost camps from their Nimpo Lake log lodge. Further south, at **Tyax Mountain Lake Resort** on Tyaughton Lake near Gold Bridge, stay at the largest log resort that is open year-round in Western Canada and enjoy a multitude of recreational activities amid mountains that soar to 3,000 meters (9,800 feet) to the usual riding and fishing opportunities, add sailing, mountain biking, tennis, gold panning, heli-skiing and camping. Contact this operation at 250/238-2221, 800/667-4854, fun@tyax.bc.ca, www.tyax.bc.ca.

If you have 10 days, plan to be in **100 Mile House** in August, for the Great Cariboo Ride, 250/791-6383, duffin@bcinternet.net. If this sounds too active, just stay put and wait for the wildlife. There are excellent wildlife viewing areas in the Cariboo: California bighorn sheep in the Junction Wildlife Management Area on Farwell Canyon Road south of Riske Creek; white pelicans at Stum and Puntzi Lakes; and all kinds of birds at Chilanko Marsh and the many lakes in the Cariboo.

FOOD

Concentrate on the ambiance when you eat your fish or steaks in the Cariboo, perhaps a floating fish resort, a working guest ranch, a chuckwagon at stampede time, or around the campfire by a secluded lake or park trail. If you must eat inside, here are some distinctive options with ambiance.

In Bella Coola, eat at the **Tallheo Cannery Inn,** a restored historic cannery that you access by water taxi from the B.C. Ferries dock, open May through September, specializes in steak and seafood, 250/982-2344. As you can expect in a rodeo town, beef is big in Williams Lake: for dinner, get steak or prime rib at the **Great Cariboo Steak House at Fraser Inn,** 285 Donald Rd., 250/398-7055; for lunch, try more family fare at the **Hearth Restaurant,** 99 Third Ave. S., 250/398-6831. This restaurant is located in a unique building that depicts an Indian Pit home and is run by the Cariboo Friendship Society. An arts and crafts shop, featuring First Nations work, is next door. The restaurant is open all week, but it closes evenings.

There are lots of choice around 100 Mile House: locals recommend **Happy Landing** on Highways 97 at 99 Mile Hill, 250/395-5359, which serves fine food Swiss style at moderate prices; **Marmot Ridge Restaurant and Lounge**, on Highway 97 at the north end of town, 250/395-6036, is named for the marmots seen as you dine on a hillside overlooking the town and the golf course. It's nicely decorated and the food is plain and affordable.

More exciting are the two restaurants at **The Hills Health and Guest Ranch** at 108 Mile Ranch, 250/791-5225, thehills@bcinternet.net, www.grt-net.com/thehills. **The 1871 Lodge,** named for the year that B.C. entered Confederation, is styled after that era: it has coffee, tea, and family lounges, the staff dresses in gold rush costume, you sear a 12-ounce T-bone steak on a hot rock near your own table, or choose the all-you-can-eat turkey, beef and veal fondue, and then top off with one of the ranch's phenomenal desserts. The **Trails End Restaurant** next door caters to the health conscious client who has come to the spa. Perhaps you should forget the phenomenal desserts and just choose an entree or two—the menu features a tantalizing mixture of ingredients, perhaps a saddle of locally raised fallow venison served with smoked bacon, wild mushrooms, and roasted pecans for $17.95.

You will be reminded again of the gold rush days in Quesnel. The **Cariboo Hotel and Saloon,** 254 Front St., 250/992-2333, is a heritage building whose restaurant serves good food at reasonable prices. At **The Hudson's Bay 1881 Heritage House Restaurant,** 102 Carson Ave., 250/992-2700, located in an old Hudson's Bay Company building, the second oldest building in B.C., all servers wear period costumes of the late 1800s.

Food is more casual in Barkerville. Copy the miners who had to work for 14 hours a day on the strength of their breakfast and go to **Wake-up Jake's** for a Boarding House Breakfast of porridge, eggs, potatoes, pancakes, and sausage served in an authentic saloon on the main street, 250/994-3259 or 250/994-3423. **Goldfields Bakery,** is noted for its excellent sourdough bread.

Hat Creek Heritage Ranch restaurant near Cache Creek, half-mile west of Highway 97 on Highway 99, 800/782-0922 or 250/457-9722, is the last intact stopping house on the Cariboo Wagon Road. It's a working farm that offers history, tours, and trail rides with lunch. Open daily mid-May to mid-October, 10 A.M. to 6 P.M. Another interesting lunch spot on a heritage site is the **Cottonwood Café** at Cottonwood House Heritage Park near Quesnel, 28 kilometers (16.8 miles) east of Highway 97 on Highway 26, 250/994-3209.

LODGING

If sleeping under the stars in the warm summer desert air of the Cariboo is not your choice, try the popular **Overlander Hotel,** 1118 Lakeview Crescent, Williams Lake, 800/663-6898 or 250/392-3321. It has three restaurants, fitness facilities, complimentary coffee, is reasonably priced and has a panoramic view of the lake and the town. Also in Williams Lake is the **Jamboree Motel,** 845 Carson Dr., 250/398-8208, which is centrally located and is even more economical.

Calling itself the "Guest Ranch Capital of North America," Clinton offers a variety of guest ranches—from a tent or teepee on the trail, to chalets, cabins, lodges, or ranch houses. Some welcome families, others are adult-oriented. Some include guests in their working operations, others don't. Meals feature cowboy breakfast rides, trail lunches, and barbecue dinners. Activities are many and varied. **The Hills Health and Guest Ranch,** 108 Mile Ranch on High-

PORT HARDY TO THE CARIBOO

N

Scale 0 — 90 KILOMETERS — 90 MILES

PLACE OF INTEREST ● / ★

PARK AREA

FERRY ······

ROAD ———

HIGHWAY ====

Map labels:

16

Willmore Wilderness Park

Jasper National Park

Bugaboo Glacier Provincial Park

Nakusp

6

Revelstoke

93

Columbia Reach

Mica Creek ■

23

Mount Revelstoke National Park

Kelowna

97A

ALBERTA

BRITISH COLUMBIA

5

Valemount

Wells Gray Provincial Park

Blue River ■

Clearwater ■

97

Vernon

5

Merritt

5

8

N

CARIBOO MOUNTAINS

YELLOWHEAD HWY

Bowron Lake Provincial Park

108 Mile House

150 Mile House

24

E

Cache Creek

Kamloops

1

H

C

K

Barkerville

Horsefly ■

B

Clinton

F

Quesnel River

L

100 Mile House

I

Fraser River

Fort St. James ■

27

Prince George

97

26

Quesnel

A

Williams Lake ■

D

Riske Creek ■

Gang Ranch ■

Garibaldi Provincial Park

99

Whistler ■

Birkenhead Lake Provincial Park

J

★

Burns Lake ■

16

Fraser Lake ■

Houston ■

Alexander Mackenzie Heritage Trail

FRASER PLATEAU

20

Chilko Lake

Tatlayoko Lake ■

Campbell River ■

19

Kitimat ■

25

Tweedsmuir Provincial Park

Dean River

Nimpo Lake ■

Hagensborg

M

G

Bella Coola

Ocean Falls ■

Namu ■

Klemtu ■

Bella Bella ■

Queen Charlotte Strait

Port Hardy ■

Vancouver Island

way 97, 250/791-5225, thehills@bcinternet.net, www.grt-net.com/thehills/, offers a world-class health spa (three times award-winner "Specialty Spa of the Year"), hay rides and horse rides, as well as its reasonably priced lodge and chalet accommodation. **The Best Western 108 Resort,** situated at 4816 Telqua Dr., 108 Mile Ranch, 800/667-5233, 250/791-5211 or www.108rst&netshop.net, is a lakeside golf and Nordic ski resort that offers a country setting of 600 acres. It's reasonably priced for the luxury you get in return. In 100 Mile House itself, your best bet is the newly renovated **Red Coach Inn,** 170 Highway 97, 800/663-8422, 250/395-2266, redcoach@bcinternet.net. This hotel is aptly named: on display in the courtyard is an original red stagecoach that traveled the Cariboo Trail until 1917. On the site of an inn built in 1863, it is in the city, yet has a country ambiance close to walking, cycling and skiing trails.

Logs mark much of the lodging in the Cariboo. In Clinton, 40 kilometers (25 miles) north of Cache Creek on Highway 97, 250/459-7992, stay at the **Cariboo Lodge** that is one of the largest log structures in B.C. and has a pub, restaurant and pool, yet is good for the budget traveler. An even larger log structure nearby is the more expensive **Tyax Mountain Lake Resort,** Tyaughton Lake Rd., Gold Bridge, about a 90-minute drive west of Lillooet, 250/238-2221, fun@tyax.bc.ca, www.tyax.bc.ca. It's a complete resort that caters to the adventurous guest who is stimulated by the stunning scenery. You can sightsee by float plane, paddle a canoe, sail a yacht, ride a horse or a mountain bike.

FOOD

- **Ⓐ** Cariboo Hotel and Saloon
- **Ⓐ** Cottonwood Café
- **Ⓑ** 1871 Lodge
- **Ⓒ** Goldfields Bakery
- **Ⓓ** Great Cariboo Steak House at Fraser Inn
- **Ⓔ** Happy Landing
- **Ⓕ** Hat Creek Heritage Ranch Restaurant
- **Ⓓ** Hearth Restaurant
- **Ⓐ** Hudson's Bay 1881 Heritage House Restaurant
- **Ⓔ** Marmot Ridge Restaurant and Lounge
- **Ⓖ** Tallheo Cannery Inn
- **Ⓑ** Trails End Restaurant

LODGING

- **Ⓗ** Beckers Lodge
- **Ⓑ** Best Western 108 Resort
- **Ⓘ** Cariboo Lodge
- **Ⓐ** Davey Mountainview Guest Ranch
- **Ⓑ** The Hills Health and Guest Ranch
- **Ⓓ** Jamboree Motel
- **Ⓓ** Overlander Hotel
- **Ⓑ** Red Coach Inn
- **Ⓒ** St. George Hotel
- **Ⓙ** Tyax Mountain Lake Resort
- **Ⓚ** Wells Hotel

CAMPING

- **Ⓒ** Barkerville Provincial Park
- **Ⓗ** Bowron Lake Lodge and Resorts
- **Ⓛ** Crystal Springs Campsite (Historical) Resort
- **Ⓜ** Tweedsmuir Provincial Park
- **Ⓝ** Wells Gray Provincial Park

Note: Items with the same letter are located in the same area.

The Wells Hotel, 2341 Pooley St., Wells, 250/994-3427 or 800/860-2299, is a newly renovated bed-and-breakfast heritage country inn established in 1933. It's a good base for trips to Barkerville or Bowron Lake. But if you want to be closer, then stay at **St. George Hotel** on Highway 26 in Barkerville, 888/246-7690, 250/994-0008, stgeorge@abccom.bc.ca, www.cariboo-net.com/stgeorge. Open May through October, weekends in December. The Wells also a renovated 1890s heritage hotel.

Nearby on Bowron Lake are some lower-budget alternatives: **Beckers Lodge** on Bowron Lake, 250/992-8864, 800/808-4761, radiophone N698552 YP Channel, beckers@beckers.bc.ca, www.beckers.bc.ca, is a good choice for some comparative luxury before or after attacking the Bowron Lake Canoe Circuit. It has a main lodge, rustic log cabins and renovated chalets in a wilderness setting with a lakeview restaurant, and a general store. You can rent canoes here. Open January through March, and May through October.

Locally recommended in Quesnel is **Davey Mountainview Guest Ranch,** 5442 Kirby Rd., 250/992-5568, dvyranch@quesnelbc.com. It's a friendly place, a homestead in a country setting with panoramic lake and mountain views, and serves a full farm breakfast.

CAMPING

The Cariboo offers comfortable camping—summers are usually dry and warm. Find a lake to yourself, put up a tent, and throw in your fishing line. **Wells Gray Provincial Park,** 250/674-2646, Clearwater Infocenter, has four main campgrounds as well as numerous wilderness camping areas and wheelchair access. **Tweedsmuir Provincial Park,** 250/398-4414, has only two campgrounds and few tenting areas. Campers need to be self-sufficient and experienced in these wilderness areas, but the scenery is worth the effort of hiking the backcountry. Fees must be paid in cash. **Barkerville Provincial Park** has three campgrounds adjacent to Barkerville, open May through October. Reserve at 181 First Avenue North, Williams Lake, British Columbia V2G 1Y8; 250/398-4414. There are 25 campsites available in **Bowron Lake Provincial Park** if you canoe the 116-kilometer (72-mile) circuit, 250/398-4414. **Bowron Lake Lodge and Resorts** is a convenient place to camp before or after you canoe the Bowron Lake Provincial Park. It offers lakeside cabins and campsites on a private sandy beach, mountain bike, boat and canoe rentals, 5 kilometers (3 miles) of hiking trails and its own airstrip, 250/992-2733.

Crystal Springs Campsite (Historical) Resort, on Highway 97, 12.8 kilometers (8 miles) north of Lac La Hache, 250/396-4497, is open April through October and offers fully equipped log chalets as well as RV sites. This is a Good Neighbor Park that gives Good Sam discounts.

NIGHTLIFE
Look at the stars and listen to singing cowboys around the campfire. And remember that after horseback-riding comes the hot tub and the spa.

7
QUEEN CHARLOTTE
ISLANDS

The Charlottes. The Misty Isles. The Canadian Galapagos. Haida Gwaii or "islands of the people" they are called by the Haida who have lived there. This archipelago of 200 storm-swept islands, 90 kilometers (56 miles) off the British Columbia coast and inhabited by 6,000 people, is one of the richest biological and cultural areas in North America. Despite its reputation for fog and rain (an average of 213 days per year), the Charlottes have become an international tourist destination. They offer remarkable trees and unique plants; an overwhelming abundance of nesting bald eagles and colorful seabirds; a rich intertidal life; excellent year-round fishing and hunting; unparalleled wilderness cruising for boaters; a bountiful paradise for scuba divers; long, sandy, deserted beaches for hikers; and the dramatic totem poles of the seafaring and artistic Haida. Its the kind of place where people who have just met you in the grocery store invite you home to give you a salmon from their freezer.

A PERFECT DAY IN THE CHARLOTTES
Sail to special places in the Gwaii Haanas wilderness of South Moresby Island on a tour boat such as the 68-foot ketch *Island Roamer.* Anchor in secluded bays, walk pristine sandy beaches, look for Japanese glass fishing floats, explore tide pools, photograph nesting puffins, and gaze at weather-worn cedar totem poles in ancient, now uninhabited Haida villages. Exult in the colorful sea stars,

urchins, cucumbers, anemones, and nudibranchs reflected in the clear waters of Burnaby Narrows at low tide; or enjoy the roar of Stellers sea lions swimming in the surf off Cape St. James; or glide into the old Haida village of Nan Sdins (Ninstints) on Anthony Island to imagine what life was like when hundreds of Haida prepared their salmon, carved their canoes, and lived in longhouses. At day's end, soak in an outdoor tub on Hotspring Island. Be sure to listen to Haida Gwaii Watchmen tell stories of their ancestral life, or longtime residents tell of homesteading in these islands of enchantment.

For *Island Roamer* information, contact Randy Burke, #3-252 E. 1st St., North Vancouver, British Columbia V7L 1B3, 604/980-3800. You can't savor all the special places of Gwaii Haanas in a day by boat—nor should you try. If you are limited to only one day, then take a helicopter tour from Sandspit to Skedans, or a float plane charter to the special places of your choice. Contact **Vancouver Island Helicopters** at Sandspit, 250/637-5344 or **South Moresby Air Charters,** Box 969, 3102 Third Ave., Queen Charlotte, B.C. V0T 1S0, 888/551-4222 or 250/559-4222.

ORIENTATION

Of the two main islands, Graham Island is the largest, most accessible, and most populated. Its communities include Skidegate (Skidegate Landing is where BC Ferries arrive), Queen Charlotte City, Port Clements, Tlell, Masset, and Old Massett. To the south of Graham is Moresby Island, whose main community is Sandspit and whose most outstanding feature is South Moresby (Gwaii Haanas) National Park Reserve/Haida Heritage Site.

The Charlottes can be reached daily by jet aircraft (Canadian Airlines) from Vancouver to Sandspit on Moresby Island; by amphibian planes daily from Prince Rupert to Sandspit, Masset, and Queen Charlotte; and by ferry (three times a week in winter, six times a week in summer) from Prince Rupert to Skidegate on Graham Island. Be prepared for rough seas on the six-hour, 93-nautical-mile crossing of Hecate Strait. The ferry has facilities for the disabled.

A smaller ferry joins Graham Island (at Skidegate) to Moresby Island (at Alliford Bay). There are few roads on the Charlottes, but on Graham Island you can drive from Queen Charlotte and Skidegate through Tlell and Point Clements to Masset, Old Massett, and Tow Hill. You must get around Moresby by boat, plane, or helicopter, since the only public road goes from the ferry terminal at Alliford Bay to the small settlement of Sandspit (a private logging road continues to Copper Bay).

Useful information: **Queen Charlotte Islands Travel Infocentre,** 3922 Highway 33, Box 337, Queen Charlotte, B. C. V0T 1S0, 250/559-4742. Sandspit

QUEEN CHARLOTTE ISLANDS

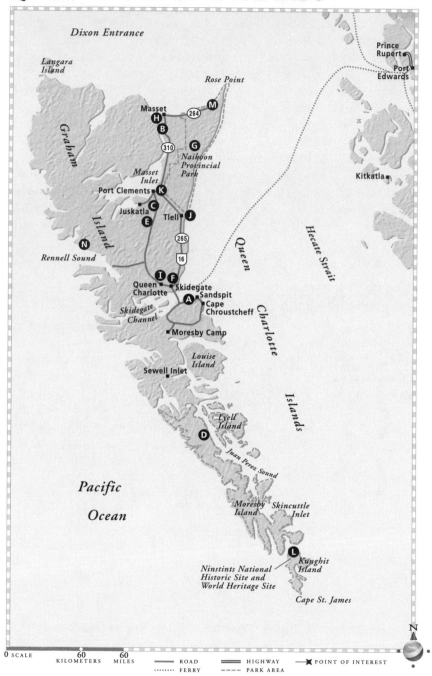

Dixon Entrance

Langara
Island

Prince
Rupert
Port
Edwards

Rose Point

Masset
H
B
M
264

Graham

310

G

Naikoon
Provincial
Park

Masset
Inlet

Kitkatla

Port Clements **K**

C

Juskatla

E

Tlell **J**

Island

265

N

16

Rennell Sound

Hecate Strait

Queen

I **F**

Queen
Charlotte

Skidegate

A Sandspit

Cape
Chroustcheff

Skidegate
Channel

Charlotte

Moresby Camp

Louise
Island

Sewell Inlet

Islands

Lyell
Island

D

Juan Perez Sound

Pacific

Moresby
Island

Skincuttle
Inlet

Ocean

L

Ninstints National
Historic Site and
World Heritage Site

Kunghit
Island

Cape St. James

N

| 0 SCALE | 60 | 60 | ROAD | HIGHWAY | POINT OF INTEREST |
| KILOMETERS | MILES | FERRY | PARK AREA |

Airport Terminal Building, 250/637-5362. **Village of Masset Tourist Infocen-tre,** 1450 Christie St., Box 68, Masset, V0T 1M0, 250/626-3982, medc@island.net.

SIGHTSEEING HIGHLIGHTS

★★★★ GWAII HAANAS NATIONAL PARK RESERVE AND HAIDA HERITAGE SITE
On South Moresby Island, 800/663-6000, 250/559-8818 or outside of North America, 250/387-1642, gwaiicom@ gcislands.net, http:fas.sfu.ca/parkscan/gwaii
It's hard to get to on your own, but do try to see some of South Moresby Islands Gwaii Haanas National Park Reserve and Haida Heritage Site, which is managed jointly by Parks Canada and the Council of the Haida Nation. The closest you can drive to the park's boundaries is 48 kilometers (30 miles) at the abandoned Moresby logging camp on Cumshewa Inlet. From there, you need a boat or kayak. A comfortable way to see Gwaii Haanas is to join a packaged tour; weather is unpredictable, and only experienced outdoors people

SIGHTS
Ⓐ Carey's Beachcombing Pacific Treasures
Ⓑ Delkatla Wildlife Sanctuary
Ⓒ Golden Spruce
Ⓓ Gwaii Haanas National Park Reserve and Haida Heritage Site
Ⓔ Haida Canoe
Ⓕ Haida Gwaii Museum
Ⓖ Naikoon Provincial Park
Ⓗ Old Massett

FOOD
Ⓐ Bun Wagon
Ⓗ Daddy Cools Neighbourhood Pub
Ⓗ Haidabucks

FOOD (continued)
Ⓘ Hummingbird Restaurant
Ⓕ Keenawiis Kitchen
Ⓘ Margaret's Cafe
Ⓘ Oceana Restaurant
Ⓙ Tlell River House
Ⓚ Yakoun River Inn

LODGING
Ⓙ Cacilias B&B
Ⓗ Copper Beech House B&B
Ⓘ Dorothy and Mike's Guest House
Ⓘ Gracie's Place
Ⓗ Harbourview Lodging
Ⓘ Hecate Inn
Ⓗ Naikoon Hotel and Hostel

LODGING (continued)
Ⓘ Premier Creek Lodging
Ⓛ Rose Harbour Guest House
Ⓐ Sandspit Inn
Ⓐ Seaport B&B
Ⓘ Sea Raven Motel and Restaurant
Ⓗ Singing Surf Inn
Ⓙ Tlell River House

CAMPING
Ⓜ Agate Beach
Ⓐ Gray Bay
Ⓙ Misty Meadows Campground
Ⓝ Rennell Sound Wilderness Campsites
Ⓗ Village of Masset RV Site and Campground

Note: Items with the same letter are located in the same area.

should travel alone. As many as 40 commercial operators offer ways to enjoy Gwaii Haanas.

At least one million sea birds nest along the shoreline of Moresby Island in summer, migratory birds pass through in spring and fall, and most of British Columbia's Peales peregrine falcon population lives there permanently. Moresby also boasts the largest sealion rookery in the province, at the **Kerouard Islands.** Try to see the sea lions at the now-automated lighthouse at **Cape St. James,** the puffins of **Flatrock Island,** and the marine life in **Skincuttle Inlet** and **Burnaby Narrows. Hotspring Island** is popular for a relaxing soak and for its rich plant life. The east coast of Moresby has innumerable coves, narrows, and islands for anchorages, beachcombing, and intertidal exploring; on the west coast, it has dramatic fjords and picturesque rockscapes, and remains of old canneries, whaling stations (**Rose Harbour**), logging and mining camps.

Try to visit at least one of the Haida village sites—Skedans, Tanu, Windy Bay, Hotspring, or Anthony Islands, and see where the old longhouses and totem poles are gradually returning to the forest. The Haida Nation still maintain summer base camps at some of these ancient villages. Although the Haida are trying to emphasize alternative villages to reduce pressure, Nan Sdins—or Ninstints as this village on Sgan Gwaii (Anthony Island) is popularly called—is still the preferred destination of visitors. It was abandoned in 1884. At that time, there were 20 houses, 25 carved poles, 20 mortuary poles, and 20 people on this secluded island at the southwest tip of the Charlottes. Nan Sdins has been declared a UNESCO World Heritage Site because it has the world's largest collection of Haida mortuary poles still standing in their original positions, all more than 100 years old. While the weather continues to erode the dozen or so that remain, efforts are being made to extend their life. Helicopters are not allowed to land, but tours by boat and fixed-wing plane (with some restrictions) may be arranged in Sandspit or Queen Charlotte, weather permitting. All visitors to the park must register and participate in an orientation session at a Parks Canada Office (Queen Charlotte City, 250/559-4496 or Sandspit, 250/559-8225).

Details: *Try South Moresby Air Charters, 888/551-4222, 250/559-4222. Air charters land at Rose Harbour on Kunghit Island, from which skiffs take you the rest of the way. Vancouver Island Helicopters, 250/637-5344, will fly you to Skedans or customize a route of your choice. Moresby Explorers, 250/637-2215 or 800/806-7633, runs one- to four-day zo-*

CAPE ST. JAMES LIGHTHOUSE

Lyn Hancock

diac boat trips that includes Nan Sdins. Bluewater Adventures, 604/980-3800, offers luxury cruises. (1 week)

★★★★ **HAIDA GWAII MUSEUM (AT QAYLLNAGAAY ON GRAHAM ISLAND)**
At Second Beach on the western edge of the Skidegate Reserve, Box 1373, Skidegate, B.C., 250/559-4643.
This distinctive cedar and glass building overlooking the waterfront contains totem poles from abandoned Haida villages, argillite (soft slate) carvings, and other First Nation artifacts. Natural history displays accompany equipment used by early settlers who tried unsuccessfully to establish farms on the eastern side of the island. Watch as Haida carve new poles in longhouse-style workshops nearby.
   Details: *Open May–Sept., Mon.–Fri., 10 A.M.–5 P.M., Sat.–Sun., 1–5 P.M. (summer); Oct. –Apr., Mon., Wed.–Fri., 10 A.M.–noon, 1–5 P.M. and Sat. 1–5 P.M., closed Tue. and Sun.; general admission $3, members free. No cameras allowed inside. (1 hour)*

★★★★ **NAIKOON PROVINCIAL PARK**
Northeast corner of Graham Island, 250/847-7320
It's largely bogland with stunted trees, but its wild, unspoiled, sandy

beaches are magnificent. You can drive on the North and South Beaches below the driftwood zone, but don't get stuck in the sand or caught by the tide (four-wheel-drive is recommended). A variety of hiking trails lead to interesting features such as the sand dunes at Rose Spit, the basalt rock column of Tow Hill, and the Blow Hole.

Details: Access to south end is at Tlell; to north end, a 25 km road from Masset causeway. Drive by or walk the beaches and trails. (1 hour to 1 day)

★★★ DELKATLA WILDLIFE SANCTUARY (GRAHAM IS-LAND)
At the head of Delkatla Inlet, Masset. Trails start from points along Trumpeter Drive and from gates along Cemetery Road, 250/557-4390 or 250/847-7320

This is a good place to see birds, especially sandhill cranes, on their spring and fall migration. The park has trails, boardwalks, and viewing platforms. Local birders can enhance your experience.

Details: Delkatla Bay Birding Tours, 250/626-5015. (1 hour)

★★★ OLD MASSETT (GRAHAM ISLAND)
3 km (2 mi) north of Masset, at the northwest end of Masset Inlet. Old Massett Village Office, 250/626-3337

The Haida village of Old Massett is worth visiting to see its artisans at work. In various gift shops and private homes Haida craftspeople fashion silver and gold jewelry or cedar canoes and totem poles. Look for poles carved by Reg Davidson at the Haida Arts and Jewelry long-house gift shop, a Haida canoe and fence designed with Haida figures at the Reg Davidson carving shed, and the totem poles and dugout canoe displayed outside the old Ed Jones Museum. For info on Haida artists, consult the Old Massett Village Office, 250/626-3337

Details: Weekdays 8:30 A.M.–noon and 1–4 P.M.. (2 hours)

★★ CAREY'S BEACHCOMBING PACIFIC TREASURES
367 Alliford Bay Rd., Sandspit

Neil and Betty Carey's front yard and fence is crammed with treasures they have collected during a lifetime living on both coasts of the Charlottes. Probably nobody has traveled these islands more thoroughly than this couple. In the lobby of the Sandspit Airport, you can see the 14-foot dugout canoe that Betty rowed between Seattle, Washington, and Ketchikan, Alaska, in 1962 and also used for her extensive explorations of the Queen Charlotte Islands. Neil's book *A Guide to the Queen Charlotte Islands* has been in print since 1975.

Details: *On the right-hand side of the beach road as you drive into town, 250/637-5492. Open year-round.(15 minutes, unless you meet the Careys...)*

★★ GOLDEN SPRUCE (GRAHAM ISLAND)
5.6 km (3.5 mi) south of Port Clements, on the Juskatla Rd., 250/557-4295

This tree, which owes its color to a lack of the pigment carotenoid (a sun damage protectant), has long been a tourist attraction on the Charlottes. To the Haida, it was a member of their band and a guardian of the Yakoun River. However, to the horror of almost everyone who has visited or lived on these islands, the tree was chopped down in January 1997, an act of vandalism that received national media attention. The Haida conducted funeral ceremonies. In efforts to grow more golden spruce, hundreds of cuttings were taken from the downed tree and grafted on a new rootstock. Secret cuttings that were taken from the old golden spruce 30 years ago and have grown into trees were resurrected and planted at the old tree site. The trail to the site of the Golden Spruce winds among giant trees to the Yakoun River. You'll arrive when you reach a bench overlooking the river and you'll look over to the site of the Golden Spruce.

Details: *(10-minute walk from road)*

★★ (THE) HAIDA CANOE
Juskatla Road, south of the Golden Spruce turnoff

This is a western red cedar dugout canoe left unfinished by its carvers in the forest after being cut, chiseled, and probed to its very heart by the Haida—a mammoth task and a mammoth heartbreak not to finish it.

Details: *Drive 8 km (5 mi) up Juskatla Rd. south of the Golden Spruce turnoff, to another well-marked trail that leads to the Haida Canoe. (10 minutes)*

FITNESS AND RECREATION
Fishing is the most popular sport on the Charlottes. From May to September, the hot spot is **Langara Island** at the northernmost tip of Graham Island, and adjacent Hecate Strait. This is the first place salmon stop on their migration back to

the rivers from the open ocean. Some say these are the best ocean salmon-fishing grounds in the world and the most popular fishing spot in British Columbia. Sportfishing facilities abound, and if you book through operators such as **The West Coast Fishing Club** and **Langara Fishing Adventures,** you can fly to Masset from the Vancouver Airport, then by helicopter to your fishing destination. It's another world: rugged seascapes and abundant wildlife—eagles, puffins, dolphins, falcons, an isolated lighthouse, the mortuary poles of Kuista; and back at the lodge, pamper yourself with massages, gourmet meals, and hot tubs.

The **West Coast Fishing Club,** 888/432-6666 (Vancouver), 416/223-5060 (Toronto), info@wcfc.ca, www.wcfc.ca, has several types of accommodations: the classy Clubhouse where you don't need to fish to have a luxury holiday; the more intimate North Island Lodge on floats in a nearby cove where you're more likely to spend time sitting in a boat reeling them in from dawn to dusk; and the new Outpost at Port Louis on the west coast of Graham Island where you have the option of halibut and freshwater fishing.

Langara Fishing Adventures also offers options: Langara Fishing Lodge, where visitors stay in a refurbished 120-foot paddle-wheeler; or Langara Island Lodge, a cedar post-and-beam building in the treetops from which you ride to a boat in an aerial tram. Prices range $2,500 to $4,200 for four- to eight-day packages, including round-trip air charter from Vancouver to Sandspit and float plane to Langara Island. For these lodges, call 800/668-7544, 604/232-5532, info@langara.com, www.langara.com. Less isolated is Kumdis River Lodge near Port Clements, 800/668-7544. New add-ons are daily eco-heliventures to the west coast of Graham Island for mountaintop hiking, kayaking, beachcombing, and more fishing—crabs, steelhead, and sea—run trout.

Do-it-yourselfers can charter or rent a boat, or stop and fish by a roadside stream. In winter, steelhead trout flourish in the Yakoun River. The Tlell River is famous for its coho salmon and steelhead trout runs. Huge halibut and lingcod also abound. So do charter boat operators. If you want to fish or explore the islands with a Haida family, call Robert Davis of **Ugolgo Boat Charters** 250/626-550 and Gilbert Parnell of **Good Spirits Touring Company**. Gilbert will sing, tell stories, take you to sacred sites and introduce you to carvers. Book with **Queen Charlotte Adventures,** 800/668-4288, 250/559-8990, qciadven@qcislands.net, www.qcislands.net/qciadven, for cultural and natural history tours by kayak, boat, vehicle or—llama! If you want llamas to do the walking and the carrying, see Island Llama Tours, 250/626-3730, www.llamatours.com, in Port Clements.

Be sure to walk the beaches of **Naikoon Provincial Park,** but watch the tides and undertow. A 16-kilometer (10-mile) round-trip hike begins at Tlell River Bridge and leads to the Pesuta Shipwreck. Continue up the coast to Rose

Spit, North Beach, Agate Beach, and Tow Hill for an 88-kilometer (55-mile) hike. Hiking south to north puts the wind at your back. Then there are new trails through the forest such as the Spirit Lake Trail, a 3-kilometer loop from Skidegate that showcases Culturally Modified Trees (CMT), trees that the Haida planned for canoes and totem poles. Birders will appreciate Bird & Breakfast given every Saturday at 8 A.M. by Delkatla Bay Birding Tours in Masset, 250/626-5015. Meet at the Stewart Tower in the Delkatla Wildlife Sanctuary, go birding, then get back to your guides for breakfast.

FOOD

Fresh salmon and halibut steaks on an open fire, a giant crab boil on the beach, a big bowl of steaming mussels, a huge seafood stew, roast venison . . . this is Queen Charlotte Islands cuisine. Do what the islanders do: gather 'round and shoot the breeze at local cafés, hangouts with good food, plenty of talk, and souvenirs, with the owner's arts and crafts, or the neighbor's jewelry for sale.

The best choice of restaurants is in Queen Charlotte City. The **Hummingbird Restaurant** at the Sea Raven Motel overlooking the harbor, 250/559-8583, is a family-style restaurant, a popular choice for lunch and dinner, and of course seafood is always on the menu. One popular dish is smoked salmon and shrimp fettuccini. Go to **Margaret's Café,** Wharf St. in the center of town, 250/559-4204, for breakfast—a platter of eggs, pancakes, sausages, and hashbrowns for less than $10. More of an institution than an eatery, it's where the locals hangout to chat about the weather. Margaret is no longer there though her table is. More upscale is the **Oceana Restaurant,** 250/559-8683, open for dinner from 5 to 11 P.M. It's a reliable place to go for Chinese food.

In Masset, try two fun places. **Daddy Cools Neighbourhood Pub,** 1993 Collison Ave., 250/626-3210, open daily from noon to 2 A.M. (Sundays to midnight) specializes in open-flame charbroiled steaks and hamburgers. **Haidabucks** (only in name is this like Starbucks) on Main St., 250/626-5548, is the new place to go for specialty coffee and frozen yogurt, as well as meals. Owned and operated by the Haida, it sells gifts, charters, and ecotours—a bit of everything in true Charlottes' style.

In Port Clements, hang out for a drink and a meal at the **Yakoun River Inn,** Bayview Dr. overlooking the Government Wharf, 250/557-4440. Locals in Sandspit rave about the mobile summertime (May through September, 11 A.M. to 7 P.M.) **Bun Wagon,** 250/637-5722, for burgers, fish and chips. In Skidegate, bypass the fast food outlets, grab three to 24 more customers and book a Haida Feast in Roberta Olsen's **Keenawiis Kitchen,** 237 Highway 33, 250/559-8347. It's a fun way of imbibing some Haida culture. Probably the most upscale dining place on the Charlottes, apart from the luxury fishing lodges, is the secluded **Tlell River House** on Beitush Road where you can sit at the window and watch anglers in hipwaders side-by-side fishing the Tlell River, 250/557-4211, rivhse@qcislands.net.

LODGING

The Charlottes offer varied accommodations, from funky bed-and-breakfasts and motel/hostels to luxury fishing lodges that cater to name-brand guests. Rates are surprisingly reasonable at most accommodations—between $35 and $100—but then there's nothing really fancy on the Charlottes and that is one of its charms.

Two of the most unusual places to stay on the Charlottes are the **Copper Beech House B&B,** 1590 Delkatla St., a funky conglomeration of tiny heritage rooms in a tangled garden near the docks in the heart of New Masset, 250/626-5441, www.bbcanada.com; and **Cacilias B&B,** a rustic, open-area, two-story log home nestled in rolling sand dunes on Hecate Strait near Tlell, 2 kilometers (1 mile) from Naikoon Park, 250/557-4664, ceebysea@qcislands.net, www.qcislands.net/ceebysea. A room at the Copper Beech House may be in the basement beside a well-stocked gourmet pantry, stuffed with antiques, surrounded by glass walls and a garden, or, according to the hosts, there is always the couch. However you experience this unique lodging, it will be memorable, especially if your host conjures up one of his lavish gourmet meals for which he is famous. Cacilias functions more like a boarding home—everybody meets everybody, and it obviously costs less. Both have that elusive element—character—that often money can't buy.

Also in Masset, is **Harbourview Lodging,** 1608-1618 Delkatla St., overlooking the Boat Harbour, 800/661-3314 or 250/626-5109. The suites are spacious and comfortable, there's lots to look at from the verandah, and the folks are friendly. **Singing Surf Inn,** 1504 Old Beach Rd., 250/626-3318, ssurfinn@island.net, is the only full-service hotel on Graham Island: It isn't much to look at, but the rooms are massive and you have all the amenities.

There's lots of choices in Queen Charlotte City. **Premier Creek Lodging,** 3101-3rd Ave., 888/322-3388, 250/559-8415 www.bizworks.com/pclodge, is one of the island's oldest buildings (1910). Fully modernized, it offers large view rooms, rooms with kitchenettes, and small budget sleeping rooms, all inexpensive. **Gracie's Place,** 8-3113 Third Ave., 888/244-4262 or 250/559-4262, is a renovated house with four antique-furnished rooms, Tiffany lamps, and down quilts. It has self-contained suites with kitchens and budget sleeping units. Gracie advertises herself as a nutty landlady and is one of the island's characters. Gracie also rents out cars, which is handy. Everybody speaks highly of bed-and-breakfasts on these islands, particularly **Dorothy and Mikes Guest House,** a private and peaceful place known for its warm hospitality at 3127 Second Ave., 250/559-8439, open April 1 to September 30. Not as colorful is the **Hecate Inn,** Box 124, right in town, three blocks west of the post office, 800/665-3350, 250/559-4543, hecatein@qcislands.net, but it offers great beds and goose-down duvets. The **Sea Raven Motel and Restaurant** at 3301 Third Ave., 800/665-9606, 250/559-4423, searaven@island.net, www.searaven.com, is also conveniently located, overlooks Bearskin Bay, is open all year, and has the fully licensed and popular Hummingbird Café on its premises.

If you want seclusion with your conveniences at an affordable price, the **Tlell River House,** a mile off the main highway in Naikoon Provincial Park, 800/667-8906, 250/557-4211, rivhse@qcislands.net, is the place for you. It is centrally located for day-tripping, overlooks the Tlell River with its year-round trout and salmon fishing, and extends to the windswept beaches for hikes of Hecate Strait. It offers cooking facilities for those wishing to prepare their own meals or there is a restaurant in the building.

In Sandspit, the **Seaport B&B,** 371 Alliford Bay, Sandspit, 250/637-5698, was the first bed-and-breakfast to open on the Charlottes. The owner, Bonnie Wasyleski, is another island character, and the rates are very reasonable for a single or double bed in one or the other separate rooms found in each of three small waterfront houses nestled beside the main house. Breakfast is self-serve. You may, however, prefer to tent right on the beach. If you want to be close to the airport in a modern hotel with every amenity, and characterized by high vaulted ceilings and a huge copper and stone fireplace then the **Sandspit Inn** is the place, 800/666-1107 or 250/637-5334.

The only private commercial facilities within Gwaii Haanas National Park Reserve are at **Rose Harbour Guest House** in Rose Harbour, 250/559-8455, or radiophone N159057 Channel 24 Cape St. James. In 1978, a group of island residents bought a former 150-person whaling station and built innovative homes amid the ruins.

CAMPING

In spite of the ruggedness of the mostly roadless terrain, especially along the west coast, the Charlottes are a friendly place for camping. Camping is available everywhere, and most of the land is publicly owned. There are few, if any, rules except in the Gwaii Haanas National Park Reserve and, to a lesser extent, Naikoon Provincial Park. Camping is not allowed in some of the Haida villages and it is discouraged in ecologically sensitive sites. The two most popular camping spots are **Agate Beach,** 250/847-7320, near Tow Hill, and **Misty Meadows Campground,** 250/847-7320, south of the Tlell River. The **Village of Masset RV Site and Campground,** 250/626-5064, 888/352-9292, medc@island.net, www.island.net/~masset has 22 shaded gravel sites opposite the Delkatla Wildlife Sanctuary on the Tow Hill Road. The sani-station is located at the Info Centre 1 kilometer away. No reservations.

Although there are few paved roads on the Charlottes, the Ministry of Forests and private logging companies maintain hundreds of miles of logging roads that may be accessed by campers and boaters. Pick up the Recreation Map of the Queen Charlotte Islands Forest District for a description of camping spots maintained by the B.C. Forest Service. Some favorites are **Rennell Sound Wilderness Campsites** on the west coast of Graham Island (be careful on the hill leading down to the beach), and **Gray Bay** on a beautiful sandy beach south of Sandspit. Phone B.C. Forest Service at 250/559-6200 or 250/559-8447 for information.

NIGHTLIFE

If you must drag yourself away from the wilderness and you're not at a fancy fishing lodge telling about the one that got away, then join the locals at **Howler's Pub and Bistro,** overlooking the harbor and docks in the heart of Queen Charlotte City, 250/559-8600. Drink and dine inside or on the deck. The pub is open afternoons and evenings until 2 A.M. (midnight Sundays), the bistro 11 A.M. to 11 P.M. seven days a week in summer.

8
NORTHERN
BRITISH COLUMBIA

Apart from hunters, trappers, and fly-in fishers, few know the breathtaking beauty of British Columbia's northern wilderness—its jumble of rugged mountains, spectacular glaciers and volcanoes, colorful lakes and rivers, and abundant and varied wildlife. It has been called North America's Serengeti Plain, a global treasure. Only three main roads traverse this vast sweep of almost roadless wilderness north of Prince George. This meeting of the Coast Mountains and the northern Rockies is the most rugged area of Canada's most mountainous province. With such a challenging topography and an area larger than England and Scotland combined, it can be intimidating. However, local guides and outfitters know where the best spots are, and they have the horses, boats, planes, and all-terrain vehicles to get there.

Hundreds of pristine provincial parks and protected areas exist in Northern British Columbia: the Tatshenshini-Alsek, Atlin, Mount Edziza, Spatsizi Plateau Wilderness, Tatlatui, and Kwadacha Wilderness in the west; and Muncho Lake, Stone Mountain, and Wokkpash Recreational Area in the east. These are the Northern Rockies, with few cars and no crowds. Here, you can truly get away from it all.

A PERFECT DAY IN NORTHERN BRITISH COLUMBIA

For a true wilderness experience in the most remote part of the Northern Rockies, fly to Chesterfield Lake in Kwadacha Provincial Park (see Photo Safari Tour, below). Soar over the Lloyd George Icefield, the centerpiece of Kwadacha Park; drop down to catch a trout or grayling on some unnamed wilderness lake of the pilot's choice; make a lunchtime campfire to cook your catch on a sandy beach; watch a grizzly with her cubs near Fern Lake; then land for supper on clear, deep, turquoise Chesterfield Lake. If time allows, return to Northern Rockies/Highland Glen Lodge on the Alaska Highway and squeeze in an evening boat ride on Muncho Lake, the end to a perfect day.

ORIENTATION

Driving your own recreational vehicle and taking flightseeing side trips with local outfitters beyond the beaten track are the best ways to explore this region. You can access Northern British Columbia by driving the Alaska Highway north from Dawson Creek to the Yukon border near Watson Lake; or Highway 37 (commonly called the Cassiar Highway) north from the Skeena River near Kitwanga to the Alaska Highway, with a side trip to Stewart on the Glacier Highway; or Highway 16—the Yellowhead Highway—from Prince Rupert east to Prince George, or from the Alberta border west to Prince George. These are truly roads to adventure; this is Western Canada's "last frontier."

A popular and more comfortable way to experience part of Northern British Columbia is to do circle routes by train: Via Rail Canada *(The Canadian)* from Vancouver northeast to Kamloops and Jasper, to contact Via Rail Canada *(The Skeena)* west to Prince George and Prince Rupert. Or BC Rail *(The Cariboo Prospector)* from Vancouver north to contact Via Rail Canada at Prince George. Phone for customized packages—Via Rail 800/665-7245, BC Rail 800/663-8238.

PHOTO SAFARI TOUR

Urs and Marianne Schildknecht of **Liard Tours**, out of Muncho Lake, Historical Mile 462 of the Alaska Highway, offer a 10-day guided photo safari. The tour begins with a flight from Vancouver to Fort Nelson and a drive on the Alaska Highway to the new Northern Rockies/Highland Glen Lodge on magnificent, 11-kilometer-long (7-mile) Muncho Lake. Each day, guests are flown over ice-capped mountain peaks, remote valleys, and secluded lakes in this little-known region—Tuchodi Lakes, South Nahanni River, Wokkpash Gorge, Kechika and

Gataga River Valleys, Stone Mountain and Kwadacha Provincial Parks. And each night under the midnight sun, guests relax in the Liard River Hot Springs, fish from lakefront wilderness cabins, or watch bush pilot films at the log lodge on Muncho Lake. For more information, contact Liard Tours, Box 8, Muncho Lake, British Columbia V0C 1Z0; 800/663-5269 or 250/776-3481.

ALASKA HIGHWAY SIGHTSEEING HIGHLIGHTS

This road, sometimes called the "Alcan," was not created for tourists. It was built in 1942 out of anger and fear that the Japanese would invade Alaska. A speedy military supply line, not scenery, was the prime motivation. The road was built wherever a bulldozer could go: through the remote mountains, muskeg, and mud of British Columbia, the Yukon, and Alaska. In eight months and 23 days, 16,000 American and Canadian soldiers and civilians finished the backbreaking work of building the highway, in temperatures that ranged from -68 degrees Celsius to -57 degrees Celsius (-90 degrees Fahrenheit to -70 degrees Fahrenheit). It was called "the premier engineering feat of the century." Upgrading has continued since World War II's end: most of the loops and wiggles have been straightened, 90 percent is paved, and it's now more of a road through wilderness than a wilderness road. For a detailed guide of the Alcan Highway, take along *The Milepost*(Vernon Publications), "the bible of northern travel." You should take a week to explore this 909-kilometer (568-mile) highway through British Columbia to the Yukon border. And if you have time, continue through Yukon to Alaska. In British Columbia, the most scenic section of the Alaska Highway is north of Fort Nelson (Historic Mile 300). Highlights include Stone Mountain Provincial Park, Summit Lake, Muncho Lake, Liard River Hot Springs Provincial Park, and Kwadacha Provincial Park.

★★★★ THE ALASKA HIGHWAY
Between Mile Zero at Dawson Creek and the Yukon border
The first 160 kilometers (100 miles) of the Alaska Highway roll through fertile Peace River Country farmlands. Stop in downtown **Dawson Creek** to photograph the famous sign that marks the **Mile Zero Cairn** and send a postcard letting the folks back home know that you are "doing" the Alaska Highway. If you have time, visit—one block north on Alaska Avenue—the **Northern Alberta Railway Park,** 250/782-9595, which houses the tourist information bureau, a museum in a restored railway station, and an art gallery in a refurbished wooden grain elevator. These are open daily in summer. Winter hours are restricted.

NORTHERN BRITISH COLUMBIA

N

ALBERTA

NW TERRITORIES

NW TERRITORIES

YUKON TERRITORY

INTERNATIONAL BOUNDARY

STATE BOUNDARY

PLACE OF INTEREST

ROAD

49

2

Fort
St. John

Peace River

Hudson's
Hope

Dawson
Creek

Chetwynd

Tumbler
Ridge

29

J

97

97

Prince
George

Sikanni Chief

Pink Mountain

A

Fort Nelson (mile 300)

Mackenzie

Fort
St. James

27

16

Liard River (mile 496)

ALASKA HIGHWAY

Stone
Mountain
Park
(mile 393)

K

E

Kwadacha
Wilderness
Park

Williston
Lake

MOUNTAINS

Houston

Babine Lake
Marine Park

G

F

Muncho
Lake Park
(mile 456)

ALASKA 97

ROCKY

BRITISH
COLUMBIA
CANADA

New
Hazelton

Smithers

16

37

Kitimat

Boya Lake Park

Tatlatui
Park

37

37

Terrace

L

H

Spatsizi
Plateau
Wilderness
Park

Khutzeymateen
River

Iskut

37A

Stewart

Prince
Rupert

Khutzeymateen
River
Recreation Area

1

37

C

Cassiar

Mount
Edziza
Park

D

Stikine River
Recreation Area

Telegraph
Creek

Stikine River

Dixon Entrance

Atlin
Lake

B

Atlin

Atlin Park

Juneau

1

8

2

ALASKA — UNITED — STATES

7

Pacific
Ocean

3

I

Tatshenshini-Alsek
Wilderness Park

0 SCALE   120   120
      KILOMETERS MILES

Also worth seeing is the **Walter Wright Pioneer Village and Mile Zero Rotary Park,** at the junction of Hart and Alaska Highways, 250/782-7144, which displays the buildings and equipment used by pioneers to homestead the area before the highway was constructed.

Stop at the **Fort Nelson Heritage Museum,** on the Alaska Highway at Historical Mile 300. Ask for Marl Brown whose long, flowing beard makes him look like Mr. Yukon, but he's actually Mr. Alaska Highway. This museum started when Marl's wife made him clear out all the Alcan memorabilia (old trucks and construction equipment) that cluttered their home. Also in Fort Nelson, you can join in the town's **"Welcome Visitors Program,"** held in the Phoenix Theatre at the impressive town square on summer evenings (Monday through Thursday, 6:45 P.M., between June and September). Listen to a talk by a Royal Canadian Mounted Police, a forester, a trapper, a dogsled racer, or see a bush pilot's slide show.

Details: Contact the Fort Nelson Travel Infocentre at Bag 399, Fort Nelson, V0C IR0, 250/774-2541; the Fort Nelson Historical Society, Box 716, Fort Nelson, V0C IR0, 250/774-3536. Open mid-May–mid-Sept. 8:30 A.M.–7:30 p.m. Admission: $2. (4 to 5 hours)

★★★ WOKKPASH RECREATION AREA
Churchill Copper Mine Rd. at Mile 382
Hike in the Wokkpash Recreation Area to view dramatic geological formations such as the *hoodoos* (erosion pillars) of Wokkpash Gorge and Forlorn Gorge. If you are adventurous and have a four-wheel-drive vehicle, access your starting point on the abandoned Churchill

---

SIGHTS

- **A** Alaska Highway
- **B** Atlin
- **C** Cassiar Highway (Hwy. 37)
- **D** Eve Cone
- **E** Kwadacha Wilderness Provincial Park and Kwadacha Recreational Area
- **F** Liard River Hot Springs Provincial Park
- **D** Mount Edziza Provincial Park
- **G** Muncho Lake
- **H** Nisga'a (First Nations) Memorial Lava Bed Provincial Park
- **I** Tatshenshini-Alsek Wilderness Provincial Park
- **J** W.A.C. Bennett Dam and Peace Canyon Dam
- **K** Wokkpash Recreation Area
- **L** Yellowhead Highway (Hwy. 16)

Note: Items with the same letter are located in the same area.

Copper Mine Road at Mile 382. Make your stream crossings early in the day at low water. Use Maps 94K/10 and 94K/7, a variably marked trail, and available cairns to climb from Wokkpash Creek into high alpine valleys, and back down again to the Alaska Highway near Mile 385 via horse trails and much-braided Macdonald Creek.

Details: *BC Parks, 250/787-3407. (2 days)*

★★★★ LIARD RIVER HOT SPRINGS PROVINCIAL PARK
Mile 497/km 800 of the Alaska Hwy.

You will appreciate stopping for a soak, camping, chatting with other travelers, enjoying the lush greenery, and perhaps watching moose. Known as the "Liard Tropical Valley," these hot springs are the second largest in Canada. Two bathing pools are linked by a boardwalk trail that leads you to viewpoints overlooking the Hanging Gardens, and wildflowers that bloom on natural terraces created by the hot springs. Join in the Visitor Program, which is held five days a week during the summer season. Most importantly, watch out for bears.

Details: *250/787-3407; park open 6 A.M.–11 P.M. (1 hour)*

★★★★ MUNCHO LAKE
Muncho Lake Provincial Park

Muncho Lake runs along the Alaska Highway between Historical Mile 436 and Mile 443, and is best known for its beautiful jade waters—colors that are due to the leaching of copper oxide into the lake. Look out for Stone sheep and mountain caribou as they approach the highway to lick the salt that's left from winter road maintenance. Animals can most likely be seen between Miles 445/Kilometer 712 and Miles 455/Kilometer 729 in the early morning or early evening. Take short loop hikes from Mile 454/Kilometer 726 to viewpoints overlooking the Trout River valley. In its mineral licks and hoodoos, its extensive alluvial fans, and its folded mountains with thrust faults and dips of limestone bedding, this area is very typical of the Northern Rockies landscape. Base yourself at **Northern Rockies/Highland Glen Lodge,** Historical Mile 462, 800/663-5269 or 250/776-3481, and fly with the pilot-owner, Urs Schildknecht of Liard Air, to other scenic spots. Alternatively, arrange a trip with Doug Andrews of Tetsa River Outfitters, Box 3182, Fort Nelson, BC V0C 1R0, 250/774-1005.

Details: *For additional information, phone the Toad River office of BC Parks, 250/232-5460. (4 days)*

★★★ KWADACHA WILDERNESS PROVINCIAL PARK AND KWADACHA RECREATIONAL AREA
South of Stone Mountain Provincial Park and Wokkpash Recreational Area in the Northern Rockies

If you really want to get further off the beaten track, take a plane or ride with guides to this wilderness area. The nearest highway is the Alaska Highway, about 80 kilometers (50 miles) to the north (Summit Lake) and 130 kilometers (78 miles) to the east (Trutch). The Lloyd George Icefield, one of the largest glaciers in the north, is the source of four northern rivers: the Tuchodi, Muskwa, Warnford, and North Kwadacha. Few people ever get into this remote area, but those who do likely land at Fern and Chesterfield Lakes. Fern Lake has rainbow trout and the only developed campsite in Kwadacha. In June and July, the area between these lakes is used by a number of female grizzlies with cubs.

Details: For additional information, phone Ministry of Forests, Fort Nelson, 250/771-3936 or 250/787-3407. Don't forget to bring the appropriate topographic maps (1 day)

CASSIAR HIGHWAY (HWY. 37) AREA SIGHTSEEING HIGHLIGHTS

The Cassiar Highway begins at Yellowhead Highway (Hwy. 16) and ends at Alaska Highway near the Yukon border. This road is rougher than the Alaska Highway route through northern British Columbia, but wilder and more spectacular. Take the Cassiar if you have to make a choice. It's best to make a circle and take both routes: north one way, and south the other way.

A popular route is to hike from Mowdade Lake to Buckley Lake, hike the west side of Mount Edziza, and exit via the Buckley Lake Route to Telegraph Creek.

★★ NISGA'A (FIRST NATIONS) MEMORIAL LAVA BED PROVINCIAL PARK

Be adventurous and access the Cassiar from Terrace by driving through the moonscape of this incredible park. This 158-kilometer (98-mile) gravel road, named the Nisga'a Highway or Nass Road, is narrow and winding with one-lane wooden bridges, but unique in commemorating where, approximately 300 years ago, a volcano erupted and destroyed villages, dammed lakes, and pushed the Nass River aside killing hundreds of Nisga'a.

Details: *The Nisga'a Visitors Centre is located about 100 kms north of Terrace on Nisga'a Hwy.; follow the signs. Reservations and a guide are required for hiking to the rim of the volcano. Guided hikes available May 1 through Aug. 31. To view the solidified outflow of lava (only), continue north by vehicle and pass over it on the road at any time in the summer. (1 day for guided hike)*

★★★★ MOUNT EDZIZA PROVINCIAL PARK
West of the Cassiar Highway

Mount Edziza Provincial Park is one of the three stunning provincial parks in this region, but to get close you must fly in to one of the park's main lakes—Mowdade or Buckley—from one of the nearest points on the highway—Telegraph Creek, Tatogga Lake, or Dease Lake. The closest connection is to get a ride with a fisherman or boater at Kinaskan Lake Park to the head of **Mowdade Lake Trail.** This 24-kilometer (14.4-mile) trail takes you to the central area of Edziza Park, which is largely an alpine plateau. The park is connected by the Stikine River to the second largest park in British Columbia, the **Spatsizi Plateau Wilderness Park,** east of the Cassiar. It is the home of red mountain goats whose wool is stained from rolling in iron oxide dust. First Nations Tahltan people from Iskut, the nearest village at Mile 250 (kilometer 405) of the Cassiar, lead trail rides into this park.

Details: *Arrange a tour on horseback or by float plane with Spatsizi Wilderness Vacations, Box 3070, Smithers, BC V0J 2N0; 250/847-9692. (1 day to 1 week)*

★★★★ EVE CONE
Mount Edziza

Eve Cone is one of several volcanoes on the flanks of Mount Edziza, which appeared as recently as 1,300 years ago. This is one of the best places to realize how volcanic action gave birth to British Columbia's staggering landscapes. The riotously colored Spectrum Range in the south end of the park was formed from lava flows through which hot sulfurous mineral waters percolated to the surface and stained the mountainsides with red, yellow, purple, and white stripes, making what looks like a vast watercolor.

Details: *Before you go, check with B.C. Parks, Area Supervisor, Box*

118, Dease Lake, V0C 1L0; 250/771-4591. Buy map 104G (1:250,000 scale) and take a compass. (1 day if you fly, 1 week or more if you hike)

OTHER SIGHTSEEING HIGHLIGHTS

★★★★ ATLIN
South from "Jake's Corner," at Mile 866 of the Alaska Hwy., and drive 93 km (58 mi)

Atlin has been called "the Switzerland of Canada" for its stunning beauty. The town overlooks the crystal-clear glacial meltwaters of Atlin Lake, the largest natural body of water in British Columbia; a lake as colorful as the Canadian Rockies' Lake Louise. This town of 500 people is surrounded by dramatic mountains, with a backdrop of glaciers that sweep down from the Juneau Ice Field at the boundary of Canada (British Columbia and the Yukon) with the Alaska. Atlin was founded in 1898 with the discovery of gold in the lake area, and gold is still mined here. Try some fishing for lake and Dolly Varden trout, arctic grayling, and whitefish. Swim in the Atlin Hot Springs at Warm Bay. View the MV *Tarahne*, a White Pass and Yukon Route vessel that once plied local waters with freight and passengers. It now sits on the lakeshore downtown.

You can get closer to the stunning scenery of **Atlin Provincial Park** south of Atlin by boat or float plane from the townsite. Fully one-third of the park's area is filled with ice fields and glaciers that shimmer in the waters of Atlin Lake. Canoes and houseboats may be rented, but strong winds on the lake make boating hazardous. Get closer to the scenery by splurging on a plane. The park has two undeveloped hiking trails: the Llewellyn Glacier Trail, which leads from the head of Llewellyn Inlet to the foot of the glacier; and the Cathedral Glacier Trail from Torres Channel to the smaller Cathedral Glacier.

Details: *Contact Atlin Visitors' Assoc., Box 365-NW, Atlin, V0W 1A0, 250/651-7522; or B.C. Parks, 3790 Alfred Ave., Bag 5000, Smithers, V0J 2N0, 250/847-7320. There is no park staff in Atlin, but you can get local info from the Conservation Officer, 250/651-7501. (1 day)*

★★★★ TATSHENSHINI-ALSEK WILDERNESS PROVINCIAL PARK

This dramatic park in the northwest corner of British Columbia protects what has been called the most magnificent river system on Earth and a step back in time to the last Ice Age. The Alsek and Tatshenshini

Rivers are a World Heritage Site for their exceptional scenery, plants, and animals, so don't miss them. It's best to leave the paddling to the experts and book a canoe or inflatable raft trip with a reputable operator. Floats down "Tat" river are so popular that private canoe and kayak operators may wait years for the necessary permits. Most tours begin at Dalton Post, Mile 99 (Kilometer 164) of the Haines Highway, which is partly in the Yukon, partly in British Columbia, and partly in Alaska. Highlights on the river include exciting whitewater (class III-IV) rapids, flower-strewn meadows, glacier-capped peaks, hikes on the Walker Glacier, a float amid icebergs that have been carved from glaciers, and grizzly bears.

Details: *Run these rivers with operators such as Whitewolf Adventure Expeditions and Nahanni River Adventures, Box 4869 Stn Main, Whitehorse, Yukon Y1A 4N6, 800/297-6927, nahanni@yknet.yk.ca, www. nahanni.com. Or Ecosummer Expeditions, 1516 Duranleau St., Vancouver, V6H 3S4, 800/465-8884 or 604/669-7741. (most tours take 12 days)*

★★★ **YELLOWHEAD HIGHWAY (HWY. 16)**
Yellowhead Highway is a major east-west route from Manitoba to Alberta and British Columbia where, except for its recent inclusion of the town of Masset on the Queen Charlotte Islands, it terminates at the coastal city of Prince Rupert. Via Rail Canada also follows this route. Its most scenic section is Smithers to Prince Rupert along the Bulkley and Skeena Rivers through the land of the Gitxskan and Tsimshian Nations. You can see dramatic evidence of their vibrant culture—elaborately carved totem poles, longhouses, and dance performances—in various villages such as Gitwangak (Kitwanga), Kitseguecla, the Hazeltons, 'Ksan, Kispiox and Kitwancool. Drive the informative 113-kilometer (68-mile) **Hands of History** tour between Kitwanga and the Hazeltons. Include the Nisga'a Highway and the Nass Forest Service Road through New Aiyansh (see above) and you have an historic First Nations circle route.

Prince Rupert is well known for its rain, but it is an important transportation hub for Western Canada. You can take the BC Ferry system west to the Queen Charlotte Islands, south along the Inside Passage to Port Hardy on Vancouver Island; or north via the Alaska Marine Highway to Skagway. Via Rail Canada and the Yellowhead Highway terminate in Prince Rupert. But this friendly port city is worth a couple of days' stay in its own right. It has excellent saltwater fishing for salmon and halibut, but you are likely to find killer whales, gray whales and humpback whales as well. **The North Pacific Cannery Village Museum** in Port Edward is worth a visit. It's B.C.'s oldest surviving salmon cannery dating from 1889 and now declared a National Historic Site. Live one-person performances bring its history to life. Open May 1 to September 30 daily from 9 to 6, admission fees are $6 adult, $3 youth, free children under 6. Phone 250/628-3538.

The Museum of Northern BC is a post-and-beam, longhouse-style building at First Avenue and McBride Street. There, you can learn the history of the Tsimshian. The museum is open year-round, 250/624-3207.

Revitalized **Cow Bay,** a 10-minute walk down Cow Bay Road to the waterfront, is a good place to watch the busy harbor activities, buy souvenirs or seafood, and visit a pub or café.

Northeast of Prince Rupert is the **Khutzeymateen Grizzly Bear Sanctuary,** perhaps the best place to observe one of the world's highest concentration of grizzly bears. Access to the estuary at the head of the inlet is restricted to authorized groups guided by commercial guides or a park ranger. It's best to go with a licensed operator, such as Ecosummer Expeditions, 800/465-8884 or 250/674-0102, or Sunchaser Charters, 250/624-5472. Another option is to charter a boat or a plane in Prince Rupert through Ecosummer or another operator. Inland Air Charters, 250/624-2577, and Harbour Air, 250/627-1341, arrange flightseeing to the sanctuary.

Details: *For more details, write New Hazelton Travel Infocentre, Box 340, New Hazelton, BC V0J 2J0, 250/842-6071. (2 days)*

★★ W.A.C BENNETT DAM AND PEACE CANYON DAM

These are major hydroelectric projects on the Peace River. Backup water from the dams form Williston Lake, the province's largest lake. W.A.C. Bennett Dam is located 24 kilometers (15 miles) west of Hudson's Hope on the Hudson's Hope Loop (Highway 29), a more scenic alternative to the Alaska Highway between Dawson Creek and Fort St. John. Peace Canyon Dam, 250/783-5211, is 1 kilometer (.6 miles) west of the ornately decorated suspension bridge over the Peace River, 6.4 kilometers (4 miles) south of Hudson's Hope.

Details: *Free underground tours of both dams are available daily May through September and on weekdays only the rest of the year.*

W.A.C. Bennett Dam: daily tours each hour on the half hours 9:30 A.M.–4:30 P.M. (2 hours)

Peace Canyon Dam: self-guided except for groups of 8 or more, daily 8 a.m.–4 p.m., the rest of the year weekdays, 250/783-5211. (1 hour)

FITNESS AND RECREATION

You don't have to look any farther than leaving your car and trying some of the sightseeing highlights outlined for this region, especially the hiking, canoeing, and horseback-riding activities in the provincial parks. It's fun to employ something else carry all your stuff in these areas; try a llama with **Northwestern Llama Ranch** from Terrace, 250/635-6910. For a different kind of recreation, the less energetic and their children will appreciate **Troy's Family Amusement Park**in Fort St. John, 250/785-8655; or horseback-riding at **Crystal Springs Ranch,** at Charlie Lake near Fort St. John, 250/787-4960. The very best way to experience the northern Rockies is by booking an organized expedition with a local guide or outfitter. In addition to the ones already mentioned, try these: **Canadian Explorer,** Hudson's Hope, 250/783-5396; **Canadian River Expeditions,** Whistler, 800/898-7238 or 604/938-6651; **Redfern Lake Adventures,** Fort Nelson, 250/774-6457; **High and Wild Wilderness Safaris,** Fort St. John, 250/787-8431 or 250/262-3287. **Seashore Charters** in Prince Rupert is a full service charter specialist, 250/624-5645 in Canada, or 800/667-4393 in the United States.

FOOD

To get anywhere in northern British Columbia, you will probably pass through Prince George, and, regardless of where you're going, head for **Esther's Inn,** dubbed a "Tropical Oasis in Northern B.C.," at 1151 NW Commercial Dr., 800/663-6844 or 250/562-4131. Sunday brunch between 10 A.M. and 2 P.M. is best, with a roasted pig, hip of beef, lavishly decorated salmon, and a smorgasbord of everything else you can think of, served in a beautiful setting of flowing water and tropical plants for not much more than $10.

Prince Rupert is another entry point into Northern British Columbia, but before you take off into the wilderness, dine at Prince Rupert's elegant **Waterfront Café,** in the Crest Motor Hotel, 222 First Ave. West, 800/663-8150 or 250/624-6771. Order the café's big halibut and salmon plate for a little more than $20, or any of the other fresh seafood specialties. Reserve a window table so you can look at the mountains, the busy harbor, and in fall, the eagles congregating to eat the spawning salmon. Not so elegant, but still good waterfront dining is a table overlooking the harbor at the popular **Cow Bay Café,** 205 Cow Bay Rd., 250/627-1212. Try its lavish, but reasonably priced seafood platter. Busier still and more casual is **Breaker's Pub** overlooking the harbor in Cow Bay at 117 George Hills Way, 250/624-5990.

As you begin a journey up the Alaska Highway, don't miss the quaint and colorful **Alaska Hotel Café and Dew Drop Inn Pub,** located 55 paces

---

south of the Mile Zero Post in the center of Dawson Creek, 250/782-7040. The atmosphere is casual, the decor is reminiscent of the pre-war days of highway construction, and you can get almost anything you want to eat for less than $20.

Despite the humble facades and ho-hum decor of most restaurants along northern wilderness highways, some are intriguing because of their history or ma-and-pa home cooking. Strike up a conversation with local residents at roadside cafés to enrich your experience. Locals and visitors like eating at the sidewalk café of the **North Peace Cultural Centre,** 10015 100th Ave., Fort St. John, 250/785-1992. Further up the Alaska Highway at Mile 72 is the **Shepherd's Inn,** known for its quality home-cooked meals and gourmet coffees. The owners specialize in making travelers feel at home. **Mae's Kitchen,** by Pink Mountain at Mile 147 on the Alaska Highway, is proud of its homemade soups, breads, pies, and pastries. You may want to buy its souvenir cookbook.

In Fort Nelson, **Dan's Neighbourhood Pub and Bistro,** on the Alaska Highway at the south end of town, is a popular gathering place, open daily. The **Fort Nelson Motor Hotel** dining room, 800/663-5225 or 250/774-6971, is unexpectedly luxurious. Walk in from a muddy or dusty street to dine in a tropical courtyard by a pool. In the 1970s, the owner was a big-game hunter; and his trophies—huge elephants, giraffes, and buffalo— hung on the walls.

LODGING

En route to the Alaska Highway is the popularly priced **Stagecoach Inn,** in the western-style, chainsaw-sculpture town of Chetwynd, 800/663-2744 (Alberta and British Columbia only) or 250/788-9666, which prides itself on being a motel with "a billion-dollar view" over the Sukunka Valley. It has a good restaurant, hot tubs, and coffeepots and alarm clocks in the rooms. Mailing address is Box 927-SM, 5413 South Access Rd., Chetwynd, V0C 1J0.

Lodge names along the Alaska Highway may conjure up images of luxury resorts, but they're not. Names on the map are often little more than service stations with cafés and rooms attached, some with campgrounds and stores. Even so, the rooms are generally clean, the food good and amply portioned, and the people friendly. Northern hospitality is special. Some places leave a note for late night travelers: "Rooms with doors open are vacant. Please help yourself and register in the morning." Talk to the locals and you will learn about the land and the people along the way.

Don't miss staying—or as the name says, dropping in—at the **Alaska Hotel Café and Dew Drop Inn,** 10213 10th St., Dawson Creek, 250/782-7040. This historic building places itself "just 55 paces from the Mile Zero Post." It's the

NORTHERN BRITISH COLUMBIA

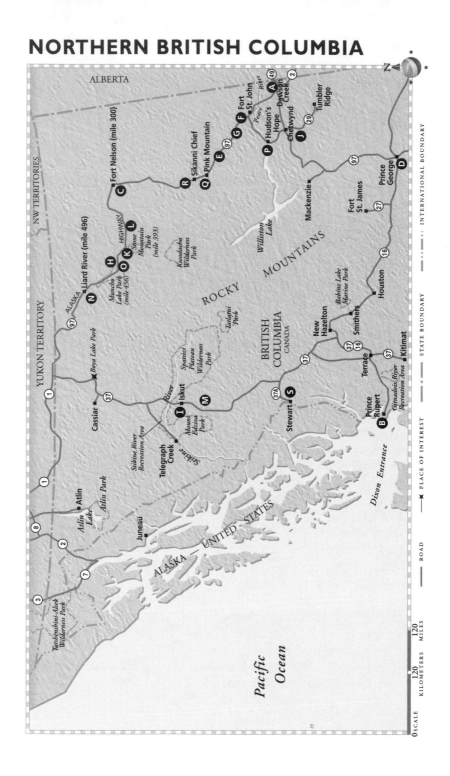

oldest continuously occupied building in Dawson Creek and displays antiques and works of art. Accommodations are basic, but dandy for those with a sense of history and place. And the price is right: Rooms start at $25.

Further north on the Alaska Highway, at Mile 72 near Fort St. John, is reasonably priced **Shepherd's Inn,** which is open 24 hours, has a restaurant and a campground attached, and is ideal for families. Write Box 6425, Fort St. John, V1J 4H8, 250/827-3676.

Don't miss the **Fort Nelson Motor Hotel** at Mile 300 for its modern rooms overlooking a tree-lined indoor courtyard, a pool, and the Tiki dining room. Rates are variable, but reasonable. Contact the hotel at Box 240-TG96, Fort Nelson, V0C 1R0, 250/774-6971 or 800/663-5225. Highway gossip reports that the grizzly burgers (no, they don't cut up grizzly bears) are great at **Summit Lake Lodge,** Historic Mile 392, 250/232-7531.

The other "don't miss" is **Northern Rockies/Highland Glen Lodge,** at Mile 462, Alaska Hwy., 800/663-5869, 250/776-3481, or by mail at Box 8, Muncho Lake, V0C 1Z0. Complementing the long-standing log chalets and motel units, the lodge's newly built main building is said to be British Columbia's largest log structure, featuring a 13.5-meter-high (45-foot) fireplace in an open-ceiling dining room. This is an all-in-one holiday resort. The owner-operator, Urs Schild-

---

FOOD

- **Ⓐ** Alaska Hotel Café and Dew Drop Inn Pub
- **Ⓑ** Breakers Pub
- **Ⓑ** Cow Bay Café
- **Ⓒ** Dan's Neighbourhood Pub and Bistro
- **Ⓓ** Esther's Inn
- **Ⓒ** Fort Nelson Motor Hotel
- **Ⓔ** Mae's Kitchen and Ed's Garage
- **Ⓕ** North Peace Cultural Centre
- **Ⓖ** Shepherd's Inn
- **Ⓑ** Waterfront Café

LODGING

- **Ⓐ** Alaska Hotel Café and Dew Drop Inn Pub

LODGING (continued)

- **Ⓑ** Coast Prince Rupert Hotel
- **Ⓤ** Eagle Bluff Bed and Breakfast
- **Ⓒ** Fort Nelson Motor Hotel
- **Ⓗ** Northern Rockies Lodge
- **Ⓑ** Pioneer Rooms
- **Ⓘ** Red Goat Lodge
- **Ⓖ** Shepherd's Inn
- **Ⓙ** Stage Coach Inn
- **Ⓚ** Stone Mountain Safaris Bed and Breakfast
- **Ⓛ** Summit Lake Lodge
- **Ⓜ** Tatogga Lake Resort
- **Ⓚ** Toad River Lodge
- **Ⓝ** Trapper Ray's Liard River Hot Springs Lodge

CAMPING

- **Ⓞ** J&H Wilderness Resort
- **Ⓑ** Park Avenue Campground
- **Ⓟ** Pine Ridge Campgrounds
- **Ⓠ** Pink Mountain Campsite
- **Ⓐ** Northern Lights RV
- **Ⓡ** Sikanni River RV Park
- **Ⓕ** Sourdough Pete's Tent and RV Park
- **Ⓢ** Stewart Lions Campground and RV Park
- **Ⓒ** Westend Campground

Note: Items with the same letter are located in the same area.

knecht of Liard Air, will fly you to any of the parks and fishing lakes in the hinterland. Despite the luxury, room rates and RV sites are middle of the road in price.

Toad River Lodge, at Mile 422 of the Alaska Hwy., 250/232-5401, is a modern motel whose slogan is "Hang Your Hat Where It's At." The lodge is known for its collection of 4,000 hats. Good sheep and caribou wildlife-viewing are nearby. New at Toad River is **Stone Mountain Safaris Bed and Breakfast,** 250/232-5469, a cedar log lodge in a ranch setting that offers horseback rides, wildlife viewing and adventure trips.

Trapper Ray's **Liard Hot Springs Lodge,** across the highway from Liard Hot Springs Provincial Park at Mile 497, is an inviting, European-style log structure with modern conveniences, including a handicapped-accessible suite and diamond willow staircase. Open year-round. Contact the lodge at Mile 497-TG96, Alaska Highway, British Columbia V I G 4J8, 250/776-7349.

On Highway 37 (the Cassiar), between Kitwanga and Watson Lake, are several wilderness lodges clustered around the small Tahltan Indian community of Iskut. They offer the usual highway-lodge amenities plus guided tours into the neighboring wilderness parks. Noteworthy is **Red Goat Lodge,** Highway 37, Box 101, Iskut, V0J 1K0; 888/733-4628, 250/234-3261, a superior bed-and-breakfast with a personally served gourmet breakfast, a hostel, and a lakeshore camp for RVs and tenters, in the shadow of Loon's Beak Mountain, open May 25 through September 15. Ask new owners Mitch and Jacquie Cunningham about reasonably priced ways to access the neighboring wilderness parks. Mitch may take you himself or rent you a boat. You won't miss the facade of moose antlers that covers the log cabin café of the **Tatogga Lake Resort,** Mile J 240.7, Box 59, Iskut, V0J 1K0; 250/234-3526. Be sure to stop for a bowl of homemade soup at the café even if you choose not to stay at the resort's cozy and colorful log cabins.

There's lots of variety in Prince Rupert. **Pioneer Rooms,** 167 Third Ave. East, 250/624-2334, is a quaint historic rooming house and as inexpensive as you can get. **Eagle Bluff Bed and Breakfast** in an original cannery resting on pilings beside the wharf at 201 Cow Bay Road in Cow Bay is another quaint and reasonably priced place, 800/833-1550, 250/627-4955, eaglebed@citytel.net. You can't beat the service or the central location at the higher-end **Coast Prince Rupert Hotel,** 118 Sixth St., 800/663-1144 or 250/624-6711.

CAMPING

Camping is the way to go in these wilderness areas, either on a guided trip or on your own at a private or provincial campground. Overnight camping is prohibited at highway turnouts, despite the temptation. In July and August it's always best to get to a campsite by midafternoon or to reserve in advance. One should consider opting for any of the provincial parks first. Of hundreds of private camping facilities available, try these.

Northern Lights RV, Box 2476, Dawson Creek, V1G 4T9; 250/782-9433; NLRV@pris.bc.ca, on Highway 97 South, 1.5 kilometers (.9 miles) south of the junction with Alaska Highway, is open 24 hours mid-April through mid-October. Not only does it have hot showers, but there are minor vehicle repair facilities, as well.

Pine Ridge Campgrounds, General Delivery, Fort St. John, V1J 4H5, 250/262-3229, on the 114-acre Bentley Ranch halfway between Hudson's Hope and Fort St. John, has attractive sites, a cookhouse, horseshoe pits, Ping-Pong tables, a childproof fence, and plenty for kids to do. It's open May 15 through September 15. Cost is $8 per vehicle (no credit cards).

At Mile 45 of the Alaska Highway near Fort St. John is **Sourdough Pete's Tent and RV Park,** 7704 Alaska Rd., Box 6911, Fort St. John, V1J 4J3; 800/227-8388 or 250/785-7664, adjacent to an amusement park and helpful for families. **Pink Mountain Campsite,** Mile 143, Alaska Hwy., 250/774-1033, is an all-encompassing place to stay, with cabins, campground, RV park, gas station, post office, store, and liquor store.

Sikanni River RV Park, Mile 162 of the Alaska Hwy., is situated at the bottom of Sikanni River Hill, 250/774-7628, and has cabins and RV vehicle sites. If you want an alternative to a hotel in Fort Nelson—and you should spend a night in this town if driving the highway—try the **Westend Campground,** Box 398, Fort Nelson, V0C 1R0, 250/774-2340, next to the museum. It offers free firewood and a free car wash, miniature golf, First Nations crafts and hides, a wildlife display, and a playground. Open April 1 through November 1.

If you can't manage a night of luxury at the **Northern Rockies/Highland Glen Lodge** at Muncho Lake, try camping at **J&H Wilderness Resort,** Box 38, Muncho Lake, V0C 1Z0, at Mile 463 of the Alaska Highway, 250/776-3453. It has a convenience store, a float plane dock, and no-nonsense dining.

Stewart Lions Campground and RV Park, Box 431, Stewart, V0T 1W0, 250/636-2537, has the usual amenities plus tennis courts, a nature walk, and a trout stream. The owners also arrange tours to the nearby Bear Salmon Glacier.

Prince Rupert's **Park Avenue Campground,** 800/667-1994, 250/624-5861, is ideal. Situated only .5 kilometers from downtown, .5 kilometers from the ferry terminals, and close to various walks and hiking trails, it boasts the beauty of the country, the convenience of the city, and all the amenities you would want.

Glacier Highway

Drive the Glacier Highway to the fjord-walled towns of Stewart and Hyder. The highlights of this stunningly scenic road are Bear Glacier and Strohn Lake (into which the glacier calves its icebergs), all of which can be easily seen from a vehicle. From Stewart, drive up a narrow, winding, 48-kilometer (30-mile) road to the abandoned Granduc minesite and Salmon Glacier. In August, watch chum and pink salmon spawning in nearby Fish Creek, and the bald eagles and black bears who feast on them. Stewart is a popular location for filmmaking. Contact the Stewart-Hyder International Chamber of Commerce, Box 306 NW, Stewart, B.C. V0T 1W0; 250/636-9224.

NIGHTLIFE

The bars in the ghost town of Hyder, Alaska (which are accessed from Stewart, British Columbia), are world famous for "Hyderizing" their patrons, who must gulp down a lot of hard liquor to earn a certificate. Hyder's nightlife has earned it the title "The Friendliest Little Ghost Town in Alaska." You will find plenty of smoke-filled, hearty local atmosphere in the bars along the wilderness roads of the north, but as an alternative, you might prefer the sound of a crackling fire by a rushing stream under the northern lights instead.

Scenic Route: Telegraph Creek and the Grand Canyon of the Stikine

The historic Telegraph Creek Road along the Tanzanilla and Stikine Rivers that leads into this area from Highway 37, is gravel and switchbacks all the way, but worth driving for its panoramic views of the Grand Canyon of the Stikine and the Tahltan Canyon. The town of Telegraph Creek, home of the Tahltan Nation, was once a telegraph communication terminal, but is now a jumping-off point for wilderness hikers and river rafters. Its main street is scarcely changed from Gold Rush days. Many residents make their living by fishing for salmon. The Grand Canyon of the Stikine is a landform unparalleled elsewhere in Canada: 80 kilometers (50 miles) long, and from 300 meters (985 feet) to as little as 2.4 meters (8 feet) wide. Experienced canoeists paddle some parts of the Stikine River, but the wild Grand Canyon section is almost impassable. The area may be accessed from Dease Lake off Highway 37 (the Cassiar) by the 113-kilometer (70-mile) Telegraph Creek Road. Phone Stikine Riversong Café, Lodge and General Store, May through September for local info, 250/235-3196. Whitewolf Adventure Expeditions and Nahanni River Adventures run annual 10 to 14 day, two-person canoe and voyageur canoe expeditions on both the Lower Stikine and Upper Stikine Rivers (see contact info above).

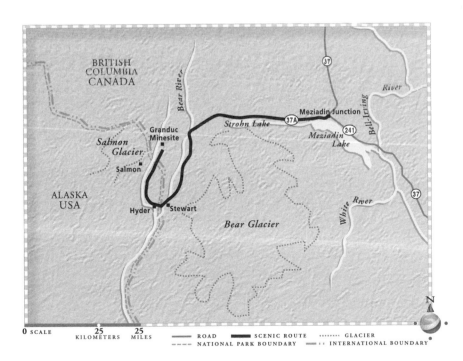

9

NORTHERN ALBERTA

Unlike Alberta's southern half, which is neatly squared off into sections, its northern half appears on the map as empty green space; and unlike northern British Columbia, Alberta's north is mostly lowland. Only three main roads pierce this emptiness: Mackenzie Highway, north from Grand Prairie and Grimshaw; Bicentennial Highway, north from Slave Lake; and Highway 63, north from Lac La Biche. The Peace and the Athabasca Rivers and their tributaries are the roads that first brought travelers into this wilderness, and are still important routes. The forest splashes with so many lakes that people call northern Alberta "Lakeland." North of Edmonton, Alberta is so vast that it could contain several European countries. Wood Buffalo National Park is the world's second-largest national park.

This is adventure country, attracting outdoor lovers all following the first traders who paddled and portaged west, then north, seeking routes to the Pacific and new fur sources. Follow them. Drive Mackenzie Highway to the Northwest Territories' Hay River, then to Wood Buffalo National Park via Fort Smith; or visit Wood Buffalo on the winter road from Fort Chipewyan. Boat from Fort Chipewyan through the Peace-Athabasca Delta, a birder's mecca. Drive Highway 63 to Fort McMurray and the world's largest oil sands. Canoe or jet-boat the Peace River. Fly to a remote fishing lodge. Ride a snowmobile to a trapline. In 1997, Fort McMurray was named The Best Place to Live for Nature Lovers by well-known *Canadian Living* magazine.

A PERFECT DAY IN NORTHERN ALBERTA

Wrest yourself away from a low-budget day in the West Edmonton Mall and spend a high-budget day getting to Wood Buffalo National Park. Although you can drive north to the Northwest Territories and access the northern end of Wood Buffalo from Fort Smith, the cheaper (though longer) method is to fly to Fort Chipewyan on the Alberta side of the park and take a boat ride with one of the native guide/outfitters through the Peace-Athabasca Delta for some bird-watching. Then, follow a park naturalist to see buffalo wallowing in the sand, and spend a couple of hours photographing white pelicans feeding and resting on ledges near the Slave Rivers Rapids of the Drowned by Fort Smith.

ORIENTATION

Northern Alberta is generally regarded as all parts of Alberta north of Edmonton as far as the Northwest Territories border, half of the entire province. It is divided into three regions: Fort McMurray and Wood Buffalo, Big Lake Country (mainly Lesser Slave Lake), and the Mighty Peace (River) Country. The favorite part for many people is Wood Buffalo National Park, which straddles the border of Alberta and the Northwest Territories. To get there, drive Highway 63 north from Edmonton to the road's end at Fort McMurray and Fort MacKay, or take one of Canadian Regional Airlines' daily flights to Fort McMurray, then fly Air Mikisew to Fort Chipewyan on Lake Athabasca, and explore the Peace-Athabasca Delta and Wood Buffalo National Park from there. Alternatively, use Highway 35 or Highway 88 to reach Wood Buffalo from the Northwest Territories. Another way to sample north-ern Alberta is to fly into one of its myriad lakes and fish, especially in June after the ice melts. Many hunting and fishing operators fly out of Fort McMurray.

For detailed information on the region, contact Alberta North Tourism Desti-nation Region, Box 1518, Slave Lake, Alberta T0G 2A0, 800/756-4351, abnorth2@agt.net. or the Fort Mc-Murray Visitors Bureau, 400 Sak-itawaw Trail, 79H 4Z3, 780/791-4336, 800/565-3947, visitors@ftmcmurray .com, www.visitors.fortmcmurray.ab.ca.

SIGHTSEEING HIGHLIGHTS

★★★★ FORT CHIPEWYAN
Use Fort McMurray Visitors Bureau 800/565-3947 for information, or Fort Chipewyan Lodge 780/697-3679

NORTHERN ALBERTA

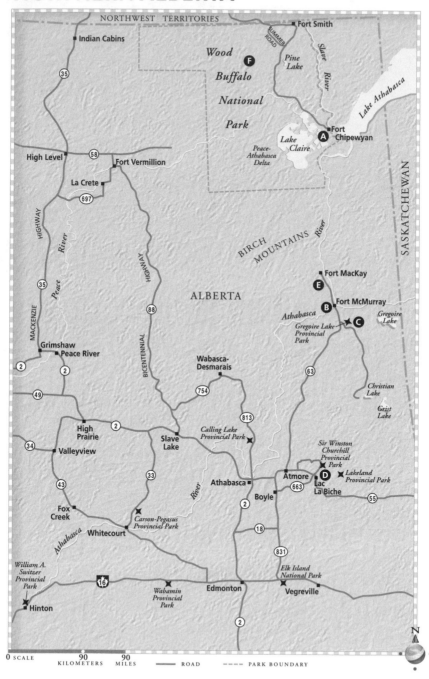

Fort Chipewyan (population 1,000) is the oldest permanently inhabited settlement in Alberta. It was designated a national historic site in 1939. Called Fort Chip, or just Chip, by the locals, this was the Northwest Company's most important northern fur trading post, built in 1798 to collect furs from the Mackenzie River basin and the Peace River country. The First Nations people who live in Fort Chip today are still trappers, hunters, and fishers who live a semitraditional lifestyle. Learn some of this history at the **Fort Chipewyan Bicentennial Museum** on Mackenzie Avenue, 403/ 697-3844, which is modeled after the Hudson's Bay Company store of 1872. It presents the history of the Chipewyan, Cree, Metis, and European settlers, and the key role Fort Chip played in Canada's early exploration and fur trade. Learn about the natural history of the region by strolling along the banks of Lake Athabasca by

Fort Chipewyan can be accessed by winter road mid-December through mid-March, 285 kilometers south to Fort McMurray, or 228 kilometers north to Fort Smith, NWT; by river late May through October (8 hours) from Fort McMurray and Fort Smith, NWT; by plane with Air Mikisew, 800/268-7112.

the **Fort Chipewyan Nature Trail and Viewing Platform.** The walk has 77 information signs describing the plant and animal life that may be seen along the way.

Details: *Museum open year-round weekdays 9 A.M.–5:30 P.M., weekends 1–5 P.M.; donations accepted. (1 hour)*

At the confluence of the Clearwater and Athabasca Rivers, Fort McMurray, located about 420 kilometers (255 miles) north of Edmonton by Highways 2 and 63, was a major depot for both the Northwest Trading Company (1790) and the Hudson's Bay Company (1870) on the supply route from northern

SIGHTS

- Ⓐ Fort Chipewyan
- Ⓑ Fort McMurray Oil Sands Discovery Centre
- Ⓒ Gregoire Lake Provincial Park
- Ⓓ Lac La Biche
- Ⓔ Oil Sands Plants (Syncrude Canada and Suncor Energy)
- Ⓕ Wood Buffalo National Park

Note: Items with the same letter are located in the same area.

Saskatchewan to Lake Athabasca. From here, people and goods traveled north by riverboat and paddle-wheeler to the Arctic via Slave River, Great Slave Lake, and the Mackenzie River. Today Fort McMurray is the service center for the giant **Athabasca Oil Sands** deposits, one of the world's largest oil deposits, which produces more than 250,000 barrels of oil per day. It's believed that these deposits represent roughly one-third of the earth's known petroleum reserves. Suncor Energy and Syncrude Canada have announced plans to expand existing facilities. Fort McMurray is one of the largest outports in Canada for fly-in fishing.

★★★★ **FORT MCMURRAY OIL SANDS DISCOVERY CENTRE**
Jct. Hwy. 63 and Mackenzie Blvd., (515 Mackenzie Blvd.), 403/743-7167, 800/565-3947 (tour reservations at Fort McMurray Visitors Bureau), www.oilsandsdiscovery.com
Through colorful, hands-on and sit-in exhibits, and multimedia presentations, you learn how oil was formed millions of years ago and how it is now extracted from the oil sands. Explore some of the massive mining equipment such as a seven-story bucket-wheel excavator in the Industrial Garden.
> **Details:** open May 15–Labor Day daily 10 A.M.–6 P.M., rest of year 10 A.M.–4 P.M.; $3 adults, $2 seniors, $1.50 ages 7–12, $8 family. (1 hour)

★★★★ **OIL SANDS PLANTS (SYNCRUDE CANADA AND SUNCOR ENERGY)**
Approximately 35 km (21.7 mi) north of Fort McMurray on Hwy. 63, 800/565-3947, 780/791-4336
Take a bus tour of either one of these mammoth operations by booking with Fort McMurray Visitors Bureau. This popular tour includes a visit to the Oil Sands Discovery Centre and the reclamation sites of both plants. You can also get a complete tour package that includes two nights' accommodation in a Fort McMurray hotel of your choice, a complimentary breakfast and a souvenir T-shirt. Even if you don't care for machinery, you will be awed by the size of the gigantic earth movers that scoop and carry rich, black oil sand to seven-story-high machines, and crush the ore into bite-sized pieces.

The **Syncrude Tour** includes a stop at **The Oil Sands Viewpoint** about 45 km (30 miles) north of the Oil Sands Discovery Center in downtown Fort McMurray and from this vantage point you can see the mine's vast production facilities and miles of conveyor belts. On the other side of the road is the **Wood Bison Viewpoint,** an interpretive area overlooking 83 hectares of reclaimed land where you get a close-up view of the Syncrude/Fort McKay wood bison herd. You also stop at the **Wood Bison Gateway**—four massive sandstone sculptures of wood bison that mark the beginning of Syncrude's mining area and the **Wood Bison Trails,** the portion of the highway that cuts through the Syncrude site. If you have your own vehicle, park it near these statues and walk these self-guided trails. The **Matcheetawin Discovery Trail** shows what the landscape will look like when Syncrude has completed mining and reclaimed the land. The **Sagow Pematosowin Trail** explores the region's First Nations heritage.

If you have your own vehicle, walk the **Crane Lake Nature Trail,** a .4 km path through one of the reclaimed areas on the **Suncor Energy** site, about 30 km north of Fort McMurray. More than 129 species of birds migrate through here each year. Viewing blind interpretive signs help you identify the commonly seen birds.

Details: Syncrude public tour dates: May–Jun., Fri. and Sat.; Jul.–Aug., Wed.–Sat.; Sep.–Oct., Sat. Suncor public tour dates: Jun., Sun. and Mon.; Jul.–Sep. Sun.–Tue. Admission. $15 adult, $12.50 seniors, no children under 12. (Tours last 3 hours)

★★★★ WOOD BUFFALO NATIONAL PARK
On the border of Alberta and Northwest Territories, Box 750, Fort Smith, NT X0E 0P0, 867/872-2349 (Fort Smith), 780/697-3662 (Fort Chipewyan)

This is Canada's largest national park. It is also a UNESCO World Heritage Site, established in 1922 to protect the world's largest free-roaming wood bison herd. The park is now home to 3,500 or more of these animals. Later, plains bison received refuge in the park, and the two species interbred to form the current hybrid herd. Join a park naturalist on a regularly scheduled summertime buffalo creep to see them close up, perhaps wallowing in a sand bath or grazing in a meadow in the subarctic boreal forest.

The park also contains the world's last nesting grounds of the endangered whooping crane and the northernmost nesting grounds of the white pelican. The **Peace-Athabasca Delta,** a massive maze of channels, islands, and marshes, is the staging ground for North America's four major waterfowl flyways, so birds are abundant. More than 500,000 waterfowl pass through the delta in spring and fall on their annual migration, and many remain to nest.

Wood Buffalo also has noteworthy landforms: extensive gypsum karst formations such as caves, sinkholes, and underground rivers; and salt plains, the remnants of an ancient seabed that once covered North America's inland prairies. If you enter the park from the Northwest Territories, drive Parsons Lake Road, which leads to the Salt Plains Overlook. These glistening plains are reminiscent of the Sahara Desert. Take the bends carefully on this narrow, winding road-buffalo may be lurking around each corner. Gravel roads open May 1–November 1 with more convenient summer access at the northern end from Fort Smith; the 400 km (250 mi) Fort Chipewyan Winter Rd. (part is on the ice) from Fort McMurray to Fort Chipewyan and Fort Smith is open December 15–March 15 weather permitting.

Details: Boating, picnicking, and camping are permitted at Pine Lake in summer: snowshoeing, cross-country skiing, and ice fishing are permitted in winter. Free. (1 day)

★★ GREGOIRE LAKE PROVINCIAL PARK
38 km (23 mi) southeast of Fort McMurray, 780/334-2222
This is the only easily accessible lake in the area, so if you can't manage a fly-in fishing trip, try here for northern pike, walleye and yellow perch. Many species of waterfowl nest here, and moose and black bear are common. Gregoire Lake has lots of camping areas, walking trails, and boat-launch facilities.

Details: (1 day)

★★ LAC LA BICHE
215 km (134 mi) northeast of Edmonton on Hwy. 55; 780/623-5235, reservations 780/623-7961, www.llbnet.ab.ca/CAP
This was originally a Hudson's Bay Company trading post, built in 1798. Father Lacombe added a mission in 1853. Today Lac La Biche is a major jumping-off point for exploring the local area. **Lakeland Provincial Park** showcases some of Alberta's best wilderness lakes and first circle-tour canoe route. **Shaw Lake Nordic Ski Area** offers 20 kilometers (12 miles) of groomed trails, and the adjacent recreation area contains four provincial campgrounds, numerous sandy beaches, and a designated trophy-fishing lake. **Sir Winston Churchill Provincial Park,** 780/623-4144, the largest of 12 islands in Lac La Biche, joins to the mainland by a causeway. Birders may view more than 200 different bird species here.

Details: (1 hour)

CONTACTS FOR GUIDED TRIPS

The northern wilderness can be a daunting place when you are going it alone. If you'd prefer to leave the driving to others, the following guide/outfitters can help. For comprehensive Northern Alberta information, contact **Alberta North,** Box 1518, Slave Lake, T0G 2A0, 780/849-6050 or 800/756-4351.

In Fort McMurray, try **Majic Country Wilderness Adventures,** 780/743-0766; **Points North Adventures,** 780/743-9350; or **Webers Tour and Charter Service,** 780/790-1777.

In Fort Chipewyan, see **Peace-Athabasca Delta Tours,** 780/697-3914; and **Fort Chipewyan Adventure Lodge,** 780/697-3679. **Mikisew Tourism Corporation,** 780/697-3740, runs a seven-day Wood Buffalo Delta Safari into the national park from Fort Chipewyan. Guided by the local First Nations people, this trip includes a boat tour of the delta and a hike across the prairie to view buffalo, eagles, waterfowl, and wolves. Things have a penchant for change in the north, so it's always advisable to make sure a business is still in operation when making travel arrangements.

The guide/outfitters in the Peace River area of northwestern Alberta will take you fishing, hunting, river cruising, wildlife-viewing, horseback-riding, and canoeing. Try **Doig River Outfitters,** 780/835-5152; **Peace Island Tours,** 780/624-4295; **Smoky River Adventure Tours,** 780/624-9416; **Outdoors Magnified,** 780/324-3602; and **Wilderness Adventures International,** 780/351-3980 or 780/551 2097. Or if you want to experience a working farm of sheep, cattle, and alpacas, try **R&R Alpacas,** 780/568-2536.

The following guides specialize in Wood Buffalo National Park, but can lead you to other destinations as well. In Fort Chipewyan, try **Scott Flett,** 780/697-3914; **Vince Vermilion,** 780/697-3661; **John Rigney,** 780/697-3740; or **Jumbo Fraser,** 780/697-3739. **John Rigney** and **Alice Marten-Marcel** run eight-hour boat tours into the Peace-Athabasca Delta. Contact them at Box 178, Fort Chipewyan, T0P 1B0, 780/697-3929. Guide/outfitters tailor trips to the individual interests of their clients, whether it's angling, wildlife-viewing, or cultural interests. Most people plan to fish, hike, and camp.

FITNESS AND RECREATION

Fort McMurray may be the province's northernmost and most isolated town, but it has every sport and sporting facility imaginable, including sled-dog races, winter bicycle rides, winter golfing, marathons, and triathlon events. Its well-connected roads and trails make it convenient to bike, hike and in-line skate, as well as ski, and snowmobile. **Skywonder Scenic Tours** (contact Sawridge Hotel 800/661-6567) takes you on a tour of the heavens to see the Aurora

Borealis (northern lights). So does **Aurora Tours of Edmonton,** 780/452-5187. Northern Lights RV Rentals rents quads (four-wheel-drives) and trikes (three-wheel vehicles)—and guides if you prefer—to explore the Athabasca Sand Dunes, 780/791-3893.

Canoeing is important in this region. The Clearwater River originates at Lloyd Lake in Saskatchewan and meets the Athabasca River at Fort McMurray. As the only major river within the western prairie region to flow west, it was an integral part of the river and lake system that brought explorers and fur traders westward during the eighteenth and nineteenth centuries. The Clearwater was declared a Heritage River in 1986 for its contributions to Canadian history. An 118-kilometer (71-mile) canoe route on this river is a popular four- to six-day paddling trip for intermediate paddlers. If you want company while you paddle the Clearwater, take a trip with **Points North Adventures** out of Fort McMurray, 780/743-9350.

The Fort McMurray-Wood Buffalo region is a well-known center for fly-in fishing and hunting. Among the lodges that cater to in-house anglers and hunters, or outfitters who fly anglers to their fish and hunters to their game animals, are **Andrew Lake Lodge,** 780/464-7537; **Christina Lake Enterprises,** 780/559-2224; **Grist Haven Lodge,** 780/594-1254; **Island Lake Lodge,** 780/743-0214; **Kimowin Lake Lodge,** 780/743-9640; **Magic Country Wilderness Adventures,** 780/743-0766; **Namur Lake Lodge,** 780/791-9299; **Northern Sport Fishing,** 780/791-3412; **Poplar Ridge Outfitters,** 780/799-9324; and **Steep Bank Wilderness Lodge,** 780/623-0636.

FOOD

Meals in northern Alberta should be fresh fish fried over an open fire—trout, Arctic grayling, walleye, perch, and whitefish—or maybe moose and caribou stew.

Dining establishments in Fort McMurray are not much different than those in a southern prairie town. This community of more than 45,000 people has nine Chinese restaurants, 10 pizza places, 23 general restaurants, and 15 fast-food outlets. It has five restaurants that advertise fine dining. If you want to get into the swing of Fort McMurray, look at old pictures on the walls, and be served by staff who have been there for decades, eat at **Cedars Steak House,** 10020 Biggs Ave., 780/743-1717. The local flavor is the same at **The Fish Place Steak and Seafood,** 412 Thickwood Blvd., 780/791-4040, it's just the decor that is different. **Mitchell's Café and Gifts,** 10015 Main St., 780/743-1665, once the old RCMP building, is popular. It's cozy and so is its food. It has a Victorian Tea House atmosphere, featuring light lunches, homemade baked goods, and specialty teas and coffees. More upscale is **Au Bon Vivant,** 10018 Franklin Ave., 780/799-4911 for fine French dining at moderate prices, and **Walter's Dining Room** in the Sawridge Hotel, 530 MacKenzie Blvd., 780/791-7900, for dinners only. For predictable food and service, Fort McMurray has reliable chains: The **Keg Steakhouse and Bar** in the Nomad Inn, 10006 MacDonald Ave., 780/791-2540, and **Earl's Restaurant,** located at 9802 Morrison St., 780/791-3275.

In cafés, be prepared for good old-fashioned food and hospitality. You'll find all that in Fort Chipewyan far to the north—at the **Athabasca Café,** 780/697-3737; and the more upscale **Fort Chipewyan Lodge** whose dining room overlooks Lake Athabasca, 780/697-3679.

In La Crete, Alberta's most northerly agricultural town and a largely Mennonite community east of High Level, try some traditional Mennonite food cooked in big outdoor ovens —perhaps roast goose during hunting season. La Crete is well known as a prime goose- hunting spot. In town, try **Country Corner Restaurant,** 780/928-3161. It has a noon buffet on weekdays and a Sunday brunch. **Dunvegan Tea Room,** 700/835-4459, near Fairview west of Peace River, is in an actual greenhouse converted to a dining room. You can pick tomatoes right from your table. In Fort Vermilion, try **M and M Family Restaurant,** 780/927-4550, for affordable home-style cooking in a relaxed setting.

LODGING

A lodge in the northern Alberta outback may be a log cabin, a shack, even a tent camp. It's surprising, therefore, to find comparative luxury in some of the northernmost hotels. The best place to stay in Fort Chipewyan is the comfortable **Fort Chipewyan Lodge,** 888/686-6333, 780/697-3679, www.AlbertaHotels.ab.ca/fortchip. It has every modern amenity, satellite TV, displays of local crafts, a full-service restaurant, and experienced guides to take you on various adventure tours—ice fishing, snowmobiling, fishing, and trapline tours with the local Cree and Chipewyan.

Fort McMurray may be isolated, but it has half a dozen good hotels in keeping with its young and aggressive image. **Sawridge Hotel,** 530 Mackenzie Blvd., 800/661-6567, 780/791-7900, is a classy, full-service hotel where kids under 12 sharing their parents' room stay free. **Mackenzie Park Inn Convention Centre and Casino,** 424 Gregoire Dr., 800/582-3273 or 780/791-7200, has a full-service casino as well as everything else you'd expect in the south, even computer facilities and video lottery terminals. Similar in style is the **Nomad Inn,** 10006 MacDonald Ave., 800/661-5029, 780/791-4770, reservations@nomadinn.com, www.nomadinn.com. The most distinctive place to stay in Fort McMurray is **Chez Dube Country Inn Bed and Breakfast,** 10102 Fraser

NORTHERN ALBERTA

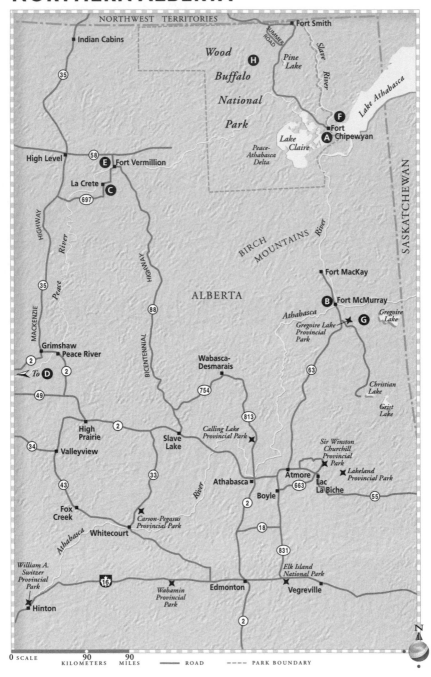

Ave., 800/565-0757, 780/790/2367, B&B@chezdube.com, www.chezdube.com. Each room is designed and decorated differently by the owner. One room even has its sitting room in a turret.

Even if you don't go to fish, stay at one of the region's adventure-travel or fly-in fishing lodges, since they have the region's best resources for wilderness exploring. Seek out **Grist Haven Lodge** and **Winefred Lake Tent Camps,** 147 kilometers (92 miles) southeast of Fort McMurray, Box 1350, Grand Centre, T0A 1T0, 780/594-1254. There are private log cabins with kitchen facilities, and are located on a sandy beaches. Fishing is good on both lakes. Guest cabins at **Gypsy Lake Lodge,** 80 kilometers (50 miles) east of Fort McMurray, 780/743-3176, are available year-round. The lodge offers a summer flyout to fish Clearwater River for walleye and Arctic grayling.

CAMPING

Northern Alberta is blessed with an abundance of campgrounds and recreational day-use areas provided by the Alberta Parks Service, the Land and Forestry Service, municipalities, and private industry. All are listed in the government's excellent camping guide, **The Alberta Campground Guide,** which is available from Travel Alberta, Box 2500, Edmonton, T5J 2Z4. **The Internet Campground Guide** can be found on the web at www.AlbertaHotels.ab.ca/campgrounds.

FOOD
- Ⓐ Athabasca Café
- Ⓑ Au Bon Vivant
- Ⓑ Cedars Steak House
- Ⓒ Country Corner Restaurant
- Ⓓ Dunvegan Tea Room
- Ⓑ Earls Resturant
- Ⓑ The Fish Place Steak and Seafood
- Ⓐ Fort Chipewyan Lodge
- Ⓑ Keg Steakhouse and Bar
- Ⓔ M&M Family Restaurant
- Ⓑ Mitchell's Café and Gifts
- Ⓑ Walter's Dining Room

LODGING
- Ⓑ Chez Dube Country Inn Bed and Breakfast
- Ⓐ Fort Chipewyan Lodge
- Ⓑ Grist Haven Lodge
- Ⓑ Gypsy Lake Lodge
- Ⓡ Mackenzie Park Inn Convention Centre and Casino
- Ⓑ Nomad Inn
- Ⓑ Sawridge Hotel
- Ⓑ Winifred Lake Tent Camp

CAMPING
- Ⓑ Centennial Park Campground
- Ⓕ Dore Lake Provincial Park
- Ⓖ Gregoire Lake Provincial Park
- Ⓑ Rotary Park Campground
- Ⓗ Wood Buffalo National Park

Note: Items with the same letter are located in the same area.

In Fort McMurray, there are several urban parks, campgrounds and developed trails in the town itself as well as another dozen parks in the Fort McMurray area. In town are **Centennial Park Campground** at the southern city limits along Highway 63, 780/743-7925, and **Rotary Park Campground** just before the airport turn-off on Highway 69, 780/790-1581. South and east of Fort McMurray on Secondary Highway 881 is highly popular **Gregoire Lake Provincial Park,** 780/334-2222. Sixty of its 140 campsites have electrical hookups. The park offers a sandy beach and grass, boat- and canoe-rental facilities, and a convenient boat launch. Firewood is available for sale. It's open year-round.

In **Wood Buffalo National Park,** 867/872-2349, there's organized camping at Pine Lake. **Dore Lake Provincial Park,** 16 kilometers (10 miles) northeast of Fort Chipewyan, has a floating boat dock, but powerboats are prohibited. There are several **Forest Service camps** on the Clearwater River and other rivers in northern Alberta.

NIGHTLIFE

You don't go this far north to find dark, noisy nightclubs—nor should you. Better to lie back in a sleeping bag by a quiet lake and take in the silence and the natural northern lights. If you do need alternative excitement, there are plenty of bars, nightclubs, lounges, bingos, casinos, billiard halls, bowling alleys, even a state-of-the-art theater, **Keyano Theatre,** 780/791-4990, in Fort McMurray. There's **Cowboys** in the Peter Pond Hotel, 9713 Hardin St., 780/791-2582. Its loud music and lively atmosphere appeals to the younger set, but the decor— the dance floor looks like a corral, real haystacks abound—is distinctive. More popular with older folks is **Paddy McSwiggins British Pub,** just off Thickwood Boulevard behind the A&W, 780/791-3687.

Scenic Route: The Deh Cho Connection

The Deh Cho (Mackenzie River) Connection is a circular drive that starts at Grimshaw, Mile 0 of the Mackenzie Highway, and follows Alberta Highway 35 north to the Northwest Territories border and Hay River. It veers west through Northwest Territories to Fort Simpson on the Mackenzie River; turns south along the Liard Highway to meet the Alaska Highway in British Columbia; continues through Fort Nelson and Fort St. John; and finishes at Dawson Creek, its other Mile 0. Total distance is about 1,800 kilometers (1,125 miles).

Some highlights near the northern Alberta section are La Crete, a mostly Mennonite community; Fort Vermilion, the oldest settlement in Alberta; Rainbow Lake, a new community developed by the oil and gas industry; Zama, another oil and gas community; and Indian Cabins, the last gas/restaurant service in Alberta before the Northwest Territory border. Of special interest in Indian Cabins is a historic log church, a grave in a box set high on the branch of a tree, and a cemetery with graves covered by spirit houses.

Compared to the Rockies, this route is not particularly scenic, but it is wild and uncrowded, and you feel like you are taking a step back in time. Take time to ferret around behind the scenes. Take every opportunity to talk to the locals.

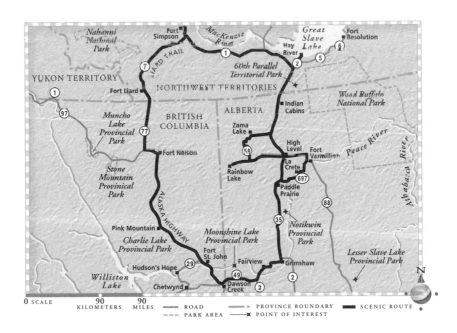

10
EDMONTON

Edmonton, situated on the high bluffs of the North Saskatchewan River, has many attractions that are the largest of their kind—at least in Canada. Nearly everyone knows about the West Edmonton Mall, the world's largest shopping and entertainment complex. But few may realize that Edmonton also has more green space and parks per capita than any other Canadian city. Edmonton exists because of abundant natural resources—furs, gold, oil—that sparked three major booms. In 1795 Hudson's Bay Company founded Fort Edmonton; traders bartered with Cree and Blackfoot for prized animal pelts. The growing settlement quickly became central to routes north and west.

From here, the first prospectors raced for Klondike gold. Realizing they'd not get rich quickly, if at all, many returned for slower but surer lifestyles. Edmonton grew six-fold, becoming a natural choice as the capital when Alberta, "Gateway to the North," was created in 1905. (Thereafter, the Edmonton-Calgary rivalry intensified.) Today's Klondike Days festivities are becoming as famous as Calgary's Stampede.

In 1915, Edmonton became the Canadian Pacific Railway's north-south/east-west crossroad. In the 1930s, bush pilots flew vital supplies to northern outposts. When Alaska Highway construction began in 1942, Edmonton was a pivotal supply center. In 1947, Leduc #1 Well, southwest of Edmonton, gushed black gold, and more than 2,250 nearby wells have been pumping oil ever since. Today only one airport remains, but with a transcontinental train station and major highways, Edmonton is an important travel center.

A PERFECT DAY IN EDMONTON

One day is not nearly enough, since the West Edmonton Mall (the biggest in the world) alone will absorb a day—it's a vacation center in itself, all under the one roof, and open 24 hours a day. Try to contain the urge to shop and sample some of the mall's Waterpark attractions, instead: swimming, riding the waves, relaxing in a deck chair, and basking in the park's constant 30-degree Celsius (86-degree Fahrenheit) heat, and the almost constant Alberta sunshine that pours through the glass roof. For convenience and fun, stay in one of the themed rooms of the mall's Fantasyland Hotel. That evening, dine in the revolving restaurant at the top of the Crowne Plaza Château Lacombe, or take a cruise along the North Saskatchewan River in the riverboat Edmonton Queen. But be back to the mall before midnight to catch the last climactic three-minute performance of Galaxyland's new fire-breathing dragon.

ORIENTATION

Edmonton is centrally located in Alberta. Two major highways run through the city: the Trans-Canada Yellowhead Highway (Highway. #16) provides access from the east and the west; Highway 2 runs north and south; and VIA Rail's "Canadian" route links Edmonton with other major Canadian cities.

It's easy to get to Edmonton—by car, bus, train, or plane—and easy to get around—by an innovative connected light rail and bus transit system, a simple road grid system if you're driving your own vehicle, and a comfortable, climate-controlled, all-weather pedway system (above and below street level covered walkways) that links key public buildings and main shopping centers. The downtown core has ample and reasonably priced "Park in the Heart" parking lots (look for the heart sign). Traffic circles reduce speeding. Edmonton Transit provides special public transportation to physically and mentally disabled individuals, 780/496-4567. A new Sky Shuttle Bus service for $11 one-way to West Edmonton Mall, the University of Alberta, and downtown hotels takes the bite out of paying for expensive cabs or limousines to and from the Edmonton International Airport 29 kilometers to the south.

SIGHTSEEING HIGHLIGHTS

★★★★ **FORT EDMONTON PARK**
SW end of Quesnell Bridge and Fox Dr., 780/496-8787
www.gov.edmonton.ab.ca/parkrec/fort
Here at Canada's largest living history museum, you will enter a world

EDMONTON

Northlands Park

To

106TH AV

112TH AV

84TH ST

98TH AV

90TH AV

83RD ST

ARGYLE RD

FORT RD

STADIUM RD

JASPER AV

CONNORS RD

82ND AV

Mill Creek

63RD AV

95TH ST

NORWOOD BLVD

110TH AV

95TH ST

99TH ST

HARBIN RD

100TH ST

SCONA RD

99TH ST

101ST ST

102ND ST

QUEEN ELIZABETH PARK RD

103RD ST ←

PRINCESS ELIZABETH AV

106TH ST

111TH AV

KINGSWAY

105TH ST

97TH AV

SASKATCHEWAN DR

104TH ST →

109TH ST

109TH ST

109TH AV

109TH ST

99TH AV

WALTERDALE HILL

109TH ST

104TH AV

100TH AV

River Valley RD

B

River

WHYTE AV (82ND AV)

109TH ST

116TH ST

JASPER AV

VICTORIA PARK RD

EMILY MURPHY PARK RD

University of Alberta

114TH ST

113TH ST

119TH ST

117TH ST

180TH AV

102ND AV

PLAIN RD

GROAT RD

SASKATCHEWAN DR

87TH AV

UNIVERSITY AV

114TH AV

BELGRAVIA RD

124TH ST

H

North

122ND ST

F

132ND ST

STONY

Saskatchewan

Whitemud Creek

D

142ND ST

149TH ST

95TH AV

8TH AV

76TH AV

111TH AV

107TH AV

156TH ST

WHITEMUD DR

MAYFIELD RD

STONY PLAIN RD

100TH AV

170TH ST

J

69TH AV

178TH ST

Scale

MILES 0 2

KILOMETERS 0 2

--- --- PARK BOUNDARY

—— ROAD

N

of the past where four periods of Edmonton's development are re-created: an 1846 Hudson's Bay Company fur trading post; an 1885 frontier settlement; the new capital of Alberta in 1905; and the city as it was in 1920. Costumed characters bring history to life by interpreting events and encouraging you to do things such as making soap, tossing horseshoes, or baking bread in an outdoor oven. Your ride in a 1908 streetcar and on a 1919 steam train is included in the admission.

Details: *Open daily late Jun.–early Sept., weekdays 10 A.M.–4 P.M., weekends 10 A.M.–6 P.M.; $6.75 adults, $5 over 64 and ages 13–17, $3.25 children, $20 families. (3 hours)*

★★★★ WEST EDMONTON MALL
8770 170th St., 800/661-8890, 780/444-5348

The number-one attraction on almost every visitor's list is the West Edmonton Mall, often described as the Eighth Wonder of the World. It's the world's best-known and largest shopping and entertainment complex, it has the world's largest parking lot, and is so huge that it covers the equivalent of 48 city blocks or 115 American football fields. It has more than 800 stores and services, more than 110 restaurants, cafés, and fast-food outlets, 19 movie theaters, and seven major attractions. Probably the most outstanding is the 2-hectare (5-acre) World Waterpark, with the world's largest wave pool, 16 breathtaking waterslides as high as 136 meters (85 feet), a bungee jump, family picnic areas, and an artificial beach.

The 25 rides and attractions of Galaxyland, the mall's amusement park include the thrills of the Mindbender (a 14-story triple-loop rollercoaster) and the Drop of Doom (a 13-story free-fall). Also interesting is the Deep Sea Adventure on the world's largest indoor lake, which features a submarine trip, five dolphin shows, and a life-

---

SIGHTS

A Alberta Aviation Museum
B Alberta Legislative Building
C *Edmonton Queen Riverboat*

D Edmonton Space and Science Centre
E Elk Island National Park
F Fort Edmonton Park
G Muttart Conservatory

H Provincial Museum of Alberta
I Ukrainian Cultural Heritage Village
J West Edmonton Mall

Note: Items with the same letter are located in the same area.

---

sized replica of Christopher Columbus's ship, the *Santa Maria*. The mall also has a new casino, a new showpiece spa that features a 144-jet massage tub (the first in Western Canada), Playdium Edmonton, (a high-tech indoor game park), Silver City (a complex of 12 new cinemas, a 3-D IMAX theater and a massive, explosive fire-breathing dragon), a new 18-hole mini-golf course, and rooftop driving range outside, and, of course, shops. Soon there will be a West Edmonton Mall Hotel, but for now, Fantasyland Hotel with its 113 intriguing theme rooms is a first class conversation piece. If you don't want to walk, rent a scooter; if you don't want to carry packages, rent a three-wheeled cart and one of the new programmable keyless lockers.

If you don't have all the fun you expect, you may still find it if you forget which exit to use, or where your car is parked, or where/when to catch the bus. So use a map. Building is open 24 hours, year-round, most stores open daily weekdays 10 A.M.–9 P.M., Saturday 10 A.M.–6 P.M., Sunday and most holidays noon–6 P.M.

Details: *Times and prices of attractions vary, for more information, 800/661-8890 or 780/444-5300. (1 day)*

★★★ **EDMONTON QUEEN RIVERBOAT**
Rafter's Landing, 9734 98th Ave., 780/424-2628, riverboat@ edmontonqueen.com, www.edmontonqueen.com
Cruising Edmonton's skyline in the ice-free season along the North Saskatchewan River in a Mississippi-style two-level paddlewheeler is a great way to see the sights while you eat, drink, and listen to live entertainment. Choose one of five daily excursions—lunch, afternoon leisure, dinner dance, a weekend midnight party, or a Sunday brunch. Dine inside or out.

Details: *Prices and times vary, cruises range from $9.95–$24.95, and times 1–2 hours, children 10 and under reduced prices, 2 and under free. (3 hours)*

★★★ **EDMONTON SPACE AND SCIENCE CENTRE**
1121 142nd St., 780/452-9100, 780/451-3344, essc/planet@eon.net, www.edmontonscience.com
This multipurpose facility houses state-of-the-art theaters and sound systems, an observatory, exhibit galleries, and live demonstrations. It contains the largest planetarium in Canada; an IMAX Theatre; the Margaret Zeidler Theatre, which presents musical laser light shows on a

23-meter (75-foot) domed ceiling; a "Learning Centre," where you can participate in simulated space missions aboard the *Challenger;* the Dow Computer Lab to explore the world of computers; and an amateur Ham Radio Station.

Details: *Open daily mid-Jun.–early Sept. 10 A.M.–10 P.M., rest of the year Tue.–Sun. 10 A.M. –10 P.M.; Challenger missions given mid-Jun.–early Sept. daily 1–4 P.M., rest of year weekends and holidays 1–4 P.M.; Admission to exhibits and planetarium or IMAX show : $7 adults, $6 seniors over 64 and ages 13–17, $5 ages 3–12, $26 family rate. Phone for rates that include IMAX show as well. (2 hours)*

★★★ PROVINCIAL MUSEUM OF ALBERTA
12845 102nd Ave., 780/453-9130

Surrounding this natural- and human-history museum is a park of sculptures overlooking the North Saskatchewan River Valley. There are four galleries: Habitat shows Alberta's four great regions—prairie, aspen parkland, mountain and boreal forest in life size dioramas; Natural History has specimens of animals and plants, past and present; Human History, the settlement of Europeans in Alberta; and the new Syncrude Gallery of Aboriginal Culture showcases one of the finest collections of First Nations tribal artifacts in North America. Facilities include guided tours, a shop, and a restaurant.

Details: *Open daily 9 A.M.–5 P.M., $6.50 adults, $5.50 over 64, $3 ages 4–17, $18 family rate. (2 hours)*

★★ ALBERTA LEGISLATIVE BUILDING
10800 97th Ave., 780/427-7362, sklem@assembly.ab.ca, www.assembly.ab.ca

Take a tour of this gracious sandstone and marble building completed in 1912 on the site of the original Fort Edmonton. It is set off by parkland, pools and fountains.

Details: *Open daily except for Saturday; phone for hours; free. (1 hour)*

★★ MUTTART CONSERVATORY
9626 96th St., 780/496-8755

Imagine four sheer glass pyramids, their reflections shimmering in a huge pool. Muttart Conservatory is just that from the outside, but on the inside each is a world within a world—a Tropical, an Arid, and a Temperate Pavilion (all with temperatures to match), and a Show Pavilion with changing seasonal exhibits. The architecture and photo-

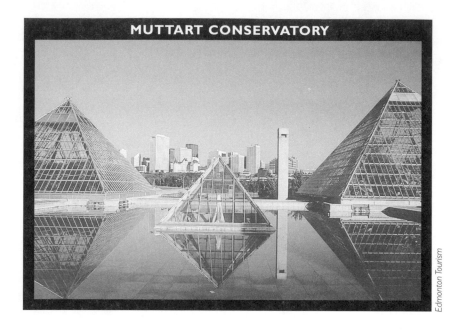

MUTTART CONSERVATORY

graphic opportunity looking past the pyramidal roofs to the city sky-line is more stunning than the plants. Good place to visit in winter.

Details: *Open daily, weekdays 9 A.M.–6 P.M., weekends and holidays 11 A.M.–6 P.M.; $4.50 adult, $2 child 2–12, $3.50, senior/youth/student, $12.50 family. (1 hour)*

★ ALBERTA AVIATION MUSEUM
11410 Kingsway Ave, 780/453-1078

This museum houses a collection of original aircraft showing the history of aviation in Alberta, particularly in Edmonton. The bush pilots of those days (like H. A. "Doc" Oaks, whose methods of engine heating and maintenance in extreme winter conditions became standards; Punch Dickens; and Wop May) created legends that thrill young and old alike.

Details: *Near City Centre Airport; open year-round, $5 adults, $4 senior/student 13–18, $3 child, $12 family, $2/person group tours. (1 hour)*

If you have time, take in a Gallery Walk 124th Street Area 780/413-6503; or a walk through Old Strathcona Historic Area, 780/437-4182 or 780/433-5866; take a look at the dramatic architecture of the Shaw Conference Centre, and

City Hall 780/496-8200; go for a 2.5 km ride in the restored High Level Street-car over the High Level Bridge across the North Saskatchewan River to get between north and south Edmonton, 780/496-1464 or 780/478-7919.

GREATER EDMONTON SIGHTSEEING HIGHLIGHTS

★★★ ELK ISLAND NATIONAL PARK
50 km (30 mi) east of Edmonton on Hwy. 16, Site 4, RR1, Fort Saskatchewan, 780/992-2961
You will probably see bison along the roadside before you see the elk for which this park was created in 1906. Have your camera handy in the car. North of Highway 16 is a herd of more than 700 free-ranging plains bison, south of Highway 16 are several hundred wood bison, a threatened subspecies. In summer, combine a walk along some of the trails through forests and meadows past lakes and ponds with a visit to the nearby Ukrainian Cultural Heritage Village for a day's respite beyond busy Edmonton. In winter, use the trails for cross-country ski-ing. There's also an interpretive center, a campground and a golf course. Watch out for the information center .8 km (.5 mi) north of Highway 16 before the park's south gate entrance.

Details: Open year-round, $4 adults, $3 seniors over 64, $2 ages 6–16, $8 admission 2–7 people in a private vehicle, $5–$14 camping fee. (1 day)

★★★ UKRAINIAN CULTURAL HERITAGE VILLAGE
35 km (25 mi) east of Edmonton along Hwy. 16, 3 km east of the gate entrance to Elk Island National Park, 780/662-3640, 780/662-3855, toll-free in Alberta 310-0000 uchv@mcd.gov.ab.ca, www.gov.ab.ca/~mcd/mhs/uchv/uchv/html
At the turn of the century, east central Alberta was home to the largest settlement of Ukrainian pioneers in all of Canada. More than 30 authentically restored buildings have been brought to the site of this lovingly recreated outdoor museum and arranged in three themed areas: a townsite, a rural community, and farmsteads. One of the most interesting buildings is a reconstructed 1,900 burdei, a mud-walled, grass-roofed sod house dug out of the ground for temporary shelter that may have lasted several years. You can stroll from one

building to another, or catch a free ride on a horse-drawn wagon. Costumed villagers take on the roles of Ukrainian pioneers as they struggled to wrest farms from the bush. Don't be shy. Act your part and engage them in conversation as if you were living at the same time. You will find them doing just what they would be doing between 1892 and 1930, perhaps weeding an authentic historic garden or baking bread in an outdoor oven.

Details: *Open May 15–early Sept. daily 10 A.M.–6 P.M., reduced hours rest of year, $6.50 adults, $5.50 seniors, $3 youth 7–17, free children under 7, $15 family of two adults and two children up to 17, reduced admission rest of year, tours available. Lunch kiosk if you don't want to bring your own picnic. (2 to 3 hours)*

FITNESS AND RECREATION

You'd expect Edmonton to have lots of recreation facilities: it's home of Wayne Gretsky, the Great One of ice hockey fame. Its other claim to fame is the **North Saskatchewan River Valley** that winds through its center and is one of the longest continuous stretches of urban parkland in North America, certainly Canada. Edmonton was the first Canadian city to be awarded a Green Survival Award for the use of its green space. Accessible from many parts of the city and easily by stairways from the Shaw Conference Centre, the Hotel Macdonald and the Crowne Plaza Château Lacombe, this oasis of parkland contains 62 miles (100 kilometers) of trails, four lake systems and 22 parks. Several of the more than 70 golf courses within an hour's drive of Edmonton are located in this river valley. You can drive this ribbon of green, but better to hike, bike, ski, snowshoe, skate, fish—or pan for gold. In June or July with up to 17 hours daylight, you can golf almost into the midnight sun. Try the **Victoria Golf Course,** 12130 River Rd., 780/496-4710, the oldest and one of the busiest municipal courses in Canada.

FOOD

There are 2,000 restaurants in Edmonton, serving more than 30 types of cuisine. It's a multicultural showcase. To help you decide which to sample, take a stroll in what is called the Avenue of Nations, an area surrounding 107 Avenue—from 95th Street to 116th Street—as you decide between Chinese, Vietnamese, Italian, Ukrainian, Polish, Japanese, and Latin American cuisine.

If you want variety, but you don't want to go all over town to find it, try one or two of the many pubs and restaurants along Bourbon Street in the West

Edmonton Mall, 8882-170th Street. It echoes New Orleans in serving Cajun to Chinese to Italian cuisine, a lively atmosphere, and reasonable prices. Outside the Mall but nearby is another fun place, **The Outback Steakhouse** at 17118-90th Ave., 780/484-5400. As well as characteristic Aussie fun, this restaurant serves "fair dinkum tucker" such as huge, well-seasoned beef steaks, seafood—and of course, lamb.

Another good area for concentrated dining is the Old Strathcona district centered on 82nd (Whyte) Avenue. You get great value for your money in **Chianti Café and Italian Restaurant** at 10501 82nd Ave., 780/439-9829, where you'll have a difficult time making up your mind between 40 homemade pastas. You may get singing waiters at Chianti, and belly dancers and zorba line dancing each weekend at **Yianna's Taverna,** the lively Greek restaurant across the street, 10444 82nd Ave., 780/433-6768. A little more sedate is **The King and I,** on nearby 8208-107 St., 780/433-2222, noted for its Thai curries.

On the outskirts of Old Strathcona is the highly regarded **Von's Steak and Fish House,** 10309 81 Ave., 780/439-0041, which specializes in prime rib, and of course, a big Alberta steak. The **Unheard of Restaurant,** 9602 82nd Ave., 780/432-0480, doesn't live up to its name because it certainly does have a national reputation with signature items such as rack of lamb, salmon, and bison, and excellent service. Try their Grand Marnier crêpes with an orange brandy sauce.

Go downtown for more elegant—and expensive—ambiance. Everyone's favorite, though it doesn't match everyone's pocketbook, is **La Ronde,** 10111 Bellamy, 780/428-6611 (more commonly known by its former name, the Château Lacombe), a revolving rooftop restaurant at the Crowne Plaza Château Lacombe. Take in the excellent views over the city and the North Saskatchewan River as you enjoy the restaurant's continental cuisine. The Harvest Room in the historic **Hotel Macdonald,** 10065 100th St., 780/424-5181, faces a large terraced garden, but it is opulent inside as well. This restaurant at "The Mac" offers a children's menu, health-conscious meals, and a popular Sunday brunch. It also specializes in Canadian dishes such as barbecued Atlantic salmon with blackberry essence, and herb-crusted lamb with parsnip bread pudding.

There are several other award-winning, high-end restaurants in the downtown area. Despite the name, the **Hardware Grill,** 9698 Jasper Ave., 780/423-0609, is the first on many taxi drivers' lips when you ask them for the best restaurant in Edmonton. Canadian dishes here include Smoky Lake bison and Alberta Angus tenderloin. You'll enjoy looking at the desserts (visual masterpieces), even if your calorie conscience tells you not to eat them. Another popular place for fine dining is the **Sawmill Restaurant,** located at 11560 104th Ave., 780/429-2816, where the steaks and prime ribs are huge and the salad bar is awesome.

EDMONTON

Northlands Park

112TH AV

106TH AV

98TH AV

84TH ST

90TH AV

83RD ST

ARGYLE RD

CONNORS RD

82ND AV

63RD AV

Mill Creek

FORT RD

STADIUM RD

JASPER AV

95TH ST

HARBIN RD

B

107TH A AV

NORWOOD BLVD

99TH ST

100TH ST

C

N

102ND ST

E

101ST ST

105TH ST

9TH AV

SCONA RD

QUEEN ELIZABETH PARK RD

WATERDALE HILL

SASKATCHEWAN DR

H

99TH ST

95TH ST

111TH AV

106TH AV

KINGSWAY

109TH ST

104TH AV

109TH ST

99TH AV

100TH AV

I

103RD ST

104TH ST

A

WHYTE

J

AV

109TH ST

PRINCESS ELIZABETH AV

124TH ST

109TH ST

116TH ST

117TH ST

118TH AV

G

JASPER AV

102ND AV

RIVER VALLEY RD

VICTORIA PARK RD

River

EMILY MURPHY PARK RD

North Saskatchewan

University of Alberta

87TH AV

O

D

114TH ST

113TH ST

M

119TH ST

UNIVERSITY AV

BELGRAVIA RD

R

To

122ND ST

SASKATCHEWAN DR

GROAT RD

PLAIN RD

GROAT RD

STONY

132ND ST

111TH AV

142ND ST

149TH ST

95TH AV

Saskatchewan

North

Whitemud Creek

To **S**

107TH AV

156TH ST

100TH AV

87TH AV

WHITEMUD DR

76TH AV

To **P**

L

MAYFIELD RD

STONY PLAIN RD

170TH ST

F

K

178TH ST

69TH AV

Q *To*

N

LODGING

Compared to other places of similar size in Western Canada, Edmonton has an impressive number of reasonably priced rooms (even in the luxury class), and many of its hotels are presently being renovated or expanded. Common now in rooms are irons and ironing boards and high-speed Internet access, with two phone lines for executives. A handy number to remember for reservations is Alberta Express Reservations, at 800/884-8803.

The **Fantasyland Hotel** is the jewel of the West Edmonton Mall, and the most exotic and fun place to stay in Edmonton. Luxury personified, it has 354 guest rooms, including 127 decorated according to different themes: Roman, Hollywood Nightclub, Polynesian, Truck, Victorian Coach, Arabian, Canadian Rail, Igloo, African, and the new Western room. Each has a full-size Jacuzzi. The Truck room features working traffic signals (turn them off or you'll be awake all night), an antique gas pump, and an imposing blue-uniformed policeman that looms over you in the mirrored Jacuzzi. In the Igloo Room, you can sleep in a snow-house, lounge on a sled, gaze at a polar bear holding up the glass coffee table and cuddle a seal by an iceberg. The hotel staff are helpful and super friendly. It's located at the west end of the mall on 17700 87th Ave., 800/661-6454, 800/737-3783, 780/444-3000, hotel@westedmall.com, www.fantasylandhotel. com. Rates are high, but packages are available that make a stay affordable.

A deluxe hotel in the traditional manner, **Hotel Macdonald,** 10065 100th St., 800/441-1414, 780/424-5181, www.cphotels.com, deserves a tour even if you don't stay there. This stately château-style Canadian Pacific Railway hotel is set picturesquely on top of a hill with a wonderful view of the North Saskatchewan River. Originally opened in 1915, it has been completely restored

FOOD
- Ⓐ Chianti Café and Italian Restaurant
- Ⓑ Hardware Grill
- Ⓒ Harvest Room
- Ⓓ The King and I
- Ⓔ La Ronde
- Ⓕ Outback Steakhouse
- Ⓖ Sawmill Restaurant
- Ⓗ Unheard Of Restaurant
- Ⓘ Von's Steak and Fish House
- Ⓙ Yianna's Taverna

LODGING
- Ⓔ Crowne Plaza Chateâu Lacombe
- Ⓚ Fantasyland Hotel
- Ⓒ Hotel Macdonald
- Ⓛ Mayfield Inn and Suites
- Ⓜ Ramada Inn and Conference Centre/Edmonton Inn
- Ⓝ Union Bank Inn
- Ⓞ The Varscona

CAMPING
- Ⓟ Kinsmen RV Park
- Ⓠ Klondike Valley Tent and Trailer Park
- Ⓡ Rainbow Valley Campground
- Ⓢ Whitemud Creek Golf and RV Park

Note: Items with the same letter are located in the same area.

and is Alberta's only four-star and four-diamond hotel. Be sure to sneak a look at the ceiling of the Wedgewood Room and the Empire Ball Room, and the Fathers of Confederation oil painting in the Confederation Lounge. There are special low rates for seniors and families. At least have Sunday brunch and a stroll through the terraced gardens.

Crowne Plaza Château Lacombe, 10111 Bellamy Hill in the heart of downtown, 780/428-6611, 800/2CROWNE, cpcl@planet.eon.net, www. coasthotels.com, is another Edmonton institution with all facilities, including a famous revolving restaurant. It's also affordable. Another reliable choice is the **Ramada Inn and Conference Centre/Edmonton Inn,** 11830 Kingsway Ave., 888/747-4114, 780/454-5454, inn@edmonton-inn.com. A large rock garden and an encircling stream enhance its entrance. This hotel has recently been renovated. The **Mayfield Inn and Suites,** 16615-109th Ave., 800/661-9804, 780/484-0821 is very popular, especially being so close to the West Edmonton Mall. It has a variety of recently renovated rooms and suites (separate rooms for kids) on 10 nonsmoking floors, live dinner theater, full-service salon, exercise and steam rooms, squash and racquetball courts, a bank, and free parking.

For something different in a boutique, European-style bed-and-breakfast, there's the downtown **Union Bank Inn,** 10053 Jasper Ave., 888/423-3601, 780/423-3600, info@unionbankinn.com, ubi@planet.eon.net, www.unionbankinn.com, is a refurbishment of a bank first built in 1911. Except for its heritage look outside, you'd never know it. Walk off the street into the hotel's elegant Madison Grill restaurant or the beautiful Givenchy Room adjacent to the reception desk then take the elevator to its uniquely designed bedrooms. Distinctive touches include a custom-built desk to accommodate spreading out of papers, white elm wood to complement street trees of Edmonton, floral fabrics to create old world appeal, a Scottish-themed room featuring tartans, framed curling boots, and a kilt pin to hold the shower curtains together. All rooms are designed to be homes away from home, especially for the woman business traveler. A particularly nice touch is the wine, cheese and fruit tray delivered to guestrooms nightly, that's more useful than a turn-down service, though you can get that, too.

Over in the Old Strathcona district at 8208 106th Street is another new boutique hotel, **The Varscona,** 888/515-3355, 780/434-6111, varscona@telusplanet.net, www.varscona.com. Distinctive features are the fireplace in the lobby, the cozy concierge room for breakfast, and hosted wine sampling at the end of the day, flowers in the bathroom, and the personalized, classy, but not stuffy service you'd expect from this kind of lodging.

For those who like chain-type accommodation, there are several **Best Western** hotels and **Travelodges** in Edmonton. Prices are lower than the boutiques and you have the comfort of the expected.

CAMPING

There are some campgrounds comparatively close to the West Edmonton Mall and most are open May through September. **Rainbow Valley Campground,** 119th St., in Whitemud Park is close to downtown and open April 15 through September 30. **Klondike Valley Tent and Trailer Park,** Highway 2 south and Ellerslie Rd., 780/988-5067, advertises itself as Edmonton's most scenic campground. It is nestled in a quiet, natural setting along Blackmud Creek, yet is within minutes of the city center and the Edmonton Mall. The **Kinsmen RV Park,** 15 minutes from the West Edmonton Mall, at 47 Riel Dr., 5 km (3 mi) north on 184th St., off Highway 16X in St. Albert, 780/419-3434, has washrooms and hot showers, some water, and power, and is open May through September for RVs only. **Whitemud Creek Golf and RV Park,** 16520 41st Ave. S.W., 780/988-6800, has 60 sites and a trout pond. It's adjacent to a nine-hole golf course and close to the West Edmonton Mall, Fort Edmonton, and the Valley Zoo.

NIGHTLIFE

Start with—where else?—the **West Edmonton Mall,** which does almost as good a job enticing you at night as it does during the day. Gamble or watch the gamblers at the **Palace Casino,** 780/444-2112. Eat, drink, listen to live bands, play billiards and cosmic bowling, or relax in the **Furnace Room** with a cigar and cognac in Red's enormous 1960s-style rec and rumpus room, 780/484-7182. Listen to standup comedy at **Yuk Yuk's Komedy Kabaret,** 780/481-9857. Watch a show with dinner at **Jubilations Live Dinner Theatre,** 780/484-2424. Of course, you could do something more ordinary such as take in a movie at one of the mall's 19 movie theaters, perhaps the new IMAX 3D Theater, and watch the new fire-breathing dragon spew smoke from the ceiling.

If you can tear yourself away from the always frenetic Edmonton Mall, the city has a myriad of other nightspots to entertain you—nightclubs, sports bars, comedy clubs, dinner theaters, pubs, casinos, and well-frequented live performances. Look in *Billy's Guide, See Magazine, Where,* and newspapers such as the *Edmonton Journal* for up-to-date arts and entertainment information.

As Canada's "Festival City," Edmonton has more live theater per capita—and for all ages—than any other Canadian city. The **Citadel Theatre** complex, downtown at 99th St. and 101 A Ave., 780/425-1820, consists of four individual theaters, an amphitheater, and a beautiful indoor atrium. For an entertaining evening in which the audience is part of the show, try the **Mayfield Dinner Theatre,** in the Mayfield Inn on 166th St. and 109th Ave., 780/448-9339. Stage Polaris offers family entertainment at 7114 98th St., 780/432-9483.

Pubs are very popular now and Edmonton has some excellent ones, several British-style Sherlock Holmes and Elephant and Castle pubs and fashionable Irish ones. Don't miss **O'Byrne's Irish Pub** in Old Strathcona next to the Vascona Hotel. Owner, Dennis Byrne, moved to Edmonton from Ireland, combined ideas from several Dublin pubs, and recreated his dream pub at 10616 82nd Ave., 780/414-6766. It features Irish food, music, and dancing, and whiskey tastings. It's crowded for good reason.

11
JASPER NATIONAL PARK

The most northerly and the largest of the four Canadian Rocky Mountain National Parks and the three B.C. Provincial Parks that make up a UNESCO World Heritage Site, Jasper National Park is as spectacularly beautiful as Banff National Park, its neighbor to the south—and fortunately less crowded. And Jasper townsite, the service center for the park, is less developed than Banff, probably because it is more remote. It takes longer to get to Jasper from Edmonton and its nearest international airport (four hours), than to get from Banff to Calgary International Airport (less than one hour).

Both the town and the park are located in the Athabasca River Valley (Athabasca Pass), a major route in the early 1800s for early explorers and fur traders on their way west. The area's value was again recognized in the early 1900s as a transcontinental railway route. To protect the area from logging, coal mining, and to make money from tourism, Jasper Forest Park was created in 1907, but not until 1930 was Jasper National Park officially established. The town of Jasper, an important railway divisional point in 1924, relies on the railway as much as tourism (a third of its residents are employed by the Canadian National Railway/CN). An appropriate way to get to Jasper is by train. You get scenery and history both.

HANDY CONTACTS

www.discoverjasper.com
www.explorejasper.com
www.skimarmot.com
www.jasperadventures.com
www.visit-jasper.com
www.worldweb.com/parkscanada-jasper

Superintendent, Jasper National Park:
  Box 10, Jasper, AB, T0E 1E0, 780/852-6176, fax 780/852-6152,
  www.worldweb.com/parkscanada-jasper.

Jasper Tourism and Commerce:
  Box 98, Jasper, AB, T0E 1E0, 780/852-3848, fax 780/852-4932.

A PERFECT DAY IN JASPER NATIONAL PARK

This is a marathon, but worth it! Get up early. Perhaps stay the previous night at the Icefields Chalet Hotel or the Columbia Icefield Campground. Start at Parks Canada's new Icefield Centre opposite the Columbia Icefield—before other tourists arrive en masse—and book your seat on the first possible Snocoach for a touching tour of the Athabasca Glacier. Alternatively, book a guided Glacier Icewalk from the Icefields Chalet Hotel. There's something awesome about walking on ice perhaps 360 meters (1,200 feet) thick, and looking at crevasses so deep they appear bottomless.

Get into your vehicle now and drive north along the Icefields Parkway (Highway 93), the 230-kilometer (144-mile) scenic mountain drive that connects Banff and Lake Louise to Jasper, probably the world's most beautiful road. The Icefields Parkway is a naturalist's dream, especially in spring and fall. Have your camera ready for wildlife and landscapes such as Stutfield Glacier, Sunwapta Falls, and Athabasca Falls.

Once in Jasper, check into Jasper Park Lodge (remember, this is a perfect day!), then drive the 48-kilometer (28.8-mile) Maligne Lake Road to take a picture of Maligne Lake, the world view for Jasper, the one you find on all the brochures and postcards. Pick a window seat for dinner at the Maligne Lake Lodge or whiz back to Jasper Park Lodge for a meal at one of their many restaurants. Of course, you could drive instead to Miette Hotsprings for a relaxing soak.... But then, Jasper is worth more than a day!

ORIENTATION

The classic way to get to Jasper is by train, from Vancouver via Kamloops on VIA Rail's Rocky Mountaineer, then rent your own vehicle to explore the park. Or

JASPER WILDLIFE

Jasper is known particularly for its easily accessible wildlife. The slopes, and particularly the surrounding meadows, are the grazing grounds of deer and elk whose disdain for motorists frequently causes lines, not necessarily because people are watching them, but because the animals are in no hurry to clear the way! Elk are particularly noticeable in the town where the life is easy—though increasing numbers of elk means increasing numbers of problems for both people and elk. Great photo opportunities, though, for tourists.

Do take care as you drive. Too many animals are killed or maimed on these roads. Moose and bear are fairly common visitors—great to photograph, but potential dangers to others even if you aren't chased or harmed. Never be the cause of someone else's injuries (or death) because you fed or approached the animals. Hunting is illegal, which is why the animals generally have little fear of humans.

drive your own vehicle through the park to the town of Jasper, which is reached from the west and from the east via Highway 16 (Yellowhead Hwy.), and from the south via the Icefields Highway (Hwy. 93). Many visitors fly into Edmonton International Airport, about 370 kilometers (234 miles) to the east, and drive or catch a shuttle bus along Highway 16 to Jasper. Since the recent twinning of the road from Edmonton to Jasper, travel time has been reduced from five hours to four hours. You can also get there by bus, from Calgary, Banff, Edmonton, and Vancouver.

To get around town, walk. To get around the park, drive, hike, bike, climb, ski, or take a tour.

SIGHTSEEING HIGHLIGHTS

★★★★ ICEFIELDS PARKWAY (HWY.93)

So, you have driven this spectacular road link from Banff and Lake Louise to the border of Banff and Jasper National Park. Continue now to Jasper with stops to look at the displays at the Icefields Centre, and to tread on the ice of the Athabasca Glacier at the Columbia Icefields

JASPER NATIONAL PARK

ALBERTA

Edson

16
47

Hinton

40

Entrance
Brule

Park Gate

Pocahontas

Jasper Lake

Jasper

Yellowhead Pass

Miette
Hot Springs

Jasper National Park

Mount
Kerkeslin

93A

Mt. Edith
Cavell

C D G H E

F Maligne
Lake

ICEFIELDS PARKWAY

Sunwapta
Falls

B Athabasca River

93

A

Athabasca
Glacier

Columbia Icefield

Mount
Columbia

Rocky Mountains Forest Reserve

HIGHWAY

11
734

DAVID THOMPSON

Recreation Area

Wildlands

Bighorn

White Goat Wilderness

BRITISH COLUMBIA

Kinbasket
Lake

Fraser River

Canoe Reach

Robson Provincial Park

Mount

16

Mount
Robson

Tete Jaune Cache

5

Blue River

Wells Gray
Provincial Park

Willmore Wilderness Park

N

SCALE
0   24
KILOMETERS   MILES
        24

━━━ ROAD   ━━━ HIGHWAY   ━━ PROVINCE BOUNDARY   ---- PARK AREA   ★ PLACE OF INTEREST to view Sunwapta Canyon, Stutfield Glacier, and Sunwapta Falls, and to look for sheep and goats at the Athabasca River. The road runs alongside a chain of ice fields that straddle the Continental Divide.

Details: *You'll need at least half a day to stop and read the interpretive signs and to take some of the interpretive walks. (half day)*

★★★★ **COLUMBIA ICEFIELDS AND ICEFIELDS CENTRE**
105 km (65 mi) south of Jasper and 125 km (78 mi) north of Lake Louise, Icefields Centre, 403/762-6735
This is one of the largest accumulations of ice and snow outside the Arctic, 389 square km (150 square miles) in area and up to 385 meters (1,270 feet) thick. The ongoing accumulation of snow feeds eight major glaciers, three of which you can see from the road —Athabasca, Dome and Stutfield. The meltwater from this icefield feeds streams and rivers that pour into three different oceans by four major river systems—the Columbia and Fraser, which flow to the Pacific Ocean; the Mackenzie, which flows to the Arctic; and the Saskatchewan, which eventually flows to the Atlantic via Hudson's Bay. The Athabasca Glacier descends from the ice field almost to road level and you can touch its "toe." As you walk toward it, notice the markers showing the rapid receding action of the glacier.

In the old days, you could peer down crevasses, but now safety rules dictate that you just step onto the ice. It's a strange thrill all the same, especially for those unfamiliar with snow country. Ice Cubed is a three-hour guided walk on the ice with Athabasca Glacier Ice Walks. Walking by yourself on the ice or peering into crevasses is dangerous— people have died doing it—so best to take one of the two tours available. Across the parkway is the new (1996) chalet-style stone building, the **Icefields Centre,** a cooperative venture between Brewster Transportation and Tours, and Parks Canada, which houses a dining room, cafeteria, snack bar, gift shop, ticket office, and a new Parks Canada Exhibit Hall (the Glacier Gallery) and information desk. It also is a hotel

---

SIGHTS

Ⓐ Columbia Icefields and Icefields Centre
Ⓑ Icefields Parkway (Hwy. 93)
Ⓒ Jasper Aerial Tramway
Ⓓ Jasper Park Lodge
Ⓔ Maligne Canyon
Ⓕ Maligne Lake
Ⓖ Marmot Basin
Ⓗ Mount Edith Cavell

Note: Items with the same letter are located in the same area.

---

if you want to stay overnight and catch the first tour in the morning. Open May 1 to mid-October.

Details: *Brewster's Columbia Icefield Snowmobile Tours 403/762-6735, leave in special Snocoaches every 15 minutes May–Sept., 9 A.M.–5 P.M., Oct., 10 A.M.–4 P.M.; $22.50 adults, $5 ages 6–15. Book ice tours with Jasper Adventure Centre, 800/565-7547, which leaves from the Toe of the Glacier car park mid-Jun.–mid-Sept., daily 11:30 A.M., except Sun. and Thur.; or "Icewalk Deluxe" a more strenuous five-hour guided walk Sun. and Thur. 11:30 A.M.; "Ice Cubed" walk $28 adults, $12 children 7–17; "Icewalk Deluxe" walk $32 adults. Reservations are essential. (2 hours)*

★★★★ **JASPER AERIAL TRAMWAY**
Whistler Mountain Rd., Box 418, Jasper, 780/852-3093,
www.worldweb.com/JasperTramway/

Just 7 km (4.2 miles) south of Jasper is the longest and highest aerial tramway in Canada. It takes just seven minutes to travel up 2,500 meters (8,100 feet) to reach the upper terminal atop Whistler Mountain, some 2,227 meters (7,500 feet) above sea level. Here you can look full-circle at five mountain ranges, two river systems, and many lakes from the glass-enclosed Sunset Dining Room in the Treeline Restaurant or from boardwalks and barbecue decks. Try the 45-minute hike to the summit. The view is worth it.

Drive three kilometers (1.4 miles) south on Hwy. 93 toward Banff, turn right at the Whistler Mountain turn-off, and follow the tranmway symbols three kilometers (1.4 miles) up the Whistler Mountain Rd

Details: *Open daily, May–Sept. 1, 8:30A.M.–10 P.M.; Sept. 2–28, 9:30 A.M.–9 P.M.; Sept. 29–Oct. 31, 9:30 A.M.–4:30 P.M.. Sunset Dinner at the Top $29.95 includes lift up and down, three-course dinner including dessert. (2 hours)*

★★★★ **JASPER PARK LODGE**
On Lac Beauvert, 7 km (4.4 mi) east of Jasper on Hwy. 16,
Box 40, Jasper, T0E 1E0; 780/852-3301 or 800/465-7547
within Alberta, or 800/441-1414, www.cphotels.ca

This impeccably landscaped world-class resort was built in the 1920s by Canadian National Railway (CN) to compete with Canadian Pacific Railway's (CP) resort hotel, Banff Springs. There's little rivalry now since CN sold Jasper Park Lodge to CP, who spent $25 million to develop and renovate it. Jasper Lake Lodge has an outstanding 18-hole golf course; riding stables; tennis courts; cycle and boat rentals; fishing

PARKS ADMISSION

There are two infocenters: one in Jasper at 500 Connaught Drive across from the CNR station, in a beautiful stone building, a National Historic site itself; and the other at Columbia Icefield, Highway 93. Park admission is $10 per vehicle (2 to 10 persons) per day, $8 for seniors over 64; on an individual basis, $5 adults, $4 seniors, $2.50 children. It is best to buy a Great Western Pass that allows entry to 11 national parks in Western Canada for $70 (2 to 10 persons), $53 (seniors); and on an individual basis, $35 adults, $27 seniors, $18 children.

The town was named for Jasper Hawes, a clerk who in the early 1800s ran a small trading post just east of present day park boundaries. Jasper's House, as it was eventually called, was a supply depot for fur traders, adventurers, explorers, missionaries, surveyors and railway people. Now Jasper is a supply depot for tourists who swell the resident population of 5,000 to 10,000 in summer. The townsite stretches around a bend in the road paralleling Highway 16 and the railway tracks. If visiting in the busy months of July and August, before you head out into the scenery, take the **Jasper Walking Tour** with a guide from "Friends of Jasper National Park," 780/852-4767.

facilities; a walking path around the lake; cross-country ski trails; and many restaurants, boutiques, nightclubs, lounges, and meeting rooms. Many international celebrities have stayed at this resort. My strongest memory of this stunning hotel is of room service waiters bicycling around the lavishly landscaped lodgings with one hand on the steering wheel and the other in the air holding a tray of drinks.

Details: *(1 hour)*

★★★★ **MALIGNE LAKE**
48 km (30 mi) southeast of Jasper on Hwy. 16 and Maligne Rd., Maligne Tours, Box 280, 626 Connaught Dr., Jasper, 780/852-3370; Maligne River Adventures Ltd. Box 280, 626 Connaught Dr., Jasper, 780/852-3370

This largest lake in the Canadian Rockies and the second-largest, and perhaps prettiest, glacial lake in the world, is one of Jasper National Park's biggest attractions, and the view of Spirit Island is world-famous, the quintessential world view of Canada. The dramatic lake offers canoes, rowboats (electric motors can also be rented), tackle, and even fishing guides. Trail rides and white-water rafting can be arranged. In winter, it's a fairyland for cross-country skiing. A day lodge, licensed cafeteria and dining room offer fabulous views as well as food.

Details: Open May–Oct. for boat and river tours. For Maligne Lake Boat Tours, trips depart daily on the hour, check details, $31 adults, $27.50 over 64, $15.50 ages 6–12. (1 hour from Jasper to Maligne Lake and 1 to 2 hours for a tour)

★★★★ MARMOT BASIN
19 km (11.4 mi) south of Jasper via Hwy. 93A and the Marmot Basin Rd. Box 1300, Jasper, 780/852-3816; Ski Jasper 800/473-8135, info@skimarmot.com, www. skimarmot.com

Arguably, Jasper National Park is best seen in winter, and if you choose to ski, you will find that Marmot Basin is one of the least-crowded ski resorts of its size in North America. Locals say, "What's a Lift Line?" Marmot has 53 runs that cover more than 1,000 acres of eye-dazzling mountain terrain that rises 2,900 vertical feet. It was updated in 1997 with a new base lodge Caribou Café that boasts "the best little breakfast joint in the mountains," a new lounge, restaurant, day-care nursery, gift and sport shop and a new Snowboard Park, and daily shuttle service from Jasper lodgings. New programs include "I've Never Skied Before." Ski Marmot in January/early February and enjoy the **Jasper in January Festival.**

Details: Open Nov.–Apr., all seven lifts open 9 A.M.–4:30 P.M.; $29–$37 adults for day, $29 seniors, $32 youth 13–17, $17 junior, but check current prices, which can be variable. (1 day)

★★★ MALIGNE CANYON
11 km (6.8 mi) east of town via Hwy. 16 and Maligne Rd.; Maligne Canyon Tours, 780/852-3370

The longest, deepest, and most impressive canyon in Jasper National Park was carved by river action. A self-guiding interpretive trail follows the canyon rim downstream to the river valley bottom. Footbridges provide stunning views down 55 meters (165 feet) into the canyon depths. In winter, go on an ice walk on the bottom of the canyon or a canyon crawl through the suspended, frozen waterfalls. A Teahouse operates in summer. Guided tours available in winter.

Details: *(1 hour)*

★★★ MOUNT EDITH CAVELL
9 km (11.8 mi) from Jasper on Hwy. 93, then Hwy. 93A, then along an access road

This 3,363-meter (10,200-foot) mountain was named to honor a British nurse who was executed by the Germans for helping Allied troops escape during World War I. On the northeast slope is Angel Glacier, which hangs over the cliff face. The 14-kilometer (8-mile) road to Cavell Lake and the mountain's north face snakes along the Whirlpool River Valley and is open June through October only. It's twisty, but like most roads in similar areas, virtually every curve brings a fantastic view, hence its reason for being. It's a worthwhile drive. Trails leads to a better view of Angel Glacier and colorful alpine flower meadows.

Details: *Access road closed in winter (make it a day trip)*

FITNESS AND RECREATION

This is the place to keep fit—hiking, climbing, fishing, mountain biking, horseback riding, canoeing, river rafting, skiing, snowshoeing, snowboarding, skating, dog sledding, sleigh riding—or to just unwind and do nothing but sit in a hot springs and drink in the scenery.

Hiking is the most popular summer activity in Jasper. The trails (1,000 kilometers) are varied and many trails are close to town. Pick up free detailed maps from Parks Canada Infocentres, including the *Day Hikers' Guide to Jasper National Park*. Overnight hikes require a $6 Wilderness Pass Parks Use Permit. Some suggested hikes include:

From Miette Hot Springs, there's a fabulous half-day hike through subalpine forests and meadows to a great view from Sulphur Ridge—and the hot springs await your return! The 8-kilometer Wilcox Pass Trail begins near the Columbia Icefield Campground in subalpine forest and ascends quickly to an alpine meadow and the ridge that provides superb views of the Athabasca and Dome Glaciers. There's a good chance that you will see mountain sheep or goats in the pass area. This can be a full- or half-day hike.

Rocky Mountain Hiking, Box 2623, Jasper, Alberta T0E 1E0, 780/852-5015, provides information on such guided hikes and also on caving. An exciting one-day trip into an ancient drainage system takes you deep into a mountain in one of Canada's largest caves. This trip is well-suited to children and adults in good health. Rocky Mountain Hiking also offers an interpretive guiding service, providing outdoor activities or natural history programs that include walks, hikes, and overnight pack trips as well as caving.

If you want a few more feet to help you hike, try horseback guided rides from one to five hours or pack trips from 1 to 14 nights. For trail rides in summer or sleigh rides in winter, and its Dine and Ride package, contact **Pyramid Stables/Horseback Riding,** 4 kilometers (2.5 miles) north on Pyramid Lake Rd., Box 787, Jasper, 780/852-3562, daily 9 A.M.–5 P.M.

Golfers will be ecstatic playing the stunning **Jasper Park Lodge Golf Course,** 780/852-3301 (see Sights). Skiers will love downhill skiing at **Marmot Basin** or cross-country skiing at **Maligne and Pyramid Lakes** (see Sights). Whitewater rafters will be excited by trips on the Maligne River with **Maligne River Adventures,** Box 280, 626 Connaught Dr., Jasper, 780/852-3370, or the Athabasca River with **Jasper Raft Tours,** 780/852-2665, jaspraft@incentre.net.

The ultimate is to heli-hike with **Canadian Mountain Holidays,** 800/661-0252, www.cmhhike.com. The best way is to land on top of the Cariboo Mountains by helicopter, hike effortlessly for the day on high ridges, past glaciers and through alpine meadows, have lunch and then at the end of the day get whisked back down to base again. You can also get a sightseeing flight for as short as 15 minutes. Phone 800/661-0252, or visit www.cmhhike.com. $255 adult, $191 children.

FOOD

Jasper Park Lodge, 780/852-6052, is the place to go in Jasper, whether you eat or not (see Sights). Like most of these grand hotel resorts, Jasper Park Lodge offers a variety of restaurants to suit your taste buds and pocketbook. Food may be more expensive than downtown, but what price can you put on view and ambiance. Don't miss Sunday brunch. If you can afford fine French cuisine, then dress up and go to award-winning **Edith Cavell Dining Room,** where you'll also be treated to the romantic sounds of a harp and the ceiling-to-floor window views of Lac Beauvert and the Rocky Mountains. The **Moose's Nook Canadiana Grill Room** offers world-famous Canadiana cuisine, and it does include more than hamburgers and maple syrup. If you manage to stay in one of the cottages, order something by room service just for the experience of having it delivered by bicycle.

You dine while a harpist plays at **Charlton's Château Jasper's** award-winning **Beauvallon Dining Room,** 96 Geikie St., 780/852-5644. It's not likely you'll be eating rabbit sausage, ostrich crêpes, guinea fowl, and deer ragout back home, so try them here. The Château specializes in wild game cuisine. The fixed-price menu, including dessert, is tops but there is a weekend buffet and a spectacular Sunday brunch with 25 selections for a lot less, and seniors and children 6 to 12 pay even less than that. Another award-winning restaurant with exotic dishes such as paté-stuffed quail and wild duck ravioli is **Walter's Dining Room and Lounge** in the Sawridge Hotel Jasper, 82 Connaught Dr., 780/852-5111 or 800/661-6427. Try the Sawridge's afford-able and good-value breakfast buffet in the **Sunrise Café.** Another fine din-ing restaurant with a master chef (also the owner) is **Andy's Bistro,** 606 Patricia St., 780/852-4559. Send Andy an email or find him on the Internet to learn of his current masterpiece: ginnya@telusplanet.net, www.visit-jasper. com/Andys_Bistro.html.

Another high-end place in summer is the **Treeline Restaurant** on top of Whistlers Mountain, which you reach by the **Jasper Tramway,** 780/852-3093. It is literally high in terms of its location, a 360-degree view overlooking six mountains, including Mount Robson, the highest mountain in the Canadian Rockies. The Sunset Dinner Package includes the tram ride and meal and is worth it. In winter, try the Dine and Ride Package offered by **Embers Restau-rant and Fireside Lounge** in the **Marmot Lodge,** 86 Connaught Dr., 780/852-4544. You have your meal then tour Jasper in a covered wagon. After the ride, go back to Embers for dessert and special coffees.

Papa George's Restaurant, in the Astoria Hotel, 404 Connaught Dr., 780/852-3351, is the traditional, tried-and-true Jasper standby, the kind of place to take Aunt Gertrude when she comes to town. Classic menu, generous por-tions, and cheesebread "to die for," says one of the locals. Like many of Jasper's restaurants that cater to hikers, Papa George's offers filling breakfasts and boxed lunches to go. **Fiddle River Seafood Co.,** 622 Connaught Dr., 780/852-3032, is also popular. It serves fresh seafood with a difference, from salmon with spinach-artichoke mousse in filo to fish and chips. You can also get landlubber steak and chicken, but go for the fish.

At the other end of the monetary scale, join the locals at the **Jasper Pizza Place,** 402 Connaught Dr., 780/852-3225, where you can get such exotic top-pings as smoked salmon, artichoke hearts, capers, scallops, and asparagus; ar-chitecturally distinctive **Spooners,** 610 Patricia St., 780/852-4046, popular for quick inexpensive lunches (try the veggie lasagna or spanakopita); **Truffles and Trout,** in the Jasper Marketplace, corner of Patricia St. and Hazel Ave., 780/852-9676, which specializes in homemade soups, "VIP" picnics and "pick-up-a-dinner" dishes, and the **Bear's Paw Bakery,** Connaught Dr. and Cedar Ave., 780/852-3233, which locals love for its fresh baked treats. Lots of take-out eateries for picnic-loving Jasperites.

JASPER NATIONAL PARK

LODGING

Jasper has a variety of accommodations, but not all are open year-round. Rooms in this resort are a bit expensive, and rates can alter with the season, so ask about them.

If you've got a lot of cash or a lot of friends and relatives, then splurge for a night or more at Jasper's best—the newly renovated **Jasper Park Lodge,** 800/441-1414. A park in itself, it is backdropped by mountains spread artistically around a lake and edged by a beautifully landscaped 18-hole golf course. It has a variety of units that include a main lodge, bungalows, and guest houses. It has seven types of specialty "cabins"—perhaps cabin's the wrong word considering the $3,800 a night price tag for Milligan Manor—but then you can fit a lot of friends and relatives into its eight bedrooms.

A downtown hotel in a more moderate price category is **Whistler Inn,** 105 Miette Ave., 800/661-1315 (W. Canada) or 800/282-9919 (Alberta), 780/852-3361. Distinctive features are the roof hot tub/steam room, The Den (a wildlife museum displaying more than 100 species of native wildlife), exterior wall murals, and a European alpine lodge atmosphere.

A favorite hangout for the locals on weekends is the even less expensive **Athabasca Hotel,** 510 Patricia St., 877/542-8422 (W. Canada), 780/852-3386, or osheas@telusplanet.net. This could be a disadvantage or an advantage, depending on your point of view. Rates range from a very affordable room with shared bath over the popular tavern to a couple of hundred dollars or more for a room on the quieter side. Built in 1929, the Atha B, as it is called locally, has

---

FOOD

- Ⓐ Andy's Bistro
- Ⓐ Bear's Paw Bakery
- Ⓐ Beauvallon Dining Room
- Ⓐ Edith Cavell Dining Room
- Ⓐ Embers Restaurant and Fireside Lounge
- Ⓐ Fiddle River Seafood Co.
- Ⓐ Jasper Pizza Place
- Ⓐ Papa George's Restaurant
- Ⓐ Moose's Nook Canadiana Grill Room

FOOD (continued)

- Ⓐ Spooners
- Ⓐ Sunrise Cafe
- Ⓑ Treeline Restaurant
- Ⓐ Truffles and Trout
- Ⓐ Walter's Dining Room and Lounge

LODGING

- Ⓒ Athabasca Falls Hostel
- Ⓐ Athabasca Hotel
- Ⓐ Bear Hill Lodge
- Ⓐ Beauty Creek Hostel
- Ⓐ Beckers Chalets
- Ⓓ Columbia Icefields Chalet

LODGING (continued)

- Ⓐ Hilda Creek Hostel
- Ⓐ Jasper International Hostel
- Ⓐ Jasper Park Lodge
- Ⓔ Maligne Canyon Hostel
- Ⓕ Mount Edith Cavell Hostel
- Ⓐ Seabolt Ridge Bed and Breakfast
- Ⓐ Whistler Inn

CAMPING

- Ⓖ Wapiti
- Ⓖ Whistler

Note: Items with the same letter are located in the same area.

---

been recently renovated in the Victorian style. There are two bars, the live entertainment side and the DA Room, short for the "Dead Animal Room," featuring the heads of stuffed animals. There are more critters in the lobby—elk, caribou, sheep, goats, moose—all road kills, the receptionist assures me.

Chalets, cabins and bungalows are popular with visitors to Jasper. If you want privacy downtown, the only bungalows in the townsite, try **Bear Hill Lodge,** Box 700, T0E 1E0, 780/852-3209, bonhomme@telusplanet.net, www.visit-jasper.com/BonhommeBungalows.html. It's in a quiet forest setting yet is on Bonhomme Street, two blocks off Connaught Drive within walking distance of the main shopping area. Accommodations range from original log cabins to contemporary chalets, many with wood-burning fireplaces and kitchenettes, and rates reflect the variety. Open April through October.

If you want privacy out of town, try favorite local standby, the moderately priced **Beckers Chalets** (formerly Beckers Bungalows), located on the Icefields Parkway, 5 kilometers (3 miles) south of the townsite and looking across to the Athabasca River. Contact Becker's at Box 579, Jasper 780/852-3779. Open May through October 15 and prices are reasonable. The old **Columbia Icefields Chalet** opposite the Athabasca Glacier and now part of the new Icefields Centre has been renovated and you can scarcely better the view if you book one of the Glacier View rooms. You can also be first on the scene for the morning tours of the glacier. Hotel is open May through October. Contacts in season: Box 1140, Banff, T0L 0C0. 780/852-6550, icefields@brewster.ca, off-season 403/762-6735 or 762-2794.

Before you make a reservation at a bed-and-breakfast, get some advice from Jasper's Private Home Accommodation Association, Box 758, Jasper T0E 1E0. The advantage at **Seabolt Ridge Bed and Breakfast,** Box 645, 780/865-5044, is that your host is a National Park warden who can offer some personalized in-depth information on the area.

For some, the best place to sleep in Jasper National Park is under the stars or in the convivial atmosphere of a hostel. Six hostels providing affordable accommodation are: **Athabasca Falls, Beauty Creek, Maligne Canyon, Mount Edith Cavell, Jasper International Hostel,** all contacted through 780/852-3215, and **Hilda Creek,** 403/762-3441.

CAMPING

There are 11 campgrounds in Jasper National Park: five serviced and six primitive. Most are located along the Icefields Parkway, and are fairly small and basic. All can be reached at 780/852-6176. As in Banff National Park, accommodations are first come, first served. They fill up quickly in summer, especially on long weekends. There is an extra fee for making a fire. Opening and closing times for the different campgrounds are variable so check *Alberta Campground Guide,* available from Travel Alberta Visitor Information Centres, or the**Alberta Hotel Association,** #401, Centre 104, 5241 Calgary Trail South, Edmonton, AB T6H 5G8, 780/436-6112, or Park Info Centres. Check the Internet at www.explorealberta.com for continually updated information.

Each campground has its own advantages—and disadvantages. **Whistler,** 3 kilometers (2 miles) south of the town on Highway 93, and open May through October, has the most services, including phones, a play area, hiking trails and coin-operated showers. It has 781 sites, 77 with power, water and sewer, 100 with electricity and 604 unserviced. **Wapiti,** 5 kilometers (3 miles) south of town on Hwy. 93, has 40 sites with electricity and 322 unserviced, and it, too, has showers. Wapiti is distinctive in that it has 268 sites, (40 with electricity and 228 unserviced), that are open in winter, October through May, for those who like winter camping.

NIGHTLIFE

Most visitors have probably seen, walked, or done enough to be contentedly tired, but there are a few noteworthy nightspots.

If you really want to kick up your heels, hang out with the locals at the historic **Athabasca Hotel,** 510 Patricia St., 780/852-3386. You have two choices: live music nightly with the younger set at the **Atha-b** lounge with its large modern dance floor and tavern, or join a slightly older crowd at the more intimate **O'Shea's,** a sports lounge decorated with antiques and sports memorabilia. Two more popular nightspots for those whom the hiking trails and ski slopes haven't worked off enough steam, are **Pete's on Patricia,** 780/852-6262, the only bar in Jasper to feature ladies' nights, and **Nick's Bar** at the Tonquin Inn, Juniper Street between Connaught and Geikie, 780/852-4966. Under its glass-enclosed atrium, Nick offers sports and ski movies on a big screen, piano music, and pub grub.

Oldies, say 35 and up, will probably prefer the quieter atmosphere, pool table, dart boards, and 10 varieties of ale in the **Whistle Stop Pub** of The Whistlers Inn, 105 Miette Ave., 780/852-3361. Or, despite its name, the **De'd Dog Bar and Grill** in the Astoria Hotel, 780/852-3351.

12
THE OKANAGAN
SIMILKAMEEN

Unlike rainy Vancouver, the Okanagan's semiarid climate records more sunshine than most of Canada. Besides more than 250 lakes and sandy beaches, it has 40 golf courses; three exceptional ski resorts; more than 25 wineries/vineyards; abundant orchards, farms, and ranches; and activities for all ages and interests. It really is an all-season playground, as the ads say.

North American tour-bus operators rate the Okanagan among the continent's top 100 destinations.

A PERFECT DAY IN THE OKANAGAN

Start in Osoyoos on a pleasant day in May, when cherry, peach, pear, plum, and apple blossoms are turning the lakeside hills into flower gardens, and drive north to Vernon along the west side of the Okanagan Valley. Pick up a calendar of events for the Okanagan Wine Festival and decide on the highlight for that day—a guided tour of several wineries with lunch or dinner included; a horse- or tractor-drawn tour of an orchard; perhaps both. Photograph the intriguing Spotted Lake near Oliver and look for birds and bighorn sheep on the bluffs of Vaseaux Lake. In the evening, dine and dance aboard the 1948 paddle-wheeler MV *Fintry Queen,* on Lake Okanagan out of Kelowna. Between courses, keep an eye out for the Okanagan's legendary sea monster, Ogopogo. He is described as a creature with a snake—like body that may include several humps, a dark green outer skin, and a head the size of a horse's. Sleep by the water, perhaps at Kelowna's sumptuous Grand Hotel. In winter, a perfect day means skiing at Silver Star Mountain Resort or Big White Ski Resort.

ORIENTATION

The Okanagan Valley (Okanagan River and Okanagan Lake) is located in the south central region of British Columbia, 400 kilometers (240 miles) east of Vancouver. It extends 250 kilometers (150 miles) from Osoyoos in the south (just minutes from the U.S. border), past the main towns of Penticton, Kelowna, and Vernon, to Enderby in the north. The Similkameen Valley (Similkameen

River) stretches 100 kilometers (60 miles) from Princeton in the west to Penticton in the east.

It can be accessed by many routes, but one of the best is via the comparatively new Coquihalla Highway (Hwy. 5) from Vancouver north to Merritt, and the Okanagan Connector (Hwy. 97C) east to Kelowna. This road cuts through alpine terrain, has few pullouts, generous speed limits (110 kilometers-per-hour), and parallels a 100-kilometer (60-mile) chain link fence with 25 wildlife underpasses and a wildlife overpass, aimed to protect animals trying to cross the road. If you have an extra hour and want a more leisurely drive from Vancouver along the Similkameen River, use the Hope-Princeton (Hwy. 3) east to Keremeos and thus Osoyoos, Oliver and Okanagan Falls. Or if you want to skip the southern section of the region, cut off at Keremeos and take Highway 3A to Kaleden and Penticton. From Calgary it's a seven-hour drive via the Trans-Canada Highway (Hwy. 1), and from Spokane, Washington State, it's a five-hour drive via Highway 97. Whatever you choose, certainly drive Highway 97 from Osoyoos and Vernon.

SIGHTSEEING HIGHLIGHTS

When driving through the Okanagan Valley, stop in the lakeside towns of Spanish-themed, desert-like Osoyoos (its sandy beaches line one of Canada's warmest freshwater lakes); Oliver, Okanagan Falls, Penticton (more relaxing than Kelowna); Summerland, Kelowna (the busy lake and activity-oriented "capital" of the Okanagan, named in 1991 by *Chatelaine* magazine, as one of the best cities to live in Canada, one in which you must walk along the lakefront of its City and Waterfront downtown parks; and Vernon (not so close to the water as the others, but surrounded by lakes and parks.

★★★★ CATHEDRAL PROVINCIAL PARK
Box 399, Summerland, V0H 1Z0; 250/494-6500, 48 km (30 mi) southeast of Princeton off Hwy. 3

There are two ways to reach this beautiful park near Keremeos. Either drive to a base camp along a 21-km (13-mi) gravel road from Highway 3 near the Ashnola River, 5km west of Keremeos, then rough it by hiking up a 15-km (9-mi) trail to the private facility (see Lodgings section) of Cathedral Lakes Lodge at 2,000 meters (7,000 feet). Or, if you want a quicker alternative to an eight-hour hike, pay for a thrice-daily, one-hour alpine taxi ride to the top in the lodge's four-wheel-drive vehicle. Even if you can't wangle a ride and you have to hike, the scenery on top is worth the climb, and private vehicles are not allowed on the park road.

Cathedral Provincial Park is a stunningly beautiful wilderness in the Cascade Mountains, which Canada shares with the United States. Jagged peaks that stand majestically against the skyline guard the park's turquoise lakes and alpine meadows. It has 85 km (53 mi) of hiking trails that lead to the park's main features—curious rock formations with names such as Smoky the Bear, Devil's Woodpile, Stone City, and the Giant Cleft. You'll probably see mule deer, mountain goats, and California bighorn sheep.

Details: *Open Jun.–Oct., but best mid-Jul.—late-Aug. Fee charged Jun.–Sept., phone for rates, cash only. (3 days)*

★★★★ **OKANAGAN FOOD AND WINE FESTIVAL**
Okanagan Wine Festivals, 102-266 Lawrence Ave., Kelowna, BC V1Y 6L3; 250/861-6654, info@owfs.com, www.owfs.com
Classified as one of the top-100 events in North America by international bus-tour organizers, this biannual festival (May and October) has become so popular that some events sell out months before they occur. Most of the wineries link up with local restaurants and tourist attractions to provide food, wine, and travel packages. During consumer tastings and wine judgings in the fall, visitors are offered such enticements as pig or pit roasts, winemasters' dinners, progressive dinner parties, salmon bakes, seafood extravaganzas, chocolate buffets, train rides, and wine biking tours. A popular event is a float plane ride to

Get your Wine Festival Passport stamped at each winery to earn prizes. For further information, contact the Okanagan Wine Festival Society, 1030 McCurdy Road, Kelowna, V1X 2P7, 250/861-6654; or the Okanagan Wine Festival Office, 185 Lakeshore Dr., Penticton, V2A 1B7, 250/490-8866 or 800/972-5151.

the top of the Kettle Valley Railway and a cycle back to town, during which riders learn a bit of history and enjoy wine and cheese in an exotic location. Fall festival recommended.

Details: *Spring festival opens May, fall festival Oct.. (2 days)*

★★★★ **OKANAGAN VALLEY WINE TRAIN**
BC Office: 991 Richter St., Kelowna, BC V1Y 2K4, 250/712-9888, 888/674-TRAK (8725), funtrain@incentre.net, www.incentre.net/funtrain

THE OKANAGAN SIMILKAMEEN

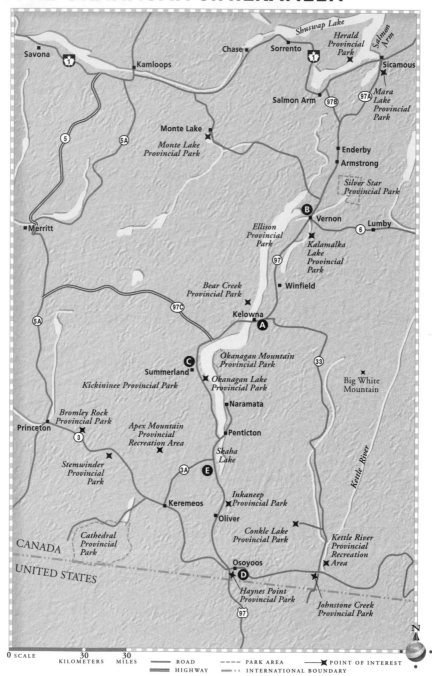

Savona

Kamloops

Chase

Sorrento

Shuswap Lake

Herald Provincial Park

Sicamous

Salmon Arm

Salmon Arm

97B

97A

Mara Lake Provincial Park

Monte Lake

Monte Lake Provincial Park

Enderby

Armstrong

Silver Star Provincial Park

Merritt

B

Vernon

Lumby

6

Ellison Provincial Park

Kalamalka Lake Provincial Park

97

Bear Creek Provincial Park

Winfield

97C

Kelowna

A

Okanagan Mountain Provincial Park

33

Summerland

C

Okanagan Lake Provincial Park

Big White Mountain

Kickininee Provincial Park

Naramata

Bromley Rock Provincial Park

Princeton

3

Apex Mountain Provincial Recreation Area

Penticton

Skaha Lake

Kettle River

Stemwinder Provincial Park

3A

E

Keremeos

Inkaneep Provincial Park

Oliver

Conkle Lake Provincial Park

Kettle River Provincial Recreation Area

CANADA

Cathedral Provincial Park

UNITED STATES

Osoyoos

D

Haynes Point Provincial Park

Johnstone Creek Provincial Park

97

N

0 SCALE

30 KILOMETERS

30 MILES

ROAD

HIGHWAY

PARK AREA

INTERNATIONAL BOUNDARY

POINT OF INTEREST

Here's something new for the Okanagan—or anywhere in BC for that matter—a seven-hour family attraction that includes a scenic vintage rail trip from 600 Recreation Avenue in downtown Kelowna through wine and orchard country to Vernon via gorgeous Kalamalka Lake. It ends with a dinner and Las Vegas-style show at the terminus of Armstrong. Guests have the option of returning to Kelowna that night and sleeping aboard. You choose between seats in the Day Coach or in the Club Galley Car where seats are more comfortable, tables are available, and there is a variety of music (big band sounds of the 1930s and 1940s, rock and roll from the 1950s and 1960s, country and western, or soft rock.

Details: Call for starting date, ends Oct. 31; Wed.–Sat. 4–11 P.M.; Sun. 11 A.M.–6 P.M. Daycoach: $64.75 adults, $60.25 senior 65+, $53.95 youth 9–18, $44.95 child 4–8; Theme Bar Car: $82.75 adults. Reduced price from Vernon, $19.95 dinner and show in Armstrong only (7 hours)

★★★ HISTORIC O'KEEFE RANCH
Located 12 km (7 mi) north of Vernon on Hwy. 97; 250/542-7868

This is a famous ranch founded in 1867 as the headquarters of a vast cattle empire. You can tour original buildings such as the O'Keefe Mansion, St. Anne's Church, the general store, and the blacksmith's shop. Guides are available. Also on the premises are a cowboy ranching gallery, a popular ranch-house restaurant, and stagecoach rides.

Details: Open mid-May–mid-Oct. daily 9 A.M.–5 P.M., $6 adults, $5 over 65 and ages 13–18, $4.50 ages 6–12, $18 families (1.5 hours)

★★★ KETTLE VALLEY STEAM RAILWAY
The Kettle Valley Railway Society, 18404 Bathville Rd. Box 1288, Summerland, BC V0H 1Z0, 250/494-8422, toll-free in BC 877/494-8424, big_ideas@bc.sympatico.ca

SIGHTS

- **A** Father Pandosy's Mission/Pandosy Mission Provincial Heritage Site
- **B** Historic O'Keefe Ranch
- **C** Kettle Valley Steam Railway
- **A** Okanagan Food and Wine Festival
- **A** Okanagan Valley Wine Train
- **D** Pocket Desert (Haynes Lease Ecology Reserve)
- **E** Vaseux Lake

Note: Items with the same letter are located in the same area.

OKANAGAN WINE ROUTE

The Okanagan Similkameen has become one of Canada's premier wine-producing regions. Among the Okanagan Similkameen's most notable wineries are the **Cedar Creek Estate** near Kelowna, 250/764-8866; the **Gray Monk Estate** in Winfield, 250/766-3168 or 800/663-4205; the **St. Hubertus Estate** near Kelowna, 250/764-7888 or 800/989-WINE; and the Sumac Ridge Estate near Summerland, 250/490-0451. The historic **Quails' Gate Estate** near Westbank, 250/769-4451 or 800/420-WINE, features an 1873 log cabin wine shop.

Most of the region's two dozen wineries are clearly marked by highway signs on the Okanagan Wine Route. Some wineries offer tastings and tours by appointment only, so it's best to phone ahead.

Spanning southern British Columbia from Hope through the Okanagan to Rock Creek at the entrance of the Kootenay region (the Coast to Kootenay Connection), this railroad was designed in 1916 to open up new mining areas, and to stave off competing American attempts to do likewise. It was known as "McCulloch's Wonder," after the Canadian Pacific Railway engineer who pushed the railway through to completion despite mudslides, avalanches, and the deaths of many construction workers. It was regarded as one of the greatest engineering feats in railway history.

By 1959, the railway was abandoned for lack of traffic and the difficulty of maintaining it under adverse conditions. The tracks have been torn up, but parts of the line have been restored for hiking, cycling, biking, and horseback riding along its railbed. Get maps from infocenters in Summerland, Kelowna, and Penticton, which will guide you to various access points. One of the most popular destinations is to Myra Canyon and its picturesque heart-stopping trestles.

In Summerland, near the Trout Creek Canyon, you can re-live that old-railway-days feeling by taking a ride in a 1924 Shay Locomotive on a 10km portion of preserved track in this area. This two-hour ride departs from the Prairie Valley Station located near the Summerland Rodeo Grounds, mostly on summer weekends, also for special events. **Details:** Open May 22–Jun. 30, Sat.–Mon.; Jul. 1–Sept. 6, Thur.–Mon.;

Sept. 7–October 11, Sat.–Mon.; 10:30 A.M.–1:30 P.M.; $11 adults, $10 seniors and ages 13–18, $7.50 children 4–12, $39 family. (2 hours)

★★ FATHER PANDOSY'S MISSION/PANDOSY MISSION PROVINCIAL HERITAGE SITE
3685 Benvoulin Rd., Kelowna; 250/860-8369

The first agricultural site and the first European settlement in the Okanagan Valley, the mission was set up in 1859 by three Oblate missionaries as a base to convert the aboriginal inhabitants, traders, and free settlers. Father Pandosy is well known for planting the first apple tree in the valley. You can tour four of the original buildings remaining, including the church.
Details: *Open Apr.-Oct., dawn–dusk, admission by donation. (1 hour)*

★★ POCKET DESERT (HAYNES LEASE ECOLOGICAL RESERVE)
Near Osoyoos Oxbows Fish and Wildlife Management Reserve, off Rd. 22, 250/494-6500

It can get so hot in Osoyoos that one visitor actually fried an egg on the sidewalk. The Pocket Desert is Canada's only true desert, the northern extremity of America's Great Basin Desert, one of the most unusual geographical locations in Canada. This area of unirrigated land extends 48 kilometers (30 miles) north to Skaha Lake and west along the Similkameen River. A federal ecological reservation, it features such rarities as spadefoot toads, Pacific rattlesnakes, and Calliope hummingbirds.
Details: *(30 minutes to 1 hour)*

★★ VASEUX LAKE
Located 14.5 km (9 mi) north of Oliver on Hwy. 97, Vaseux Lake Provincial Park, 250/494-6500

In this excellent wildlife-viewing area that is a federal wildlife and migratory bird sanctuary are mountain goats, California bighorn sheep, and a wide variety of bird life. Trails access nearby Vaseux Lake Canadian Wildlife Service Sanctuary and Vaseux Lake Provincial Park. You can swim and fish in the lake for largemouth bass and rainbow trout.
Details: *(30 minutes)*

AGRITOURS

Many Okanagan Valley ranches and farms welcome visitors. Try a tour and sample some cheese at the Armstrong Cheese Factory, 3155 Pleasant Valley Rd.,

Armstrong, 250/546-3084. Have a honey farm vacation at Honey Farm Vacation Tours, a working bee-farm bed-and-breakfast, 2910 North Glenmore Rd., Kelowna, 250/762-8156. Feed and milk the dairy goats at Paradox Farm, Enderby, 250/838-7766. Catch trout and sample venison at the Fink Trout, Deer, Elk, and Bison Farm, Mabel Lake Rd., Enderby, 250/838-7621. Watch how raw fiber is spun into wool at the Okanagan Alpaca Company, 11014 Bond Road, Winfield, 250/766-3175. Take a hike with High Country Llama Adventures, Meadow Valley, Summerland, 250/494-8329. Visit the Okanagan Crockers Ostrich Farm, 112 Westside Rd., Kelowna; call ahead, 250/769-6693. Take the self-guided walking tour of Davison Orchards, RR4, Davison Rd., Vernon, V1T 6L7, 250/549-3266. There is a tremendous choice of farms, orchards, farmers' markets, and apiaries in the Okanagan.

Lots of people tour the Okanagan Similkameen in fall to take advantage of fresh fruits and vegetables from roadside stands. Keremeos is known as the Fruit Stand Capital of the World, with more than 25 stands in town. Stop and tour one of the orchards—it's a fun way to get your produce and learn something of the process. Try the Kelowna Land and Orchard Company, 2930 Dunster Rd., Kelowna V1Y 7R2, 250/763-1091, for a wagon ride on a working orchard. You'll learn the Oriental way of growing apples—in paper bags right on the tree—in order to produce flawless fruit. Following the tour are free samples.

FITNESS AND RECREATION

Now that you've eaten and imbibed your way around the Okanagan Similkameen, you'd better concentrate on getting in shape. So forget sun-bathing on the sandy beaches and go for another swim. There are dozens of places to stop for a swim along the west side of Okanagan and Skaha Lakes. Try Kalamalka Lake, "the lake of many colors," on the outskirts of Vernon. Stop at the viewpoint on Highway 97, 5 kilometers (3 miles) south of 25th Avenue in Vernon, to take panoramic photos. Look over the lake to **Kalamalka Lake Provincial Park,** popular with swimmers, boaters, and cross-country skiers who want to avoid the biggest crowds.

Families love the Okanagan as there's so much to do especially in the outdoors. Kids will have fun at one of the many Okanagan waterslides: **Wonderful Waterworld,** Penticton, 250/493-8121; **Wild Waters Waterslide Park,** Kelowna, 250/765-9453; **Atlantis Waterslides and Recreations,** 7 kilometers (4 miles) north on Highway 97A at Pleasant Valley Road, outside of Vernon, 250/549-4121. **Okanagan Bobsliding,** 8 kilometers (5 miles) north of Vernon on Highway 97A, 250/542-0104, offers a 580-meter (1,903-foot) ride down a stainless steel bobslide. A mechanical lift takes riders to the lift site.

Residents and visitors alike make the most of water in the sunny Okanagan. If they're not swimming, boating, skiing, sliding, and fishing it, they're floating it. The Okanagan River Channel, a 6-kilometer (3.8-mile) canal that connects Skaha and Okanagan Lakes, is a drawing card for anyone with a flotation device, including rented tires. Locals love it. As many as 30,000 people float it on a hot summer weekend. You can rent dinghies and tire tubes. You can also stroll, bike and jog along the channel's banks.

The Okanagan Similkameen is determined to catch up to Whistler in the current expansion of ski facilities at its three main ski destinations: **Silver Star Mountain Resort** near Vernon, Box 2, Silver Star Mountain, V0E 1G0, 250/542-0224 or 800/663-4431; **Big White Ski Resort** near Kelowna, Box 2039, Station R, Kelowna, V1X 4K5, 250/765-3101 or 800/663-2772; and **Apex Resort** near Penticton, Box 1060, Penticton, V2A 7N7, 250/492-2880 or 800/387-2739. All three have recently upgraded their facilities, and all three are within an hour's drive of a city. I like Silver Star for its 1890s Gaslight Era village, which reminds me of the days of the Old Canadian West.

FOOD

When you're tired of roadside stands but still want to feel you're in the outdoors, settle by the creek that runs through the **Garden Cafe and Courtyard Dining Room** in the Best Western Vernon Lodge and Conference Centre, 3914 32nd St. (Hwy. 97), Vernon, 250/545-3385 or 800/663-4422. Dine in a magnificent three-story indoor courtyard atrium filled with tropical plants, swim in the pool, or sit in the whirlpool. In such a setting the food may be secondary, but here you won't compromise on taste or service.

Kelowna, which is the largest and most centrally located of all cities in the Okanagan, has, naturally, the greatest variety of restaurants. One of the most elegant of Kelowna's restaurants is the **Vintage Dining Room** at the Coast Capri Hotel, 1171 Harvey Ave., 250/860-6060, ext. 229. Specialties such as escargots, châteaubriand, and lobster tails may be fairly expensive, but the meal will be memorable. Lunch Monday through Friday, dinner every day, Sunday brunch recommended.

The Aberdeen family, pioneers of the Okanagan's fruit-growing industry, built Guisachan House, now a historic site, in 1891. It houses the upscale **Guisachan House Restaurant,** 1060 Cameron Ave. at Gordon Dr., Guisachan Heritage Park, 250/862-9368. Lunch is served daily and dinner Thursday to Sunday. If you eat only once in Kelowna, choose this one, and after your meal, stroll through the perennial gardens (plants are labeled).

In Penticton, another heritage house and landmark restaurant, **Granny**

Bognor's, at 302 Eckhardt Ave. West, 250/493-2711, is noted for desserts and artistic presentation. Duckling and veal sweetbreads are specialties of its wide menu. Prices are fairly high but typical of all elegant and intimate restaurants. Open for dinner Tuesday through Saturday. With its whitewashed walls, red tiled floors, heavy rough-hewn beams, and tree-lined staircase, **Theo's Greek Restaurant,** 687 Main St., Penticton, 250/492-4019, looks like an outdoor patio in the Greek Islands. Rabbit and octopus are the specialties of this popular restaurant, and entrées are reasonable in price. One of the best deals in Penticton is **Mickey Finn's Restaurant,** 57 Padmore Ave., 250/493-3883, which has had loyal clientele since 1977. A seven-ounce steak meal, including vegetables, soup, a salad bar, bread, and choice of potato, rice, or French fries, is very affordable. A casual, fun and friendly eatery in Penticton is **Salty's Beach House,** 1000 Lakeshore Dr. West, Penticton, 250/493-5001, right on the water.

A unique feature of **Shaughnessy's Cove Waterfront Pub and Restaurant,** 12817 Lakeshore Dr. North in Summerland, 250/494-1212, is its free shuttle service from homes or hotels. If you like dining over water, Shaughnessy's is as close as you can get. Try their fish 'n' chips or stew served in hollowed bread. Lunch and dinner are served daily, and meals are inexpensive. On the other side of the lake at Naramata is **The Country Squire,** an old standby where dinner of several entrées and several hours (you can certainly get pheasant under glass here) is practically a choreographed event, and you can go for a walk between courses.

LODGING

What could be grander than the **Grand Okanagan Lakefront Resort and Conference Centre** on the shores of Okanagan Lake and within walking distance of downtown Kelowna? Among 10 hectares (25 acres) of beach, parkland, and lagoons, this luxury hotel at 1310 Water St., 250/763-4500 or 800/465-4651, offers a variety of units at variable prices. **Lake Okanagan Resort,** on a steep hillside at 2751 Westside Rd., Kelowna, 250/769-3511 or 888/888-4374, is a destination in itself: it has a golf course, tennis courts, marina, summer camp, naturalist programs, horseback-riding, cycle and heli-tour packages, and lodgings that are more affordable than the Grand.

Hotel Eldorado, 500 Cook Rd., Kelowna, 250/763-7500, www.sunnyokanagan.com/el, has an excellent reputation and is the one that locals promote first. It has a waterside boardwalk and café; cozy antique-filled rooms; and a lakeside dining room, bar, and grill. Room rates are reasonable considering the location and ambiance, especially in the off season. **Borgata Lodge** at the Quail Ridge Golf and Country Club close to the Kelowna Airport, 3200 Via

Centrale, 250/765-5655, 800/765-7720, is very popular, especially with golfers. More affordable and a good choice for families is clean, friendly and convenient **Stay 'n' Save Motor Inn,** 1140 Harvey Ave., Kelowna, 250/862-8888, 800/663-0298, staynsave@staynsave.com, www.staynsave.com.

In Vernon, bed-and-breakfasts are abundant, reasonably priced, and several have that extra ambiance that sets them apart. Try the **Castle on the Mountain B&B,** 8277 Silver Star Mountain Rd. (close to skiing), S-10, C-12, 250/542-4593 or 800/667-2229, castle.eskila@bc.sympatico.ca, www.pixsell.bc.ca/bb/3221.html. This imposing house includes an outdoor Jacuzzi and the Eskila Gallery, showing artworks by the host and other B.C. artists. Standard double rate is medium-priced, but stretch the budget a little more and take the stargazer's tower suite. **Lakeside Illahee Inn,** 15010 Tamarack Dr. Vernon (on beautiful Kalamalka Lake), 250/260-7896, 888/260-7896, is a bit expensive, but it gets rave reviews.

If you're thinking of honeymooning in Penticton, the **Best Western Inn** at Penticton, 3180 Skaha Lake Rd., 250/493-0311, 800/668-6746, has a fabulous suite with a canopied bed. If you're a naturalist, especially a birder, then head for **Three Gates Farm B&B,** 533A, CC2, RR 1, Kaleden (it's not far from Penticton), V0H 1K0, 250/497-6889, threegates@img.net. For the budget conscious in Penticton, try **Shoreline Resort Condominiums** at 926 Lakeshore Dr., 250/492-7113, 800/663-1900 (you have a kitchen and a waterfront location). For the really budget-conscious, try Hostelling International—Penticton located at 464 Ellis St., 250/492-3992, penticton@hihostels.bc.ca, www.hihostels.bc.ca.

There are some interesting places to stay away from the central Okanagan core. Families appreciate **Sandy Beach Lodge and Resort,** 4275 Mill Rd., Box 8, Naramata, on the east side of Okanagan Lake, 250/496-5765, www.sandybeachresort.com. Reservations may be necessary a year in advance for the peak summer season as it has so many repeat guests. Facilities include croquet, horseshoes, tennis courts, rental boats, a swimming pool, and 410 feet of sandy beach. Just beyond the boundaries of the Okanagan is **Quaaout Lodge,** a small, secluded and medium-priced lodge on Little Shuswap Lake Rd., 8 kilometers (5 miles) east of Chase. It's close to the world-famous Adams River salmon run and features a restaurant with First Nations cuisine. Write Box 1215, Chase, V0E 1M0; or 250/679-3090 or 800/663-4303.

The grand finale of your trip to the Okanagan-Similkameen should be to leave the lakes and the crowded beaches below, and head up to the mountain lakes of Cathedral Provincial Park (see Sights). **Cathedral Lakes Lodge** features 50 kilometers (31 miles) of hiking trails, four trout-stocked lakes, and free canoes. You can choose a cabin, a room in the chalet, or the lodge itself. It's

THE OKANAGAN SIMILKAMEEN

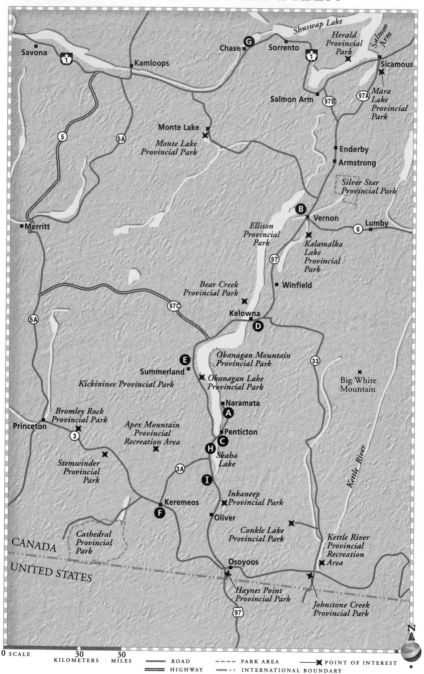

Savona

Kamloops

Chase Sorrento **G**

Shuswap Lake

Herald Provincial Park

Sicamous

Salmon Arm

Salmon Arm 97B

97A *Mara Lake Provincial Park*

Monte Lake

Monte Lake Provincial Park

Enderby

Armstrong

Silver Star Provincial Park

5

5A

Merritt

B Vernon Lumby

Ellison Provincial Park

6

Kalamalka Lake Provincial Park

97

Bear Creek Provincial Park

Winfield

5A

97C

Kelowna

D

Okanagan Mountain Provincial Park

33

E

Summerland

Kickininee Provincial Park

Okanagan Lake Provincial Park

Big White Mountain

Naramata

A

Bromley Rock Provincial Park

Princeton

3

Apex Mountain Provincial Recreation Area

Penticton

C

H

Skaha Lake

Stemwinder Provincial Park

3A

I

Inkaneep Provincial Park

Keremeos

F

Oliver

Kettle River

CANADA

Cathedral Provincial Park

Conkle Lake Provincial Park

Kettle River Provincial Recreation Area

UNITED STATES

Osoyoos

Haynes Point Provincial Park

Johnstone Creek Provincial Park

97

N

0 SCALE   30   30
KILOMETERS   MILES   ROAD   PARK AREA   POINT OF INTEREST
HIGHWAY   INTERNATIONAL BOUNDARY

nothing fancy, but you get three meals a day, hot water, wonderful views, and the price is worth it. It's open June 1 to October 15 and reservations are recommended. No credit cards, but checks accepted. Contact the lodge by writing Cathedral Provincial Park, Site 4, Comp 8, Slocan Park, V0G 2E0; 250/226-7560, 250/492-1606, 888/255-4453, Journey@wkpowerlink.com, www.cathedral-lakes-lodge.com. Alternatively, try 250/499-5848 or cellular phone 250/492-1606 off-season; or write RR1, Cawston, British Columbia V0X 1C0.

CAMPING

Dry, sunny weather encourages camping in Okanagan Similkameen. For BC Provincial Parks reservations, phone **Discover Camping,** 800/689-9025. **Okanagan Lake Provincial Park,** on Okanagan Lake 11 kilometers (7 miles) north of Summerland on Highway 97 is open March through November. It has a good beach, a boat launch, and hot showers. Similar conditions prevail at **Bear Creek Provincial Park,** 9 kilometers (6 miles) west of Kelowna on Westside Road off Highway 97, 250/494-6500. If you want to watch wildlife, choose **Vaseux Lake Provincial Park** at the north end of Vaseux Lake, 4 kilometers (2 miles) south of Okanagan Falls, 250/494-6500. If you want all beachfront campsites go to Haynes Point Provincial Park, two kilometers north

---

FOOD
- Ⓐ The Country Squire
- Ⓑ Garden Cafe and Courtyard Dining Room
- Ⓒ Granny Bognor's
- Ⓓ Guisachan House Restaurant
- Ⓒ Mickey Finn's Restaurant
- Ⓒ Salty's Beach House
- Ⓔ Shaughnessy's Cove Waterfront Pub and Restaurant
- Ⓒ Theo's Greek Restaurant
- Ⓓ Vintage Dining Room

LODGING
- Ⓒ Best Western Inn
- Ⓓ Borgata Lodge
- Ⓑ Castle on the Mountain B&B
- Ⓕ Cathedral Lakes Lodge
- Ⓓ Eldorado Hotel
- Ⓓ The Grand Okanagan Lakefront Resort and Conference Centre
- Ⓓ Lake Okanagan Resort
- Ⓑ Lakeside Illahee Inn
- Ⓖ Quaaout Lodge
- Ⓐ Sandy Beach Lodge and Resort
- Ⓒ Shoreline Resort Condos
- Ⓓ Stay 'n' Save Motor Inn
- Ⓗ Three Gates Farm B&B

CAMPING
- Ⓔ Bear Creek Provincial Park
- Ⓓ Hiawatha RV Park
- Ⓑ Lakeshore Tent and RV Park
- Ⓑ Okanagan Lake Provincial Park
- Ⓘ Vaseux Lake Provincial Park

Note: Items with the same letter are located in the same area.

---

of the U.S. border/two kilometers south of Osoyoos on Osoyoos Lake, where you can wade chest-high three-quarters across the lake by a distinctive sand spit. Ask for the "Corner Suite" campsite (campsites are named rather than numbered). Phone 250/494-6500.

There are many private campgrounds in the Okanagan. Some of the best are: **Lakeshore Tent and RV Park,** 15419 North Lakeshore Dr., RR1, Summerland, 250/494-8149-open May through September, this park has 120 meters (394 feet) of beach for swimming and boating, a playground, and game room; **Hiawatha RV Park,** 3787 Lakeshore Rd., Kelowna, is quiet, family-oriented, and near a sandy beach open March 15 through October 15. Security is important, and the gate is closed at night 250/861-4837.

NIGHTLIFE

Opt for a nightly dinner-dance cruise on Lake Okanagan aboard the **MV** *Fintry Queen* from Kelowna 250/763-2780. Those who like to gamble can play blackjack, roulette, Sic Bo, Red Dog, and Caribbean stud poker at **Lake City Casinos** in Kelowna, 250/860-9467; in Vernon, 250/545-3505; and in Kamloops, 250/372-3334. There are enough pubs, bistros, coffeehouses, and clubs in Okanagan Similkameen to satisfy summer and winter vacationers, but the region is known for its appreciation of the arts as well: sample **Vernon's Powerhouse Theatre,** 250/542-6194; **Newport Beach Resort's Sen'Klip Native Theatre,** 250/549-2921; and **Armstrong's Caravan Farm Theatre,** which puts on several productions a year from its base on a working organic farm, 250/546-8533.

13
THE KOOTENAYS
(BRITISH COLUMBIA
ROCKIES)

The dramatic but unhurried Kootenays, part of the Rocky Mountains in south-eastern British Columbia, is reminiscent of Vancouver Island as it used to be, before the crowds, before development. The Kootenays, west and east, are still pristine despite a late 1800s influx of miners seeking gold, silver, lead, zinc, and copper; and another influx in the early 1900s of Doukhobors-Russian immigrants escaping religious persecution—and now the encroachment of loggers and dam builders. Its dramatic scenery—parallel ranges of massive, glacier-clad mountains, rugged peaks, wilderness forests, long rivers, elongated lakes, and copious hot springs—stand out in a province famous for its scenery. Though all roads lead to the Kootenays, the region is still a quiet and unspoiled backwater that attracts artists and lovers of the outdoors.

In addition to the fabulous scenery, the Kootenays are also rich in history. Ghost towns, abandoned mines and smelters, restored paddle-wheelers, heritage buildings, and living museums attest to the area's mining-related boom-and-bust economy.

There are no freeways, but plenty of good two-lane highways, logging roads, hiking trails, cross-country ski trails, and free ferries. Circular driving routes ranging 70 to 450 kilometers (42 to 315 miles) allow convenient access to the region's on- and off-road attractions.

A PERFECT DAY IN THE KOOTENAYS

Many people dream of scooting around the Kootenays by helicopter, but opt to drive it instead. Circular routes loop mountains, lakes, and rivers, but choosing the best of the loops is difficult. Try this one—a 323-kilometer (202-mile) drive that blends history and beauty. Start early in Nelson and take a tour by streetcar, or with a costumed guide, of some of its beautiful heritage buildings. If there's time, walk the waterfront. Then travel west on Highway 3A and north on Highway 6 along the (Silvery) Slocan River Valley, the route taken by thousands of fortune-seeking miners in the 1890s. Stop at the Slocan Lake Viewpoint that some say is the most spectacular view in the West Kootenay, sidle along the east shore of Slocan Lake and look up at the rugged mountains of Valhalla Provincial Park. Turn east on Highway 31A and stop at the ghost town of Sandon then take a 12-kilometer (7.5-mile) gravel road to Idaho Peak Lookout to see the much-photographed alpine flowers (in season).

After driving Highway 31 from Kaslo to Balfour, which some have described as a "narrow ledge" along the west side of Kootenay Lake, enjoy a relaxing soak at the Ainsworth Hot Springs before returning to Nelson and a healthy dinner at the All Seasons Restaurant.

ORIENTATION

The Kootenay region is a quiet backwater best explored by road in your own vehicle. The Trans-Canada Highway crosses the northern section of the region with access from Vancouver and Calgary. Highway 3 (the Crowsnest Hwy.) crosses the southern section, paralleling the U.S. border, with access from the Okanagan and Southern Alberta. But because of the north-south alignment of the mountains, lakes, and rivers, and the conspicuous broad valley known as the Rocky Mountain Trench (1,600 kilometers/960 miles long and 3 to 16 kilometers/8 to 9.6 miles wide), the roads are aligned north-south, too. From west to east, Highways 23, 6, 31, and 93/95 find narrow routes along the lakes and rivers. Ferries that cross the waterways are free, though they operate on a first come, first served basis.

Fly into Castlegar and Cranbrook from Vancouver and Calgary via Canadian Regional Airlines and Central Mountain Air, or fly into Nelson and Creston from Vancouver via North Vancouver Air.

The Kootenay is handy to both British Columbia and Alberta, a convenient base for touring all the Rockies. But remember that east of Creston you must put your clocks ahead one hour from Pacific time to Mountain time.

SIGHTSEEING HIGHLIGHTS

★★★★ **CRESTON VALLEY WILDLIFE MANAGEMENT AREA**
On Hwy. 3, 10 km (6 mi) northwest of Creston; Box 640, Creston, V0B 1G0, 250/428-3260, www.cwildlife.bc.ca; Creston and District Chamber of Commerce, 250/428-4342, www.crestonvalley.com
During spring and fall, more than 250,000 birds-migratory ducks, geese, and swans—fly into this 6,880-hectare (17,000-acre) bird refuge/outdoor education center to feed and rest. This preserve has the highest density of osprey in the world. It offers a variety of nature hikes and canoe trips and operates a campground for people exploring the marshlands and taking part in the nature programs. It's best to walk the boardwalk over the marsh or take a guided canoe trip.
Details: *Area open every day year-round, Interpretive Centre open last weekend of Apr.–Labour Day in Sept. daily 8 A.M.–6 P.M., day after Labour Day–Oct. 31, Wed.–Sun. 9 A.M.–4 P.M.; $3.50 adults, $2 ages 2–18, $9 families. (1.5 hours)*

★★★★ **FORT STEELE HERITAGE TOWN**
On Hwy. 93/95, 3 km (2 mi) southwest of Fort Steele; 250/489-3351
The park represents an East Kootenay town from 1890-1905. Fort Steele began in 1864 as Fisherville when gold was discovered at nearby Wild Horse Creek. More than 60 buildings have survived or been restored or reconstructed. Street dramas, quilting demonstrations, stagecoach rides, steam-train rides, and live theater help re-create that life of a hundred years ago, when Fort Steele was the site of the first Northwest Mounted Police post in British Columbia. The fort was named after Samuel Steele, the mountie who peacefully settled tensions between Kootenay Indians and newcomers bent on mining and farming.
Details: *Living history programs presented mid-June–mid-Sept. daily 9:30A.M.–5:30P.M.; mid-Oct.–mid-May daily dawn–dusk; rest of year 9:30 A.M.–dusk; $5.50 adults, $3.25 over 64 and ages 13–18, $1 ages 6–12, $10.75 family rate. (half day)*

★★★★ **KIMBERLEY**
28 km north of Hwy. 3/95 junction, Infocentre, 350 Ross St. 250/427-3666 or 250/427-4881. Kimberley Vacations, 340 Spokane St., V1A 2E8, 250/427-4877, 800/667-0871

THE KOOTENAYS (BRITISH COLUMBIA ROCKIES)

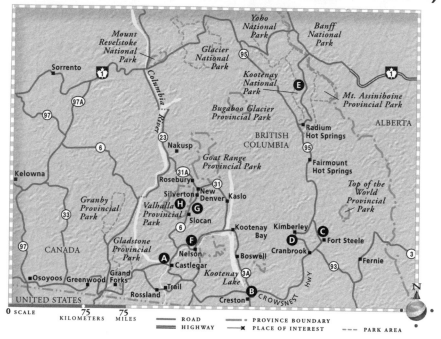

SIGHTS

- **A** Castlegar
- **B** Creston Valley Wildlife Management Area
- **C** Fort Steele Heritage Town
- **D** Kimberley
- **E** Kootenay National Park
- **F** Nelson
- **G** Slocan Valley ("Silvery Slocan")
- **H** Valhalla Provincial Park

Note: Items with the same letter are located in the same area.

Kimberley is the home of the Sullivan Mine, the world's largest underground silver, lead, and zinc mine, and it is named after the diamond mining capital of South Africa. But mines close (the Sullivan Mine is scheduled to close in 2003) so Kimberley, a picturesque town that calls itself the "Bavarian Town of the Rockies," is concentrating on tourism. Many of its buildings have a Bavarian Alpine decor, and its pedestrian-only downtown shopping area known as the Platzl features

Canada's largest operating cuckoo clock. Stroll the footpath from the Platzl to the Cominco Gardens and have a cup of tea at the teahouse, 250/427-2203.

Just two blocks from the Platzl is the Bavarian City Mining Railway. Take an interesting 9-kilometer (6-mile) ride on this line through switchbacks, a tunnel, steep slopes and sharp curves to learn about Kimberley's mining history. Visitors can disembark to take a tour of Cominco's original Power House of the Sullivan Mine, which is the first phase of the Sullivan Mine Interpretive Centre, 340 Spokane St., Kimberley, B.C. V I A 2E8, 250/427-53 I 1, www.bcrockies.com. Kimberley Ski and Summer Resort, a 5-minute drive from town, has an Alpine Slide (.5-miles long). A chairlift ride takes you up North Star Mountain and you can choose to hike or bike down the mountain or take the lift back to the bottom.

Details: *Alpine Slide open late Jun. to early Sept. daily I 0:30A.M.–7:30 P.M., $4 single ride. Downhill skiing Dec.–Apr. Mining Railway and Power House Tour $6 adult I 9–59 return, $5 one-way; $5 ages I 3–18 and 60 and over, return, $3.50 one-way; $3 children 6–I 2 return, $2 one-way; $ I 8 family return, $ I 2 one-way. (I day)*

★★★★ **KOOTENAY NATIONAL PARK**
On the western slopes of the Rocky Mountains adjoining Banff and Yoho National Parks. West Gate entrance at Radium Hot Springs I km north of Hwy. 3/95 jct. Kootenay National Park, Box 220, Radium Hot Springs, V0A I M0, 250/347-9505 (Jun.–Sept.), 250/347-9615 (year-round) or 800/748-7275

This park, a World Heritage Site, is the third most visited national park after Banff and Jasper. Highway 93 following the Kootenay and Vermillion Rivers slices through the middle of the park. This was a travel corridor for local First Nations people long before it was the first road built by European newcomers through the central Rocky Mountains. Every twist and turn reveals something interesting to explore-gray-white-striped limestone Marble Canyon; towering red sandstone cliffs of the Redwall Fault; ochre-tinted Paint Pots cold springs once used by First Nations people to make body paint, decorate their teepees, and draw their rock paintings; and at the park's southern end, popular Radium Hot Springs, which has both a hot pool (35-47° Celsius/95-117° Fahrenheit) and cool pool. Of the numerous hiking trails, two of the best are Floe Lake Trail and Stanley Glacier Trail. The park is open year-round, three campgrounds operate mid-May to late September. Visitors must obtain a park motor vehicle pass at the entrance, and backcountry campers must obtain a wilderness pass.

Details: *Daily admission for private motor vehicles is $10 adults, $8 senior citizens (bring the grandparents), or $70 annual permit for all four western national parks. Radium Hot Springs pools, 250/347-9485, are open daily 9 A.M.–10:30 P.M., $5.50 adults, $5 seniors and children, $16.50 a family of four. (1 day)*

★★★★ NELSON
41 km northeast of Castlegar on Hwy. 3A; Nelson and District Chamber of Commerce, 225 Hall St., B.C. V1R 5X4; 250/352-3433

Situated on a steep hillside overlooking the west arm of Kootenay Lake, this was once an iron- and silver-mining boom town. Today it has the second-highest concentration of heritage buildings (350) per capita in British Columbia. Francis Rattenbury, the famous architect of Victoria's Parliament buildings and the Empress Hotel, designed Nelson's impressive courthouse and city hall. Most of the town's historic buildings are open to the public, with free guided (early July through Labor Day) and self-guided tours highlighting Nelson's arts, crafts, and antiques. Nelson may have more artists and craftspeople per capita than any other city in Canada, so expect lots of theater, musical events, art galleries, bookstores, and marble sculptures in parks and along boulevards, plus two colleges. It's a great place for strolling, especially the waterfront, but also take a ride on restored Streetcar 23 along the shores of Kootenay Lake. Seek out local locations for movies you may have seen, films shot in Nelson such as Steve Martin's Roxanne.

Details: *(1 day)*

★★★ CASTLEGAR
At jct. Hwys. 3, 3A and 22; Chamber of Commerce and Travel Infocentre, 1995 Sixth Ave., V1N 4B7, 250/365-6313

On the west bank of the Columbia River, Castlegar is the "crossroads of the Kootenays." It is surrounded by Doukhobor "farm communes." In the 1920s, British Columbia held about 90 such communes, each occupied by about 60 people who cleared the virgin forest to farm, build sawmills, plant orchards and gardens, operate jam factories, and try to remain as independent as possible from outside influences. Their motto was "Toil and a Peaceful Life," and their communes' Russian names translate as "Blessed," "Meadowland," "The Beautiful," and "The Cross." In Brilliant, at the bottom of Airport Hill in Castlegar, is a Doukhobor suspension bridge across the Kootenay River, built of hand-poured concrete in the early 1900s to connect with the old Doukhobor settlement of Ootischeniye ("Valley of Consolation"). Nowadays, many Doukhobors are dispersed and integrated into the mainstream of provincial life.

Visit the Doukhobor Historical Village across from Castlegar Airport just off Highway 3A, 250/365-6622. This group of buildings is a replica of a communal settlement of Doukhobors, a pacifist group of unorthodox Russian immigrants who lived here from 1908 to the 1930s. Descendants guide visitors and explain their customs.

Details: *Open May–Sept. daily 9 A.M.–5 P.M.; $3 adults, $2 ages 6–18, $3 family rate ($3 first adult, $2 each additional member)*

Accessible by a pedestrian suspension bridge, Zuckerberg Island Heritage Park and Chapel House at Seventh Ave. and Eighth St., near the confluence of the Columbia and Kootenay Rivers. Phone Castlegar City Hall, 250/365-7227, or Zuckerberg Island, 250/365-5511.

Details: *Open daily dawn–dusk, Chapel House open noon–dusk, donations (30 minutes)*

★★★ SLOCAN VALLEY ("SILVERY SLOCAN")
Tour along Hwys. 31, 23 and 6. Trail guide available from Valhalla Wilderness Society, Box 224, New Denver, B. C. V0G 1S0; or B.C. Parks, RR3, Nelson, B. C. V1L 5P6; 250/825-4421

Most towns in the Slocan Valley owed their existence to the nineteenth-century silver rush. Mines around Slocan, New Denver, Silverton, and Sandon worked until high production costs and low ore prices ended the boom. Logging, milling, and tourism are now the valley's three main industries. Visit Sandon ghost town, once the wealthiest mining community on the whole continent. A 2-kilometer (1.3-mile) trail from Sandon takes you up through alpine meadows to Idaho Peak Lookout for wonderful views and wildflowers, especially late July through mid-August. In New Denver, visit the **Nikkei Internment Memorial Centre,** 306 Josephine St., 250/358-7288, for the story of Japanese internment during World War II.

For a change of pace, explore part of Valhalla Provincial Park, which encompasses most of Slocan Lake's western shore. In Norse mythology Valhalla was "heaven" (a magnificent palace), and reaching Valhalla was the greatest honor a Norse warrior could attain. Wilderness en-thusiasts say the same about Valhalla Park's rock palaces. Although Highway 6 along Slocan Lake's eastern shore gives superb views of the rugged Valhalla Range mountains to the west, you need a boat to cross the lake and reach the park's main trailheads. Valhalla's most pop-ular hike is the Evans Creek-Beatrice Lake Trail, reached from the vil-lage of Slocan by a connecting trail.

Relax afterward with a soak at **Ainsworth Hot Springs,** 250/229-4212 or 800/668-1171, in a horseshoe-shaped cave with sta-lagmites and stalactites.

Details: *Nikkei Internment Memorial Centre, open May 15—Sept. 15, daily 9:30 A.M.–5 P.M., $4 adults, $3 over 55 and ages 13–17, $2 ages 3–12, $10 families. Ainsworth Hot Springs, open daily 10 A.M.–9:30 P.M., $6 adults, $5.50 ages 13–15, $5.50 over 65, $4 ages 3–12; $10 day passes, $9 ages 13–15, $8.50 over 65, $6.50 ages 3–12. Nakusp Hot Springs, open Jun.–Sept. daily 9:30 A.M.–10 P.M., rest of year, 11 A.M.–9:30 P.M., $5.15 adults, $4.21 over 64 and ages 6–18, $7.48 day pass, $6.55 over 64 and ages 6–18. Whole driving tour approx. 450 km/280 mi. (2 days)*

FITNESS AND RECREATION

Many of the miners who flooded into Kootenay country a century ago—as well as the loggers and railroaders who followed—came from Scandinavia, bringing skiing to this region and building the first lifts. Skiing is the passionate in-terest of current residents; Canada's most famous skier, Nancy Greene, came from Rossland.

For its area, **Red Mountain,** in Rossland, 250/362-7384, 800/663-0105, redmtn@ski-red-com, has more advanced and expert terrain (60 percent) than any other ski resort in British Columbia. Panorama Mountain Village in Panorama, 17.5 kilometers (11 miles) west of Invermere, off Hwy. 95, is a luxury wilderness resort that has the second-highest vertical drop in B.C. next to Whistler-Blackcomb, with daily helicopter ski packages, 250/342-6941, 800/663-2929, paninfo@panoramaresort, www.panoramaresort.com.

Golfing is big in the Kootenays, and few places have better scenery. Courses carved from the forest are surrounded by towering mountains punctuated with shimmering glacier-fed lakes. Some offer RV facilities and other course-side ac-commodation that allows you to golf longer. **Kokanee Springs Golf Resort** Box 96, Crawford Bay, V0B 1E0, 250/227-9226 or 800/979-7999, sets the stan-dard. New in 1999 is the **Greywolf at Panorama** golf course, 800/663-2929, www.panoramaresort.com.

CANADIAN MOUNTAIN HOLIDAYS

The next best thing to dying and going to heaven has got to be a heli-hiking trip in the Kootenays with Canadian Mountain Holidays.

Each day, you are transported by helicopter to a mountaintop ridge to start your hike. Depending on the terrain, and your interests and abilities, this may be for an hour or a day. Try rock or mountain climbing, too. Needless to say, it's very satisfying to be on the roof of Canada surrounded by glaciers, snow-capped peaks, glistening lakes, gurgling boulder streams and alpine meadows . . . the Canada everybody expects to see. Later, back comes the helicopter to whisk you to the lodge.

You may stay at the one lodge or you may go lodge-hopping—by chopper, of course. The lodges match the beauty of the mountains: many have stone fireplaces, natural wood furniture, sundecks, saunas, a warm friendly ambiance, and healthy gourmet cuisine.

Trips begin at Calgary and Banff, then 5- to 8-day packages are available, based on staying at one or more of the following lodges: Bobbie Burns and Bugaboo Lodges in the Purcell Mountains, Cariboo Lodge and Valemount Lodge in the Cariboo Mountains, and Adamant Lodge in the Selkirk Mountains. Peak season is July and August; prices range from about $1,500 (5-day) to $3,000 (8-day) adventure vacations. Canadian Mountain Holidays Heli-Hiking/Heli-Skiing, Box 1660 Banff, Alberta, Canada T0L 0C0, 403/762-7100, www.cmhhike.com, www.cmhmountaineering.com.

Abundant lakes, streams, and rivers give Kootenay country an edge for boating and fishing. Christina Lake on the western boundary could well be the clearest, warmest lake in the province. Some of the largest freshwater sport fish in North America are found in the ice-free waters of Kootenay Lake, including the largest breed of rainbow trout in the world. Other fishing hot spots are Arrow Lakes, and Columbia and Kootenay Rivers, where you can fly-fish for sturgeon, walleye, and kokanee salmon.

The many parks and trails in this region allow a variety of hiking and climbing opportunities. Try **Valhalla Provincial Park, Kokanee Glacier Provincial Park, Top of the World Provincial Parks,** and the **Pur-**

cell **Wilderness Conservancy.** Further north, try **Mount Revelstoke National Park; Yoho National Park**—a great family hike is the 5-kilo-meter (3.1-mile) Emerald Lake Circuit; and **Mount Robson Provincial Park** (Robson is the Canadian Rockies' highest peak). For a different kind of hiking, go for a guided spelunking adventure in **Cody Caves Provincial Park,** near Ainsworth Hot Springs. For information, contact Kokanee Creek Provincial Park, RR3, Nelson, British Columbia V1L 5P6, 250/825-3500 or 250/353-7425.

After days spent on these activities, the Kootenay has a variety of hot springs for relaxation; **Ainsworth Hot Springs,** Box 1268, V0G 1A0, 250/229-4212, 800/668-1171, reservations@hotnaturally.com, www.hotnaturally.com; **Fairmont Hot Springs,** Box 10, V0B 1L0, 250/345-6311, info@fairmontresort.com, www.fairmontresort.com,); and **Radium Hot Springs,** Kootenay National Park, 800/767-1611.

FOOD

In the 1970s, the Kootenays attracted hippies and alternative lifestyle seekers, who have left their mark on the region's restaurants. You may not find a lot of high-end fine dining, but reasonably priced good food, much of it vegetarian, is served in inviting and intriguing places.

Due to its large Doukhobor population, Russian food is readily available, especially in Grand Forks and Castlegar. Don't skimp on the borscht, a regional specialty.

Nelson has many good eateries. The well-respected "funky-moving-to-classy" **All Seasons Restaurant,** 620 Herridge Ln., 250/352-0101, offers what it calls its "left coast inland cuisine" menu that covers all of Western Canada. Meals are memorable and emphasize local and vegetarian ingredients, the portions are mountain-sized, the prices fair, the wine list award-winning in competition with the best of Vancouver hotels, and the chefs are topnotch. The restaurant is open every night from 5 P.M., plus Sunday brunch from 10 A.M. Don't miss it. Another well-loved Nelson restaurant is **Fiddlers Green** at 2710 Lower 6 Mile Rd., 250/825-4466, lynda@netidea.com. It is set in a 1929 heritage home surrounded by perennial gardens. Vegetarians like this restaurant. Try its baked eggplant stuffed with ratatouille and feta cheese. The **Rice Bowl** at 301 Baker St., 250/354-4129, is now one of the hottest places to eat. Its floor-to-ceiling windows on the main street make it a good place to hang out and watch people. It specializes in sushi, whole grains and organic foods-organic venison from the north is the latest dish on the menu. Try the hot and sour coconut Thai soup. **Max and Irma's,** 515A Kootenay St., 250/352-2332, is a good mid-range restaurant noted for its thin crust pizzas and calzones (try smoked salmon and peppercorn pizza).

In Castlegar, you'll find **Gabriel's,** a French restaurant at 1432 Columbia St., 250/365-6028. It's comfortable atmosphere makes for fine dining, definitely the "in" spot to take visitors. Families seeking good, plain and affordable food-and the biggest menu in town-will like **Gardeli's Restaurant** (and pub next door) at 1502 Columbia St., 250/365-7006. It's a fun place with neon-lit cartoon figures on the walls, such as a kangaroo with a bowling pin in its paw. **Café Friends,** 1102 Third St., 250/365-0846, is a popular lunch spot in Castlegar. Try the borscht.

In Rossland, budgies (the new name for present-day hippies) like the food, the portions, and the prices at the **Sunshine Café,** 2116 Columbia St., 250/362-7630. Have the popular budgie burger (grilled boneless chicken breast with ham and cheese). **Olive Oyl's,** 2167 Washington St., 250/362-5322, is known for "incredibly good food" and gets rave reviews. Snack while you read.

In New Denver, the unpretentious, but popular **Apple Tree** in a century-old building (with tilted floors) at 210 Sixth Ave., 250/358-2691, is an excellent choice for coffee, homemade soups, sandwiches, and baked goods. Ask for a bowl of Bombay Bisque. Open 7 A.M. to 4 P.M.

Eat around an actual tree at the popular **Treehouse Restaurant,** 419 Front St., Kaslo, 250/353-2955. It's the place everybody in Kaslo heads to first. It epitomizes the Kootenay spirit—a comfortable ambiance and simple food that tastes good. Another popular choice in Kaslo is **Sternwheelers Family Pool Parlour,** 344 Front St., 250/353-7422, which has the advantage of tables on the Kootenay lakefront in summer. Another restaurant very popular with families is the **Colander Restaurant,** 1475 Cedar St., 250/364-1816. For not much more than $10, you get all-you-can-eat spaghetti with two pieces of chicken, two meatballs, jo-jos (potatoes), salad, bread, and tea or coffee. The owners are proud that the Colander was chosen 12th out of 40 of the best places to dine out in a recent *Beautiful BC Magazine* competition.

LODGING

The Kootenay isn't known for its four-star luxury resorts, but there is an abundance of charming, old world chalets, cottages, and inns; plenty of motels; and lots of basic accommodations. Given the nature of this region, it's easy to choose something cozy. Compared to the rest of British Columbia, and especially the world-renowned Rockies, prices are moderate. Ask if golf or ski packages are available. Reservations are recommended during July and August, especially in Nelson and Cranbrook. Here are some of the more distinctive lodgings.

THE KOOTENAYS (BRITISH COLUMBIA ROCKIES)

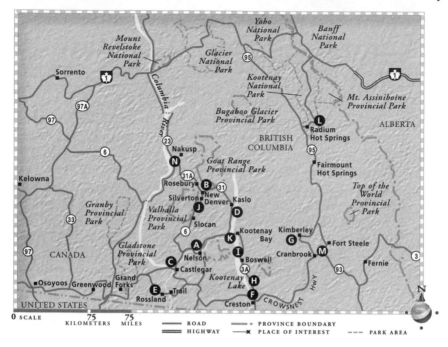

Legend: ROAD — HIGHWAY — PROVINCE BOUNDARY — PLACE OF INTEREST — PARK AREA

0 SCALE 75 KILOMETERS 75 MILES

FOOD

- **Ⓐ** All Seasons Restaurant
- **Ⓑ** Apple Tree
- **Ⓒ** Café Friends
- **Ⓓ** Colander Restaurant
- **Ⓐ** Fiddlers Green
- **Ⓒ** Gabriel's
- **Ⓒ** Gardeli's
- **Ⓐ** Max and Irma's
- **Ⓔ** Olive Oyl's
- **Ⓐ** Rice Bowl
- **Ⓓ** Sternwheelers Family Pool Parlour
- **Ⓔ** Sunshine Café
- **Ⓓ** Treehouse Restaurant

LODGING

- **Ⓕ** Bavarian Orchard Motel

LODGING (continued)

- **Ⓖ** Boundary Street Bed and Breakfast
- **Ⓗ** Cathan's Grand Escape B&B
- **Ⓐ** Dancing Bear Inn
- **Ⓘ** Destiny Bay Resort
- **Ⓐ** Emory House B&B
- **Ⓐ** Heritage Inn
- **Ⓖ** House Alpenglow Bed & Breakfast
- **Ⓐ** Inn the Garden B&B
- **Ⓙ** Mistaya Country Inn B&B
- **Ⓑ** Ram's Head Inn
- **Ⓑ** Sweet Dreams Guest House
- **Ⓚ** Tara Shanti Retreat
- **Ⓚ** Wedgwood Manor Country Inn

CAMPING

- **Ⓛ** Canyon RV Resort
- **Ⓔ** Christina Lakeside Resort RV Park
- **Ⓜ** Cranbrook City Centre Campground
- **Ⓝ** Halcyon Hot Springs
- **Ⓐ** Kokanee Creek Provincial Park Campground
- **Ⓐ** Nelson Tourist Park

Note: Items with the same letter are located in the same area.

In Nelson, the **Heritage Inn,** centrally situated at 422 Vernon St., 250-352-5331, info@heritageinn.org, www.heritageinn.org, is a big, old hotel with period rooms (1898) that are sensibly priced. Its Library Lounge is a popular meeting place. Also close to downtown in a beautifully restored Victorian heritage home is **Inn the Garden B&B,** 408 Victoria St., 250/352-5331, 800/596-BEDS (2337), www.innthegarden.com. It includes a three-bedroom self-contained cottage. Everybody thinks highly of **Emory House B&B,** another beautiful heritage home overlooking Kootenay Lake at 811 Vernon St., V1L 4G3, 250/352-7007, www.bbcanada.com/189.html. Hostelers and other budget-conscious travelers get excellent value at **Dancing Bear Inn,** 155 Baker St., 250/352-7573, dbear@netidea.com. It's a warm, friendly place where guests cook in the communal kitchen, swap stories around the fireplace, and join organized activity programs.

Typical of Kootenay charm with a European flavor is **Tara Shanti Retreat,** 134 Riondel Rd., Kootenay Bay, 250/227-9616, 800/811-3888, tara@netidea.com. www.tarashanti.bc.ca. It has a sun deck, sauna, and hot tub with views of Kootenay Lake and Kokanee Glacier. **Wedgwood Manor Country Inn,** 16002 Crawford Creek Rd., Box 135, Crawford Bay, V0B 1E0, 250/227-9233, 800/862-0022, www.bctravel.net/wedgwood, is a Victorian-era house on a 20.2-hectare (50-acre) country estate with extensive gardens and hiking and bicycling trails. Rates are reasonable and include complimentary breakfast and evening tea. Open April to mid October.

Destiny Bay Resort, 11935 Highway 3A, Box 6, Boswell, 250/223-8234 or 800/818 6633, destinyb@kootenay.com, www.crestonbc.com/destiny, has sod-roofed cottages with lake-view verandahs overlooking Kootenay Lake. No TV or phone ensures tranquillity. The price seems high for the Kootenay, but includes a value-added gourmet four-course dinner and a buffet breakfast for two.

Mistaya Country Inn B&B, Highway 6, Box 28, Silverton, 250/358-7787, is a secluded bed-and-breakfast ranch on 36 hectares (90 acres) in the Slocan Valley. It offers easy hiking access to Valhalla and Kokanee Glacier Provincial Parks and is near Slocan Lake for swimming, canoeing, and fishing. Rates are very affordable. **Sweet Dreams Guest House,** a restored heritage house on Slocan Lake, 702 Eldorado Ave., 250/358-2415, jbus@wkpowerlink.com, www2.wkpowerlink.com/sweetdreams, has romantic views of the Valhalla wilderness with equally reasonable rates. Note that bathrooms are shared.

In Rossland, the well-known **Ram's Head Inn** is set in a forest at the base of Red Mountain on Highway 3B, 3 kilometers (2 miles) west of town, Box 636, V0G 1Y0, 250/362-9577. If you are skiing, ask for package deals. For Creston, choose between two orchard settings: the **Bavarian Orchard Motel,** 3205 Highway 3, Box 1364, V0B1G0, 250/428-9935, 800/663-9544; or **Cathan's**

Grand Escape B&B, 4749 Lower Wynndel Rd. RR1 Site 23B, Box 17, Wynndel, V0B 2N0, the best of Canadian and Dutch hospitality with lots to do-golf, canoeing, birding and fishing.

Beautiful Kimberley has two highly recommended B&Bs. **Boundary Street Bed and Breakfast,** 89 Boundary St., V1A 2H4, 250/427-3510, is in a heritage home within walking distance of the Platzl, You get a private bathroom, a shared sitting room, and a three-course breakfast for an affordable price. The Bavarian-styled **House Alpenglow Bed & Breakfast,** at 3 Alpenglow Court, 250/427-0273, 877/257/3645, alpenglow@rockies.net, is also within walking distance of the Platzl and Trickle Creek Golf Resort. All rooms share a sitting room, enclosed patio, hot tub, and TV room.

Visit www.bcrockies.com for more information on accommodation in this region.

CAMPING

Provincial and national parks provide the best campgrounds in that their locations are selected to be near hiking, swimming, boating, or fishing. Most campsites have road access, but you'll have to boat, ski, or hike in to wilderness backcountry spots. Sites may not have electrical hookups or shower facilities, but most parks have developed hiking trails, and parks officers offer excellent free interpretive programs. It's wise to reserve space in July and August. For provincial campground reservations anywhere in the province, keep handy the **B.C. Parks' Discover Camping** phone number: 800/689-9025. Another useful number to find out if a campsite is full or not, is **West Kootenay Parks and Outdoor Recreation District Office,** 250/825-4421 or visit www.camping.bc.ca.

The Kootenay is popular camping country, so many commercial private campgrounds stay open in spring and fall as well as summer. Keep in mind, too, the B.C. Forest Service wilderness campsites. For maps and other information, write to **Regional Recreation Officer,** Ministry of Forests, 518 Lake Street, Nelson, British Columbia V1L 4C6, or call 250/354-6200.

Christina Lake at the western boundary of the Kootenay's region is a very popular camping area. A good location for RV vehicles-1200 feet of private sandy beach and fully serviced sites-is **Christina Lakeside Resort RV Park,** 1835 Highway 3, Christina Lake V0H 1E2, 250/447-9213, clresort@wkpowerlink.com. If you don't have your own RV, rent one of theirs.

New to Nakusp is **Halcyon Hot Springs,** 68 km (40.8 mi) south of Revelstoke on Highway 23, Box 37, Nakusp, V0G 1R0 250/265-3554, 888/689-4699, halcyon2@cancom.net. It has about everything-lakeshore, hot springs, campsites, cabins and RV sites, wellness treatments, hiking and horseback riding, boats, skis, and snowmobiles-obviously open year-round. The **Canyon RV Resort on Sinclair Creek,** Box 279, Radium Hot Springs, V0A 1M0, 250/347-9564, is prettily situated in a private little valley right in town, close to hot pools and golf courses, with lawns, gardens, and lots of flowers.

It can be handy to have a campsite close to town. **Nelson Tourist Park,** 90 High St., 250/352-7618 (summer), 250/352-5511 (winter), www.city.nelson.bc.ca, is downtown and open April through October. Seniors get a discount and children under 14 are free. **Cranbrook City Centre Campground,** 250/426-2162 is within walking distance of a mall and golf course, and has both indoor and outdoor pools, and a softball field. It's open March through November. Note that no credit cards accepted, but kids stay free.

Kokanee Creek Provincial Park Campground, on Highway 3A, RR3, Site 8, Comp 5, 20 km (12 mi) east of Nelson, 250/825-3500, is popular. It has sandy beaches, nature trails, a playground, and a visitor center.

Crescent Pass Route:

From Cranbrook, go east along Highway 3 to Fernie and Sparwood, then to Coleman and Blairmore, and on to either Waterton Lakes National Park, Calgary, or the Drumheller area. This road winds (and I mean winds) through some of the most spectacular mountain scenery, going over Crowsnest Pass (1,396 meters/4,580 feet). This is one of only three passes that cut through the Canadian Rockies. About 35 kilometers (22 miles) inside the Alberta border is the town site of Frank, which was obliterated in 1903 by a 74-million-ton rockslide. The slide tore off the top of Turtle Mountain and swept 1.6 kilometers (1 mile) across the valley to bury roads, rail lines, homes, and whole farms, leaving the area so unstable that the remaining mountain continues to be monitored.

Kootenay Lake Route:

From Creston drive Highway 3A north along the eastern shore of Kootenay Lake to Kootenay Bay and take the free ferry across the lake to Balfour. Go north again on Highway 31, which parallels the lake's western shore for 70 km (44 mi) to the community of Meadow Creek. The road becomes gravel, but is still good in all weather, and

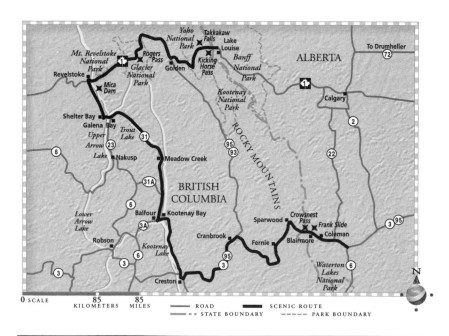

skirts Trout Lake to Galena Bay, where you take another free ferry ride to Shelter Bay (check for ferry times before beginning). Drive north on Highway 23 to Revelstoke.

A brief detour will take you to Mica Dam, for free guided tours at 11 A.M. and 1:30 P.M. or self-guided tours daily: from 8 A.M. TO 8 P.M. mid-June through mid-September; 9 A.M. to 5 P.M. mid-Sept through October 31 and mid-March through mid-June. Here are lighted displays, topographical maps, and audiovisuals on the design, construction, and function of the dam, 250/837-6515.

Roger's Pass Route:
From Revelstoke, follow the Trans-Canada Highway via Mount Revelstoke National Park and Roger's Pass to Glacier National Park and Golden, then through Yoho National Park and Kicking Horse Pass to Lake Louise. A mini-side trip in Yoho Park will take you to Takkakaw Falls, at 305 meters (1,000 feet) it's the highest sheer waterfull in Canada. "Yoho" is an exclamation of wonder in the Kootenay Indians' language, and translates, roughly, to "O wowee!"

14
BANFF NATIONAL PARK (INCLUDING LAKE LOUISE)

The transcontinental railway tracks were edging their way toward the forbidding Rocky Mountains in 1883 when three workers discovered hot water simmering in the ground. Banff was born—and so was tourism! Two years later, the area was protected as a tourist mecca to help pay for the new Canadian Pacific Railway. Banff is the oldest and most visited of Canada's national parks, and, like Jasper, it is a World Heritage Site in recognition of its outstanding scenery.

At 1,372 meters (4,530 feet), Banff is the highest townsite in the country. It sits beside the Bow River, cradled by mile-high mountain peaks: to the north, the Cascade Mountains and Mount Norquay; to the south, the Sulphur Mountains; to the east, Mount Rundle. Chateau Lake Louise and the Victoria Glacier are 58 kilometers (36 miles) to the northwest. Add a red canoe and a mountie in his red serge, and you have the world's view of Canada. It is a picture-perfect scene that attracts more than 4 million visitors a year.

A PERFECT DAY IN BANFF/LAKE LOUISE

One day in this area is like offering only one selection from a newly opened box of mixed chocolates! Try catching the 7:30 A.M. eight-minute gondola ride up Sulphur Mountain and hiking one of the trails to build a good appetite for breakfast at The Summit, Canada's highest restaurant. Then drive Highway 1A, known as the Bow Valley Parkway, to the village of Lake Louise.

BANFF NATIONAL PARK

At Lake Louise, take an obligatory picture of the famous turquoise-colored lake from the Château, then rent a red canoe and paddle Louise's waters, enjoying a closer look at Victoria Glacier. Later in the afternoon, drive the 14-kilometer (8.4-mile) road to Moraine Lake, set below the Valley of Ten Peaks, a lake that rivals Lake Louise in both beauty and fame.

It would be a tossup whether to stay at Château Lake Louise that night for the dawn over Victoria Glacier and the lodge's special early bird breakfast, or return to the Banff Springs Hotel for a pampered soak in its Solace Spa. If you are not going to spend the night in the $3,000 Presidential Suite, at least walk through the hotel's legendary halls.

ORIENTATION

You can drive, fly and drive, bus, or take a train to Banff, but once there, you'll want to get around in a car, then walk, canoe, ski, or climb. Banff boasts that you can get there from almost anywhere in the world in less than 24 hours.

Calgary, 120 kilometers (75 miles) to the east via the all-weather, four-lane Highway 1 (Trans-Canada Hwy.) is a popular gateway to the Banff townsite. Fly to Calgary International Airport then rent a car or take a shuttle bus for the 90-minute journey via Canmore. From British Columbia, take Highway 1, the

Trans-Canada; from Jasper, take Highway 93; and from Red Deer and Rocky Mountain House, take Highway 11.

If coming by bus, there is scheduled van and motor coach service several times a day from Calgary International Airport and downtown Calgary to Banff and Lake Louise. A spectacular way to arrive is by train from Vancouver and Kamloops, B.C. Between May and October, Rocky Mountaineer Railtours runs two-day sightseeing trips by daylight through the Rockies. Phone Rocky Mountaineer Railtours, 800/665-7245, reservation@rkymtnrail.com.

BANFF TOWNSITE SIGHTSEEING HIGHLIGHTS

The scenery in Banff National Park is spectacular, but the town of Banff, sitting beside the Bow River at the base of Sulphur and Tunnel mountains, is unable to expand because of national park policy. Consequently, it is very crowded, especially in summer. Explore the Banff Springs Hotel, take a gondola ride up Sulphur Mountain, soak for a while in the Upper Hot Springs Pool, take a photo of Cascade Mountain from Cascade Gardens looking down Banff Avenue, take in a museum or two if it is raining—then drive out of town. In winter, take advantage of the snow and ski.

Useful contacts: Banff Visitor Centre, 224 Banff Ave. Banff, T0L 0C0, 403/762-1550; Banff/Lake Louise Tourism Bureau, 223 Banff Ave. Banff, T0L 0C0, 403/762-8421; Banff National Park, Box 900, Banff, T0L 0C0, www.worlddweb.com/ParksCanada-Banff/parks.html.

★★★★ **BANFF SKI AREAS: BANFF MOUNT NORQUAY AND BANFF SUNSHINE VILLAGE**
Banff Mount Norquay, Box 219, Ste. 7000, Banff, T0L 0C0, 403/762-4421, info@banffnorquay.com, www.banffnorquay. com. Banff Sunshine Village, Box 1510, Banff, T0L 0C0, 403/762-6500, reservations@skibanff.com, www.skibanff.com
Banff Mount Norquay, 6.5 kilometers (4 miles) from Banff townsite is the park's oldest ski resort and the choice of local families, but it has been totally redesigned and expanded with a new timber frame day lodge at the base of the mountain and a new, improved snowboard park on Mount Standish. The season spans from early December to mid-April. Banff Sunshine Village is the highest ski resort in the Canadian Rockies and has the only "ski-in, ski-out" resort hotel (Sunshine Inn) in Banff National Park. Banff Sunshine Village season runs mid-November to late May, which rivals Lake Louise. It wins awards for Canada's best snow.

Details: Banff Sunshine Village open mid-Nov.–late May, lifts $46 adult, $15 children 6–12, $38 student/senior, packages available. Banff Mount Norquay open early Dec.–mid-Apr., lifts $35 adult, $15 children 12 and under, packages available. Free daily tours of the mountains. (1 day per area)

★★★★ BANFF SPRINGS HOTEL
Box 960, T0L 0C0, 400 Spray Ave., 403/762-2211 or 800/441-1414

This imposing stone castle in the clouds—another of the grand "don't miss" Canadian Pacific hotels—is a blend of German baronial and French château charm. It is a National Historic Site. Its past clientele was the rich and famous—Winston Churchill, Marilyn Monroe, and the King of Siam. It still is, but current guests are more likely to be early rising tour bus passengers. In 1885, the first visitors went to Banff to "test the waters," that is, the natural mineral waters springing out of a cave at the base of Sulphur Mountain. In 1995, the hotel added The Solace-The Spa at Banff Springs, 403/762-1772, which covers 3,270 square meters (35,000 square feet) and cost $12 million to build. Services range from simple massages to aroma- or hydrotherapy to facials that cost $60 and more.

Incredibly distracting mountains and a resident herd of elk are two of the natural hazards to playing golf on The Banff Springs Golf Course, 403/762-6801. The hotel is a city in itself. For the indoor-inclined, it has 17 restaurants, 50 shops and boutiques; and elegant historic rooms. For the outdoor-oriented, it has its own horse corral, 403/762-4551, as well as swimming pools, saunas, whirlpools, health club, and tennis courts. Pick up the brochure *Banff Springs Hotel Walking Tour,* conveniently divided into time slots from 10 minutes to one hour, and use it to explore the place. An expensive place to stay, but for a once-in-a-lifetime splurge, well worth it.

Details: Open year-round. Explore package deals and off-season discounts.

★★★★ BANFF SULPHUR MOUNTAIN GONDOLA
At the top of Mountain Ave., 3.2 km (2 mi) south of downtown Banff, Box 1258, Banff, T0L 0C0, 403/762-2523, amoberg@banffgondola.com, www.banffgondola.com

The glass-enclosed Sulphur Mountain Gondola is an eight-minute ride up Sulphur Mountain to 2,451 meters (8,040 feet). At the summit, en-

BANFF NATIONAL PARK (INCLUDING LAKE LOUISE)

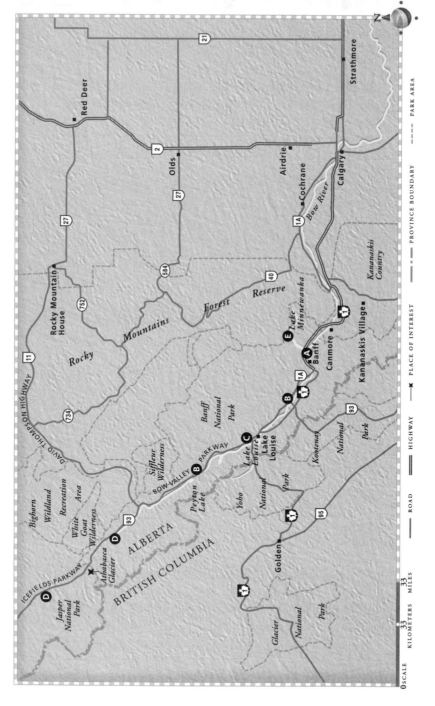

joy the view of surrounding mountains and valleys or the miniaturized town beneath. You can stroll the promenade walkway, hike an alpine trail or dine at the Summit or Panorama Restaurants.

Details: *Open May 8–Jun. 18 8 a.m.–8 p.m., Jun. 19–Aug 22, 7:30 A.M.–9 P.M., otherwise varies; $12 adults, $6 children. (30 minutes to 2 hours)*

★★★ UPPER HOT SPRINGS POOL
To the right along Mountain Ave., 4.5 km (2.8 mi) from Banff townsite, 403/762-1515, 403/760-2500 (massage)
Bathe in the 40-degree C (104-degree F) large outdoor pool while gazing up at Mount Rundle. This site has been renovated with chang-

---

SIGHTS
- **A** Banff Ski Areas: Banff Mount Norquay and Banff Sunshine Village
- **A** Banff Springs Hotel
- **A** Banff Sulphur Mountain Gondola
- **B** Bow Valley Parkway
- **A** Buffalo Nations Luxton Museum
- **C** Château Lake Louise
- **D** Icefields Parkway (Hwy. 93)
- **C** Lake Louise (the lake)
- **C** Lake Louise (village and ski area)
- **E** Lake Minnewanka
- **A** Upper Hot Springs Pool

FOOD
- **A** Alberta Room
- **C** Alpine Lounge
- **C** Baker Creek Bistro
- **C** Brewster Cowboy's BBQ and Dance Barn
- **A** Bumper's the Beef House

FOOD (continued)
- **A** Craig's Way Station
- **C** Edelweiss
- **F** Glacier Saloon
- **C** Glacier Scoop
- **A** Grizzly House
- **A** Koffie Huis
- **A** Le Bistro Restaurant
- **C** Moraine Lake Lodge Atrium Dining Room
- **A** Parls's Restaurant
- **A** Pavillon
- **G** Puppy Room
- **A** Restaurant Le Beaujolais
- **A** Ristorante Classico
- **A** Rob Roy
- **A** Samurai
- **C** Station Restaurant
- **A** Ticino Swiss Italian Restaurant
- **C** Tom Wilson Dining Room
- **C** Victoria Dining Room
- **A** Waldhaus
- **C** Walliser Stube

LODGING
- **A** Banff Springs Hotel
- **A** Banff International Hostel
- **C** Baker Creek Chalets and Guest Lodge
- **A** Castle Mountain Hostel
- **C** Chateau Lake Louise
- **A** Douglas Fir Resort and Chalets
- **A** Eleanor's House
- **C** Lake Louise International Hostel and Alpine Centre
- **C** Moraine Lake Lodge and Cabins
- **F** Post Hotel
- **C** Skoki Lodge
- **A** Y Mountain Lodge

CAMPING
- **C** Lake Louise 1
- **C** Lake Louise 2
- **A** Tunnel Mountain Trailer Court
- **A** Tunnel Mountain Village 1
- **A** Tunnel Mountain Village 2

Note: Items with the same letter are located in the same area.

---

ing rooms, bathing suit and towel rentals, lockers and therapeutic massage (reserve ahead), an interpretive display, and wheelchair accessibility. The co-ed Pleiades Spa offers wrap bed, steam room, and aromatherapy.

Details: *Opens for the summer on May 24, 10 A.M.–10 P.M., Fri.–Sat. to 11 P.M.; $7 adults, $6 seniors and ages 3–16, free children under 3, $20 family rate, reduced rates rest of year. (1 hour)*

★★ BUFFALO NATIONS LUXTON MUSEUM
1 Birch Ave., 403/762-2388

Kids will love the stockade fence enclosing this museum. The history of Native Indians of the Canadian Rockies and Northern Plains is told through life-size scenes depicting teepees, travois, and ornamental costumes. Wheelchair accessible.

Details: *Open summer daily 9 A.M.–7 A.M., winter 1–5 P.M.; $5 adults, $3.75 seniors and students, $2 children, free under 6. Adults $5, seniors and students $3.75, children $2, under 6 free, $11.50 families. (1 hour)*

SIGHTSEEING HIGHLIGHTS BETWEEN BANFF AND LAKE LOUISE

★★★★ BOW VALLEY PARKWAY (Hwy 1A)

This parkway is a more leisurely route between Banff and Lake Louise than the Trans-Canada Highway 1 that parallels it on the other side of the Bow River Valley. It is only 58 kilometers (34 miles) long, but drive it slowly to savor the views and wildlife. Watch for elk, deer, bighorn sheep, coyotes and bears. Animals are best viewed at dawn or dusk. The road from its eastern access to Johnston Canyon is closed to the public 6 P.M.–9 A.M. March through June to allow resident wildlife a chance to reproduce without human disturbance. For most of the route, the speed limit is 60 kilometers per hour (36 mph).

Not to be missed is Johnston Canyon and two waterfalls, 7 kilometers (3.5 miles) southeast of Castle Junction, the halfway point at which you have the opportunity to loop back to Banff. Walk the trails and the spectacular boardwalk anchored to the canyon wall.

Details: *You'll need 90 minutes to return to the upper waterfalls and three hours to return to the Ink Pots brilliantly colored mineral springs. During winter, White Mountain Tours, 403/678-4099, guides ice walks into the canyon. (3+ hours)*

★★★★ **ICEFIELDS PARKWAY (HWY. 93)**
Scenic road link between Lake Louise, 229 km (138 mi) north to Jasper

The Icefields Parkway has been called the most scenic mountain road in North America, some say the world. It follows the valleys of the North Saskatchewan, Sunwapta and Athabasca Rivers, climbs two passes, (Bow and Sunwapta), straddles the ice fields and glaciers of the Continental Divide, spans both Banff and Jasper National Parks, and provides the backdrop for a welter of wildlife such as mountain sheep and goats.

Stop at all the marked viewpoints if you can, but definitely take a photograph of the intense aquamarine of Peyto Lake at the Bow Summit; step onto the ice cap at the Columbia Icefield, and have a look at the new Parks Canada Icefield Centre (See JASPER).

Details: *Open year-round, but use snow tires and carry chains in winter; book a 90-minute snow coach tour with Columbia Icefield Snocoach Tours, Box 1140, Banff, T0L 0C0, 403/762-6735, 888/350-7433, icefield@brewster.ca, www.brewster.ca, open May 1–Oct. 15, 9 A.M.–5 P.M.; $23.50 adults, $5 children. For more info contact Lake Louise Visitor Centre, Samson Mall 403/522-3833. (half to 1 day)*

LAKE LOUISE SIGHTSEEING HIGHLIGHTS

★★★★ **CHÂTEAU LAKE LOUISE**
5 km west of the Lake Louise Village and Hwy. 1. Address: Canadian Pacific Hotels, Lake Louise, T0L 1E0, 403/522-3511, 800/441-1414, cll@cphotels.ca, www.cphotels.ca

Like Banff Springs Hotel, Château Lake Louise is one of the grand hotels that one must at least look at and walk through, even if one can't afford the stay. Recently renovated, it has the top rating of any hotel in Canada. Everything about this 515-roomed hotel is grand and grandiose. Walk its halls, stroll its gardens, dine in one of its restaurants, browse through its arcade of shops.

Details: *Open year-round. (1 hour)*

★★★★ **LAKE LOUISE (THE LAKE)**
Located 4.5 km (2.8 mi) west of the Transcanada Hwy. 1, near its jct. with Hwy. 1A and Hwy. 93

This lake is a rare jewel, the most famous glacial lake in the Canadian Rockies. It's the quintessential image of Canada—stunning turquoise water framed in front by the waving orange and yellow poppies of stately Château Lake Louise in summer (ice carvings in winter) and set against a spectacular tiara of glaciers and mountains. It's probably the most photographed scene in the Rockies. CPR scout Tom Wilson originally named it Emerald Lake for its emerald green and aquamarine color. The name was changed later to Louise to honor Queen Victoria's daughter, and the glacier that rises behind it was renamed to honor the queen herself. One of the most popular trails goes 3 kilometers (2 miles) around the lake to the foot of the glacier. Two other trails lead to teahouses, an appropriate reward for your walk.

Details: *(half to 1 day)*

★★★★ **LAKE LOUISE (VILLAGE AND SKI AREA)**
Bounded by the Bow River and Hwy. 1 at the jct. of Hwys. 1 and 1A., 56 km north of Banff, 186 km from Calgary.
Lake Louise Village (pop. 1,500) is a quiet little sister to Banff (pop. 4,000). It has a handful of small hotels, chalets and condos, a youth hostel, 20 secluded bars and restaurants (many within the lodgings), one mall, and one stoplight. From June through September, get the aerial view, a wide angle view of the lake and a telescopic look at the village's surrounding glaciers and mountains, by taking the 14-minute ride with Lake Louise Summer Sightseeing Lift, 403/522-3555, up Whitehorse Mountain in a glass-enclosed gondola, a bubble chair, or an open chair. At the top, explore trails and nature displays, or take a guided walk. The Whitehorse Lodge has a licensed teahouse and an outdoor terrace. Back at the base of the gondola, celebrate the scenery with a meal at the new log Lodge of the Ten Peaks.

Moraine Lake, located 15 kilometers (9 miles) southwest of the village of Lake Louise at the end of Moraine Lake Road, is a must-see and rivals the beauty of Lake Louise. It is a stunning emerald set beneath 10 glaciated peaks (Valley of the Ten Peaks). At one time the much-photographed view of Moraine Lake appeared on the Canadian $20 bill. For close-up views of the Ten Peaks, walk the 1.5 km (1 mi) lakeshore trail. The Larch Valley Trail 2.4 kilometers (1.5 miles) further on is popular in fall when the larch trees turn golden.

In winter, Lake Louise Ski Area is consistently voted as North America's most scenic ski area. There's considerable rivalry between Banff and Lake Louise. Lake Louise boasts the largest natural snow fields spread across four mountains of the Continental Divide, backed by Canada's largest snowmaking system, giving it a six month ski season from early November to early May. It prides itself on Alberta's highest lift capacity (11 interconnecting lifts): if you can't get out of the base area in ten minutes, you'll get a refund. Shuttles between accommodations and the ski area, minutes from the town, are complimentary. Contact the Parks Canada Visitor Centre (Lake Louise Visitor Reception Centre) for more information 403/522-3763, Skiing Louise Ltd. Box 5, Lake Louise, T0L 1E0, 403/522-3555, reservations 800/258-7669, vertical@skilouise.com, www.skilouise.com

Details: *Summer sightseeing lift open daily Jun.–Sept., 8:30 A.M.–6 P.M. Jun. 1–30 and from 8 A.M.–6 P.M. Jul.–Aug., 8:30 A.M.–6 P.M. Sept. 1–26; ride only rates: $10.95 adults, $9.95 seniors and students, $7.95 youth 6–15, free under 5. Ten Peaks Restaurant open 7:30 A.M. year-round. Ski lifts: adult $46 a day, children $15 a day, packages available. Free daily tours of the ski mountains.*

★★ LAKE MINNEWANKA
Located 8 km (5 mi) northeast of Banff on Lake Minnewanka Loop Road.

This is the largest lake in Banff National Park, measuring 19.7 kilometers (11.8 miles), and the only one where power boats are permitted. The lake, and especially the boat tour, allows you to see spectacular scenery in a comfortable way with the chance to do some fishing on the side. Minnewanka Boat Tours, 403/762-3473, takes you on a 90-minute cruise in heated, 48-passenger, glass-enclosed launches to Devil's Gap beneath mountain peaks and hoodoos, and often past deer and bighorn sheep. It also offers half- and full-day fishing tours, as does **Banff Fishing Unlimited,** 403/762-4936. The **Boathouse at Lake Minnewanka,** 403/762-3473, rents fishing boats and sells licenses and tackle if you want to do it on your own.

Details: *Cruises leave daily at 10:30 A.M., 12:30, 3, and 5 P.M., mid-May–Oct. with a 7 P.M. sunset cruise in Jul. and Aug.; $26 adults, $13 ages 5–11. (2 hours)*

FITNESS AND RECREATION

Fitness and recreation possibilities are endless in the Banff-Lake Louise area. Summer visitors will enjoy walking, hiking, cycling, canoeing, golfing, kayaking, white-water rafting, horseback-riding, rock climbing, ATV tours, fishing, climbing, helicopter touring, and wildlife viewing. In winter, downhill, helicopter and cross-country skiing, tobogganing, dog-sledding, snowshoeing, and ice-climbing lure thousands. Banff and Lake Louise used to shut down in winter, but now they are all-season playgrounds. There are tours or outfits offering just about everything. For one-stop shopping, try **Banff Adventures Unlimited,** 403/762-4554.

Parks Canada offers interpretive hikes, June through September, 403/762-1550 or 403/762-1500 (Banff) or 403/522-3833 (Lake Louise). Canadian Rockies Mountaineering and Interpretive Hiking Program, a Canadian Pacific Hotels Heritage Program, carries on the Canadian tradition of mountaineering and hiking by offering tours led by professional mountain guides. Pick up a brochure from Banff Springs Hotel or Château Lake Louise (or Jasper Park Lodge), choose your tour, and meet your guide. Recommended is The Two Teahouse Tour from Lake Louise. Phone Banff Springs Hotel, 403/762-2211, or Château Lake Louise, 403/522-3511.

The 7 P.M. to 8 P.M. sittings are the busiest, so eat earlier or later if you can. Be sure to reserve at the fancier restaurants, try for window tables, and phone first to check the variable times of operation.

Be very Albertan and go by horse. **Holiday on Horseback,** 403/762-4551, offers hourly to multiday pack trips, breakfast rides, evening steak fries, and overnights. The Explorer is a full-day trip, lunch included. Accommodation in backcountry lodges is provided on longer trips. **Brewster Lake Louise Stables** offer trips to the Plain of Six Glaciers and Lake Agnes Teahouse, all-day trips to Paradise Valley, as well as hourly rides, overnight trips and western barbecues, 403/762-5454.

It's easier to fly, of course. **Alpine Helicopters,** 403/678-4802, based in Canmore, offers reasonably priced flightseeing tours from 20 minutes to one hour. Especially recommended is **CMH Heli-Hiking,** 403/762-7100, which operates multiday helicopter-assisted adventures from its fantastic backcountry lodges west of Banff National Park. Take any chance to get closer to these mountains by hiring a chopper.

The park and Canada's history is not all based on the mountains. River-rafting trips vary from gentle floats down the Bow River to white-water adventures on the Kicking Horse River west of the national parks. Local companies include **Hydra River Guides,** 403/762-4554, **Rocky Mountain Raft Tours,** 403/762-3632, and **Western Canadian Whitewater,** 403/762-8256.

In winter, in addition to skiing and other snow sports, return to the traditions of trappers and mounties by dog sledding. Contact **Mountain Mushers Dog Sled Tours,** 403/762-3647.

FOOD

Although Banff National Park is mecca for the rich and famous, it has well over a hundred restaurants. For an authentic Western meal in the Rockies, take a horseback or covered-wagon ride to a wilderness cookout. Between June and September, **Brewster Cowboy's BBQ and Dance Barn,** 403/522-3511, ext. 1210, or 403/762-5454 offers a ride around Lake Louise followed by a barbecued steak dinner for a reasonable price. Holiday on Horseback, 403/762-4551, takes guests to Sundance Canyon for a Mountain Breakfast Ride, a covered-wagon luncheon cookout, or an evening steak fry. Steaks are accompanied by cowboy beans, spuds, and Caesar salad.

Banff has far more to chose from than Lake Louise. Starting at the top, find something to your liking at the Banff Springs Hotel, Spray Ave., 403/762-6860. The **Rob Roy** is the hotel's signature venue and offers a panoramic view of the Bow Valley, along with nightly entertainment and dancing. Dress up for this one and be prepared to pay upscale prices though it has an affordable evening buffet during July and August. The **Alberta Room** is a more casual and less expensive alternative for breakfast and dinner buffets, yet you get even grander surroundings and still with nightly entertainment and dancing. Try the famous Sunday brunch. You can eat around the world and all under one roof at this hotel: Japanese food at the **Samurai;** Italian food at the **Pavilion;** German food, fondues, and entertainment at the **Waldhaus.** Hours at these three are 6 to 10 p.m. For all day affordable eating, go to the **Koffie Huis.**

As at the Banff Springs Hotel, you get elegant ambiance, a superb view of the Bow Valley (and Mount Rundle) and this time fine Italian cuisine, at **Ristorante Classico** in the beautiful Rimrock Resort Hotel, Mountain Ave., 403/762-3356.

Most things French are expensive, but **Restaurant Le Beaujolais** on the corner of Buffalo St. and Banff Ave., 403/762-2712, has been serving fine French food for more than 17 award-winning years. Its more economical affiliate is the popular **Le Bistro Restaurant,** on the corner of Wolf and Bear Sts., 403/762-8900. In this cozy, casual spot, you get a lot of variety at affordable prices: hearty bouillabaisses, seafood crêpes, and excellent steaks, salads, and salmon. **Paris's Restaurant** sounds French, but it isn't. This longtime Banff restaurant on 110 Banff Ave., 403/762-3554, has been around since 1963. Here, in the Euro-Canadian tradition, you get schnitzel with steak and seafood.

Highly recommended by the locals is **Ticino Swiss Italian Restaurant,** 415 Banff Ave., 403/762-3848. It's noted for its Swiss decor, Swiss-dressed wait staff, and well-prepared food. But probably the first restaurant that comes to everybody's lips in Banff is **Bumper's The Beef House,** 603 Banff Ave., 403/762-2622. "If you haven't been to Bumpers, you haven't been to Banff."

Bumper's is a family restaurant that offers top service and good value, with Alberta beef specials-prime ribs, steaks, and baby back ribs-B.C. salmon, an all-you-can-eat salad bar, and a children's menu. Perhaps the second is **Grizzly House,** 207 Banff Ave., 403/762-4055. Anything goes here—a madcap menu—from pork and beef to buffalo, ostrich, and rattlesnake—a zany decor, and phones at every table. Another talked-about choice is **Craig's Way Station,** 461 Banff Ave., 403/762-4660, a popular diner known for its legendary all-day breakfasts and its long menu that includes a special seniors' menu and menus for Little Pardners—and it's cheap.

With its superb scenery you get a lot of value-added atmosphere when you dine in the Lake Louise area. As at Banff Springs Hotel, there are several restaurants in Château Lake Louise, 403/522-3511. You'll pay top prices at the **Victoria Dining Room,** which has been restored to its 1913 opulence, with wood paneling, hand-painted motifs on the walls and vaulted ceilings. The **Tom Wilson Dining Room** accompanies its fine dining with a panorama of the lake. The elegant **Edelweiss** serves innovative European food while offering the same spectacular views. Less expensive is the **Poppy Room,** which serves family fare. **Walliser Stube** is the place for fondues of every kind. At the **Glacier Saloon,** you get light meals while you dance; and at the **Alpine Lounge,** finger foods while you drink. My favorites are the early bird breakfasts to see dawn on the Victoria Glacier, and lunch in the garden on the Lakeside Terrace. If you just want an ice cream, go for the **Glacier Scoop.**

You have a choice of ambiance at the **Station Restaurant** at Lake Louise, 200 Sentinel Rd. on the Bow River, 403/522-2600: roadside dining in a 1920s log railway station or elegant eating in a vintage dining car with wood paneling, immaculate linen, silverware, and perhaps the sound of a transcontinental train passing by. The menu reflects the difference from pizzas, burgers, and home-made soups, to fresh salmon, red spring trout, and honey-mustard curry organic chicken.

You get an awesome view at lovely **Moraine Lake Lodge Atrium Dining Room** on Moraine Lake Road, 13 kilometers (8 miles) from the Village of Lake Louise, 403/522-3733. In summer, sit in a casually elegant atrium dining room (or café or outdoor patio) overlooking the lake set below the Valley of Ten Peaks. The lodge's breakfast buffet consists of muesli, fruit, croissants, and muffins for a very reasonable price, and the dinner menu features game paté, tenderloin beef, caribou, salmon Wellington, lemon chicken, or grilled sea bass.

Partway between Banff and Lake Louise, closer to Lake Louise, is the **Baker Creek Bistro,** an intimate log cabin restaurant so popular that you must reserve even if you are staying in the nearby Baker Creek Chalets, Box 57, Lake Louise, Alberta T0L 1E0, 403/522-2182.

LODGING

Without doubt, **Banff Springs Hotel,** 405 Spray Ave. (only 500 meters from downtown), 403/762-2211 or 800/441-1414, Banff's picture-postcard perfect castle in the clouds since 1888, is the biggest and the best. Its Presidential Suite with a private glass elevator rents for several thousand dollars a night, Canada's most expensive accommodation. But you can also get a room for as "little" as $200 in the off-season. In winter, the hotel offers an all-inclusive "winter wonderland experience" starting about the same price for deluxe accommodation, daily use of Solace Spa and Fitness Centre, three meals a day in your choice of hotel restaurant, plus activities such as skiing, skating, snowshoeing, dog sledding, and sleigh riding. Not a bad deal for a day, except that the days may not be long enough to fit everything in. All rooms have minibars; the hotel has outdoor and indoor pools, a golf course, tennis courts, riding stables, exercise rooms, and a new and comprehensive spa.

The Rockies' other castle is newly renovated **Château Lake Louise,** on the shores of Lake Louise looking across to Victoria Glacier. It has nearly the same amenities as Banff Springs but not quite the same opulent ambiance inside. For me, Château Lake Louise has the edge over Banff because of its stunning scenery, its numerous and convenient trails, and its greater distance from downtown, albeit measured in minutes. Be sure to ask for a room overlooking the lake. Address: Box 178, Lake Louise, Alberta T0L 1E0, 403/522-3511 or 800/441-1414.

A lot smaller than the two signature hotels of the Rockies, but with the charming, elegant and expensive ambiance of the world-renowned Relais-and-Châteaux inns is the **Post Hotel,** 200 Pipestone Road in the village of Lake Louise, 403/522-3989 or 800/661-1586, posthotel@telusplanet.net

You can't beat the architecture at the **Moraine Lake Lodge and Cabins** located on Moraine Lake, Box 70, Lake Louise, Alberta T0L 1E0, 403/522-3733, info@morainelake.com, www.morainelake.com. It's expensive, but the lake is one of the most beautiful and the buildings were designed by Arthur Erickson, famous architect of the new Canadian Embassy in Washington, D.C. And you do get complimentary afternoon tea and pastries, as well as evening brandy and sherry.

A little easier on the budget and often chosen for weddings for its romantic atmosphere is **Baker Creek Chalets and Guest Lodge,** on the Bow Valley Parkway between Banff and Lake Louise, Box 66, Lake Louise, 403/522-3761. Chalets have red roofs, red shutters with hand-painted flowers, decks and flower boxes, fireplaces, and kitchens. Cute. Fun for the family is the **Douglas Fir Resort and Chalets,** on Tunnel Mountain Rd., Box 1228, Banff, Alberta T0L 0C0, 403/762-5591 or 800/661-9267. A unique feature is its two giant indoor water slides to keep the kids busy. The resort has a variety of rooms, from studios to A-frame chalets to suit many tastes, all with kitchens and fireplaces.

Bed-and-breakfasts are less expensive alternatives to the landmark hotels. Try **Eleanor's House,** 125 Kootenay Ave. between the center of Banff and Banff Springs Hotel, 403/760-2457, info@bbeleanor.com. Eleanor House (yes, that's her name, really!) calls her home "Alberta's finest." Check her Web site at www.banff.cyberstream.net/eleanor.

For the budget-conscious, there are several hostel-type accommodations: **Lake Louise International Hostel and Alpine Centre** in the townsite, 403/522-2200; **Banff International Hostel,** on Tunnel Mountain Rd., 403/762-4122; and **Castle Mountain Hostel,** in Banff, 403/762-4122. A little more expensive, but with a variety of room types is the **Y Mountain Lodge,** at 102 Spray Ave. in downtown Banff, 403/762-3560. It used to be a hotel.

If you want backcountry privacy, **Skoki Lodge,** 14.5 kilometers (9 miles) from the Lake Louise Ski Area, 403/522-3555, is a beautiful 1930's log lodge with cabins, open Christmas through April and June through September. However, you can't drive to Skoki—you'll have to hike or ski. But the awesome food, they say, that is waiting for you at your destination makes it all worthwhile.

CAMPING

The 15 public campgrounds in Banff National Park are available on a first-come, first-served basis. No reservations are accepted, so it's wise to settle into a site early in the day and stay awhile. If you want to stay overnight in the backcountry, you must get a backcountry permit obtainable at information centers in the Banff and Lake Louise townsites. Rates vary according to the location and services available. All Banff-area campsites listed can be reached at 403/762-1550. For the Lake Louise campgrounds call 403/522-3980.

Tunnel Mountain Trailer Court has 321 RV-only sites, tap water, flush toilets, sewage disposal, all services, and is wheelchair accessible. It's 2.5 kilometers (1 mile) northeast of Banff on Tunnel Mountain Road, open mid-May through late September. It's the closest to the town.

Tunnel Mountain Village 1 has 618 RV-only sites, tap water, showers, flush toilets, sewage disposal, and phone, and is wheelchair accessible. With good hiking trails and an interpretive amphitheater, it's 4 kilometers (2.5 miles) northeast of Banff on Tunnel Mountain Rd., open mid-May through late September. **Tunnel Mountain Village 2** has 222 designated and walk-in sites, tap water, power only, phone, wheelchair accessibility, and an interpretive amphitheater. It's 2.5 kilometers (1.6 miles) northeast of Banff on Tunnel Mountain Rd. and open year-round; winter camping is permitted.

Lake Louise 1, in Lake Louise on Hwy. 1, has 189 sites, tap water, phone, sewage disposal, hiking, fishing, and winter camping in the RV area. Open mid-

May through early October. Lake Louise 2 has 220 tent-only sites, tap water, and flush toilets. Open mid-May through early October.

NIGHTLIFE

After a hard day on the hiking trails or the ski slopes, opt for a hot tub and duvet, but if you insist, then you're sure to find a pub, a club, a bar, or a saloon in your own hotel. If you want to explore further, here's a couple of recommendations. The most talked about is **Wild Bill's Legendary Saloon,** upstairs at 201 Banff Ave., 403/762-0333, featuring country western, rock, folk, and blues bands. **St. James's Gate Olde Irish Pub,** 205 Wolf St., in Banff, 403/762-9355, has traditional decor, occasional Celtic and Maritime bands and lots of variety in its libations. Or go for an elegant dinner accompanied by a soft piano at Banff Springs Hotel or Château Lake Louise, or, at the other extreme, something at **Brewster Cowboy's BBQ and Dance Barn,** 403/762-5454.

If timed right, you can attend a number of festivals. In the second week of June, the **Banff TV Festival** showcases the world's best TV productions. The **Banff Festival of the Arts** presents a variety of performances, including jazz, dance, chamber music, musical theater, and drama, with solo and ensemble performances, between early June and the end of August. For two to three days each in early November, the **Banff Festival of Mountain Films and Festival of Mountain Books** previews and honors top mountaineering and adventure films from around the world. Phone 403/762-6157 for more information.

15
KANANASKIS COUNTRY

Kananaskis, Alberta, is remarkable in many ways. Its 4,250 square kilometers (1,540 square miles) of wilderness and prime four-season recreational area are easily accessible from Calgary, only about 90 kilometers (54 miles) away. But most tourists drive right by it as they hurtle along the Trans-Canada Highway to Banff and Lake Louise. Until the 1988 Winter Olympic Games were held in Calgary and Canmore, the region was little known except by Calgarians. Now, as Banff and Jasper National Parks become increasingly overcrowded, Kananaskis commands more attention.

Kananaskis means "meeting of the waters." The Bow and Kananaskis Rivers and their tributaries provided the corridor that led Captain John Palliser through the Rockies between 1857 and 1860, just as they had for the First Nations people more than 10,000 years before. Except for Kananaskis Village, there are no townsites, no thousands of international tourists looking for shops and quick scenery fixes. Rather, the area has abundant and unparalleled opportunities to appreciate the outdoors. Once, after a painful slog up a mountain in Sheep Valley behind a pack of barking hounds, I looked up a tree and saw three wild cougars—a thrilling experience. In many ways, the foothills of the Rockies in Kananaskis Country and the rivers that slice through them are just as satisfying as the Rockies themselves.

A PERFECT DAY IN KANANASKIS COUNTRY

Choose a day in mid-September, when crowds have thinned, the skies are deep blue, and the autumn colors are most intense, and prepare to move like a whirlwind. It's possible to drive around Kananaskis Country from Canmore to Canmore via Highway 40 in three hours, but don't. Start at the northern end where Highway 1 meets Highway 40 and head south along the Kananaskis River, a route called the Kananaskis Trail.

Take time to notice how the colors change, from the lime gold poplars of the valley to the blood red willows to the burnt gold alpine larches. In Peter Lougheed Provincial Park, turn right at the Kananaskis Lake Trail on a 40-minute detour to the parking lot between Upper and Lower Kananaskis Lakes for one of the day's many Kodak moments—the view to the southwest of mountain—framed Mangin Glacier. Back down Highway 40, take the gravel road to the left over Elpoca Creek for another short detour. Stop near the bridge and look up at the cliff face for mountain goats. Another rewarding stop is further south along Highway 40 through the Highwood Pass, which, at 2,206 meters (7,280 feet), is the highest driveable pass in Canada. Hike the 5.6-kilometer (3.5-mile) Ptarmigan Cirque Trail on the left side of the road. Beside the stepped waterfalls, you're likely to see hoary marmots and lots of fossils. Back on the road, stop for pie or muffins and coffee at nearby Highwood House. Complete the loop back to Canmore to Calgary through the cattle and cowboy country of the foothills.

ORIENTATION

Kananaskis begins south of Highway 1 between Canmore and Bragg Creek, and extends south on Highway 40 to the intersection of Highways 532 and 940. It encompasses three provincial parks—Bow Valley, Peter Lougheed, and Bragg Creek— with hundreds of kilometers of hiking and cross-country ski trails, a complex network of bike paths, areas for horseback riding and ATV driving, dozens of lakes stocked with fish, and a world-class 36-hole golf course. On its northern outskirts is the artists colony of Bragg Creek and the service center of Canmore. Parts of Highway 40, from Peter Lougheed Provincial Park to Highway 541, are closed December 1 through June 15. From the east, you can access the area via Highways 1, 8, and 66 from Calgary, Highway 549 from Okotoks, Highway 546 from Turner Valley, and Highway 541 from Longview. From the west, access the area from Banff and Canmore via Highway 1.

Driving a truck and camper with a canoe on top is the best way to travel through Kananaskis Country. Or stay at one of the luxury hotels in Kananaskis Village and let the locals be your guide.

KANANASKIS COUNTRY

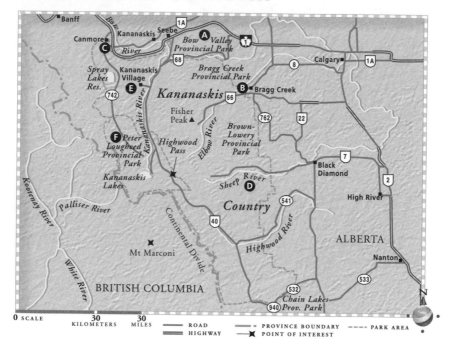

SIGHTS

A Bow Valley Provincial Park and Bow Valley Corridor

B Bragg Creek
C Canmore
D Elbow/Sheep Wildlands Provincial Park

E Kananaskis Village
F Peter Lougheed Provincial Park

Note: Items with the same letter are located in the same area.

For local convenience, the area has been divided into eight zones: Bow Valley Provincial/Bow Corridor, Barrier Lake/Ribbon Creek, Sibbald, Elbow River Valley, Sheep River Valley, Highwood/Cataract, Spray Lake, and Peter Lougheed Provincial Park.

GETTING AROUND KANANASKIS COUNTRY

The following contacts will help you get around the area: Canmore Chamber of Commerce, 403/678-4094, Barrier Lake Information Centre, 403/673-3985;

Kananaskis Village Information Centre, 403/591-7555; Peter Lougheed Provincial Park Information Centre, 403/591-6322; Kananaskis Country Canmore office, 403/678-5508. You can visit Kananaskis Country vicariously on the Internet at www.gov.ab.ca/env/parks/prov-parks/kananaskis.

Be sure to stop at all information centers in each zone, see the interpretive displays and stock up on trail guides.

SIGHTSEEING HIGHLIGHTS

★★★★ KANANASKIS VILLAGE
Kananaskis Village Information Centre, Alberta, T0L 2H0, 403/591-7555

This is less a village than a central square surrounded by three ritzy hotels and impeccably landscaped grounds with ponds, waterfalls, and gardens: the **Lodge at Kananaskis** and **Hotel Kananaskis,** both part of the Canadian Pacific Hotels and Resorts chain, 800/441-1414, and the **Kananaskis Inn Best Western,** 800/528 1234. Kids from the Calgary Children's Hospital visit each year to fish out the rainbow trout that are stocked in the hotel ponds in the spring.

Adjacent to the hotels is the **Village Centre,** which consists of a convenience store, a leisure center, a sports equipment rental shop, the start of interconnected hiking and skating trails, and a 36-hole championship golf course. **Kananaskis Country Golf Course** was designed by Robert Trent Jones, who planned every tee shot to line up with a different mountain peak. Every drive is a painting, making it difficult to keep your eyes on the ball. Locals advise players at the fourth hole on the Mount Lorette side of the course to watch out for grizzly bears. They've been seen on the slopes above the course. For tee times, call 403/591-7272.

About five minutes from the Village Centre off Highway 40 is the **Nakiska Ski Area,** on Mount Allan, 403/591-7777, which was one of the venues for the 1988 Calgary Winter Olympics. Winter activities include downhill and cross-country skiing, skating, sleigh riding, and dog sledding. In summer, use the trails for hiking and biking.

Details: *Write to Nakiska at Box 100, Kananaskis Village, Alberta T0L 2H0; 403/591-7495; open year-round. (half day; 2 days if golfing)*

★★★★ PETER LOUGHEED PROVINCIAL PARK
Kananaskis Village Box 130, Alberta T0L 2H0,

403/591-7227; campground reservations, 403/591-7226; Visitor Centre, 403/591-6322

At more than 500 square kilometers, this was the largest provincial park in Alberta until the recent declaration of the Elbow-Sheep Wildlands Provincial Park, also in Kananaskis Country and now a globally recognized Special Place. Glacial streams, evergreen valleys, clear sparkling lakes, and towering mountains leave an indelible impression. Go to the Park Visitor Centre for orientation, maps, and detailed information on trails and campsites. The hiking trails vary from barrier-free trails for persons limited in mobility to high alpine backcountry adventures. There are 85 kilometers (53 miles) of groomed cross-country ski trails, 12 kilometers (7.5 miles) of paved biking trails, and one equestrian trail. Campgrounds vary from rustic walk-in tent-type to pull-through trailer sites. See A Perfect Day for suggested activities. For a bite to eat, stop in at the Boulton Creek Trading Post and Highwood House.

One of the most special places in Peter Lougheed, and perhaps the world, is **William Watson Lodge,** a special needs facility that provides accommodations in a mountain setting for people with physical, mental, or sensory limitations. The lodge has eight cabins that house two to four apartments, all of which are self-contained and wheelchair accessible at a minimum cost ($25 to $35 a night for up to eight people). It has two campgrounds, one with plug-ins that have oxygen units to recharge wheelchair batteries. Reservations are essential.

Details: (1 day)

★★★ CANMORE

Northwest corner along the Trans-Canada Hwy., 106 km (66 mi) west of Calgary, 22 km (13 mi) east of Banff; Canmore Chamber of Commerce, Box 1178, T0L 0M0, 403/678-5277

In 1883, Canmore was a coal mining region. Today, it is a fast-growing service center or jumping-off point for attractions in Kananaskis Country and Banff National Park. It is just off Highway 1, or the Trans-Canada, the major artery into the Rockies. It is headquarters for the Alpine Club of Canada and is a popular mountain climbing location. Because of its position at the foot of the Rocky Mountains, it is called "The place to look up." Leave the business strip and browse around shops, eateries, ponds, and pathways of the Towne Center. It hasn't any stoplights, nor does it have any parking meters. Visitors are thrilled.

Park at the IGA grocery store and walk the Boardwalk Trail along Policeman's Creek to look for birds and watch ducks. In fall, you'll see monster three-foot brown trout in this skinny waterway. Also in fall, watch for migrating golden eagles; 7,500 a year have been counted in Canmore. The **Canmore Nordic Centre,** with its 56 kilometers (35 miles) of groomed woodland skiing, biking, hiking, and orienteering trails, was built for the 1988 Winter Olympics, but it provides excellent recreation facilities for all seasons. The Nordic Centre is on the Smith Dorrien/Spray Trail, 403/678-2400.

Details: (1 day)

★★ BOW VALLEY PROVINCIAL PARK AND BOW VALLEY CORRIDOR

The park is located at the north end of Kananaskis Country at the confluence of the Kananaskis and Bow Rivers; the corridor follows the Bow River, and both are bisected by the Trans-Canada Hwy., 80 km (50 mi) west of Calgary and 28 km (17 mi) east of Canmore, 403/673-3663 and 403/673-2163

This trail to the Rockies has been a traditional travel route for 10,000 years—and it still is. Highway 1A parallels the north shore of the Bow River and Highway 1 the south shore. Try fishing for trout and whitefish in the Bow River and bike the paved trails. Stay the night at one of the two excellent campgrounds—Willow Rock and Bow Valley—and listen to an interpretive program.

Details: Park is open year-round, campgrounds Apr./May–Oct. 31. (3 hours)

★★ BRAGG CREEK

40 km (25 mi) southwest of Calgary on Hwy. 22, Chamber of Commerce, White Ave., T0L 0K0, 403/949-0004

The rural hamlet Bragg Creek is known as Gateway to the Kananaskis. It has been a year-round recreation mecca for Calgarians since the 1920s. It is still a favorite weekend drive for city dwellers, but it has now developed into a shopping and cultural center as well. Its main street, known as Heritage Mile, is lined with craft shops, antique emporiums, and restaurants. It has several bed-and-breakfasts and a popular restaurant, Barbecue Steak Pit, 43 White Ave., 403/949-3633. In mid-November, Bragg Creek puts on an Artisans Arts and Crafts Show and Sale.

Details: (half day)

★★ ELBOW/SHEEP WILDLANDS PROVINCIAL PARK

Encompasses the Elbow River Valley and the Sheep River Valley in eastern Kananaskis Country, crossed by Hwy. 66 southwest of Bragg Creek (Elbow Valley Visitor Centre, 403/949-4261), and Hwy. 546 west of Turner Valley (Sheep River Valley, 403/949-3754)

This new park combines the grasslands, forests, and alpine peaks of the Elbow River Valley with the peaks, gorges and meadows of the Sheep River Valley—varied landscapes that you can explore by well-connected trails in a day, a weekend or longer backcountry trip. Lots of day use areas and close enough to Calgary to be a favorite week-end destination for hikers, mountain bikers, cross-country skiers and equestrian users. The Sheep River Valley area is especially known for its abundance of bighorn sheep, which you can easily see grazing in the valley or scrambling up the rocks on either side of the river. Bighorn Lookout in the Sheep River Wildlife Sanctuary has a meadow observation blind overlooking a popular bighorn gathering site. Because of its varied wildlife—sheep, cougars, ground squirrels, dippers, grouse—the University of Calgary established a Biological Field Station here.

Details: Information Centre, Bag 1, Bragg Creek, Alberta T0L 0K0; 403/933-7172. Or contact Fish and Wildlife in Calgary at 403/297-6423. *(half day)*

FITNESS AND RECREATION

There's lots to keep you fit in Kananaskis Country; the whole region is geared toward physical activity, both indoor and outdoor in all seasons. Major activities are skiing and hiking, but there's probably nothing you can't do here—either independently or as part of an organized group. Facilities such as **Nakiska Ski Area,** at Mount Allan, adjacent to Kananaskis Village, 403/591-7777; **Canmore Nordic Centre,** 403/678-2400; and **Fortress Mountain,** near Peter Lougheed Provincial Park, 403/591-7108 or 403/264-5825, are modern, all-encompassing, and well-organized to provide both winter and summer activities. To get the flavor of Kananaskis Country, make sure to walk a trail, ski a slope, ride a horse, and kayak a lake; if you can, climb a peak, too. Try trekking with llamas and **Bragg Creek Tours and Travels,** 403/949-3400. Others won't want to miss golfing at the spectacular **Kananaskis Country Golf Course,** adjacent to the Lodge at Kananaskis, 403/591-7071 or 403/591-7070.

For one-stop shopping—whitewater rafting, hiking, canoeing, cross-country skiing—let an operator be your guide. Try **Mirage Adventure Tours,** Box

8097, Canmore, 888/312-7238 or 403/678-4919, mirage@telusplanet.net, www.miragetours.com. Check at your lodging for other local guides and tours.

FOOD

Canmore is said to have more restaurants per capita than anywhere else in North America and, compared to Banff and Calgary, prices are very reasonable. You'll dine well in luxurious surroundings amid spectacular mountain scenery at any of the restaurants in either of the two hotels in Kananaskis Village. Sunday brunch at **The Peaks** in the Lodge at Kananaskis, 403/591-7171, is especially recommended. At other times, if price is important, watch for specials. Meals at the **Kananaskis Golf Course,** 403/591-7070, are quite reasonable considering its country club atmosphere. A large bowl of seafood chowder is good value for around $5, and a bonus is the possibility of seeing elk or grizzly bears from the clubhouse windows. You can have pheasant under glass inside and grizzlies through glass outside!

On the other hand, you won't find the following restaurants advertised in the glossy magazines, but they are places locals swear by. They say the food, service, and scenery at the **Boulton Creek Trading Post** on the Kananaskis Lakes Trail in Peter Lougheed Provincial Park, 403/591-7678, is as good as anywhere. The menu is standard burgers, lasagna, pizza, and roast chicken, but you can get a lunch for $6 to $11, and the servers take the trouble to recognize clients and make them feel welcome. Try the rhubarb strawberry muffins and chocolate cake served regularly at **Highwood House** a humble eatery at the junction of Highwood with Highway 40, 403/558-2144. Also highly praised are the barbecued steaks and cowboy fare of beans, buns, and spuds at the **Boundary Ranch,** on the east side of Highway 40 near Kananaskis Village, 403/591-7171. And locals like dining on the deck of **Mt. Engadine Lodge,** on the Spray Lake Rd., 403/678-2880, because the setting in this wildest part of Kananaskis Country is so incredible, as is the food.

The best deal in town is lunch at the **Drake Hotel,** 909 Railway Ave., 403/678-5131. Lunch specials, including soup, salads or fries, and entrées such as *nasi goreng* (an Indonesian rice dish) and calamari, are affordable and the portions are large. For a friendly English pub atmosphere, though not necessarily English food (which to this writer is a plus), try the **Rose and Crown Restaurant and Pub,** 749 Railway Ave., Canmore, 403/678-5168. **Sherwood House** at the corner of Eighth St. and Eighth Ave., 403/678-5211, is a colorful old log cabin with a popular patio, frequent entertainment, and a granola-type menu that appeals to the younger set. **Zonas Bistro,** 710 Ninth St., 403/609-2000, is another heritage-type house. Its menu is distinctive and popular with vegetarians.

A little further up the price scale is the cozy **Gasthaus Restaurant,** 1723 Mountain Ave., 403/678-5000, which serves authentic European cuisine.

KANANASKIS COUNTRY

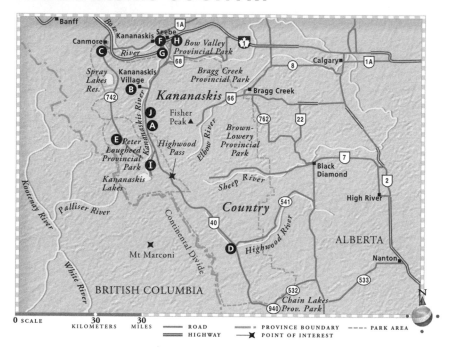

FOOD

- **A** Boulton Creek Trading Post
- **B** Boundary Ranch
- **C** Drake Hotel
- **C** Gasthaus Restaurant
- **D** Highwood House
- **B** Hotel Kananaskis
- **B** Kananaskis Country Golf Course
- **E** Mt. Engadine Lodge
- **B** The Peaks
- **C** Rose and Crown Restaurant and Pub
- **C** Sherwood House
- **C** Sinclairs
- **C** Zonas Bistro

LODGING

- **C** Akai Motel
- **F** Bow Valley Motel
- **G** Brewster's Kananaskis Guest Ranch
- **C** High Country B&B
- **B** Hotel Kananaskis
- **B** Kananaskis Inn Best Western
- **C** Kiska Inn B&B
- **B** Lodge at Kananaskis
- **H** Rafter Six Ranch Resort
- **B** Ribbon Creek Hostel
- **C** Stockade Log Cabins

CAMPING

- **I** Boulton Creek Campground
- **I** Canyon Campground
- **I** Cataract Creek Campground
- **I** Elkwood Campground
- **I** Interlakes Campground
- **I** Lower Lake Campground
- **A** Mount Kidd
- **I** Mount Sarrail
- **J** Sundance Lodges (Teepees) and RV Park

Note: Items with the same letter are located in the same area.

Try Bavarian liver dumpling soup, grilled bratwurst or schnitzel, followed by hot apple strudel. Enjoy mountain views, casual elegance, and innovative cuisine at **Sinclairs,** 63 Eighth St., 403/678-5370. Here you can select from a varied menu made from fresh ingredients, even if it is relatively expensive and portions are small.

LODGING

If you can't camp in the great outdoors, pick a place with an intimate view of mountains close to outdoor activities. New accommodations and restaurants are being developed all the time. The three big all-season luxury hotels are in Kananaskis Village: the two regal Canadian Pacific hotels, the newly renovated **Lodge at Kananaskis,** 403/591-7171 or 800/441-1414, and **Hotel Kananaskis,** 403/591-7711 or 800/441-1414; and the **Kananaskis Inn Best Western,** 403/591-7500. Rates are high, but worth the splurge for these world-class facilities. Go for it.

A more authentic Western feel is found at **Brewster's Kananaskis Guest Ranch,** two kilometers (1.3 miles) from the Trans-Canada Highway in Seebe, 403/673-3737 or 800/691-5085. It's an oldie, but a goodie. It belongs to the famous Brewster family, some of whom took the tourist route from carriages to buses, and others of whom stayed in horses. From your renovated cabin or chalet, you can go horseback-riding, rafting, jet-boating, heli-hiking, and fly-fishing in addition to the usual hotel amenities of swimming in the pool or soaking in the hot tub. The Brewsters can handle group barbecues of up to 1,200 people—fancy events that include rodeos, gunfighters, cowboy poets, and native dancers. Ten-day packages are available and prices are reasonable.

The **Rafter Six Ranch Resort,** 2 kilometers (1.3 miles) south of the Trans-Canada at the Seebe exit, 403/673-3622 or 888/26RANCH, also has a heritage atmosphere and Western feel. In fact, it's motto is "Where the West stays alive." It consists of a log lodge and cabins and offers trail and pack trips, hay and carriage rides, an antique photo parlor, and a dance hall. Another attraction is their Passing of the Legends Museum, which houses First Nations and pioneer relics.

In Canmore, there are many choices. For economy and character, try a teepee or log cabin at **Stockade Log Cabins,** Box 575, in the Canmore Harvie Heights part of town, 403/678-5212 or 800/330-3824. For economy without the character, try the **Akai Motel,** Box 687, 403/678-4664. The **Bow Valley Motel** has a convenient downtown location at 610 Eighth St., Canmore Alberta, T1W 2B5, and is also very affordable, 403/678-5085 or 800/665-8189.

There are many bed-and-breakfasts in Canmore. Reserve through a registry such as **High Country B&B,** Box 772, Turner Valley, 888/509-1965. The themed rooms (Haida or Voyageur) in **Kiska Inn B&B,** at Deadman's Flats in Canmore, are intriguing. So is Kiskas decadent hot gourmet breakfasts such as stuffed fruit crêpes drizzled with a special chocolate sauce. Contact Kiska at 403/678-4041, 888/533-7188, or www.info&kiska.ab.ca on the Internet. Rates are reasonable. A useful hostel located on the access road to Kanaskis Village is **Ribbon Creek Hostel,** 403/762-4122. Rates are $12 for members, $16 for nonmembers.

CAMPING

As expected, there are lots of campgrounds in Kananaskis Country. Most are not fancy, but you go to this region for the outdoor experience, not for the sophistication of the campsite. There are six campgrounds in Peter Lougheed Provincial Park, 403/591-7226. Families prefer the two largest ones—**Boulton Creek** and **Elkwood,** which have tap water and amphitheaters that put on award-winning interpretations. The others **Canyon, Cataract, Interlakes, Lower Lake,** and **Mount Sarrail** are smaller, pump water, and sell firewood.

    Mount Kidd RV Park, on Highway 40, 28 kilometers (17.5 miles) south of the Trans-Canada near Kananaskis Village, is more of a resort than a campground. This is high-end camping. It offers facilities for every possible type of recreational vehicle and tents, many designed for winter use. The park features saunas, showers, a whirlpool, game room, lounge, and fast-food counter inside— and tennis courts, bicycle and walking paths, children's play areas, wading pool, and outdoor amphitheater. Mount Kidd even has a gift shop, an arcade, and banking. Box 1000, Kananaskis Village, Alberta T0L 2H0, 403/591-7700, open year-round.

    Sundance Lodges (Teepees) and RV Park, 403/591-7122, on Highway 40, 21 kilometers (13 miles) south of the Trans-Canada near Kananaskis Village, offers camping with a difference. Apart from regular campsites, it features handpainted teepees with wood floors, beds, and mattresses (rent bedding and cook kits), lanterns, hot showers, groceries, and the opportunity for horseback-riding, rafting, golfing, hiking, and fishing.

NIGHTLIFE

You should be too tired out taking in K-Country scenery to do anything but sleep, but if you do want some other nightlife, try **Woody's Pub** at the Best Western Kananaskis Inn in the Village.

DRUMHELLER VALLEY

Drumheller, a town of 7,000 people on the Red Deer River, is a convenient location from which to explore Alberta's Badlands. The rolling farmland east of Calgary suddenly drops from the prairie to the river through a skeleton of steep, dry canyons that Albertans call *coulees*. These are the Badlands, where stark layers of multicolored rock, bared by the eroding forces of wind, water, and ice over 70 million years, tell the story of time through the fossilized remains of gargantuan creatures that once roamed this river valley.

This is Dinosaur Country, where in 1884 Joseph Tyrrell discovered the skull of a dinosaur, and where the town of Drumheller now houses the world-famous Royal Tyrrell Museum. As you look down into the arid coulees or up at the rock-capped hoodoos, it is hard to believe that this semidesert was once a forested swamp.

More than 650,000 people visit the Drumheller Valley annually. More 50 intriguing attractions located within a 100-square-kilometer (60-square-mile) area await them. You can return to the Badlands time and time again and still be as intrigued as the first time you visited.

A PERFECT DAY IN THE DRUMHELLER VALLEY
Spend the morning at the Royal Tyrrell Museum and the afternoon on either or both of the loop drives. Such is the landscape and its interpretation that it doesn't take much imagination to see this barren, moon-like world clothed in forests

and swamps and filled with the bellows of huge, rampaging beasts? It's humbling to think how insignificant any of us really are. Some day it will be our turn to become the subject of discovery, excavation, and conjecture.

Out on the North Dinosaur Trail, meditate a moment in the Little Church, pause long enough at Horsethief Canyon to get some of the best of the Badlands on film, and stop again on the South Dinosaur Trail on the way back to Drumheller to photograph the Red Deer River Valley from the Orkney Hill Viewpoint. On the second loop, the East Coulee/Hoodoo Trail, focus the camera on the famous Hoodoo sandstone columns.

If you have time, take an evening side trip along Highway 10X to Wayne and relax with a drink in the Last Chance Saloon, followed by a do-it-yourself barbecue at the Rosedeer Hotel. If traveling in July, skip Wayne and see the Canadian Badlands' Passion Play in Drumheller.

ORIENTATION

It's easy to navigate Alberta as most of the roads are laid out grid-fashion. Perhaps the best way to get to Drumheller is by Highway 9 (138 kilometers/82 miles) from Calgary, or by Highway 56 from Red Deer (163 kilometers/97 miles). The most dramatic introduction to this destination is to stop along Highway 9 at Horseshoe Canyon, 19 kilometers (11.4 miles) west of Drumheller. The best way to see the sights in Drumheller is to drive your own vehicle. That way, you can stop on any whim. Spend the most time at the Royal Tyrrell Museum of Paleontology on the westernmost of the two loop drives.

SIGHTSEEING HIGHLIGHTS

★★★★ CANADIAN BADLANDS PASSION PLAY
Performed at 17th St. SW and South Dinosaur Trail; mailing address: Box 457, Drumheller, T0J 0Y0; 403/23-7750, www.agt.net/public/dandann/passion

The Passion Play that portrays the life and passion of Jesus Christ, is set in an outdoor amphitheater just south of Drumheller, where you are seated quite comfortably on wooden-backed benches. Including intermission, the performance takes all of three hours and has been described as a "life-changing and moving experience." Tickets go on sale at the beginning of November at the Passion Play office. Seating is assigned, and tickets are mailed to you after payment. One free ticket is given to each group purchasing 15 or more.

Details: Afternoon and evening performances in July, check dates with the Canadian Badlands Passion Play Society at addresses above. Admission, $18 adults, $9 children 12 and under; no GST in price (3 hours)

★★★★ EAST COULEE/HOODOO TRAIL (LOOP DRIVE)
Begins at Hwy. 10 at the junction of Hwy. 9, continues east along Hwy. 10 to East Coulee, west on Hwy. 569 to Dalum, north on Hwy. 56 to Hwy. 10, followed by a side trip on Hwy. 10X to Wayne before returning to Drumheller

Stop first at the Rosedale Swinging Suspension Bridge that miners crossed on their way to work in the now-buried Star Coal Mine. It was originally built without "sides" so imagine yourself walking across that! Cross the Red Deer River at Cambria and stop to photograph one of the Badland's most famous trademarks, The Hoodoos, sandstone columns capped by harder rock that has withstood the ravages of wind and rain erosion. And then it's on to East Coulee, a coal-mining town with a museum and cultural center inside a 1930s school. Across the river is the Historic Atlas Coal Mine that has all of the above-ground buildings much as they were when the mine closed in the early 1980s.

On the way back to Drumheller, take a side trip on Highway 10X to Wayne. The road winds and weaves along and across the Rosebud River (a tributary of the Red Deer River), using 11 uniquely narrow bridges in a very short distance (sufficiently unique that this stretch of road and bridges is featured in *Ripley's Believe it or Not*). At the small community of Wayne (pop. 70)—where films *Running Brave, Draw*, and *2001: A Space Odyssey* were filmed—the whole family can safely enjoy the "pleasures" of the Rosedeer Hotel and the Last Chance Saloon.

Details: Contact Drumheller Regional Chamber of Development and Tourism, Box 999, Drumheller T0J 0Y0, toll-free in Alberta 310-0000, ask for 823-7707 or from outside, 888/440-4240, www.dinosaurvalley.com, or call Drumheller Regional Chamber of Commerce, 60 1st Ave. West, 403/823-3100. (half day)

★★★★ HORSESHOE CANYON
19 km (11 mi) west of Drumheller on Hwy 9. Horseshoe Canyon Interpretive Centre, 403/823-2200, winter 403/282-4812, nodwells@cadvision.com

DRUMHELLER VALLEY

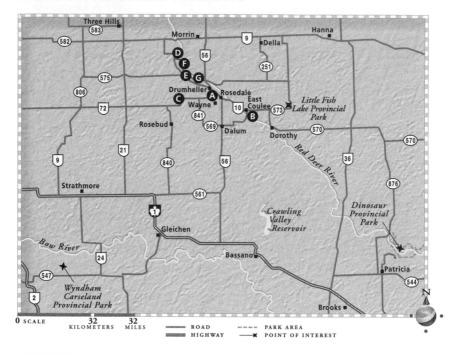

0 SCALE 32 KILOMETERS 32 MILES

━━━ ROAD ▬▬▬ PARK AREA
━━━ HIGHWAY ──✶ POINT OF INTEREST

SIGHTS

Ⓐ Canadian Badlands
Passion Play
Ⓑ East Coulee/Hoodoo
Trail (Loop Drive)
Ⓒ Horseshoe Canyon

Ⓓ Horsethief Canyon
Ⓔ Little Church
Ⓕ North and South
Dinosaur Trails (Loop
Drive)

Ⓖ Royal Tyrrell Museum
of Paleontology

Note: Items with the same letter are located in the same area.

For most visitors, this is their first experience of the Badlands as they
drive north on Highway 9 from the Trans-Canada. A typically straight
and seemingly never-ending prairie road takes a sudden, sharp right
turn at a rough-grassed parking lot—and there is the canyon. Although
it can be viewed almost from your vehicle, it's best to walk down to
the canyon floor to really appreciate the sedimentary strata and al-
ternating layers of volcanic ash that form the steeply banked cliffs. Hiking, walking, and scrambling up and down the cliffs are very popular in

this area, but take special care! In wet weather these slopes become treacherous. The soil is actually bentonitic clay, used in lubricating oil drills and (hold your breath!) in manufacturing toothpaste and cosmetics. When wet, this clay can swell to ten times its volume, becoming soggy glue. In such weather it's unwise (to say the least) to park or drive off the road—your car may well remain "glued" there until conditions are much drier.

If you walk for any distance or time, always take a canteen of water—temperatures are often considerably hotter "down there" in the canyon or coulee. But do walk. It's an experience well worth the time, effort, and perspiration. It's one of Canada's mini-Grand Canyons. For background, visit the Horseshoe Canyon Interpretive Centre

Details: Open May 15–Sept. 10 A.M. daily, hours vary, admission free. (1 hour)

★★★★ NORTH AND SOUTH DINOSAUR TRAILS (LOOP DRIVE)
A 60 km (37 mi) loop along both sides of the Red Deer River Valley that starts and ends in Drumheller

Head out on Highway 838 along the north bank of the Red Deer River and stop where you like—the Homestead Antique Museum, Midland Provincial Park Interpretive Centre, McMullen Island Picnic Site, (a delightfully cool surprise after the dry and often hot badlands), Royal Tyrrell Museum of Paleontology, the Little Church, and Horsethief Canyon Viewpoint.

Details: Contact Drumheller Regional Chamber of Development and Tourism, Box 999, Drumheller T0J 0Y0, toll-free in Alberta: 310-0000, ask for 823-7707 or from outside, 888/440-4240, www.dinosaurvalley.com, or call Drumheller Regional Chamber of Commerce, 60 1st Ave. West, 403/823-3100. (1 day)

HIGHLIGHTS OF NORTH AND SOUTH DINOSAUR TRAILS LOOP DRIVE

★★★★ HORSETHIEF CANYON
Located on Hwy. 838

Highway 838 changes direction suddenly as it climbs out of the valley and leads you to Horsethief Canyon. Follow the trails from the parking lot to get closer to the canyon. Here are the best views of the multilayered cliffs so typical of these Badlands. Another two sharp turns later and the road drops back again to the Red Deer River. At the halfway point on the loop, the little cable-operated free Bleriot Ferry takes you across the river to a sharp climb up to the flats and Orkney Viewpoint, where marvelous views of the Red Deer River Valley may be captured before you go back to Drumheller via the Canadian Badlands Passion Play Site.

Details: *(1 hour)*

★★★★ LITTLE CHURCH (CHAPEL OF CONTEMPLATION)
Located near the Royal Tyrrell Museum on Hwy. 838
This tiny church billed as the World's Largest Little Church is visited by tens of thousands of people a year—six at a time—as it measures only 7' x 11' with six one-person pews. It was the inspiration of Reverend Edgar O'Brien and local carpenter Trygve Seland to provide some peace and comfort to travelers and inspire more people into going to their own churches.

Details: *(15 minutes)*

★★★★ ROSEBUD DINNER THEATRE IN ROSEBUD
On Hwy. 840, 30 min southwest of Drumheller; mailing address Box 654, Rosebud T0J 2T0, 403/677-2001 or 800/267-7553
The Rosebud Dinner Theatre in the tiny town of Rosebud is a very popular year round event. Country-style meals are served accompanied by live music, then guests enjoy either family theater or a variety show in the Rosebud Opera House put on by the Rosebud School of the Arts. Other local attractions are Akoiniskway Gallery, Rosebud Craft Shop, and the Centennial Museum. The Rosebud Hotel looks much as it did in the 1920s. These dinner shows are extremely popular, so purchase your tickets early.

Details: *Open year-round, Wed.–Sat., phone for show dates and times. Box office open Mon.—Sat. 9A.M. to 5P.M. by phone at 800/267-7553 from Alberta, 403/677-2350 from elsewhere. Admission includes dinner, $34 matinees, $39 evenings with special rates for children. (3 to 4 hours)*

★★★★ ROYAL TYRRELL MUSEUM OF PALEONTOLOGY
On Hwy. 838, 6 km (4 mi) northwest of Drumheller, Box 7500, Drumheller, T0J 0Y0, 403/823-7707, 888/440-4240, www.tyrrellmuseum.com
This world-famous complex in Midland Provincial Park displays life-

size models, full skeletons, fossils, hands-on exhibits, computer simulations, films, a preparation laboratory, and an indoor science garden that illustrate millions of years of geological and biological progressions, all of which are updated as soon as new information becomes available. Good free parking, a cafeteria, and a picnic area are available; an excellent souvenir/bookstore keeps browsers browsing. It is possible—advisable for a first visit—to have a guided tour by appointment (phone ahead for reservation), but audio guides are available, too.

Details: *Open year-round, summer daily 9 A.M.–9 P.M., winter Tue.–Sun. 10 A.M.–5 P.M.; $6.50 adults, $5.50 seniors, $3 children, $15 family (3 hours)*

FITNESS AND RECREATION

Drumheller has good hiking, swimming, fishing, and golfing; and some campsites and parks have fitness trails. Don't miss seeing (even if you don't play) the **Dinosaur Trail Golf Course** on Highway 838 on the north bank of the Red Deer River, 403/823-5622 or 403/823-5621. Nine of the 18 holes are shaped by the unique rock formations, coulees and plateaus of the Badlands One of the toughest but best kept courses in Alberta. Open April through October.

Back to Nature Trail Rides, 28 kilometers (18 miles) from Drumheller, 403/823-8760, offers one- to two-hour guided trail rides spring to fall, through scenic spruce coulees where deer, beaver and many kinds of birds are likely to be found. Rustic camping is also available. Try camping in teepees. For comprehensive touring, try **Drumheller Valley Tours,** 570 3rd Ave. W, 403/823-4738 or 403/820-7121. To find your own fossils, check out the **Royal Tyrrell Museum's** dinosaur digs, 888/440-4240, in Alberta, 310-0000, ask for 823-7707; or **Groundwork Adventures in Paleontology,** Box 516, East Coulee, T0J 1B0, 403/822-3976, www.alberta.com/c/dr/ground.html.

ESPECIALLY FOR KIDS

Badlands Go-Kart Park on the North Dinosaur Trail, 4 kilometers (2.4 miles) west of the Royal Tyrrell Museum, 403/823-7352, gives a fast, fun ride over 1,700 feet of track, is open all week from May through September 10 A.M. to 9 P.M. Youngsters can burn off energy at **Funland Amusement Park,** 901 North Dinosaur Trail, 403/823-5201.

FOOD

Despite its small size, Drumheller has a good variety of restaurants, ranging from Greek to Chinese to Western, with the usual fast-food outlets for the famished. Smorgasbord lunches are reasonably priced and if you want elegance, you can get that, too.

Starting at the top of the price scale, try the **The Drumheller Inn,** 100 South Railway Ave. SE, 403/823-8400, which has a delightfully elegant Skylight Dining Room with a bar. Meals here are excellent and variably priced. **The Falcon,** 298 Centre St., 403/823-8441, is known for its Friday night seafood buffet (as well as the more ordinary daily one) and Sunday brunch (it also has a popular karaoke lounge).

Places to take the whole family? For Greek and Italian dishes and what some people think are the best steaks in Drumheller, go to the **Stavros Family Restaurant,** 1103A Highway 9 South, 403/823-6362, stavs@telusplanet.net. Or the **Yavis Family Restaurant,** in the Valley Plaza Shopping Centre, 403/823-8317, which has a family area rather like a European roadside café, along with the Prop Room, a pool room decorated with an aircraft propeller, a lounge and sports bar. Awesome burgers are served here, according to enthusiastic locals. Entrées are varied and affordable, with special dishes for seniors and children. **Fred and Barney's Family Restaurant,** 1222 Highway 9 South, 403/823-3803, is another excellent smorgasbord spot, offering a selection of 45 items including soup, salad bar, and a wide variety of Chinese and Western foods.

Drumheller has a couple of reliable and reputable restaurants specializing in Chinese food. **Diana Restaurant,** 388 Centre St., 403/823-3030 and **Sizzling House,** 160 Centre St., 403/823-8098. And everybody talks about **Whifs Flap Jack House** at the Badlands Motel, 801 Dinosaur Trail, 403/823-7595, even if, like me, they don't care for pancakes. Try the alternatives behind the name: W for waffles, H for hamburgers, I for ice cream, F for flapjacks, yes, and S for salads, anything you can eat between 6 A.M. and 2 P.M. when Whifs is open. There are big lineups on Sundays. Children love it because they can watch the model trains run along tracks that hang from the ceiling. Another fun place is **Old Grouch's Cozy Café**—eat in or take out, bake shop, deli, and gift shop—at 87 Bridge St., 403/823-3803. Everything's made from scratch, prices are unbeatable, and patrons choose the Old Grouch of the Year. It pays to be a grouch as you get a dollar off your already reasonable meal.

Outside Drumheller, there are interesting choices as well. **Mother's Mountain Tea House and Country Store,** 102 First Ave. West, Delia, 403/364-2057, spent two years restoring an old Crown Lumber building to its former glory, now it's complete with antique furniture and gleaming maple floors.

Breads, soups, sandwiches, salads, and light meals are freshly homemade, whether for family orders, groups, or whole busloads. Teahouse prices are reasonable, it is licensed, and wheelchair accessible. The store is filled with craft items from around Alberta and prides itself on old-fashioned country atmosphere. The owners speak English, German, and French.

Rosedeer Hotel, 1 Jewel St., Wayne, (beside the Last Chance Saloon), 403/823-9189, wants your steak to be done the way you like it, so you have the option of doing it yourself! Decor includes such memorabilia as a boar's head, stuffed rattlesnakes, traps, and music boxes.

The Prairie Inn in Morrin, where you can also see a prairie sod house, is reputed to serve the best hamburgers in the world—huge and affordable.

LODGING

Drumheller has lots of intriguing bed-and-breakfast places. The **Inn at Heartwood Manor,** 320 N. Railway Ave., 403/3823-6495, is an outstanding place to stay. It looks a bit garish from the outside, but is warm and comfortable inside. All ten of its rooms have private baths, nine have whirlpool tubs, five have fireplaces, and two have wheelchair access. Rates are affordable and include a large pancake breakfast. The Inn also offers a full spa, with emphasis on Asian healing arts; packages include a full-body massage, makeovers, pedicures, glamour photography, and manicures.

Several of these establishments are historic. **Taste the Past B&B,** 281 2nd St. W., 403/823-5889, was built by a Drumheller coal baron in the early 1900s. It's an original mansion, with each room decorated in period antiques. **Victorian House B&B,** 541 Riverside Dr. W., 403/823-3535, overlooks the Red Deer River and the Badlands. **Rosebud Country Inn and Tea Room B&B,** on Highway 840 in the village of Rosebud near the popular **Rosebud Theatre,** 403/677-2211, is a beautiful place in which each of the ten bedrooms has a queen-size sleigh bed, antique furnishings, private bath, and balcony with scenic view. And there's the new **Sky T*Rex,** Twp Rd., 30-4 at Rge Rd 19-2, near Michichi, 403/364-2297. Be prepared to get up at 2 A.M. and look at the stars as there's an observatory and planetarium on site with telescopes readily available. Rates at all of these are very reasonable, considering their uniqueness (at Sky T*Rex you get a planetarium show included). For information about other B&Bs in the area, write Drumheller B&B Association, Box 865, Drumheller, Alberta T0J 0Y0.

Motels in Drumheller can also be a little different. Apart from its comfortable rooms, the **Badlands Motel,** in a country setting at 801 Dinosaur Trail, 403/823-5155, is well known for its café Whifs (see FOOD section).

DRUMHELLER VALLEY

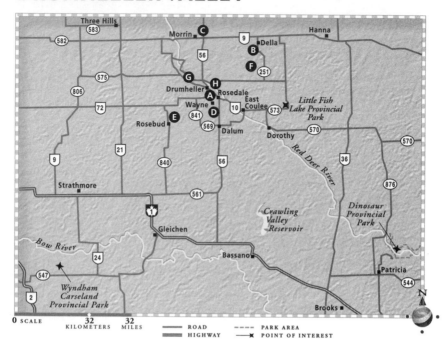

FOOD

- Ⓐ Diana Restaurant
- Ⓐ Drumheller Inn
- Ⓐ The Falcon
- Ⓐ Fred and Barney's Family Restaurant
- Ⓑ Mother's Mountain Tea House and Country Store
- Ⓐ Old Grouch's Cozy Café
- Ⓒ Prairie Inn
- Ⓓ Rosedeer Hotel
- Ⓐ Sizzling House
- Ⓐ Stavros Family Restaurant
- Ⓐ Whifs Flap Jack House
- Ⓐ Yavis Family Restaurant

LODGING

- Ⓐ Badlands Motel
- Ⓐ Best Western Jurassic Inn
- Ⓐ Drumheller Inn
- Ⓐ The Inn at Heartwood Manor
- Ⓔ Rosebud Country Inn and Tea Room B&B
- Ⓕ Sky T*Rex
- Ⓐ Taste the Past B&B
- Ⓐ Victorian House B&B

CAMPING

- Ⓖ Dinosaur Trailer Park
- Ⓖ Dinosaur Trail RV Resort
- Ⓗ Kokopelli Kampground and RV Park
- Ⓐ River Grove Campground and Cabins

Note: Items with the same letter are located in the same area.

SIDE TRIP: DINOSAUR PROVINCIAL PARK

Dinosaur Provincial Park is a natural preserve that is designated a UNESCO World Heritage Site because of the richness and diversity of the 35 dinosaur species (75 million years old) already found there, as well as those still embedded in its deeply eroded Badlands. Indeed, the fossilized remains of nearly 300 species of Cretaceous-period animals and plants have been discovered here. Many of the specimens displayed in the Royal Tyrrell Museum came from here, and the museum conducts major digs every summer in this area.

The park covers more than 7,300 hectares (more than 18,000 acres) with self-guiding trails to reveal its natural and cultural history. Lying alongside the Red Deer River, the park is approximately 150 km (95 mi) southwest of the Royal Tyrrell, but it's well worth the additional driving distance or taking one of the special interpretive tours, some of which are wheelchair accessible.

The Badlands Bus Tour takes you on a two-hour ride (led by a park staff member) into the very heart of Dinosaur Provincial Park to see and hear what's so unique about it—and why it's a World Heritage Site. Because not all of the buses can accommodate wheelchairs, phone ahead, 403/387-4342, to make necessary arrangements.

The Centrosaurus Bone Bed Hike takes a little more than two hours and goes to a weirdly shaped area about the size of a football field, where you see firsthand one of the world's most exciting excavation sites. The Fossil Safari Hunt is also a two-hour hike to a micro-vertebrate fossil site in the Natural Preserve to see fossils and discover exciting new facts about the creatures that lived in this river delta 75 million years ago. Guides lead both of these hikes. Remember to wear proper walking shoes and a hat, and bring sunscreen, binoculars, a camera, and water.

Tickets for these three tours are sold at the Field Station (located in Dinosaur Provincial Park) at 8:30 A.M. for the morning tour and 12:30 P.M. for the afternoon tour. Tours are limited to 17 to 24 participants, so in July and August especially, plan to arrive 30 minutes early. Tickets cost $4.50 adults and $2.25 ages 6–17; youths under 6 are free but require a ticket stub.

Further information is available from the Bookings Officer, Royal Tyrrell Museum, P.O. Box 7500, Drumheller, T0J 0Y0, 403/823-7707, rtmp@dns.magtech.ab.ca.

If you want a full service hotel, your two choices are the **Drumheller Inn,** 100 S. Railway Ave. (Hwy. 9), 403/823-8400, a large complex with 100 rooms, the Skyline Dining Room, Jessie's Restaurant and Pub 57; and the **Best Western Jurassic Inn** at 1103 Highway 9 South, 403/823-7700, 888/823-3466.

CAMPING

These campgrounds are all pleasantly quiet and offer scenic walks particularly suited for late afternoons or evenings. Both **Dinosaur Trailer Park,** 403/823-3291, and **Dinosaur Trail RV Resort,** 403/823-9333, are along Dinosaur Trail North; **River Grove Campground and Cabins,** 403/823-6655, is on Poplar St., north of the bridge in town. Each sits alongside a river, which adds to the walks' scenery.

In Rosedale just five minutes from Drumheller is **Kokopelli Kampground and RV Park,** 403/823-2890. It's off the beaten path, nestled under giant cottonwood trees on the west side of the Rosebud River. A nice place to bird-watch.

NIGHTLIFE

Dream of dinosaurs!

17
CALGARY

Set between rolling foothills to the west and the prairie plains to the east, Calgary offers the best of two worlds: big-city stimulation and accessible wilderness serenity. Images of cowhands, chuckwagons, oil wells, and ski slopes identify Calgary as friendly, energetic, and progressive. The United Nations has recognized it as one of the best cities in the world.

Calgary appeals to both sophisticated and unsophisticated tastes with fashionable shops; a variety of theaters for drama, ballet, symphony, and opera; ultramodern works of art; and restaurants offering every cuisine imaginable—Old World to indigenous people to Asian to sizzling, lean Alberta steaks. For those who prefer outdoor pursuits, Calgary has a zoo, a prehistoric park, a pioneer village, botanical gardens, walks along two sparkling rivers, and awesome, hot-air-balloon views of the city and countryside.

Calgary also has other extraordinary assets: the enviable reputation of being the least-expensive city of its size on the entire North American continent and more hours of sunshine each year than anywhere else in Canada. That's a big reason why Calgarians are so outdoorsy. All told, Calgary, for its size, has the best variety of activities, parks, golf courses, and restaurants of any city in Canada.

A PERFECT DAY IN CALGARY

Begin with breakfast at the Panorama Restaurant in the Calgary Tower for an overview of the city, then drive to Fort Calgary Historic Park to recall the times when Sam Livingston, Calgary's first settler, confronted the Northwest Mounted Police when they came to his land to build a fort. Then, go south, as Sam did, down the Elbow River to where Glenmore Reservoir has now flooded "his" valley, and visit Heritage Park—the Livingston House is part of this pioneer village, and effigies of Sam and his wife are on display.

In the afternoon, head for Canada Olympic Park to get the feel of bob sled-racing and ski-jumping with simulators, and if you have the courage, take a thrilling luge run. Back in town for a change of pace, meander through the Calgary Zoo, Prehistoric Park and Botanical Gardens, or the Devonian Gardens. In the evening, buy a big juicy charbroiled steak, probably at Hy's or the Keg, and finish the day at one of Calgary's nightclubs, dancing to western music and trying to become part (if only temporarily) of "cowboy and cattle country."

The best time to visit Calgary is in July during the Calgary Stampede. Dress western like everybody else, start the day with a pancake breakfast on the street, watch the kick-off parade, go to the rodeo in the afternoon, and watch the chuckwagon races and grandstand stage show in the evening. In between, meet and mingle with some of Calgary's friendly locals. In Calgary, people can be a drawing card as much as the place—and there's no better time to meet them than Stampede time.

ORIENTATION

It's easy to get to and around Calgary, which is situated at the confluence of the Bow and Elbow Rivers. Banff is 120 kilometers (80 miles) west, Edmonton is 294 kilometers (176 miles) north, and the U.S. border 244 kilometer (151 miles) south. Passengers rank Calgary International Airport as the third best airport in the world for overall performance. Adults like it because it's easy to get around, and kids love it for Kidsport, a play area on the departures' level that contains a mini-Jumbo jet, a mock runway with step-activated lights and a playroom featuring toys and movies. It's cheap to get downtown by shuttle bus only 20 minutes away.

Getting there by road is easy as well. Major highways run through the city. Highway 2 (16th Avenue) runs north/south through the city and Highway 1 (9th Avenue)—the Trans-Canada Highway—runs east/west. This makes a nice quadrant (grid) with Centre Street separating east from west and the Bow River/Memorial Drive separating north from south. Streets run north/south; avenues run east/west, numbering starts at the center of the grid and moves outward. Special trails—Crowchild Trail, Macleod Trail, Deerfoot Trail—provide handy overrides.

MOUNTIES AT THE CALGARY STAMPEDE

Lee Foster

Calgary has both bus and light-rail rapid transit (C-train), the latter is free in the downtown area. Handi-bus provides transport for the physically and mentally impaired (visitors and residents alike). Downtown is busy and has a number of attractions that are easily accessible by foot or on the C-train. It's a friendly city for a walk. Take the self-guiding tour of Stephen Avenue, a pedestrian mall that extends from Macleod Trail west along Eighth Avenue to Third Street SW and look at all the historic buildings.

SIGHTSEEING HIGHLIGHTS

★★★★ CALGARY EXHIBITION AND STAMPEDE
14th Ave. and Olympic Way SE, 403/261-0101, 800/661-1260, www.calgary-stampede.com

This world-renowned international rodeo occurs for 10 days within the first two weeks of July and must be booked months ahead to obtain better seats for events you really wish to see. The entire city becomes a ten-day Wild West show—flapjacks, chuckwagons, casinos, a midway, and street dancing create a festival atmosphere that's unparalleled anywhere. Popular rodeo events include wild horse racing, wild cow milking, bull riding, bareback riding, but most popular are the

CALGARY

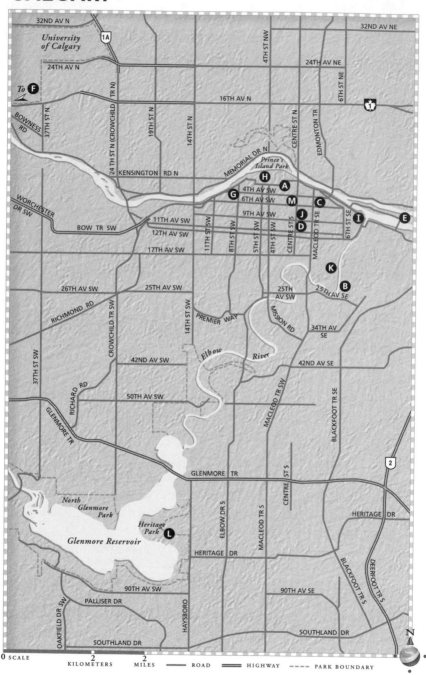

32ND AV N
University of Calgary
1A
32ND AV NE
24TH AV N
24TH AV NE
To **F**
16TH AV N
4TH ST NW
6TH ST NE
BOWNESS RD
37TH ST N
24 TH ST N (CROWCHILD TR N)
19TH ST N
14TH ST N
Centre St N
EDMONTON TR
1
KENSINGTON RD N
MEMORIAL DR N
Prince's Island Park
WORCHESTER DR SW
H
A
BOW TR SW
11TH AV SW
4TH AV SW
G
6TH AV SW
M
C
12TH AV SW
9TH AV SW
J
17TH AV SW
11TH ST SW
8TH ST SW
5TH ST SW
4TH ST SW
Centre St S
Macleod TR SE
6TH ST SE
I
E
D
26TH AV SW
25TH AV SW
25TH AV SW
25TH AV SE
K
B
RICHMOND RD
CROWCHILD TR SW
14TH ST SW
PREMIER WAY
MISSION RD
34TH AV SE
RICHARD RD
42ND AV SW
Elbow River
42ND AV SE
37TH ST SW
50TH AV SW
MACLEOD TR SW
BLACKFOOT TR SE
GLENMORE TR
GLENMORE TR
2
North Glenmore Park
ELBOW DR S
MACLEOD TR S
CENTRE ST S
HERITAGE DR
Heritage Park
L
BLACKFOOT TR S
DEERFOOT TR S
Glenmore Reservoir
HERITAGE DR
OAKFIELD DR SW
90TH AV SW
90TH AV SE
PALLISER DR
HAYSBORO
SOUTHLAND DR
SOUTHLAND DR

N

0 SCALE
2 KILOMETERS
2 MILES
ROAD — HIGHWAY ■■■ PARK BOUNDARY

chuckwagon races. Your ticket to the races is also your ticket to the grandstand stage spectacular in the evening. The Stampede is an unforgettable experience. For the rest of the year, the park also hosts thoroughbred and harness racing, horse shows, agricultural shows and various trade shows.

Details: *Admission varies according to events and seating. (5 days)*

★★★★ CALGARY TOWER
101 9th Ave. SW, 403/266/7171

This 191-meter (627-feet) tower will give you a spectacular view of Calgary and the Rocky Mountains from the Observation Terrace or the revolving restaurant, which serves dishes as superb as the views.

Details: *Open May daily 8 A.M.–11 P.M.; $5.90 adults, $4 ages 13–18, $3.75 over 64, $2.70 ages 2–17. (1 hour, longer if you dine)*

★★★★ CALGARY ZOO, BOTANICAL GARDENS, AND PREHISTORIC PARK
1300 Zoo Rd. NE, 403/232-9300, 800/588-9993, www.calgaryzoo.ab.ca

This complex is world-renowned, famous for conservation, scientific studies, education, and recreation (rated among the top-ten zoos in North America). It is unique in combining a zoo, a botanical garden and a prehistoric park. Enjoy Breakfast with the Gorillas every second Saturday from 7 to 9 A.M. The Prehistoric Park has 23 life-size dinosaur replicas. Only a few minutes from downtown, the park is fully wheelchair-accessible, and largely built on islands within the Bow River, this complex is a must-see! Guided tours available.

Details: *Open daily at 9 A.M. year-round, closing time varies seasonally; admission May–Sept. $9 adults, $4.75 over 64, $4.75 ages 2–17,*

SIGHTS

- Ⓐ Calgary Chinese Cultural Centre Museum
- Ⓑ Calgary Exhibition and Stampede
- Ⓒ Calgary Police Service Interpretive Centre
- Ⓓ Calgary Tower
- Ⓔ Calgary Zoo, Botanical Gardens, and Prehistoric Park
- Ⓕ Canada Olympic Park
- Ⓖ Devonian Gardens
- Ⓗ Eau Claire Market
- Ⓘ Fort Calgary Historic Park
- Ⓙ Glenbow Museum, Art Gallery, Library and Archives
- Ⓚ Grain Academy
- Ⓛ Heritage Park Historical Village
- Ⓜ Lunchbox Theatre

Note: Items with the same letter are located in the same area.

*Tue.–Thu.; admission rest of year, $8 adults, $4 over 64, $4 ages 2–17,
Tue.–Thu. (4 hours)*

★★★★ FORT CALGARY HISTORIC PARK
750 Ninth Ave. SE, 403/290-1875, www.fortcalgary.ab.ca

Many Calgarians have passed this spot at the confluence of the Bow
and Elbow Rivers without realizing that their city began as a fort here
in 1875. The spot is marked by gateways, log stumps, and plaques, and
the story is told by audiovisual presentations at the interpretive center.
Presently, the fort is being rebuilt with 1875 tools (watch it happen)
and includes hands-on interactive displays. A good place to use your
imagination. On Fridays between May and October, at the Deane
House Historic Site and Restaurant, just across the Elbow River, visitors can enjoy an evening of mirth and mayhem at the Friday Night
Mystery from History Dinner Theatre.

> **Details:** *Open May–mid-Oct. daily 9 A.M.–5 P.M.; $5 adults, $4.25 over
> 64, $2.50 ages 7–17. (1 hour)*

★★★★ GLENBOW MUSEUM, ART GALLERY, LIBRARY, AND ARCHIVES
**130 Ninth Ave. SE, across from the Calgary Tower,
403/268-4100 (for latest exhibitions and programs),
403/237-8988, www.glenbow.org**

This is Western Canada's largest museum and naturally focuses on the
settlement and development of the west, with rare manuscripts,
books, photo collections, artifacts, art, special international collections,
as well as pre-contact history. Here you have it all. Food and guided
tours available.

> **Details:** *Open daily year-round Jun.–Oct. 9 A.M.–5 P.M., rest of year
> Tue.–Fri. 9 A.M.–5 P.M. (i.e. closed Mon. except during the summer when it's
> open daily). Admission: $8 adults, $6 over 64, students with ID and ages
> 7–18. (2 hours)*

★★★★ HERITAGE PARK HISTORICAL VILLAGE
**1900 Heritage Dr. SW, 403/259-1900, 403/259-1910
(special events line), heritage@heritagepark.org,
www.heritagepark.ab.ca and www.heritagepark.org**

Set on a 25-hectare (60-acre) site near the Glenmore Reservoir on
Heritage Drive, this park is a re-creation of pre-1914 prairie life and
Canada's largest living historical village. Most of its buildings are orig-

inals that have been moved to the park—a general store; a black-smith shop; a Hudson's Bay Company trading post; the Wainwright Hotel; and the Big House, once the home of Calgary's first settlers, Sam and Jane Livingston, and their 14 children. For a history of Calgary from the Livingston viewpoint, see the book *Tell Me Grandmother*. Costumed interpreters bring the village to life through role-playing. You can ride in a horse-drawn wagon, ride the rails behind a steam locomotive of the period, cruise an active stern-wheeler, and thrill to an antique midway. Guided tours are available. The TV series *Lonesome Dove* was filmed here.

Details: *Open Victoria Day in May–Labour Day in Sept. daily 9 A.M.–5 P.M.; weekends and holidays plus after Labour Day–mid-Oct., 10 A.M.–5 P.M.; admission with rides: $17 adults, $13 ages 3–16; village only (no rides) $10 adults, $6 ages 3–16. All tickets include a free Stampede-style breakfast if you get there 9–10 A.M. (3 hours)*

★★★ CANADA OLYMPIC PARK

88 Canada Olympic Rd. SW, 403/247-5452, www.coda.ab.ca

This venue for 1988's XV Olympic Winter Games is now a year-round premier sport and tourist attraction. Guided bus tours are available daily for a close up look at the facilities and the breathtaking view from the top of the 90-meter (295-foot) ski-jump tower. The ski hill offers alpine and cross-country skiing and snowboard programs in winter. The Olympic Hall of Fame and Museum pay homage to Canada's athletes; and if you seek thrills (not recommended for young children), you can hurtle down the Bobsleigh Bullet ride in winter and the luge in summer. In the Olympic Hall of Fame, one simulator re-creates the thrills, twists, turns, and high speeds of bobsleigh racing; another, the 70-meter (230-foot) "flight" of a ski-jumper.

Details: *Open May–Sept. daily 8 A.M.–9 P.M., and the rest of the year 10 A.M.–10 P.M.; admission self-guided tour, $5 adults, $18 family (2 adults and their kids); guided tour $10 adults, $28 family. Olympic Hall of Fame admission included in Canada Olympic Park admission. Bobsleigh Bullet ride $39 Nov.–Mar.; luge $13 mid-Jun.–Aug. (2 hours)*

★★★ DEVONIAN GARDENS

Downtown Calgary at Eighth Ave between Second and Third Sts, 403/268-5207 or 403/268-3888 (events schedule)

This one-hectare (2.5-acre), glassed-in gardens holds more than 20,000 plants as well as reflecting pools, bridges, waterfalls, an art gallery, and a play area for the youngsters. Occasional noon-hour stage performances enhance your visit.

Details: *Open daily year-round 9 A.M.–9 P.M.; free. (2 hours)*

★★★ EAU CLAIRE MARKET
At Second Ave. and Second St. SW adjacent to Prince's Island Park, 403/264-6460, marketing@eauclaire.com

Worth a walk around this fresh food market and food court as a change of pace from museums. This new attraction is also full of specialty shops, restaurants, feature film and IMAX movie theaters. Clowns, musicians and bands provide ongoing entertainment. Good for atmosphere and some exercise.

Details: *(1 hour)*

★★ CALGARY CHINESE CULTURAL CENTRE MUSEUM
197 First St. SW, 403/262-5071

Set in Calgary's Chinatown is this unique museum—the only one in Canada to present Chinese culture exclusively. Exhibitions, an arts and crafts store, and an authentic Chinese restaurant are found in a delightful architecturally correct setting that is wheelchair accessible. It's worth seeing for its six-story hall modeled after the Temple of Heaven in Beijing. Guided tours available.

Details: *Open year-round daily 11 A.M.–5 P.M.; $2 adults; $1 seniors, students, and children 6–12. (1 hour)*

★★ LUNCHBOX THEATRE
205 Fifth Ave SW, second level, 403/265-4297

Professional one-act plays, musicals, revues, and comedies are produced Monday through Saturday—special evening shows, too—at Canada's longest-running noontime theater.

Details: *Open Sept.–May, Mon.–Sat., noon–1 P.M.; $7/person. (1 hour)*

★ CALGARY POLICE SERVICE INTERPRETIVE CENTRE
Level 2 of 316 Seventh Ave. SE, at the City Hall C-Train stop, 403/268-4566

Kids will like to try on police uniforms, sit at the wheel of a computer-equipped police car, and match wits with interactive computer/video displays in this crime museum.

Details: *Phone for times of operation, $2 adults, free seniors and youth. (1 hour)*

For a dramatic photograph of sculptures, point the lens at the Family of Man outside the Calgary Board of Education Building at 515 Macleod Trail, SE. Nude and 6.5 meters (21 feet) tall, they extend their arms and hands in gestures of goodwill and friendship, an appropriate sculpture for a friendly city such as Calgary.

★ **GRAIN ACADEMY**
At the main entrance of Stampede Park off Fourth St. SE on the second floor of Round Up Centre, 403/263-4594
If you or the kids want to know how grain gets from the field to the table, this is the place. Highlights include a miniature grain elevator and working model of a train, which depicts how grain gets from the prairie to the Pacific coast.

Details: Open weekdays 10 A.M.–4 P.M., rest of the year Sat. noon–4 P.M.; free. (1 hour)

FITNESS AND RECREATION

Calgary has more than 300 kilometers (200 miles) of pathways along riverbanks and through parks for safe and extensive walking, jogging, in-line skating and cycling—along the Bow River, Elbow River, Fish Creek, Nose Creek, around the Glenmore Reservoir and through Fish Creek Provincial Park. Buy a pathway map for a dollar and GO! Phone **Calgary Parks and Recreation Information Services** 403/268-3888 for further details. Particularly pleasant is the **Inglewood Bird Sanctuary,** 2425 Ninth Ave. SE, on the Bow River. Look for some of the 250 species of birds and mammals that have been spotted along the self-guiding trails that wind through the forest. The visitor center is open daily dawn to dusk, 403/269-6688. Free.

In addition to its natural areas, the city has many artificial facilities for indoor and outdoor recreation year-round. Its experience as host for the 1988 Winter Olympics boosted its inventory. Several "leisure venues" are scattered around the city. **Village Square Leisure Centre Indoor Water Park,** 2623 56th St. NE, 403/280-9714, has a wave pool, one of North America's longest indoor water slides, one which is six stories high (568 feet/173 meters), two ice arenas, arts and crafts rooms, weight training rooms, racquet courts, gyms with rock-climbing walls, and sports halls. **Eau Claire YMCA** is an exceptional full-service fitness facility located downtown on the banks of the Bow River, 101 Third St. SW, 403/269-6701.

There's lots more to do in this sports-oriented city. To find an operator that suits you, ask the Calgary Convention and Visitors Bureau, 800/661-1678, or locally 403/263-8510, www.tourismcalgary.com. Kids will love **Calaway Park,** 11 kilometers (8 miles) west of Calgary on Highway 1, Western Canada's largest amusement park. General admission is $18.50 (reduced for kids and seniors) and includes all rides and special shows, 403/240-3822. In Calgary, there's something for everyone.

FOOD

Calgary is home to big juicy Alberta beefsteaks, barbecue, prime ribs, and stacks of syrup-sloshed flapjacks served from a chuckwagon at the Calgary Stampede. Enjoy the city's western flavor at its many steakhouses, where you'll get a country atmosphere, a saloon, reasonable prices, and free two-step lessons.

Billy MacIntyre's Cattle Company, in the Brentwood Village Mall, Crowchild Trail N.W., 403/282-6614, prides itself on being Alberta's most award-winning restaurant. It gets attention with its reasonable prices and drinks such as "Skip and Go Naked." Its Rattlesnake Saloon is especially popular after dinner for country and new music dancing. **Ranchman's Restaurant,** 9615 Macleod Tr. S., 403/253-1100, has an authentic Western saloon, a dance hall, and a museum of rodeo memorabilia and photographs to enliven its western menu. Real local cowboys go to this saloon, and Thursday is Ladies' Night, with free admission for women all night and free admission for everyone before 8 P.M. **Dusty's Saloon,** 1088 Olympic Way SE, 403/263-5343, serves excellent homemade sausage and buffalo burgers and offers country and western dancing on the city's largest floating dance floor—as well as free two-step lessons on Tuesday and Wednesday. **Buzzard's Cowboy Cuisine,** 140 10th Ave. SW, 403/264-6959, offers contemporary versions of actual chuckwagon-style recipes from the open plains. Serves bison as well as beef, and their own Buzzard's Breath Ale.

Of course, to relish unadulterated Grade A Alberta beef, you can always go to the reliable steakhouses. At **Hy's Steakhouse,** 316 Fourth Ave. SW, 403/263-2222, dinners are fairly expensive, but early bird specials are offered regularly. There are at least four Keg Restaurants in Calgary, and their steaks and salad bars are predictably good and well-priced. Try the Billy Miner Mud Pie at **Keg Restaurant Glenmore,** corner of 11th Ave. and Fifth St. SW, 403/226-1036.

For traditions of another kind, sample First Nations cuisine of buffalo, bannock, venison, and rabbit at the **Chief Chiniki Restaurant and Handicraft Centre**, on the Trans-Canada Highway at Morley, 403/881-3748. **Dante's Café and Wine Bar,** 210, 513 Eighth Ave. SW, 403/237-5787, specializes in wild game such as wild boar, reindeer, pheasant, and buffalo. The host is author of a wild game cookbook. For those seeking old-fashioned cooking of another sort, check out the **Arden Diner** serving macaroni and cheese, and tuna casserole. Singing star Jann Arden and her brother are co-owners of the restaurant and have adapted their mother's recipes to appeal to aging baby boomers raised on simple home-style cooking. You'll find them at 1112 17th Ave. SW, 403/228-2821.

There are many Italian restaurants in Calgary. **La Dolce Vita Ristorante Italiano** in Calgary's "Little Italy," at 916 First Ave. NE, 403/263-3445, offers fresh seafood, pasta, quail, and veal cooked to perfection, but at the high end of the cost scale. A little cheaper is **Teatro,** 200 Eighth Ave. SE. The chef uses a woodburning oven to prepare inventive renditions of Italian traditions that he calls "Italian Market cuisine." The restaurant is in the historic Dominion Bank building, across from the Centre for Performing Arts. It's a very hip place to be seen. A new kid on the block is **Centini,** 1202 First St. SW, 403/262-6622. Created by well-known local restaurant designers, Mike and Sylvia Baboushkin in partnership with chef Fabio Centini, this boldly decorated restaurant is classy. Food is imaginative and features chicken, seafood, and of course, Alberta beef.

As everywhere in Western Canada, Thai food is a favorite. Many like the **Thai Sa-on,** 351 10th Ave. SW, 403/264-3526, for consistent quality. Others prefer **The King and I,** 822 11th Ave. SW, 403/264-7241, for such exotics as marinated chicken wrapped in pandulus banana leaves. Even more exotic is the **Sultan's Tent,** 909 17th Ave. SW, 403/244-2333, Calgary's first Moroccan restaurant, which is made to look like the inside of a Berber tent. Try the six-course, two-and-a-half-hour "Sultan's Feast." Chinese restaurants have been around a long time in Calgary. One of the favorites is **Regency Palace,** a large seafood restaurant on top of Dragon City Plaza, 403/777-2288, where buffets offer good value and daily dim sum is popular.

Although eating out can be fairly cheap in Calgary, here are some choices that give the most for your money. **Mother Tucker's,** 345 10th Ave. SW, 403/262-5541, has a children's menu and an extensive salad bar. Dinners run $11 to $20. There is a fresh and healthy multiethnic menu and low prices (under $10 entrees) at the **4th Street Rose Restaurant,** 2116 Fourth St. SW, 403/228-5377. The best value is the ever-changing gourmet menu at **SAIT (Highwood Dining Room Hospitality Careers),** a world-class, student-

CALGARY

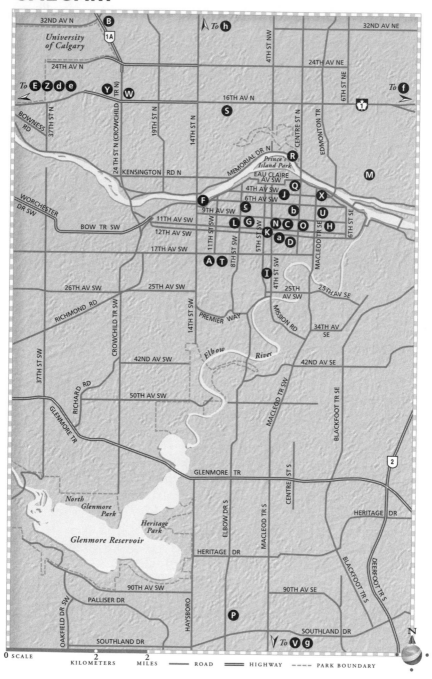

operated training facility at 1301 16th Ave. NW, 403/284-8612. Don't count on it at weekends, despite the lavish five-course meals served weekdays.

Making a quick jump sky-ward in the price scale, but worth it for a special occasion, is the **Panorama Dining Room,** atop the Calgary Tower in Palliser Square at 101 Ninth Ave. SW, 403/266-7171. The restaurant revolves slowly in order to offer fabulous views of the city and the surrounding countryside, the foothills, and the Rockies. Dishes are not cheap and it costs $5.50 extra to ride the elevator whether dining or not, but it's worth the splurge.

You know there's got to be something good about a restaurant when all it needs in a magazine ad is its name. This is the **River Café,** located across the bridge from Eau Claire Market in Prince's Island Park, 403/261-7670. Its setting, in a city park beside the river, is quiet, romantic and perfect for summertime people-watching. The food is imaginative, especially the daily specials, breads and desserts. It's a Calgary favorite. Another upscale riverside restaurant is **The Cross House Garden Café** on the Bow River at 1240 Eighth Ave. SW, 403/531-2767. It is the historic home of A.E. Cross, one of the Big Four, Founders of the Stampede. It has excellent nouvelle cuisine prepared by an award-winning chef.

FOOD

- Ⓐ Arden Diner
- Ⓑ Billy MacIntyre's Cattle Company
- Ⓒ Buzzard's Cowboy Cusine
- Ⓓ Centini
- Ⓔ Chief Chiniki Restaurant and Handicraft Centre
- Ⓕ Cross House Garden Café
- Ⓖ Dante's Café and Wine Bar
- Ⓗ Dusty's Saloon
- Ⓘ Fourth Street Rose Restaurant
- Ⓙ Hy's Steakhouse
- Ⓚ Keg Restaurant Glenmore
- Ⓛ The King and I

FOOD *(continued)*

- Ⓜ La Dolce Vita Ristorante Italiano
- Ⓝ Mother Tucker's
- Ⓞ Panorama Dining Room
- Ⓟ Ranchman's Restaurant
- Ⓠ Regency Palace
- Ⓡ River Café
- Ⓢ SAIT
- Ⓣ Sultan's Tent
- Ⓤ Teatro
- Ⓥ Thai Sa-On

LODGING

- Ⓥ Babbling Brook Bed and Breakfast
- Ⓦ Best Western Village Park Inn
- Ⓧ Delta Bow Valley

LODGING *(continued)*

- Ⓨ Econolodge
- Ⓩ Four Points Sheraton Hotel and Suites
- ⓐ Holiday Inn Calgary Downtown
- ⓑ Palliser
- ⓒ Ramada Hotel Downtown

CAMPING

- ⓓ Calaway Park RV Campground
- ⓔ KOA Calgary West
- ⓕ Mountain View Farm Campground
- ⓖ Pine Creek RV Campground
- ⓗ Symon's Valley BBQ Ranch and RV Park

Note: Items with the same letter are located in the same area.

LODGING

As you'd expect in a large city, accommodation ranges from deluxe to bare-bones. There tends to be a lack of small, family oriented hotels in the city center, and, oddly, considering the city's reputation for hospitality, there are few bed-and-breakfasts. How to choose one place over another? You may want to consider distance from downtown, the airport, or the light-rail transit system; fitness facilities; or proximity to parks and riverbank trails.

Probably the oldest (1914) and best known is the **Palliser,** a typically regal Canadian Pacific Hotel. The Palliser is a large, renovated, turn-of-the-century hotel that attracts visiting dignitaries. Located at 133 Ninth Ave. SW, 403/262-1234 or 800/441-1414, it is conveniently connected via skywalk to the convention center, the performance center, and the Glenbow Museum. Rates are expectedly at the high end, but they can change according to demand, and there's a discount for seniors.

Chains are the way to go in Calgary. A first-class downtown hotel is the **Delta Bow Valley,** at 209 Fourth Ave. SE, 403/266-1980 or 800/268-1133 (Canada), or 800/877-1133 (U.S.). It has fully equipped fitness facilities and an award-winning dining room, The Conservatory. Children are welcome. The hotel has a Kids Creative Centre, and those under 6 eat free. The **Ramada Hotel Downtown,** 708 Eighth Ave. SW, 403/263-7600 or 800/661-8684, is only two blocks from the Eaton Centre and half-a-block from the light-rail. It has an outdoor heated pool, poolside rooms, and the usual fitness facilities.

There are four Best Western hotels, but in terms of ambiance, the best choice is the **Best Western Village Park Inn,** 1804 Crowchild Trail NW, 403/289-0241 or 800/528-1234. It is the smallest of the four, has a lovely atrium, and the rates are slightly lower than the others (children stay free). Among the few smaller downtown hotels is the **Holiday Inn Calgary Downtown** at 119 12th Ave. SW, 403/266-4611 or 800/661-9378. This is the closest nice hotel to the Stampede rounds and is just a short walk from downtown's shopping and offices. Facilities include a small outdoor pool located in the hotel's central courtyard, a bar, and a cheerful café.

A new hotel on the Calgary scene is the **Four Points Sheraton Hotel and Suites,** 8220 Bowridge Crescent NW across from Canada Olympic Park, 877/288-4441. It's a family-style hotel en route to Banff, which makes it convenient, yet it has presidential and honeymoon suites that include fireplaces and jetted tubs, complete health and fitness facilities, plus a water slide, and an on-site massage therapist.

There are many options for the budget-conscious. The **EconoLodge** at 2440 16th Ave. NW, 800/553-2666, has attractive rooms with complimentary coffee. A bed-and-breakfast with a memorable name is the **Babbling Brook**

Bed and Breakfast, at 939 124th Ave. SW, 403/251-0340. Its yard overlooks a brook and walking trails and is close to Fish Creek Park. For names of other B&Bs, contact the B&B Association of Calgary, Box 1462, Station 'M,' Calgary, Alberta T2E 1P3, 403/531-0065.

CAMPING

With the sunniest skies in Canada and friendly people, Calgary is attractive to campers. Here's suggestions for each quadrant, from whichever way you enter the city.

KOA Calgary West is at the western city limits on Highway 1, at Box 10, Site 12, RR1, Calgary, T2M 4N3, 403/3288-0411, reservations 800/562-0842. Like most KOAs, it offers full hookups, tent and trailer space, RV supplies, LP gas, laundry facilities, a recreation room, heated pool, minigolf, nature walks and trails, plus shuttle services to the Stampede, downtown, the zoo, and Heritage Park. It's a pretty good deal. Open April 15 through October 15.

Calaway Park RV Campground is in a country setting located at RR 2, Site 25, Comp 20, 403/249-7372, www.calawaypark.com, yet only 10 kilometers (6 miles) west of the city on the Trans-Canada Highway. Within walking distance are a driving range and Calaway Park, Canada's largest amusement park. It offers a shuttle service to the Stampede grounds, a grocery store, coin laundry and free showers. Open late May to late September.

For Internet surfers, check out the Internet Campground Guide, at www.AlbertaHotels.ab.ca/campgrounds.

Mountain View Farm Campground is open year-round, and is just 3 kilometers (2 mi) east of Calgary, at Site 8, Box 6, RR6, T2M 4N3, 403/293-6640, fax 403/3293-4798. It has a coin phone, laundry, firewood, propane, videos, mini golf, a petting zoo, and a barbecue and dance in the evenings. It offers tours, and German is spoken.

Pine Creek RV Campground, just 1.6 km (1 mi) south of the city on Highway 2, is fully fenced and has a security gate. It's in a country setting near Spruce Meadows Equestrian Centre, golf courses, shopping centers, restaurants, and churches; it also offers pull-throughs, hookups, TV lounge, billiard room, horseshoe pits, pitch 'n' putt golf, and immaculate washrooms, showers, and laundry facilities. Wheelchair accessible. Box 174, De Winton, T0L 0X0, 403/256-3002. Reservations suggested. Rates quoted on inquiry.

To the north is **Symon's Valley BBQ Ranch and RV Park,** RR4, T2M 4L4, 403/274-4574. It offers all the usual facilities plus a shuttle service to the Stampede.

SIDE TRIP: THE WESTERN HERITAGE CENTRE

The Western Heritage Centre, located 2 km (1 mi) north of Cochrane and 40 km (24 mi) west of Calgary on Highway 22, 403/932-3514, is a cowboy ranch, and rodeo interpretive center, which through exhibits, touch-screen technology, and hands-on participation, lets you explore the past, present, and future of western life. You can brand cattle, shear sheep, and rope calves or watch films about it. If you ever wanted to try the life of a cowboy or rancher, this is your chance. Open Victoria Day in May to Labour Day in September daily 9 A.M. to 8 P.M., rest of year 9 A.M. to 5 P.M.; $7.50 adults, $5.50 over 59 and ages 12–17, $3.50 ages 7–11, $20 family rate. Allow 45 minutes if you don't watch the films, two hours if you do.

NIGHTLIFE

Calgary offers nightclubs with music and meals to suit just about every taste—from the **Mercury,** a stylish lounge catering to a young sophisticated crowd at 801b 17th Ave SW, 403/541-1175, to the blues and jazz of **Mad Jack's Saloon,** 438 Ninth Ave. SE, to alternative music catering to Calgary's subculture at places such as **Republik,** 219 17th Ave. SW, 403/244-1884, or **The Ship and Anchor Pub,** 534 17th Ave. SW, 403/245-3333. But beware—if you're over 25 you may get laughed right out of these college-oriented bars. One of the busiest and best nightclub strips is the Eau Claire neighborhood. **The Palace Nightclub,** found on 219 Eighth Ave. SW, 403/263-9980 or 403/263-9981, www.palaceclub.com, is a restored theater from about 1920, open for lunch weekdays, and though I wouldn't use it, it has a members-only cigar lounge.

More mainstream is the country and western style that stamps the city. The must-go bar during Stampede time is **Dusty's Saloon,** 1088 Olympic Way SE, 403/263-5343. It boasts the city's largest floating dance floor, live country bands playing weekend evenings and free line-dancing lessons. The younger crowd loves **Cowboys Dance Hall,** 826 Fifth St. SW, 403/265-0699, www.CowboysNiteClub.com. It's a bar and dance hall that accommodates up to 1,200 people. **The Ranchman's,** 9615 MacLeod Trail South, 403/253-1100, which plays live music six days a week, has been rated as Calgary's top country and western nightclub.

Irish pubs are all the rage. The best is the **James Joyce** situated in the historic Toronto Bank building at 114 Stephan Ave. SW (Stephan Avenue Walk), 403/262-0708. It's a traditional Irish pub with Irish staff, Guinness is served at three temperatures, ordinary pub fare such as shepherds' pie, liver and onions, and Irish stew, and sometimes a live Celtic band. Another authentic Irish pub (the staff was brought over from Ireland to run it) is **Fionn McCool's Irish Pub** on 255 Barclay Parade in the Sheraton Suites Calgary Eau Claire Hotel, 403/517-6699.

APPENDIX

Consider this your travel toolbox. Use it along with the material in the Planning Your Trip chapter to craft the trip you want. Here are the tools you'll find inside:

1. Planning Map. Make copies of this map and plot out various trip possibilities. Once you've decided on a route, write it on the original map and refer to it as you travel.

2. Mileage Chart. This chart shows the driving distances (in miles) between various destinations throughout the province and region. Use it in conjunction with the Planning Map.

3. Special Interest Tours. If you'd like to plan a trip around a certain theme-such as nature, sports, or art—one of these tours may work for you.

4. Calendar of Events. Here you'll find a month-by-month listing of major area events.

5. Resources. This guide lists various regional chambers of commerce and visitors bureaus, provincial offices, bed-and-breakfast registries, and other useful sources of information.

PLANNING MAP: Western Canada

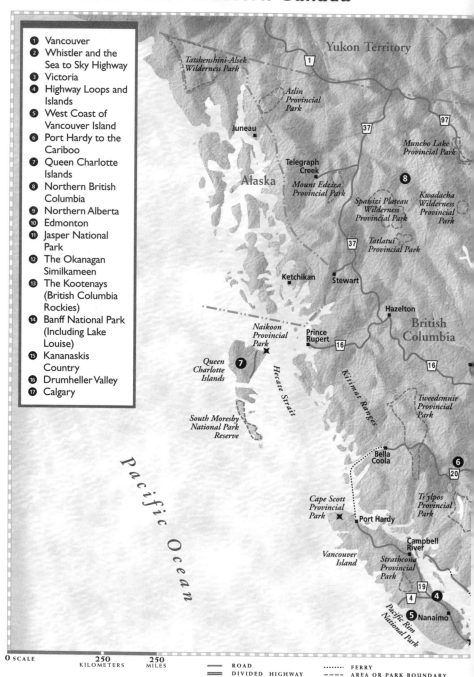

1. Vancouver
2. Whistler and the Sea to Sky Highway
3. Victoria
4. Highway Loops and Islands
5. West Coast of Vancouver Island
6. Port Hardy to the Cariboo
7. Queen Charlotte Islands
8. Northern British Columbia
9. Northern Alberta
10. Edmonton
11. Jasper National Park
12. The Okanagan Similkameen
13. The Kootenays (British Columbia Rockies)
14. Banff National Park (Including Lake Louise)
15. Kananaskis Country
16. Drumheller Valley
17. Calgary

Yukon Territory

Tatshenshini-Alsek Wilderness Park

Atlin Provincial Park

Juneau

Muncho Lake Provincial Park

Telegraph Creek

Alaska

Mount Edziza Provincial Park

Spatsizi Plateau Wilderness Provincial Park

Kwadacha Wilderness Provincial Park

Tatlatui Provincial Park

Ketchikan

Stewart

Hazelton

British Columbia

Naikoon Provincial Park

Prince Rupert

Queen Charlotte Islands

Hecate Strait

Kitimat Ranges

Tweedsmuir Provincial Park

South Moresby National Park Reserve

Bella Coola

Cape Scott Provincial Park

Port Hardy

Ts'ylos Provincial Park

Campbell River

Vancouver Island

Strathcona Provincial Park

Pacific Ocean

Nanaimo

Pacific Rim National Park

O SCALE

250 KILOMETERS

250 MILES

ROAD

DIVIDED HIGHWAY

FERRY

AREA OR PARK BOUNDARY

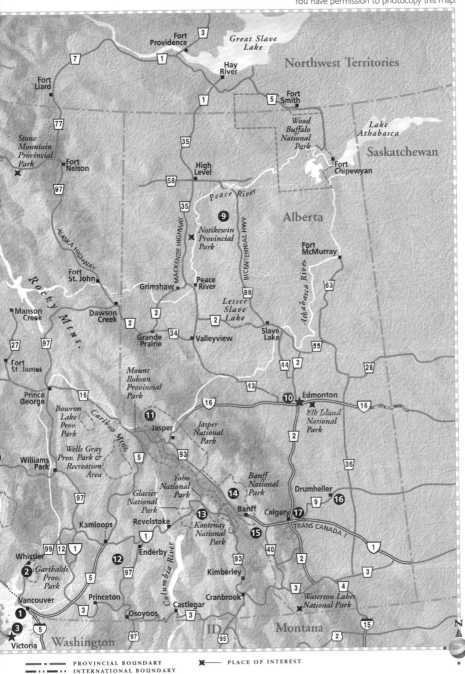

Fort Providence [3]

Great Slave Lake

[7] [1]

Hay River

Northwest Territories

Fort Liard

[1] [5] Fort Smith

[77]

Wood Buffalo National Park

Lake Athabasca

Stone Mountain Provincial Park

Fort Nelson

High Level

Fort Chipewyan

Saskatchewan

[35]

[97]

[58]

Peace River

[35]

9

Notikewin Provincial Park

Alberta

BICENTENNIAL HWY

Fort McMurray

ALASKA HIGHWAY

Fort St. John

Grimshaw

Peace River

Fort McMurray

[63]

MACKENZIE HIGHWAY

Rocky Mtns.

Manson Creek

Dawson Creek

[2]

Grande Prairie [34]

Valleyview

[88]

Lesser Slave Lake

Slave Lake

Athabasca River

[27] [97]

Fort St. James

[2]

[55]

[28]

Prince George

Mount Robson Provincial Park

[16]

[13]

[44] [2]

Edmonton

[10]

[16]

Bowron Lake Prov. Park

Cariboo Mtns.

11

Jasper

Jasper National Park

Elk Island National Park

[16]

Wells Gray Prov. Park & Recreation Area

Williams Park

[97]

[5]

[93]

Yoho National Park

Banff National Park

14

[2]

Drumheller

[36]

Glacier National Park

Kamloops

Revelstoke

13

Kootenay National Park

Banff

Calgary

17

[9] **16**

[99] [12] [1]

[1]

Enderby

15

TRANS CANADA 1

Whistler

2 Garibaldi Prov. Park

12

[97]

Columbia River

[93]

Kimberley

[40]

[2]

[1]

[5]

[3]

Vancouver

Princeton

Cranbrook

[3]

[4]

Waterton Lakes National Park

1

[3]

Castlegar

[3]

3 [5]

Osoyoos

ID

Montana

[15]

Victoria

Washington

[97]

[95]

[2]

N

	Calgary	Drumheller	Edmonton	Fort McMurray	Jasper	Kananaskis Village	Kelowna	Nelson	Prince George	Prince Rupert	Terrace	Vancouver	Watson Lake	Whistler	Williams Lake
Banff	128/80														
Calgary	263/164	138/86													
Drumheller	401/249	295/183	279/174												
Edmonton	840/522	733/456	703/475	439/273											
Fort McMurray	287/179	413/257	547/340	361/225	796/495										
Jasper	257/160	129/80	249/155	339/211	778/484	372/231									
Kananaskis Village	474/295	602/374	740/460	897/558	1314/817	602/374	559/348								
Kelowna	496/309	624/388	762/474	919/572	1336/831	701/436	581/361	338/210							
Nelson	661/411	789/491	927/577	737/458	1206/750	376/234	746/464	685/426	979/609						
Prince George	1385/861	1513/941	1651/1027	1461/909	1930/1201	1100/684	1470/914	1409/876	1703/1059	724/450					
Prince Rupert	1238/770	1366/850	1504/935	1314/817	1155/718	1687/1049	794/494	932/580	657/409	778/484	147/91				
Terrace	847/527	975/606	1113/692	1155/718	1687/1049	794/494	932/580	395/246	657/409	778/484	1502/934	227/141			
Vancouver	1889/1175	1870/1163	2008/1249	1575/980	2104/1309	1604/998	1974/1228	1913/1190	2207/1373	1228/764	988/615	1500/933	1492/928		
Watson Lake	967/601	1095/681	1233/764	1275/793	1807/1124	914/569	1052/654	515/320	777/483	898/559	1622/1009	308/192	192/119	2126/1322	
Whistler	779/485	907/564	1045/650	904/562	1444/898	543/338	864/537	447/278	741/461	238/148	962/598	757/471	583/363	1466/912	660/411

SPECIAL INTEREST TOURS

With *Travel Smart: Western Canada* you can plan a trip of any length—a one-day excursion, a getaway weekend, or a three-week vacation—around any special interest. To get you started, the following pages contain five special interest itineraries geared toward a variety of interests. For more information, refer to the chapters listed-chapter names are in boldface, and chapter numbers appear inside black bullets. You can follow a suggested itinerary in its entirety, or shorten, lengthen, or combine parts of each, depending on your starting and ending points.

Discuss alternative routes and schedules with your travel companions—it's a great way to have fun even before you leave home. And remember: Don't hesitate to change your itinerary once you're on the road. Careful study and planning ahead will help you make informed decisions as you go, but spontaneity is the extra ingredient that will make your trip memorable.

THE BEST OF WESTERN CANADA TOUR

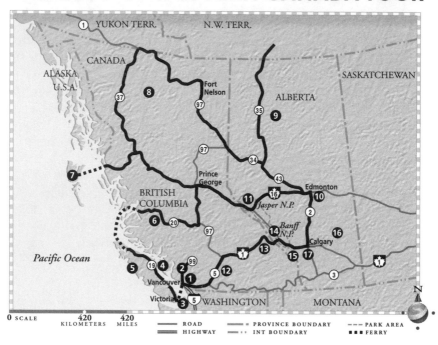

- ❶ Vancouver
- ❷ Whistler and the Sea to Sky Highway
- ❸ Victoria
- ❹ Highway Loops and Islands
- ❺ West Coast of Vancouver Island
- ❻ Port Hardy to the Cariboo
- ❼ Queen Charlotte Islands
- ❽ Northern British Columbia
- ❾ Northern Alberta
- ❿ Edmonton
- ⓫ Jasper National Park
- ⓬ The Okanagan Similkameen
- ⓭ Kootenay Country
- ⓮ Banff/Lake Louise
- ⓯ Kananaskis Country
- ⓰ Drumheller Valley
- ⓱ Calgary

Time needed: 3 to 4 weeks

NATURE LOVER'S TOUR

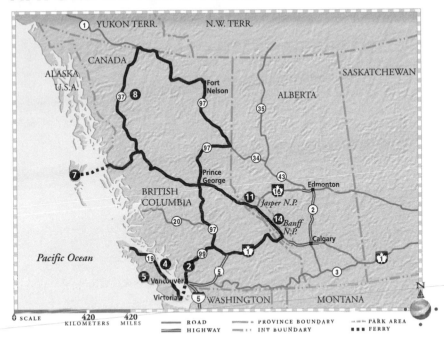

The whole of Western Canada is a nature lover's tour, from the rich marine life, rugged fjords, and forests of the West Coast to the lakes and rivers of the semi-desert interior; from the glaciers and ice sheets of the Rocky Mountains to the rolling prairie beyond.

- ❷ **Whistler and the Sea to Sky Highway** (parks, wintering eagles)
- ❹ **Highway Loops and Islands** (whales, wintering sea birds, spawning salmon, marmots, Nanaimo Sea Lion Festival)
- ❺ **West Coast of Vancouver Island** (Cathedral Grove, Pacific Rim National Park Reserve, Pacific Rim Whale Festival)
- ❼ **Queen Charlotte Islands**

(Gwaii Haanas National Park Reserve, Naikoon Provincial Park, Delkatla Wildlife Sanctuary)
- ❽ **Northern British Columbia** (Photo Safari Tour, provincial parks)
- ⑪ **Jasper National Park** (Icefields Parkway, Columbia Icefield, Mount Edith Cavell, Maligne Lake)
- ⑭ **Banff/Lake Louise** (Bow Valley Parkway, lakes, hot springs)

Time needed: 3 weeks

FIRST NATIONS CULTURE TOUR

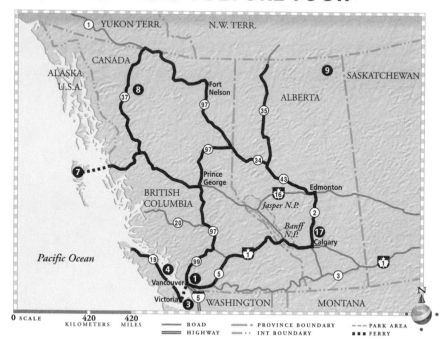

With land claims negotiations as a background, there has been a recent resurgence of interest and pride in First Nations (formerly called *Indian*) culture. Visit the following museums, cultural centers, and villages to learn more about Western Canada's indigenous people.

- ❶ **Vancouver** (UBC Museum of Anthropology)
- ❸ **Victoria** (Royal British Columbia Museum, Thunderbird Park)
- ❹ **Highway Loops and Islands** (Native Heritage Centre, U'mista Cultural Centre, Duncan City of Totems)
- ❼ **Queen Charlotte Islands** (Gwaii Haanas National Park Reserve, Haida Gwaii Museum, Ninstints, Old Masset)
- ❽ **Northern British Columbia** (Hands of History tour through Gitskan Wet-Suweten villages)
- ❾ **Northern Alberta** (Fort Chipewyan)
- ⑰ **Calgary** (Head-Smashed-In Buffalo Jump near Fort McLeod)

Time needed: 10 days

WINE LOVER'S TOUR

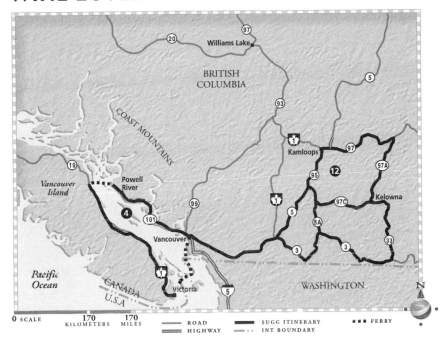

Take this tour in October, when the Okanagan Similkameen has its annual wine festival. Drive Highway 3 through the Similkameen to the Okanagan Valley; follow the highway signs to the wineries of your choice (there are more than 25), pick up local guides at various information centers along the way, and stop often to participate in wine tastings, special dinners, vineyard picnics, and horse-drawn orchard tours.

- **❶ Highway Loops and Islands** (Mill Bay, Cobble Hill, Cowichan Valley, Duncan)
- **⓬ The Okanagan Similkameen** (Keremeos, Osoyoos, Okanagan Falls, Naramata, Summerland, Peachland, Westbank, Kelowna, Vernon)

Time needed: 1 to 2 weeks

FAMILY FUN TOUR

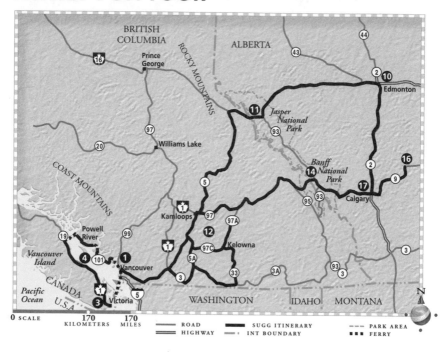

- **①** **Vancouver** (Public Aquarium, Stanley Park, Science World, Kids Festival)
- **③** **Victoria** (Old Town, Royal B.C. Museum, Craigdarroch Castle)
- **④** **Highway Loops and Islands** (Newcastle Island Provincial Marine Park, Coombs Emporium, Cyber City Adventures)
- **⑪** **Jasper National Park** (camping, canoeing, white-water rafting)
- **⑩** **Edmonton** (Space and Science Center, West Edmonton Mall, Valley Zoo, Alberta Aviation Museum, Klondike Days in July)
- **⑰** **Calgary** (Calgary Science Centre, Stampede, Calgary Zoo, Heritage Park Historical Village, Aerospace Museum, Calaway Park)
- **⑯** **Drumheller Valley** (Rosebud Theatre, Royal Tyrrell Museum, Dinosaur Museum, Reptile World, Badlands Go-Kart Park, Funland Amusements, Drumheller Aquaplex, Dinosaur Provincial Park)
- **⑭** **Banff/Lake Louise** (hiking, fishing, wildlife watching, gondola riding)
- **⑫** **The Okanagan Similkameen** (swimming, boating, water sliding, ballooning, Kettle Valley Steam Railway)

Time needed: 2 to 3 weeks

SKIER'S TOUR

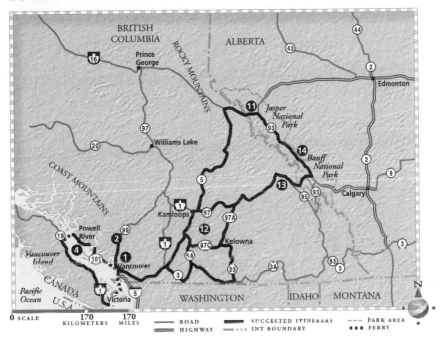

With its many mountains, high plateaus, mild climate, and staggering scenery, Western Canada is a skier's paradise.

- ❶ **Vancouver**(Grouse Mountain)
- ❷ **Whistler and the Sea to Sky Highway** (Whistler Resort)
- ❹ **Highway Loops and Islands** (Mount Washington Ski Resort)
- ⓫ **Jasper National Park** (Marmot Basin)
- ⓮ **Banff/Lake Louise** (Mount Norquay, Sunshine Village)
- ⓭ **Kootenay Country** (Red Mountain)
- ⓬ **The Okanagan Similkameen** (Silver Star Mountain Resort, Big White Ski Resort, Apex Resort)

Time needed: 2 weeks

CALENDAR OF EVENTS

Practically every town in Western Canada puts on some kind of celebration during the year, especially the hectic days of July when the kids are out of school and families are looking for diversions whether they stay at home or travel. There are folk festivals, literary festivals, music festivals, wildlife festivals, cowboy festivals, arts and crafts festivals, storytelling festivals, children's festivals, wine festivals, Oktoberfest beer festivals, First Night/New Year's Eve festivals, winter festivals, sports festivals of different kinds, Parks Day celebrations every summer in mid-July, and festivals devoted to children. Not to be missed are the Calgary Stampede, the Brackendale Eagle Festival, the Edmonton Heritage Festival, Edmonton's Fringe Theatre Event, Canadian Badlands Passion Play, the Pacific Rim Whale Festival, the Symphony of Fire in Vancouver, the Okanagan Wine Festivals, Edmonton's Klondike Days, and anything in Vancouver, Whistler, Victoria, Banff, and Jasper.

January
Banff-Lake Louise Winter Festival, (Banff) 403/762-0270 or
403/762-8421
A torchlight parade, a Town Party, a Mountain Madness Relay Race, a Lake Louise-Banff cross-country ski race, as well as barn dances, and wine tastings.

Ice Magic International Ice Sculpting Competition, (Banff)
403/762-0270 or 403/762-8421
Teams transform blocks of ice into works of art. Weather permitting, the sculptures remain until March.

Jasper in January, (Jasper) 780/852-3858
Prices of ski lift tickets and lodgings drop for two weeks.

Kelowna Snowfest, (Okanagan Similkameen) 250/768-4130
Building snow castles, fishing and swimming in the lake (not yet iced over), and racing beds on wheels.

Polar Bear Swim, (Vancouver) 604/665-3424
On New Year's Day, crowds congregate in the West End to watch the Polar Bear Swim Club (and any other brave souls) dip into the frigid English Bay.

February

Calgary Winter Festival, (Calgary) 403/543-5480
For the first two weeks in February, Calgarians make the most of winter with snow and ice sports and all sorts of entertainment.

Cariboo Cross-Country Ski Marathon, (Port Hardy to the Cariboo) 250/395-3487
Competitors come from all over for cross-country ski racing.

Chinese New Year, (Vancouver) 604/687-0729,
www.vancouverbc.com/Tourism
Crowds gather to celebrate Chinese New Year and to watch the traditional Dragon Parade wind through the streets of Chinatown.

Cowboy Festival, (Calgary) 403/261 8510, 800/822-2697,
www.tourismcalgary.com
In typical Calgary western style, at the Calgary Convention Centre.

International Sled Dog Classic, (Kananaskis Country) 403/762-9277 or 403/678-2400
More than 100 international teams compete in eight classes of dogsled racing.

March

Fort Chipewyan Winter Carnival, (Northern Alberta) 780/697-3682 or 780/697-3600
A good time to mix with First Nations people and participate in their native lifestyle is during the three days of festival time. You can join in activities such as bannock-making, sled dog and snowmobile racing.

Fort Nelson Trappers' Rendezvous, (Northern British Columbia) 250/774-2541
Sled-dog racing, beard-growing contests, and a northern version of Keystone Kops who put you in street jails if you don't show your Rendezvous passport.

Local Heroes International Screen Festival, (Edmonton)
780/421-4084 or 780/496-8400, gateway@ede.org
For those who don't like outdoor winter sports, you can cozy up in

doors watching the best in independent short- and feature-length movies from Canada and around the world.

Pacific Rim Whale Festival, (Vancouver Island) 250/725-3414 or 250/726-4641
More than 20,000 gray whales return to northern feeding grounds from Mexico. Operators with small boats will take you for a closer look..

Vancouver Storytelling Festival, (Vancouver) 604/876-2272
For three days translators assist in several different languages to entertain audiences with stories from around the world.

April

B.C. Tel World Ski and Snowboard Festival, (Whistler and the Sea to Sky Highway) 604/932-3928, info@sea2sky.com
A nine-day athletic competition featuring 2,500 athletes and accompanying celebrity events, film festivals, demo days, and live music.

Brant Wildlife Festival, (Highway Loops and Islands)
The Mid-Island Wildlife Watch Society arranges goose-viewing stations during the migration of thousands of brant (black) geese, birding competitions, nature talks, and displays of wildlife arts and crafts and photography.

Easter Sunrise Service at the Passion Play Site, (Drumheller)
403/823-8100, trex@dinosaurvalley.com
A particularly moving event held annually on Easter Sunday.

Heritage Festival, (Banff) 403/762-0270
This celebration of Canada's western heritage includes an artisan fair, readings by cowboy poets, and a Saturday night concert.

Snow Goose Festival, (Edmonton) 780/662-3269, 780/496-8400, gateway@ede.org
Thousands of migrating geese, cranes, swans, and shorebirds make a magnificent aerial display. Visitors also take in tours, an art show and sale, and a kids' environmental center and activities.

May

Okanagan Spring Wine Festival, (Okanagan) 250/860-5999,
info@ThompsonOkanagan.com
In early May wineries provide tours and tastings; hotels and restaurants
prepare special meals that feature wine.

Clinton Ball, (Port Hardy to the Cariboo) 250/459-2478
In the 1860s this was the social event of the year in the Cariboo; it is re-
putedly the oldest annual event in B.C. Also includes a rodeo.

Dreamspeakers Festival, (Edmonton) 780/471-1199, fax 780/474-3250
For one week annually, this event is an international celebration of
First Nations culture by artisans, filmmakers, and performing artists.

Vancouver International Children's Festival, (Vancouver) http://youngarts.ca/vicf
A great seven-day festival of entertainment, arts, crafts, games, story
telling, and lots of tents full of fun in Vanier Park off English Bay.

Victoria Days and Parade, (Victoria) 250/953-2033
Victoria is named after England's Queen Victoria, and her birthday,
May 24, makes a great reason to throw a city party.

June

This is the month for jazz festivals: Vancouver 604/687-0729, Victoria 250/413-
3144, and Calgary each have their own version.

Banff Festival of the Arts, (Banff) 403/762-6300 or 800/413-8368
More than 1,000 artists from around the world come together to per-
form and give workshops in music, opera, voice, dance, and drama.

Banff TV Festival, (Banff) 403/762-2211, 800/422-2633, or 800/441 1414
View some of the best television from around the world at public
screening rooms when film producers, broadcasters,
directors, writers, and actors discuss their works and present their
programs in competition.

Calgary International Jazz Festival, (Calgary) 403/249-1119,
403/263-8510, alan@calgarycvb.com
Enjoy the concerts, cabarets, dance parties, and free downtown performances as leading musicians play a variety of music from jazz to gospel.

Canadian International Dragon Boat Festival, (Vancouver)
604/688-2382, www.vancouver-bc.com/Tourism
More than 2,000 local and international paddlers race each other in
boats decorated with colorful dragons on their prow.

Du Maurier International Jazz Festival, (Edmonton) 250/432-7166,
780/496-8400, gateway@ede.org
An annual celebration of jazz and blues features local, national, and international artists.

Victoria Folkfest, (Victoria) 250/413-3144, bcode@tourvic.com,
www.tourvic.com
Various ethnic groups share their culture with displays of food, music,
and dancing.

July
B.C. Open Sandcastle Competition, (Highway Loops and Islands)
250/752-9532
About 40,000 people gather on the beach in Parksville to watch "artists"
of all ages build massive life-like images out of sand—everything but castles.

Benson and Hedges Symphony of Fire, (Vancouver) 604/876-2272
English Bay streets are cordoned off for four nights of fireworks and
music.

Calgary Exhibition and Stampede, (Calgary) 403/261-0101,
800/661-1260, alan@calgarycvb.com
Ten days of events such as chuckwagon races, stage spectaculars, a
casino, stock show, and many other city-wide celebrations and events.

Canadian Badlands Passion Play, (Drumheller) 403/823-7750
Enjoy the drama and music as the life of Jesus Christ is brought to life in
an outdoor amphitheater.

Edmonton International Street Performers Festival, (Edmonton)
780/425-5162, gateway@ede.org
Parks and streets come alive for 10 days as street performers—magicians,
clowns, jugglers, mime artists, comics, and musicians—give free shows.

Nanaimo Marine Festival, (Highway Loops and Islands) 250/756-0106, info@tourismnanaimo.com
Activities such as the Silly Boat Race (you have to make and race a boat all in the one morning) culminate in the Nanaimo Bathtub Race between Nanaimo and Kitsilano Beach in Vancouver.

Pysanka Festival, (Edmonton) 780/632-2777
A *pysanka* is a decorated Ukrainian Easter egg and you can see a giant one at this cultural festival—8 meters (24 feet) long, weighs 2.270 kg (5 lb), and turns in the wind like a weathervane. Experience the music, dance, and color of Ukrainian heritage or learn to paint your own Easter egg.

August
There are lots of folk festivals at this time of year in Western Canada—Calgary, 403/233-0904 (end of July) and Edmonton,780/429-1899.

Abbotsford International Air Show Festival, (Vancouver)
604/852-8511
This week-long event attracts 300,000 people with its latest in aircraft technology and daredevil aerial acrobatics.

Canmore Heritage Days Folk Festival, (Kananaskis Country)
403/678-3561 or 403/678-5623
Folk music by national and international performers with accompanying music workshops, an arts and crafts display, and a food fair. It is the longest-running folk festival in Alberta.

Edmonton Heritage Festival, (Edmonton) 780/488-3378
One of the best, it's been around for 22 years. For three days, more than 50 outdoor ethnic pavilions feature non-stop international sights, sounds and tastes.

First Peoples Festival, (Victoria) 250/413-3144, bcode@touvic.com
In early August, this festival is one of the only exclusively tribal-run arts and cultural events in Canada. Enjoy live demonstrations of traditional pursuits of the region's indigenous people such as dancing and carving.

Gold Panning Championships and Raft Race, (Northern British Columbia) 250/789-9015

If you're driving up or down the Alaska Highway in August, stop at Taylor, 56 km(35 mi) north of Dawson Creek, and try your luck at gold panning.

International Fringe Theatre Event, (Edmonton) 780/448-9000, 780/496-8400, gateway@ede.org
One of the largest presentations of innovative drama and music in North America—1,200 performances of 160 productions.

Sechelt Festival of the Written Arts, (Vancouver) 604/885-3100
Canada's writers converge on this picturesque seaside community for a week in mid-August to read and teach and share their writings.

September

Canmore Highland Games, (Kananaskis Country) 403/678-3561, 403/678-5623, info@tc.com
A day of Highland flings, eating (haggis, of course), tug-of-war, tossing the caber, and other Scottish games.

Indy Vancouver Car Race, (Vancouver) 604/684-4639
Streets are cordoned off for three days of car racing by the world's best.

Kimberley's International Folk Dance and Oktoberfest, (Kootenay) 250/427-4877
A Bavarian background and Autumn foliage complement entertainment by ethnic dancers, bagpipe bands, choristers, art displays, sidewalk sales, food booths—oh, Oktoberfest right? There's a "refreshment" garden in the *Platzl* (town square).

The Masters at Spruce Meadows, (Calgary) 403/974-4200
For horse lovers, this event features an equestrian trade show with hundreds of exhibits and seminars.

Pacific National Exhibition, (Vancouver) 604/253-2311, www.pne.B.C.ca
Called the PNE by Vancouverites, this 90 year-old event heralds the end of summer with agricultural exhibits, midway rides, daily parades, and musical entertainment.

World Championship Sand Competition, (Vancouver) 604/826-0029
Some of the most imaginative sand sculptures are created, judged, and

awarded. Since there is no tide in this location, some of the sculptures last well into October—a bonus for the competitors.

October
Festival of the Eagles, (Kananaskis) 403/678-1878
Birders gather to witness the annual migration of at least 500 eagles. Accompanying the eagle watching opportunities are natural history exhibits and demonstrations and evening slide and film presentations.

Okanagan Wine Festival, (Okanagan Similkameen) 250/861-6654
For 10 days, wineries, hotels, and restaurants put on a lavish all day and night party with wine tastings, gourmet meals, progressive dinners, salmon bakes, pig roasts, wine auctions, and a host of entertainment.

World's Largest Garage Sale, (Calgary) 403/261-0101
Only Calgarians could think this one up! If you have any room left in your luggage, go down to the Calgary Stampede Grounds and see what treasures you can find.

November
Canadian Finals Rodeo, (Edmonton) 403/471-7210
This is the final rodeo of the Canadian Pro Rodeo Circuit, so if you missed the Calgary Stampede, try this to see the best of the Canadian cowboys in action.

Banff Festival of Mountain Books, (Banff) 403/762-6125
Geared toward those interested in mountains and mountaineering, this literary festival features guest speakers, readings, book launches, book signings, and a mountain publishers' book fair.

Banff Festival of Mountain Films, (Banff) 403/762-6125
Ditto for films. Same time, same place as the Book Festival. This is one of the most prestigious film festivals of its kind. It previews and honors top mountaineering and adventure films from around the world.

Cornucopia, (Whistler and the Sea to Sky Highway) 604/932-3434
Whistler celebrates the harvest of the Pacific Northwest with a weekend of gourmet dining to showcase the region's best wineries and chefs.

Snow Goose Festival, (Vancouver) 604/946-6980
Birders throng to the George C. Reifel Migratory Bird Sanctuary to
watch migrating snow geese.

December

Carol Ships, (Vancouver) 604/878-9988
Christmas is celebrated all month in Vancouver. Take a mini-cruise to the
decorated carol ships or take your own boat out into English Bay and
Burrard Inlet to listen to Christmas carols. Visit VanDusen Gardens for its
fairyland of lights, 604/878-9274 and Canada Place for displays of lovely
Yuletide scenes called Christmas Under the Sails, 604/666-8477.

Edmonton's First Night Festival, (Edmonton) 780/448-9200
For more than 10 years, Edmonton has been presenting a family oriented, alcohol-free New Year's Eve celebration that includes music, theater, dance, street performers, and films. The party culminates with
rooftop fireworks around Churchill Square.

Whistler's First Night Festival, (Whistler and Sea to Sky Highway)
604/932-3434
Family-oriented entertainment on several outdoor stages that has everybody dancing in the streets, including the little ones if they haven't gone
to the kids' activity tent. The celebrations peak with fireworks.

Whistler Winter Start Festival, (Whistler and the Sea to Sky Highway)
604/932-3434
This is the best in freestyle skiing and snowboarding, along with live
music, fine food and wine, and some of the most spectacular scenery in
the world.

RESOURCES

There are several resources for people planning trips to Western Canada; this book will help you make some sense out of the chaos. British Columbia is divided into nine official tourism regions, each led by a local tourism association. Alberta has six tourism regions, with similar agencies. In addition, many communities open summer travel infocenters. So first, gather the free maps and literature provided by Tourism British Columbia and Travel Alberta, and, if you're a member, get a copy of the free handbook, maps, "trip-tiks," and other material provided by the British Columbia and Alberta Automobile Associations. Then use this book to make choices. Here are some important contacts:

TRAVEL INFORMATION

Alberta Economic Development and Tourism, 10155 102nd Street, Edmonton, Alberta T5J 4L6; 403/427-4321 or 800/661-8888

British Columbia Ferries, 1112 Fort Street, Victoria, British Columbia V8V 4V2. Recorded schedule information: Nanaimo 250/753-6626, Vancouver 604/685-1021, and Victoria 250/656-0757

Calgary Convention and Visitors Bureau, Main Floor, Calgary Tower, Tower Centre, 9th Avenue and Centre Street, South Calgary, Alberta T2G 0K8; 403/263-8510 or 800/661-1678

Cariboo Tourism Association, 190 Yorston Street, Box 4900, Williams Lake, British Columbia V2G 2V8, 250/392-2226 or 800/663-5885.

Edmonton Tourism, 104-9797 Jasper Avenue, Edmonton, Alberta T5J 1N9; 403/496-8400 or 800/463-4667

Guides and Outfitters Association of B.C., Box 94675, Richmond, British Columbia V6Y 4A4; 604/278-2688, GOABC@dowco.com

Heritage Canada, 800/651-7959. Call for National Park information

Kelowna Visitor's and Convention Bureau, 800/663-4345; Penticton Information Centre, 800/663-5052; Vernon Tourism, 250/542-1415; Vernon Reservations, 800/665-0795

Travel Alberta—Northern Alberta Tourism, 800/661-8888 or 800/756-4351

Tourism British Columbia, Parliament Buildings, Victoria, British Columbia V8V 1X4; 800/663-6000, international and local callers, 604/663-6000. In the United States, write Box C-34971, Seattle, Washington 98124-1971. In England, write 1 Regent Street, London, England SW1Y 4NS. Advance reservations for accommodations, advice on British Columbia travel, events, points of interest, publications

Tourism Rockies, Box 10, Kimberley, British Columbia V1A 2Y5; 250/427-4838 or 250/427-3344

Travel Alberta, Box 2500, Edmonton, Alberta T5J 2Z4; 800/661-8888, 403/427-4321, www.discoveralberta.com/ATP

Vancouver Infocentre, Plaza Level, Waterfront Centre, 200 Burrard Street, Vancouver, British Columbia V6C 3L6; 604/683-2000, from the United States 800/888-8835

Victoria Infocentre, 812 Wharf Street, Victoria, British Columbia V8W 1T3; 250/382-2127

DISABLED TRAVELERS

The Canadian Paraplegic Association, 780 South West Marine Dr., Vancouver, British Columbia V6P 5Y7; 604/324-3611 for wheelchair-accessibility information

SPARC, 106-2182 West 12th Avenue, Vancouver, British Columbia V6K 2N4; 604/736-4367 parking permits for people with physical disabilities available

PARKS, RECREATION, WILDLIFE AND ENVIRONMENTAL INFORMATION

Alberta Environmental Protection Fish and Wildlife Services, 9920 108th Street, Edmonton, Alberta T5K 2M4; 403/944-0313

Alberta Environmental Protection Parks Service, Standard Life Centre, 10405 Jasper Avenue, Edmonton, Alberta T5J 3N4; 403/427-6781

British Columbia Forest Service, Recreation Section, 4595 Canada Way, Burnaby, British Columbia V5G 4L9; 604/660-7500

British Columbia Provincial Parks, 800 Johnson St., Victoria, British Columbia V8V 1X4; 250/387-5002

Canadian Parks Service, Information Services, Western Regional Office, Room 520, 220 4th Ave. SE, Box 2989, Station M, Calgary, Alberta T2P 3H8; 403/292-4401

Department of Fisheries and Oceans, 555 West Hastings Street, Vancouver, British Columbia V6B 5G3; 604/666-3545

Discover Camping British Columbia, 800/689-9025. Call for booking campsites between March 15 and October 15

Ministry of the Environment, 780 Blanshard Street, Victoria, British Columbia V8V 1X4; 250/387-9717

INDEX

MAP INDEX

ABOUT THE AUTHOR

Born and raised in Australia, Lyn Hancock has been living in and writing about Western Canada for more than 38 years. She has traveled widely throughout the region and recorded her adventures in thousands of international newspaper and magazine articles. Her many book titles include *There's a Seal in My Sleeping Bag, Yukon, Nunavut, Northwest Territories,* and *Winging It in the North.* She has won numerous awards for writing and photography. In addition to traveling and writing, Hancock gives lectures throughout Canada, Australia, and the United States.

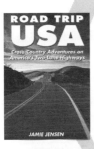